The Chinese economy, because of its vast size, growth in foreign trade and FDI inflows, has become an influential force in the global economy. China's entry into the World Trade Organization (WTO) represented a huge stride in the country's economic development.

This is a timely study of China's rapidly changing economy after entering WTO. It provides an in-depth analysis of the path China is taking in the globalization process and an understanding of the risks and opportunities that market participants will encounter in the process. Chapter authors include leading scholars in international economics and the study of Chinese economic issues. This comprehensive study covers most key topics on China's globalization process from the perspectives of economics, political science, sociology, and regional sciences. It looks at recent financial reforms and economic, industrial, and agricultural performance. It also provides theoretical frameworks for analyzing opportunities and challenges faced by China after WTO accession and derives practical policy guidance for dealing with this transition to economic integration.

China and the Challenge of Economic Globalization

The Impact of WTO Membership

Edited by

Hung-Gay Fung,
Changhong Pei, and Kevin H. Zhang

An East Gate Book

Routledge
Taylor & Francis Group

LONDON AND NEW YORK

An East Gate Book

First published 2006 by M.E. Sharpe

Published 2015 by Routledge
2 Park Square, Milton Park, Abingdon, Oxon OX14 4RN
52 Vanderbilt Avenue, New York, NY 10017

First issued in paperback 2020

Routledge is an imprint of the Taylor & Francis Group, an informa business

Copyright © 2006 Taylor & Francis. All rights reserved.

Library of Congress Cataloging-in-Publication Data

China and the challenge of economic globalization : the impact of WTO membership /
edited by Hung-Gay Fung, Changhong Pei, and Kevin H. Zhang.
   p. cm.
An East Gate Book.
Includes bibliographical references and index.
ISBN 0-7656-1468-5 (alk. paper)
1. World Trade Organization—China. 2. China—Commerce. 3. China—Economic
conditions—2000- I. Fung, Hung-gay. II. Pei, Changhong. III. Zhang, Kevin H.

HF3836.5.C4583 2005
330.951—dc22   2004022521

ISBN 13: 978-0-367-66973-7 (pbk)
ISBN 13: 978-0-7656-1468-1 (hbk)

Contents

List of Tables and Figures   vii

Introduction   xi
Hung-Gay Fung, Changhong Pei, and Kevin H. Zhang

**Part I   Economic Performance After China's Accession to the
World Trade Organization**

1. An Analysis of China's Foreign Trade After WTO Accession   3
    Changhong Pei and Jinjian Shen
2. Foreign Direct Investment: Opportunity or Challenge for China
    After WTO Membership?   23
    Kevin H. Zhang
3. China's WTO Compliance: Commitment and Progress in the
    Initial Stage   36
    Penelope B. Prime
4. After Accession to the WTO: Foreign Direct Investment Flows
    in Western China   51
    Ying-Qiu Liu

Part II The WTO and China's Economic Welfare

5. Foreign Direct Investment and Income Inequality   61
    Xiaodong Wu
6. A New World Factory and China's Labor Force   83
    Yan-Zhong Wang
7. China's WTO Membership: Commitments and Challenges   96
    Nini Yang
8. Corporatism: Rebuilding the Framework of China's Welfare Regime 108
    Bing-Wen Zheng

9. China's Trade-Related Investment Measures and Their
   Development Following WTO Accession   121
   Jian Zhang
10. China's Employment and WTO Accession   134
    Ju-Wei Zhang

Part III Financial Reforms and Capital Markets

11. China's Financial Reform in Banking and Securities Markets 145
    Hung-Gay Fung and Qingfeng "Wilson" Liu
12. How Do Chinese Firms Raise Capital? An International
    Comparison   164
    Hung-Gay Fung, Wai Kin Leung, and Stanley J. Zhu
13. The Debt Financing Gap for Small Business in China   183
    Changwen Zhao and Kun Li
14. Institutional Reform in the Chinese Banking System and China's
    Implementation of Commitments to the WTO   207
    Mei Liao

Part IV Industrial and Agricultural Development

15. Openness and China's Industrial Locations: An Empirical
    Investigation   235
    Ting Gao
16. Agricultural Policy Developments After China's
    Accession to the WTO   253
    Francis Tuan, Agapi Somwaru, and Xinshen Diao
17. The Impact of China's Accession to the WTO on
    Chinese Agriculture and Farmers   273
    Xiao-shan Zhang
18. Recent Development of the Petroleum Industry in China   282
    Wai-Chung Lo

About the Editors and Contributors   301
Index   305

List of Tables and Figures

Tables

1.1 Import and Export of Processing and Assembling Products
as a Percentage of China's Total Imports and Exports 7
1.2 China's Import and Export Business with its Main
Trading Partners, January–June 2003 16
1.3 Increased Value in Percentage of Various Trade Sectors,
2002–2003 17
1.4 Comparison of Increases in Trade Value by Type
of Enterprise 17
1.5 Increased Value in Percentage of Imports and Exports with the
United States, Japan, and the EU in the First Half of 2003 18
1.6 Foreign Trade, 2003 20
1.7 Primary Trading Partners, 2003 21
2.1 Key Changes Promised by China upon WTO Accession 25
2.2 Conflict Between MNCs and China in the Establishment
Process of Foreign-Invested Enterprises (FIEs) 29
4.1 Comparison of Land Values in Various Regions of China
in 2004 52
4.2 FDI Flows in Eastern, Central, and Western China, 2001–2003 56
6.1 Development of China's Foreign Trade and Changes in
Export Dependence 85
6.2 Development of the Exportation of Industrial Products 86
6.3 The Changing Pace of Foreign Companies' Technology
Transfers to China 87
6.4 Increase of China's Labor Force and GDP Growth, 1952–2001 88
6.5 The Contribution of Increased Labor and Capital to
GDP Growth, 1953–1997 89
6.6 Labor Force and Wages in Urban Areas and in Township and
Village Enterprises 90

6.7   Average Weekly Wages of Labor in the Manufacturing
      Sector in Some Asian Countries and Regions   91
6.8   Statistical Number of Employed Persons in Foreign Funded
      Units (including Hong Kong, Taiwan, and Macao)   93
7.1   China's Top Ten Trade Partners   97
7.2   China's FDI Growth (2001–2003)   98
7.3   Prospective Global Impacts of China's WTO Membership   99
7.4   The United States' Top Ten Trading Partners (2003)   101
7.5   The World's Top Fifteen Exporters to the United States   102
7.6   The World's Top Fifteen Importers from the United States   102
7.7   Recent History of the U.S. Trade Balance with China   103
7.8   Top U.S. Exports to China   104
7.9   Top U.S. Imports from China   104
10.1 Change of Employment Elasticity, 1979–2000   137
11.1 The Four Asset Management Companies   148
11.2 Mid-Year Report Summary for the Five Listed Banks in 2003   151
11.3 The Weights of Banks and Securities Markets: China vs.
      Other Countries   155
11.4 Summary Data of the Shanghai and Shenzhen Stock Exchanges   156
11.5 A Summary of China's Fund-Management Industry in
      September 2003   160
12.1 Financing Patterns in Developing Countries   166
12.2 Comparison of Financing Patterns Between Developed and
      Developing Countries   166
12.3 Financing Patterns in the United States   167
12.4 Financing Patterns in Developed Countries   167
12.5 Capital Structure of Listed Chinese Companies   169
12.6 Sources of Fixed Asset Investment in China, 1996–2002   170
12.7 Sources of Fixed Asset Investment by Firm Type in 2002   171
12.8 Capital Raised by Non-Financial Enterprises and Institutions   172
12.9 Capital Raised by Listed Chinese Companies   172
12.10 Capital Raised by Listed and Non-Listed Chinese Companies   173
12.11 IPO Issues in China, 1992–2002   175
12.12 Seasoned Equity Offerings in China, 1993–2002   175
12.13 Bond Market Summary, 1998–2002   177
12.14 Trading Volume of Securities in China, 1998–2002   178
12.15 The Mean and Median Values of ROE for the Listed
      Firms in China, 1997–2002   179
12.16 P/E Ratios in China, 1997–2002   179
13.1 Distribution of Financial Resources in China's Financial
      Institutions and Capital Market   187

13.2 The Capital Structure of Enterprises in China,
October 1999–October 2000   188

13.3 Rejected Business Loan Applications in China,
October 1999–October 2000   189

13.4 Business Applications for Bank Loans in China,
October 1999–October 2000   190

13.5 Distribution of Assets, Deposits, and Loans by Type of
Financial Institution in 2001   195

13.6 The Growth Rate of Bank Loans in Some Asian Countries
and Areas   197

13.7 The Size of the Innovation Fund for Small
Technology-Based Firms   199

13.8 Investment of Innovation Funds for Small
Technology-Based Firms   200

14.1 Operational Efficiencies of Major Commercial Banks
in China, 1997–1998   217

14.2 Operational Efficiencies of Major Commercial Banks
in China   218

14.3 Commercial Banks: The Ratio of Lending to Saving,
1997–1998   219

15.1 Regional Shares of Population and Industrial Output   238

15.2 Regional Shares of FDI, Exports, and Imports   239

15.3 Regional Shares of Output in Manufacturing Industries,
1985 and 1997   241

15.4 Variables and Definitions   245

15.5 Openness and the Regional Distribution of Industries, 1997   247

15.6 Openness and Changes in Regional Distribution of
Industries, 1985–1997   249

16.1 China's WTO Chronology   254

16.2 China's Tariff Rate Quota System for Major Agricultural
Products after WTO Accession   255

17.1 The Structure and Change of the Chinese Rural Labor
Force   275

17.2 The Structure of Rural Households   277

18.1 Production, Imports, and Exports of Oil (10,000 metric
tons), 1985 and 1990–2001   285

18.2 Imports and Exports of Crude Oil, 1990–2002   286

18.3 Imports and Exports of Finished Oil Products, 1990–2002   287

18.4 Descriptive Statistics on the Prices of Diesel Oil in
Shenzhen, New York, Rotterdam, and Singapore   290

18.5 Tariff Reductions in the Sino-U.S. WTO Agreement   292

Figures

1.1   The Total Growth of Imports and Exports in China, 1998–2002   5
1.2   China's Surplus Trade, 1998–2002   5
1.3   China's Top Ten Trade Partners   8
1.4   China's Exports   9
1.5   Provinces' Exports According to Resource Location   10
5.1   China's Gini Index of Income Distribution   64
5.2   Foreign Capital Invested in China   66
5.3   Annual Growth Rate of Long-Term Employees by Ownership   67
5.4   Sectoral Composition of the Largest Foreign-Funded
       Enterprises in Manufacturing by Country Group   69
5.5   Annual Growth of Real Average Wage   70
5.6   Annual Growth of Real Average Wage and FDI   75
5.7   Average Nominal Wage by Sector   76
10.1   Economic Growth, Employment Growth, and Employment
       Elasticity   136
10.2   Ratio of Employment Share to GDP Share by Industry   138
12.1   Liability to Asset Ratio: Change of Liability to Asset Ratio
       for 5,000 Large-Scale Industrial Enterprises in China   169
12.2   Shenzhen and Shanghai Composite Indices, 1991–2002   174
12.3   Capital Raised in the B- and H-Share Markets   176
12.4   Lending Rates in China   178
12.5   Stock Indices for Various Markets   180
14.1   Structure of the Chinese Banking System   210
16.1   Corn Exports: China and Argentina, 1992–2003   258
16.2   The Decline of China's Soybean Imports, 1988–2003   258
16.3   China: A Net Wheat Exporter in 2003   259
18.1   Net Imports of Crude Oil and Finished Oil Products,
       1990–2002   288
18.2   Diesel Prices in Shenzhen, New York, Rotterdam, and
       Singapore, October 2000–April 2002   290
18.3   Price Differentials in Shenzhen, New York, and Singapore
       Using Rotterdam Prices as a Benchmark   291

Introduction

*Hung-Gay Fung, Changhong Pei,
and Kevin H. Zhang*

China emerged as the largest recipient of foreign direct investment (FDI) and the fifth largest trading nation in the world in 2002. China's entry into the World Trade Organization (WTO) represents a huge stride forward in its reform efforts. These reforms include liberalization and modernization of China's economy (in industrial, services, and agricultural sectors) and trading activities.

China's growing economy, its international trade, and its large inward FDI have significantly affected the growth of global trade, the distribution of global direct investments, and the pace of expansion of global output. There is no other country in history, as a WTO member, to have achieved such expansion in a comparable time period. China is expected to be influential in future rounds of WTO trade negotiations. As the only major trading nation that is not classified as an advanced industrial economy, China is bringing an unparalleled perspective to the negotiations and exerting its power on matters important to its trade. China, as a new WTO member, is posing momentous opportunities and challenges to the United States and other countries.

A study of the Chinese economy after entering the WTO should be of importance to practitioners, scholars, and policymakers because of China's vast size, its rapid growth in foreign trade and FDI inflows, and the unprecedented speed of its integration into the world economy. The high quality of the chapters within this volume and their authors' expertise unite to make this book a most timely contribution to our understanding of China's rapidly changing economy and its transformation toward globalization after entering the WTO.

This volume is divided into four parts. The first part deals with economic performance after China's accession to the World Trade Organization. The second part relates to the WTO and China's economic welfare. The third part deals with China's financial reforms and capital markets, and the last part discusses China's industrial and agricultural development. In total, we have eighteen chapters that will shed light on the Chinese economy and the challenges posed by WTO membership.

The first chapter, "An Analysis of China's Foreign Trade after WTO Accession," by Changhong Pei and Jinjian Shen, shows that the year 2002 was a year of harvest in the development of foreign trade for China. Becoming a WTO member in 2001, China quickened its pace in both reforms and opening markets. The total foreign trade value of China reached US$620.8 billion at a growth rate of 21.8 percent, while the export value reached US$325.6 billion at a growth rate of 22.3 percent. The import value reached US$295.2 billion with a cumulative US$30.4 billion of trade surplus. There are seven main reasons for the rapid growth of Chinese trade: (1) the demand of domestic economic growth; (2) the strengthening of the export refund policy; (3) improvement of the structure of export commodities; (4) the depreciation of the U.S. dollar; (5) membership in the WTO; (6) policy encouraging foreign trade exports; and finally, (7) export growth by foreign invested enterprises in China.

In the second chapter, "Foreign Direct Investment: Opportunity or Challenge for China After WTO Membership?" Kevin H. Zhang presents his view of how China deals with the challenges of using foreign direct investment (FDI) after entering the WTO. China's entry into the WTO is bringing both opportunities and challenges in the use of foreign direct investment. With WTO commitments to further liberalization of the FDI regime and to allow more penetration by multinational corporations (MNCs) in China's markets, the dangers and negative effects of FDI seem to be increasing. While mutual benefits of FDI exist, the conflicts between China and the MNCs tend to be intensifying over time. China hopes to exchange its domestic market with MNCs for advantaged technology and to promote exports through offering MNCs cheap labor and other resources. MNCs want to control China's huge market and use China as a manufacturing base at the lower end of the value chain. The outcome depends in large part on how China balances technology transfers and domestic market protection. China should take full advantage of its large market to shape MNC activities. A strong and competent central government needs to remain in order to bargain with Western MNCs. FDI from overseas Chinese should be continuously encouraged with various incentives.

In the third chapter, "China's WTO Compliance: Commitment and Progress in the Initial Stage," Penelope B. Prime surveys China's WTO commitments for the first two years of membership and evaluates broadly the progress toward meeting those commitments. This evaluation takes into account views on compliance from both inside and outside China, as well as developing the international and national economic context within, while this process is unfolding. After introducing the key issues, the chapter summarizes the nature and extent of China's initial commitments. It later describes the monitoring infrastructure that has emerged. Monitoring compliance itself is part of the institution building that is required of a WTO member, and is an important piece of the adjustment process. Another section analyzes the progress and problems with compliance, taking different reference points into account. The final section draws some conclusions in light of the experiences of other countries and China's task ahead.

The fourth chapter, "After Accession to the WTO: FDI Flows in Western China," by Ying-Qiu Liu explains two important recent events that occurred in China. One was the decision by the central government of China to implement the strategy of the Western Development Program from the middle of 1999. The other is China's decision to become a member of the WTO toward the end of 2001. China's WTO accession will facilitate more flow of foreign direct investment into China than before, but also the growth of FDI flowing into western China. Because the comparative advantage of an abundant low cost labor supply in eastern and Central China is diminishing, there are advantages that can attract FDI into western China. It explains the current flow into western China, and illustrates the main obstacles preventing the flow of FDI into western China. Finally, the chapter offers some advice for making wise FDI investment decisions in western China.

The fifth chapter, "Foreign Direct Investment and Income Inequality," by Xiaodong Wu, demonstrates that one of the biggest concerns about China's accession to the World Trade Organization is that of the relative wage of skilled labor versus unskilled labor and the potential for increasing wage inequality in China as China lowers its restrictions on trade and foreign direct investment. This chapter analyzes the impact of different types of foreign direct investment on the relative return to skill. A general equilibrium trade model is used to demonstrate that foreign direct investment into different industries can have varying impacts on wage inequality. More foreign direct investment may not necessarily lead to more social inequality if foreign direct investments are channeled into the appropriate industries. These policy implications will apply not only to China but also to any developing country that is not strong enough to affect the world terms of trade.

The sixth chapter, "A New World Factory and China's Labor Force," by Yan-Zhong Wang, discusses China's accession to the WTO, which means that the Chinese economy will be further incorporated into the world economic system, speeding up further combinations between international capital and the industrial labor force of China, and accordingly becoming the new starting point for China to conduct its international labor market. The speedy rise of Chinese manufacturing suggests China possesses the developmental prospect of being a "world factory." China has many industrial labor resources, which are inexpensive but of high quality. It is important for China to carry out industrialization and to participate in international labor division.

The seventh chapter, "China's WTO Membership: Commitments and Challenges," by Nini Yang, investigates the ongoing debates over China's accession to the World Trade Organization from three perspectives: major opportunities and challenges from China's perspective, the controversy from the United States perspective, and the potential impacts from a global perspective. China has much to learn about WTO rules and mechanisms for the effective management of emerging trade-related conflicts and resolutions, while developing effective use of its natural, financial, and human resources.

The eighth chapter, "Corporatism: Rebuilding the Framework of China's Welfare Regime," by Bing-Wen Zheng, first discusses the basic features of corporatism and their implications for China's welfare. He then concludes that the newly issued Trade Union Law Amendment shall go down in the annals of New China as the first time legislation has allowed for the role and status of the trade union in "collective negotiation." China will enter a historical stage, build a modern welfare regime and social security system, and set up a legal foundation for the structure of a "micro-corporatist" social security system.

In the ninth chapter, "China's Trade-Related Investment Measures and Their Development Following WTO Accession," Jian Zhang discusses the Trade Related Investment Measures (TRIMs) in the World Trade Organization agreement and their impacts on China after it becomes a WTO member. In most industries, China has more opportunities to access global markets, but this access also challenges the existing Chinese political and economic system. Accession to the WTO implies a relatively dramatic economic structural adjustment in China. Highly protected agriculture and some of the capital-intensive industrial sectors will suffer, while the labor-intensive sectors such as textiles and manufactured clothing will be the main beneficiaries.

The tenth chapter, "China's Employment and WTO Accession," by Ju-Wei Zhang, discusses employment issues in China. More than 10 million enter the labor force every year; around 150–200 million rural laborers are eager to migrate to urban areas. More than 9 million laid-off urban workers were waiting for jobs by the end of 2000. Employment not only affects the ordinary life of every household but is also crucial to the stability and development of the country. WTO membership will not change the trend of economic development in China but will consolidate comparative advantages in labor-intensive industries. By looking at the change in the employment structure in the last two decades, the author does not envisage any net negative effect of WTO on employment either in the long or short run. WTO entry does have a strong structural impact on employment, and the extent of the impact varies in different industries. As a result, job switching will accelerate and temporary unemployment will become a more severe problem in the WTO era.

In the eleventh chapter, "China's Financial Reform in Banking and Securities Markets," Hung-Gay Fung and Qingfeng "Wilson" Liu present the recent reforms of China's financial market. These reforms include the rules governing the operation of the stock market with regard to A- and B-shares, and the operation of the banking sector, where foreign banks have become increasingly important. Establishing a good corporate governance structure is essential to the success of financial market reforms. This chapter also discusses recent developments and implications of foreign participation in China's stock market in open- and closed-end funds, and the implementation of the qualified foreign institution investor (QFII) rule.

The twelfth chapter, "How Do Chinese Firms Raise Capital? An International Comparison," by Hung-Gay Fung, Wai Kin Leung, and Stanley J. Zhu, explains the behavior of Chinese firms raising capital in China. The traditional pecking order theory suggests that debt is the least expensive source of external financing, while common equity is the most expensive because of tax and risk considerations. The common practice in China's capital markets appears to be different. The chapter analyzes the various methods for raising capital by firms listed on the Chinese stock exchanges between 1995 and 2002. The dominance of equity offerings can be explained by the cost of capital, corporate control, and market maturity in China. Each firm's choice of capital raising methods is closely related to frequent changes in associated Chinese policies.

The thirteenth chapter, "The Debt Financing Gap for Small Business in China," by Changwen Zhao and Kun Li, illustrates the financing problems for small business in China. Commercial banks are usually reluctant to lend to small businesses. The fundamental problem for small business debt financing is the high cost and information asymmetry that banks have to face in providing loans. The controlled interest rate, the underdevelopment of the financial market and small banks, and the absence of reliable credit rating systems make the debt-financing gap for small business in China even more serious than in other countries. To reduce the debt-financing gap for small business in China, the government needs to play a more active role and speed up the reform of the financial sector. China's entry into the WTO also opens up more opportunities for improved financing for small and medium enterprises (SMEs).

The fourteenth chapter, "Institutional Reform in the Chinese Banking System and China's Implementation of Commitments to the WTO," by Mei Liao, explains the financial system in China, which has evolved from a one-bank system under the central government with certain mechanisms incompatible with a market economy. It requires a huge effort to correct its deficiencies in structural, operational, and management mechanisms, and to build up its capital capacity, supervisory oversight mechanisms, and an efficient operational structure. The accession to the WTO and the schedule of China's commitments put its not-yet-ready banking sector in a critical position for survival.

The fifteenth chapter, "Openness and China's Industrial Locations: An Empirical Investigation," by Ting Gao, examines the effects of regional openness to trade and foreign direct investment on the cross-province distribution of manufacturing industries in China and its recent changes. Data are presented to show that significant adjustments in the industrial sector occurred during the period of 1985–1997. As southeast China gained in importance in almost all manufacturing industries, empirical evidence from data on 2–digit Chinese manufacturing industries indicates that the distribution across provinces, as well as changes in the distribution over the 1985–1997 period, were positively associated with provincial participation in trade and foreign direct investment, even after a host of other location factors were included.

The sixteenth chapter, "Agricultural Policy Developments after China's Accession to the WTO," by Francis Tuan, Agapi Somwaru, and Xinshen Diao, presents China's agricultural policy after accession to the WTO. China applied to become a member of the World Trade Organization in 1986 and officially joined the organization in December 2001. As a result, the country committed to reducing trade-distorting barriers that fall into three main categories: non-tariff trade barriers, domestic agricultural support, and export subsidies. A couple of years after accession to the WTO, China's trade of major agricultural products, such as corn, wheat, and soybeans, ran counter to expectations. So, why was China's trade of major agricultural commodities in 2002 and 2003 so different from what most trade analysts and economic models previously estimated? This chapter explores and analyzes recent changes in agricultural policies and/or other factors that affected China's agricultural trade in the short term, as well as in the long run. The chapter also discusses what other policy alternatives China has recently implemented or is currently experimenting with that could lead the nation to sustain its high degree of food self-sufficiency in the future.

In the seventeenth chapter, "The Impact of China's Accession to the WTO on Chinese Agriculture and Farmers," Xiao-shan Zhang first presents problems and challenges to the Chinese agricultural sector after its entry into the WTO. The key issue is whether economic development can provide Chinese farmers with more non-farming employment opportunities to raise the competitiveness of the farming sectors. A set of institutional arrangements is proposed as a national policy framework, including the possibility of organizing farmers to develop (a) farmers' trade associations, (b) rural specialized cooperatives or other kinds of organizations, and (c) sufficient power to enter into the domestic and world markets as a group and protect their own interests when facing non-tariff barriers or trade wars initiated by foreign countries.

The eighteenth chapter, "Recent Development of the Petroleum Industry in China," by Wai-Chung Lo, reviews the reform of the oil industry in the last two decades and discusses the implications of the WTO accession for China's oil industry and the prospects of its future development. Restructuring improved the industry's efficiency as well as creating a few sizable petrochemical enterprises for international competition deemed vital for the nation's long-term energy security. The WTO accession will step up the integration of domestic oil markets with international markets. The pricing system established in 1989 and revised in 2001 was the initial step to liberalize the domestic market. In 2004, the State Council approved the re-launch of oil futures. As the upheaval of the oil futures in the mid-1990s plainly exhibited, without a genuine commitment to price liberalization, government had to respond with price intervention in order to maintain industry stability when oil prices became too volatile. The brief history of oil futures from 1993–1995 shows that a futures exchange would not be able to function properly without a fully liberalized and competitive domestic market. The objective of the 1998 restructuring of the petroleum industry is to create regional monopolists with size and scope comparable to the international petroleum majors. A highly concentrated industrial structure will be a challenge for an effective futures market, price discovery, and risk management.

Part I

Economic Performance After China's Accession to the World Trade Organization

1

An Analysis of China's Foreign Trade After WTO Accession

Changhong Pei and Jinjian Shen

The year 2002 became the year of harvest in the development of China's foreign trade; it was the first year of China's membership in the World Trade Organization (WTO). Since then, China has quickened its pace in both reforms and opening, especially in imports and exports trade. The total foreign trade import-export value of China reached US$620.8 billion in 2002 with a growth rate of 21.8 percent over the previous year and it exceeded US$600 billion for the first time. The export value reached US$325.6 billion at a growth rate of 22.3 percent over the previous year and exceeded US$300 billion for the first time. The import value increased by 21.2 percent over the previous year and reached US$295.2 billion, while a trade surplus of US$30.35 billion was realized.

There are eight primary reasons for the rapid growth of Chinese trade after WTO accession. First, with rapid economic growth China has stimulated the demand for goods from overseas markets. Second, the strengthening of the export refund policy has promoted the growth of foreign trade exports. Third, the structure of export commodities has improved to meet the demands of the international market. Fourth, the world economy resurged mildly and the depreciation of the U.S. dollar helped the growth of trade. Fifth, the foreign trade environment of China was improved to some extent by its membership in the WTO. Sixth, the policy encouraging foreign trade exports helped the formation of a mutually beneficial foreign trade pattern. Seventh, enterprises invested in directly by foreign capital became the most important economic form of export trade. Finally, disproportionate growth in the export of mechanical and electrical equipment and products represented the largest share of total exports.

This chapter analyzes China's trade patterns after its WTO accession. We focus on the structure of trade growth and its trading partners. In addition, we shed light on the nature of Chinese trade as well as some of the reasons behind China's dramatic growth in trade.

Characteristics of China's Trade in 2002

With the help of the worldwide recovery in 2002, the demand of international markets was strong; import growth was maintained and export growth was much better than expected. Compared with the gross domestic product (GDP), the total of Chinese imports and exports in 2002 was 13 percent higher than the growth of the GDP. The characteristics of trade in 2002 were as follows.

The Positive Effect of Net Export Contributions on Economic Growth

Figure 1.1 shows the 1998–2002 trade figures and Figure 1.2 shows the trade surplus in China. From 1998 to 2002, China's imports and exports jumped to US$3 billion, comparable to the U.K. and France, thus becoming a major world trade country. Compared with the previous three years, the net exports in 2002 made a positive contribution to China's economic development. The GDP increased by 8 percent in 2002 with a benefit of US$3 billion and a net increase of US$0.8 billion compared with 2001.[1]

Trade Growth Benefits from High Export Growth

In its first year of WTO membership, China's accumulated export growth showed a steady increase after an initial decline of 10 percent in the first quarter. Export growth did not meet the expected 14 percent increase in the second quarter, or the expected 19.4 percent at the end of the third quarter. However, it did increase over 30 percent in the fourth quarter resulting in an overall increase of 22.3 percent for the year. Exports have become an important factor driving the continued growth of GDP in China.

The surplus in 2002 was US$30.4 billion, increasing by US$7.8 billion over the prior year. Imports reached US$28.73 billion, with an increase of 28.3 percent as compared with the same month of the previous year. Although five thousand types of import tariffs were reduced in 2002 and some import quotas abolished, with average tariffs down by 3 percent, the rate of imports fell by 3.6 percent, especially those ordinary imports demanded by

Figure 1.1 **The Total Growth of Imports and Exports in China, 1998–2002** (US$ billions)

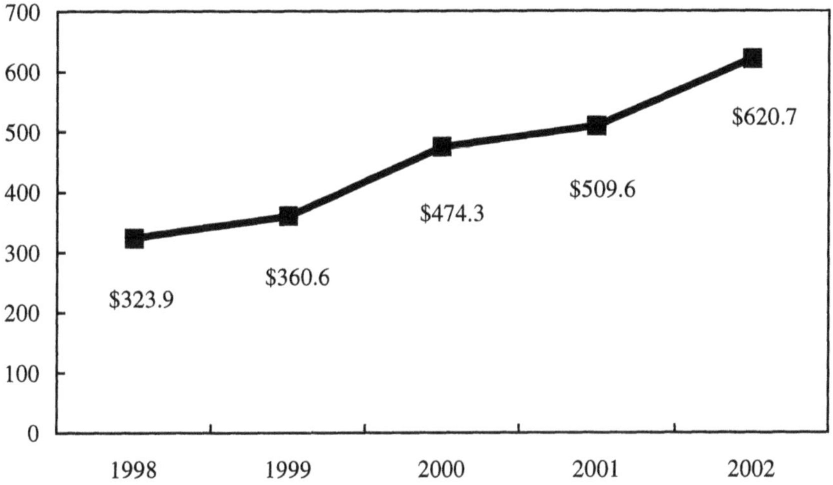

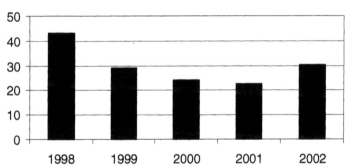

Source: PRC General Customs Administration, *China's Customs Statistics (1998–2003)*.

Figure 1.2 **China's Surplus Trade, 1998–2002** (unit: US$ millions)

Source: PRC General Customs Administration, *China's Customs Statistics (1998–2003)*.

the domestic market, which only increased by 4.8 percent, a rate reduction of 18.3 percent over the previous year.[2]

Trade in Processing and Assembling Products (PAP) Is Growing More Rapidly Than Ordinary Trade

Open policies for foreign funds has attracted a large amount of FDI into China and more and more multinational enterprises (MNEs) intend to move their manufacturing facilities into China, thereby providing impetus to the import and export growth of the processing and assembling trade. In 2002, the total value of imports and exports in PAP trade was US$302.2 billion in China, comprising 48.8 percent of China's total value of imports and exports—an increase of 25.2 percent over the previous year. PAP exports alone were US$180 billion, an increase of 22 percent, that is, 55.3 percent of the total value of exports in China, nearly the same as the previous year. The total value of PAP imports was US$122.2 billion, an increase of 30.1 percent over 2001, amounting to 41.4 percent of the total value of China's imports, an increase of 2.8 percent over the previous year (see Table 1.1).

The total value of imports and exports of ordinary trade was US$265.3, or 42.7 percent of the total value of China's import and export value, an increase over the previous year of 17.7 percent. Ordinary exports amounted to US$136.2 billion, 41.8 percent of the total, an increase over the previous year of 21.7 percent. In 2002, China's ordinary imports and exports totaled US$129.1 billion—43.8 percent of the total value of China's imports and exports, maintaining a growth rate of 13.8 percent.[3]

Rapid Growth of Trade by Non-State-Owned Enterprises (SOEs)

According to Chinese customs statistics, while imports and exports by foreign investment enterprises (FIEs) experienced stronger growth, the imports and exports of other non-state-owned enterprises increased more rapidly. In 2002, the processing foreign investment enterprises maintained strong growth with a total value of US$330.2 in imports and exports, an increase of 27.5 percent. Exports were US$170 billion, an increase of 27.6 percent, and imports totaled US$160.28, an increase of 27.4 percent. In the same year, the total value of imports and exports by SOEs was US$237.4 billion, an increase of 9.5 percent. SOE exports were US$122.9, an increase of 8.5 percent, while imports were US$114.5 billion, an increase of 10.6 percent.

The collective-owned enterprises, individual private enterprises, and other types of non-SOEs now have fewer obstacles to their import and export activities. The growth trend of imports and exports for collective-owned and individual enterprises has become stronger. In 2002, the total value of imports and exports reached 53.2 billion, an increase of 57.1 percent. Total exports were 32.8 percent, an increase of 66.5 percent, while total imports were US$204.5 billion, an increase of 43.9 percent.[4]

Asian Countries Rise in Importance Among Major Trade Partners

In 2002, trade development between China and its trading partners showed a strong trend over 2001. With the exception of Canada, bilateral trade

Table 1.1

Import and Export of Processing and Assembling Products (PAP) as a Percentage of China's Total Imports and Exports (US$ billion)

Year	Total PAP Imports and Exports (A)	Total Chinese Imports and Exports (B)	Column A/B (%)	PAP Exports (C)	Total of China's Exports (D)	Column C/D(%)	Total PAP Imports (E)	Total of China's Imports (F)	Column E/F (%)
1991	57.51	135.70	42.4	32.39	71.91	45.1	25.12	63.79	39.4
1992	70.85	165.53	42.8	39.62	84.94	46.6	32.13	80.59	38.8
1993	80.43	195.70	41.1	44.25	91.74	48.2	36.18	103.96	34.8
1994	104.35	236.62	44.1	56.98	121.01	47.1	47.37	115.69	41.0
1995	132.00	280.85	47.0	73.71	148.78	49.5	58.29	132.08	44.1
1996	146.33	289.88	50.5	84.13	151.07	55.7	62.19	138.83	44.8
1997	169.81	325.06	52.2	99.60	182.70	54.5	70.21	142.36	49.3
1998	173.03	323.95	53.4	104.47	183.71	56.9	68.57	140.24	48.9
1999	184.49	360.65	51.2	110.87	194.93	56.9	73.64	165.72	44.4
2000	230.21	474.30	48.5	137.65	249.20	55.2	92.56	225.09	41.1
2001	240.01	509.77	47.1	147.45	266.16	55.4	92.57	243.61	38.6
2002	302.17	620.79	48.8	179.94	325.57	55.3	122.23	295.22	41.4

Source: PRC General Customs Administration, *China Customs Statistics (1991–2002).*

Figure 1.3 **China's Top Ten Trade Partners** (Unit: US$ millions)

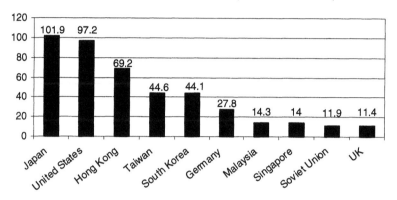

Source: PRC General Customs Administration, *China's Customs Statistics (1998–2003)*.

with top ten countries grew to two digit numbers, amounting to 85.2 percent of China's total imports and exports. Among them, Japan is China's largest trade partner with a bilateral trade volume of US$101.9 billion, breaking a US$100 billion record, and amounting to 16.4 percent of total volume of imports and exports, an increase of 16.2 percent. The second- and third-highest trade partners are the United States and the EU. China-U.S. trade totaled US$97.2 billion in volume, and China-EU trade totaled US$86.8 billion. Examining trading partners by country and region, it can be seen that China's Asian partners are playing an increasingly important role (see Figure 1.3)

The bilateral trade with Asian countries has been developing quickly. The value of imports and exports with Asian countries reached US$54.8 billion, an increase of 31.7 percent, while the total of trade with the EU increased by only 13.2 percent. The export volume to ASEAN members, South Korea, and Taiwan increased 400 percent (see Figure 1.3).[5]

Trade Surplus Comes Mainly from the United States and Hong Kong

China's top ten export markets are the United States, Hong Kong, Japan, South Korea, Germany, the Netherlands, the U.K., Taiwan, Malaysia, and Italy (see Figure 1.4). Figure 1.4 shows China's exports to different countries. China's trade surplus is mainly with the United States (US$42.7 billion), Hong Kong (US$47.7 billion), and as well as Japan, Russia, and Germany (US$5 billion each). China's trade showed a deficit in the amount of US$32 billion with Taiwan and US$13 billion with South Korea.

Figure 1.4 **China's Exports** (unit: US$ billions)

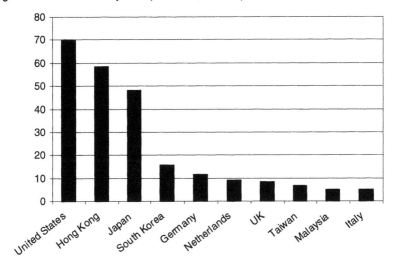

Source: PRC General Customs Administration, *China's Customs Statistics (1998–2003).*

The Eastern Area, Coastal Provinces, and Cities Remain Important Players

If examined according to resource locations, we see that the eastern areas, border provinces, and cities continued to play an important role in the general trade growth of 2002. But the growth in western areas was also fast; for instance, Sichuan's exports increased by 56.1 percent and those of Xinjiang by 93.1 percent in (see Figure 1.5).

The Importance of Trade in Machine Tools and Electronics

The export value of machine tools and electronics was US$157.1 billion, constituting 48.2 percent of the total export volume. Exports of machine tools and electronics were 3.6 percent higher in volume compared with the level in 2001, an increase of 32.3 percent. After China joined the WTO, other member countries reduced or eliminated their quota limit for some products from China and broadened the range of allowable traditional products to be exported. The export of gross goods in 2002 was much better than that in 2001. The garment export value was US$41.2 billion, an increase of 12.7 percent. The export of textiles and related products was US$20.6 billion, an increase of 22.2 percent. Shoe exports were valued at US$11.1 billion, increasing by 9.9 percent. The export of plastic products reached US$6.1 bil-

Figure 1.5 **Provinces' Exports According to Resource Location**
(Unit: US$ billions)

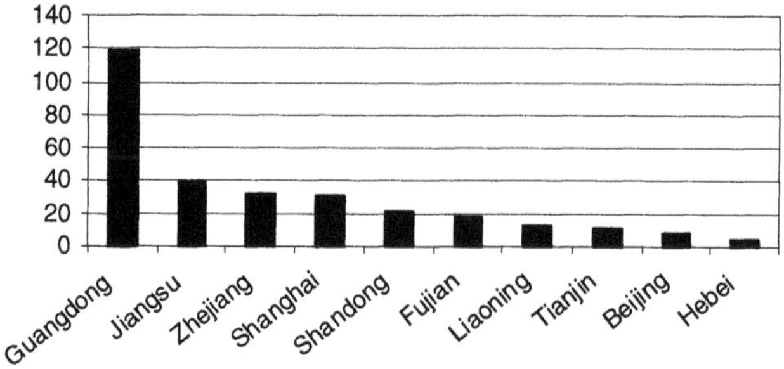

Source: PRC General Customs Administration, *China's Customs Statistics (1998–2003)*.

lion, an increase of 18.8 percent. Toy exports totaled US$5.6 billion, an increase of 7.9 percent.[6]

An Analysis of China's Trade Growth

China's trade growth mainly benefited from its microeconomic environment and favorable policies. The current recovery of the world economy and China's admission into the WTO improved the international environment and was favorable for China's imports and exports.

Domestic Economic Growth Increases the Demand for Overseas Markets

In 2002, the growth rate of total social investment to capital assets continued to be over 10 percent, reaching 21.5 percent during the first half of the year. The growth rate of industrial production climbed to 12 percent. The growth rate of added value in the secondary industry was 12.3 percent. The domestic supply still showed a strong upward turn and, as a result, the volume of commodity retail sales only increased by 10 percent while the consumer price index fell by 0.8 percent. The domestic market revealed that supply was greater than demand. Despite falling prices for exports, demand grew in the industrial sector for overseas markets.

Export Refund Policy Promotes Foreign Trade Growth

The government introduced a set of policies to promote exports and achieved a sound response. In 2002, the value of the export refund reached RMB125.9 billion, an increase of 17.1 percent (that is, RMB18.8 billion). Some local governments put more effort into supporting exports than ever before, thus stimulating the export market. In order to promote exports, China introduced the export refund system, raised the refund rate for textile products, and initiated other measures to encourage exports. The State Council took active measures, including exemptions to offset export duties. The total value of all export exemptions, offsets, and refunds increased 62 percent in 2001 and 100 percent in 2002 (this includes all export enterprises, both those that manufacture and export and those that only export). Industrial enterprises were better capitalized than ever before, which proved beneficial to export expansion.

The export refund became an important resource for industrial enterprises. The total volume of profit realized in the first quarter of 2002 was RMB79.9 billion after offsetting benefits and losses, a reduction of 9.1 percent from the previous year. Among them, the state-owned or the state shareholding enterprises realized profits of RMB33.7 billion after offsets, 30.1 percent less than the previous year. But the total of export refunds in the first quarter was RMB40.5 billion, an increase of RMB197 billion compared to the same quarter in 2001, that is, an increase of 95 percent. This shows the importance of the export refund for profit-seeking enterprises. The volume of export refunds reached half the total profit of industries during the same period of 2002, amounting to 120 percent of the total profit of state-owned or state shareholding enterprises for 2002. Encouraged by the export refund policy, enterprises are focusing on expanding their exports.

The Improved Export Structure

With the improved structure for the export and import of commodities, the export of those value added items such as high-end, new technological products and mechanical and electrical equipment, China's ability to compete in the international markets has improved. In 2002, the growth rate of mechanical and electrical equipment industries reached 32.3 percent, much higher than average levels. These products comprised 48 percent of total exports. The total export of high-end, technological products in 2002 increased to 46 percent, amounting to 20.8 percent of the total exports for that year.

China has gained a strong productive capability in IT products, which allows China increased international trade opportunities to attract additional FDI. The shift from the semi-processing of raw materials to value added production shows that the structure of the export commodities industry is adjusting and upgrading. These changes not only increase the ability to export but also upgrade the level of production and management. However, all of the major trading countries are strong in their manufacturing industries. In its efforts to increase trade with these powerful countries, the Chinese manufacturing industry must continue to develop and promote its mechanical and electrical exports.

The World Economic Recovery and the Depreciation of the U.S. Dollar

Two factors combined to promote export growth: the world economy began to recover and the U.S. dollar depreciated. In 2002, the economy in the EU, the United States, and other regions was better to varying degrees. The demand for China's exports was stronger. The demand for China's commodities increased. In 2002, the growth of GDP in the United States increased by 5.8 percent in the first quarter, 1.3 percent in the second quarter, and 3.1 percent in the third quarter (on an annualized basis). The economic recovery in the EU also became more rapid. The depreciating Japanese yen helped to mitigate downward economic pressure on that country. The economies in South Korea and Thailand were recovering to varying degrees. The demand in the international market for middle- and low-level consumer goods increased with the international economic recovery. In addition, the depreciation of the U.S. dollar had an active effect on China's exports. In 2002, due in part to the impact of 9/11, the U.S. dollar was weakening relative to the euro and the Japanese yen, as well as against other major currencies. Because the exchange rate of the RMB is directly linked to the U.S. dollar, the depreciation of the U.S. dollar leads to the depreciation of the RMB relative to other international currencies, resulting in a competitive advantage for China's exports in international and U.S. markets.

China's Improved Foreign Trade Environment

China's export sector benefited not only from the world economic recovery but also from China's participation in the WTO. Since 2002, China's WTO membership and the impact of import and export measures allowed China to maintain a high rate of export growth, exceeding expectations. On the one hand, the WTO membership decreases labor costs. Product quality and function advanced to meet international standards, and the export environment for mechanical and electrical products improved greatly. Export volume expanded rapidly within a short period. On the other hand, the export of traditional textiles, garments, and light industrial products also benefited steadily from the reduction or elimination of many tariff and non-tariff expenses. These changes will continue to benefit China's export growth.

The rewards to China after its first year of WTO membership were sweet. In the past, some had anticipated that WTO membership would strike a harsh blow to China's imports and exports, causing a sharp dip in China's surplus. They did not understand what the WTO means for China's economic development. WTO membership did negatively affect China's service sector, due to strenuous competition from FIEs, but since the majority of the service industry is domestic, it constitutes only a very small proportion of exports.

WTO membership has had an active effect on China's manufacturing industry. Manufacturing products make up the majority of exports. The manufacturing industry in China is strongly competitive and holds a position of dominance in the domestic economy. Joining the WTO provides increased growth opportunities for China's manufacturing industry in the export of its products.

China's legal system and government structure have been improved since joining the WTO. Government services and the competitive capability of enterprises have been enhanced. China has opened its market to the members of WTO and gained more access to theirs. The big retailers around the world come to China for their purchases, thus stimulating China's exports. The inflow of FDI is showing tangible results. Benefits from tariff reductions and changes in non-tariff measures are reflected in a mild increase in imports. The slower rise in imports helps China to maintain a trade surplus.

Restrictions on China's imports and exports by other countries were reduced. Although protectionism, trade tariffs, and environmental barriers involving "green" products still restrict imports and exports to a degree, these are less problematic among WTO members in general. Restrictions on China by many other countries have been comparatively lifted, especially those on products such as China's textiles, which were heavily restricted in the past.

In 2002, China's exports experienced tangible growth and a much broader international market. More important, China's export commodities' structural adjustments achieved a successful result. Some highly technical products found their market. In the first ten months of 2002, exports of high-tech products broke the highest historical record. Although the production of high-tech products in China is still smaller in size and weaker in capability compared with that of its foreign competitors, China's high-tech industry shows great potential and staying power. The emergence of many additional high-tech companies in China implies a global trend toward high-tech processing and increased demand for economic structural adjustment in China. The enhanced development of this industry will promote rising exports and continue to make a strong contribution to continuing economic growth.

Multipurpose Trade Services Development

In 2002, China's exports were able to maintain high growth in spite of the weak global economy and subsequent reduction in exports by major trade countries. In the beginning of the 1990s, China introduced a policy to expand export markets and a strategy of market diversification in order to reduce export risk. During the ten years that followed, the government established a financial services system to aid in developing markets and reducing business risk. China has gradually established a fund for small and medium-size enterprises to assist them in developing international markets; for example, the government has established a joint and cooperative fund for external aid, a special fund for contracted projects, and a medium- or long-term loan with interest deducted in RMB for overseas processing plants. China also has set up an export insurance system to support financing for all kinds of enterprises developing international markets and commodity distribution centers in other countries to enhance their export capabilities. There are six independent trade centers already established in Barcelona, Budapest, Johannesburg, and Moscow. Their main function is to provide business enterprises with support services to develop local markets in those countries and expand export markets.

The government in China also supports overseas expansion and encourages trade development by its enterprises. Since this policy was introduced in 1999, business enterprises have been able to apply for government loans designed to encourage processing production and export expansion in Africa. The total trade development fund is about RMB2 billion. During the ninth five-year plan (1996–2000), half the average annual growth rate came from overseas investment. The total value of signed investment agreements overseas reached US$1.5 billion. By the end of 2000, there were 1,458 Chinese enterprises overseas, with a total investment of US$2.2 billion.

A trade information service system was established to provide businesses with free information from China and other countries. These information service agencies facilitate the organization of large-scale international trade exhibitions for overseas sales and encourage businesses to participate in internationally known professional exhibitions to identify overseas markets. They actively seek various opportunities for trade and economic cooperation and expansion. After ten years' efforts, they have made progress. Now reciprocal worldwide market alliances have been formed with the United States, Japan, the EU, Hong Kong, and Taiwan.

The Importance of Foreign Capital

An important catalyst to trade development is direct foreign investment. In 2002, its value in China was US$5.3 billion, making China the highest recipient of FDI in the world. Now, four hundred MNEs from five hundred of the world's largest corporations have established facilities in China. These FIEs played a major positive role in driving China's export trade. In 2002, the total export value generated by FIEs reached US$169.9 billion, or 52 percent of total exports, an increase of 27.6 percent from 2001 if compared with state-owned enterprises, which generated a total export value of 37.7 percent with a growth rate over 2001 of 8 percent. The growth of other non-state-owned enterprises was faster but constituted a smaller share of the total. FIEs have become an import factor in export trade in China.

Characteristics of China's 2003 Trade

According to China's customs statistics from January to June 2003 (see Table 1.2), imports and exports totaled US$376.1 billion, an increase of 39 percent over 2002. Exports were US$190.3 billion, an increase of 34 percent over 2002, and imports totaled US$185.8 billion, an increase of 44.5 percent. The cumulative deficit was US$449.9 million. From January to June of 2003, the average monthly import and export growth rate remained above 30 percent, the accumulated growth rate in June reached 39 percent, while the accumulated import and export growth rate for the corresponding period in 2002 was only 12.3 percent. The import growth rate remained above 40 percent from the beginning to the end of this six-month period, and the cumulative growth rate in June reached 44.5 percent, which was higher than the export growth rate by 10 percent, but the cumulative import growth rate for the same period in 2002 was only 10.4 percent.

From January to June 2003, the total of general imports and exports reached US$168.4 billion, an increase of 45.3 percent over the same period in 2002. Within those figures, the value of exports was US$81.3 billion, an increase of 36.5 percent over the previous year, and imports totaled US$87.2 billion, increasing by 54.4 percent. These two increases were 2.5 percent and 9.9 percent respectively higher than the general import and export level of 2002. From April to June 2003, the total value of processing trade imports and exports reached US$173.9 billion, an increase of 31.5 percent over 2002. Within that figure, exports amounted to US$103.4 billion, and imports were US$70.5 billion, an increase of 31.5 percent over 2002, lower than the increase in general imports and exports.

Table 1.3 shows the increased value of the different trade pattern. General trade increased by 49.8 percent in 2003 as compared with 2002, and increased 28.2 percent in 2002 as compared with the same period in 2001, reflecting substantial growth . However, the processing trade growth of 39.4 percent in 2003 was smaller than the 66.5 percent increase in 2002 from 2001.[7]

Table 1.4 shows the trade patterns of different types of firms during the period from January to June in 2002 and 2003. In 2003, the total imports and

Table 1.2

**China's Import and Export Business with Its Main
Trading Partners, January–June 2003**

Country (region)	Value (bn RMB)				+− % Increase or decrease compared with same period in 2002		
	Imports and Exports	Exports	Imports	Difference	Imports and Exports	Exports	Imports
Total Value	376.14	190.32	185.82	4.50	3.90	3.40	4.50
Japan	60.91	27.10	33.80	−6.70	3.61	2.54	4.61
EU	55.51	31.20	24.46	6.797	4.42	4.83	3.93
U.S.	56.40	39.93	16.47	23.50	3.44	3.37	3.61
Total of Japan, EU, U.S.	172.81	98.18	74.63	23.55	3.80	3.55	4.16
Proportion of Japan, EU, U.S.	4.59	5.16					
Hong Kong	38.09	32.74	5.34	27.40	2.31	2.60	1.01
East Asian Countries	32.24	13.77	20.47	−6.70	4.53	3.24	5.60
Korea	27.47	8.73	18.79	−10.10	4.41	2.70	5.37
Taiwan	26.65	3.99	21.66	−17.67	3.06	4.23	2.87
USSR	6.81	2.10	4.71	−2.60	2.48	6.09	1.34
Australia	6.05	2.62	3.42	−08.00	3.19	3.77	2.09
Canada	4.57	2.52	2.05	0.467	2.71	3.27	2.09
Total of above 10 countries	31.56	16.46	15.10	13.54	3.60	3.31	3.95
Proportion of above top 10 countries	8.39	8.65	8.13				
Other countries	60.47	25.72	34.76	−9.04	5.68	4.04	7.14

Source: PRC General Customs Administration, *China's Customs Statistics (January–June 2003)*.

Table 1.3

Increased Value in Percentage of Various Trade Sectors, 2002–2003 (%)

Trade sector	2003	2002
General trade	49.75	28.17
Processing trade	39.39	66.52
Other trade	10.86	5.31

Source: PRC General Customs Administration, *China's Customs Statistics (1998–2003)*.

Table 1.4

Comparison of Increases in Trade Value by Type of Enterprise (%)

Type of enterprise	January–June 2003		January–June 2002	
	Exports	Imports	Exports	Imports
State-owned enterprise	15.4	32.1	3.2	3.6
Cooperative joint venture	15.0	17.1	10.2	0.5
Enterprise joint venture	30.3	36.9	7.2	-3.6
Foreign-owned enterprise	49.0	57.7	27.7	32.6
Collective enterprise	31.2	46.5	29.1	11.5

Source: PRC General Customs Administration, *China's Customs Statistics (1998–2003)*.

exports of SOEs reached US$132.3 billion, an increase of 23.5 percent over 2002. Exports totaled US$64 billion, an increase of 15.6 percent over 2002, and imports totaled US$68.3 billion, increasing by 32.1 percent from the previous year.

Comparing the period January to June in 2003 with the same period in 2002, according to China's customs statistics (as seen in Table 1.4), the total value of imports and exports from FOE (foreign-owned enterprises) in China reached US$203.39 million, an increase of 43.3 percent. Among FOE exports reached US$ 60.71 million, an increase of 49 percent, and their imports totaled US$ 59.53 million, increasing by 57.7 percent. The total value of imports and exports of collective enterprises was US$17.21 million, with exports comprising US$10.95 million of that figure, an increase of 31.2 percent, and imports totaling US$6.28 million, an increase of 46.5.1 percent.[8] Import growth among enterprise joint ventures and cooperative joint ventures exceeded export growth in 2002 and the first six months of 2003, indicating their confidence and interest in investment in China.

Table 1.5 shows China's trade relationships with three of its major trading partners. The increased value of imports and exports with Japan, the United States, and the EU from January to June 2003 reached US$47.6 billion,

Table 1.5

Increased Value in Percentage of Imports and Exports with the United States, Japan, and the EU in the First Half of 2003 (%)

Countries	Imports	Exports
USA	45.11	28.28
Japan	53.21	35.88
EU	38.28	17.4

Source: PRC General Customs Administration, *China's Customs Statistics (1998–2003)*.

US$25.7 billion, and US$21.9 billion respectively, with respective percentage increases in imports over the period of 45.1 percent, 53.2, and 38.3 percent. These reflected increases of 16.8 percent, 17.3 percent, and 20.9 percent respectively compared with the same period last year.

Economic recovery in the United States, Japan, and the EU played an important role in pulling up China's exports. China experienced an increased rate of trade with ten of the economically biggest countries in the world. The total value of imports and exports with Japan, the United States, and the EU was US$17.3 billion, an increase of 38.2 percent over 2002. Of this total, exports totaled US$98.2 billion, an increase of 35.5 percent, and imports totaled US$74.6 billion, an increase of 41.6 percent. In terms of the total value of imports and exports from 2002 to mid-2003, China's leading trade partners were the United States, with 45.9 percent, Japan, with 51.6 percent, and the European Union, with 40.2 percent .

China's import and export structure has been upgraded. The growth rate of mechanical and electrical equipment and products, high-tech, and new products is higher than the general trade growth rate and their proportion of the total export value is over 50 percent. From January to June 2003, the export of mechanical and electronic products reached US$19.5 billion, increasing 45.2 percent, comprising 51.7 percent of the total imports and exports, 2.2 percent higher than 2002. Among them, exports were US$96.3 billion, an increase of 41.5 percent, making up 50.6 percent of China's total exports, a 2.8 percent increase over 2002. The value of imports was US$98.2 billion, an increase of 49.1 percent, making up 52.7 percent of China's total imports, a 1.4 percent increase over 2002. The export and import values, as well as the growth rate of imports in mechanical and electronics products are higher than the general growth rate in total imports and exports.

There are several reasons for the high rate of export increases during the first half of 2003. First, depreciation of the U.S. dollar improved China's balance of trade. From July 2001 to June 2003, depreciation of the U.S. dollar compared with the euro reached 40 percent, a new record exchange rate of 1:1.9. Because the exchange rate of the RMB is linked to the U.S. dollar, exports to the EU increased significantly by 44.2 percent from January to June in bilateral trade. Of that, exports were up 48.3 percent, 9 percent higher than the growth of total imports and exports.

Second, tariffs were lowered and some non-tariff measures were abolished, improving conditions for imports and exports. In addition, the fast growth of domestic investment and the Chinese national economy, due in part to companies from developed countries shifting to China at a rapid pace and the quickly increasing rate of FDI, directly affected the growth of the processing trade and the demand for imports.

Third, although the normal import and export activity was affected by SARS, domestic and international supply and demand were not. The ability of enterprises to perform in the import and export sector did not weaken.

In addition, influenced by the war between the United States and Iraq and the outbreak of the SARS epidemic during the first half of 2003, the economic recovery of the United States, Japan, and Europe was not as strong as expected. In contrast, the effect of these factors on China's economic growth and the growth of its import and export sector was far lower than expected by the major worldwide economic research institutions and some pessimistic domestic scholars. China's overall economy continues to grow at a rate of 8.2 percent, and its import and export growth rate continues at 40 percent.

A fall in crude oil prices is improving the imbalance of trade. The war between the United States and Iraq has caused the price of crude oil and other raw materials to rise. This is the main reason for a decline in China's trade surplus. According to China's customs statistics, the increased import value of crude oil and refined oil reached US$5.4 billion, and the import value of steel, natural rubber, and certain plastics reached US$5.4 billion in the first half of 2003. Since May, the price of crude oil and refined oil fell once again. The average price of crude oil in June fell by 11.9 percent from that in April and the average price of refined oil fell by 14.6 percent from that in April. Natural rubber prices fell 4.8 percent from that in April. With the export of crude oil from Iraq resuming in the second half of 2003, the price of crude oil and related products may still fall a bit. This may help improve the balance of trade situation.

China's economy began a new growth stage in 2003. That is, China's economy entered into a new round of high growth—consumer upgrading resulted in industrial upgrading promoting the development of sectors such as housing, automobiles, communications, high-grade electronic goods, and so forth, plus the growth of demand and supply in the international market-

Table 1.6

Foreign Trade, 2003

	Value (US$ billion)	Growth (%)
Total Imports and Exports	851.2	37.1
Exports	438.4	34.6
General Trade	182.0	33.7
Processing Trade	241.8	34.4
Mechanical and Electrical Products	227.5	44.8
Hi-tech Products	110.3	62.2
Imports	412.8	39.9
General Trade	187.7	45.4
Processing Trade	162.9	33.3
Mechanical and Electrical Products	225.0	44.6
Hi-tech Products	119.3	44.0

Source: "Statistical Communiqué of 2003 and Social Development Compiled by Yu Shujun," *Beijing Review* 47, no. 10, March 11, 2004.

place. Most of China's export goods are final consumer goods and raw materials, therefore, the consumption of China's export markets is not likely to be weakened even when there are some uncertain factors in the world economy. If investors buy with large amounts of euros or the Japanese yen for the sake of avoiding risk, the yuan may be devalued indirectly. This may help to further promote Chinese exports.

The trade imbalance between China and the United States, the EU, and Japan is widening and may affect future trade. As for Sino-American trade, the gap in China's favor reached US$103.1 billion (according to U.S. statistics). American companies asked for limits on Chinese imports after protective measures were introduced in 2002.

Despite SARS and the Iraq war, by the end of 2003 Chinese exports and imports had reached US$851.2 billion, an increase of 44 percent compared to the first half of 2003 and 37.1 percent over the previous year. Exports reached US$438.4 billion, increasing 43.4 percent over the first half of 2003 and 34.6 percent over 2002. Imports reached US$412.8 billion, increasing 45 percent over those in the first half of 2003 and 39.9 percent over 2002 (see Table 1.6).[9]

Exports of China's mechanical and electronics products increased in 2003 by 44.8 percent and imports increased by 44.6 percent. Exports of hi-tech products increased by 62.2 percent and imports increased by 44 percent. These increases indicate that the structure of China's imports and exports is

Table 1.7

Primary Trading Partners, 2003

Country	Exports (US$ billions)	Growth (%)	Imports (US$ billion)	Growth (%)
US	92.5	32.2	33.9	24.3
HK	76.3	30.5	11.1	3.7
EU	72.2	49.7	53.1	37.7
Japan	59.4	22.7	74.4	38.7
ASEAN	30.9	31.1	47.3	51.7
ROK	20.1	29.4	43.1	51
Russia	6	71.4	9.7	15.7

Source: "Statistical Communiqué of 2003 National and Social Development Compiled by Yu Shujun," *Beijing Review* 47, no. 10, March 11, 2004.

changing from general trade and processing trade to hi-tech and mechanical and electronics products. China's industries have been upgrading from processing to hi-tech production since the country joined the WTO.

The United States still ranks first among the primary trading partners of China. Hong Kong and the EU are ranked second and third, and Japan ranks fourth. ASEAN and Korea rank fifth and sixth, with Russia ranking seventh. China's trade with the East Asian region and the EU is developing rapidly, especially with Russia. The growth of exports to Russia increased by 71.4 percent, to the EU they increased by 49.7 percent, with ASEAN by 31.1 percent, and 30.5 percent with Hong Kong. Still, China imports the most from Japan (see Table 1.7).[10]

An Overview of China's Trade Progress Since WTO Membership

The continuing growth of exports in China demonstrates a successful industrial structural adjustment and a shift of export direction. There are many factors that have contributed to the growth pattern. China's rapid domestic economic growth stimulated the demand for foreign technology and products. The strengthening of the export refund policy promoted increased foreign trade exports. The improved structure of export commodities began to meet the demands of the international market. The mild recovery of the world economy and the depreciation of the U.S. dollar, with the Chinese currency stable and pegged to it, positively influenced China's trade growth. The foreign trade environment of China was improved to some extent by its WTO membership.

Foreign investment enterprises and non-state-owned enterprises also each played an increasingly important role in promoting China's exports. The revised macroeconomic policy and the encouraging upward movement of exports created a sound environment for increased business exports. The governmental policy encouraging foreign trade helped to stimulate various service-related industries and also facilitated trade growth. China's membership in the WTO provides many domestic enterprises with opportunities in the overseas market and has forced them to upgrade their products to meet the competitive demands of the international market.

Notes

1. PRC General Customs Administration, *China's Customs Statistics (1998–2003)*.
2. Ibid.
3. Ibid.
4. Ibid.
5. Ibid.
6. Ibid.
7. PRC General Customs Administration, *China's Customs Statistics (January–June 2003)*.
8. Ibid.
9. "Statistical Communiqué of 2003 and Social Development Compiled by Yu Shujun," *Beijing Review* 47, no. 10, March 11, 2004.
10. Ibid.

References

Jiang Xiaojuan. 2002. "A General Introduction to Foreign Investment in China in 2001 and the Trend in 2001." *Finance and Economy*, no. 2.

Ministry of Foreign Trade and Economic Cooperation, Foreign Investment Department. 2002. *2002 Statistics on Foreign Investment in China*. Beijing.

National Bureau of Statistics. 2001–2003. *China Statistical Yearbook*. Beijing: China Statistics Press.

PRC General Customs Administration. *China's Customs Statistics. 2001, 2002, 2003*.

Qu Weizhi, ed. 2001. *A Report on a Study of the Exportation of High-Tech Electronic Products. Electronics*. Beijing: Industry Publishing House.

2

Foreign Direct Investment

Opportunity or Challenge for China After WTO Membership?

Kevin H. Zhang

China's accession to the World Trade Organization (WTO) in 2001 has created not only opportunities to attract more foreign investors but also potentially dangerous challenges from foreign direct investment (FDI). It is estimated that China could attract about US$100 billion in FDI annually after 2007, due to an increasingly liberalized FDI climate following China's commitment to the WTO and its subsequent rapid economic growth. Many analysts view China as one of a few countries in the world that have been successful in attracting and utilizing FDI (Hale and Hale 2003; Lardy 1995; Zhang 1999, 2001a, 2001d; Zhang and Song 2000). By the end of 2003, the accumulated FDI in China was over $500 billion. The role of FDI in the Chinese economy may be suggested from the following figures. In 2001, FDI inflows constituted over 10 percent of gross fixed capital formation; 29 percent of industrial output was produced by foreign investment enterprises (FIEs); and half of China's exports were created by FIEs (National Bureau of Statistics 2003; United Nations Conference on Trade and Development [UNCTAD] 2003). However, can China survive with its FDI-led growth strategy as a WTO member?

Some dangers associated with the increasing presence of multinational corporations (MNCs) in China have been emerging for a few years (Huang 2003). The Chinese economy has been more dependent on foreign capital and experienced more volatility from changes in world markets. Foreign firms have gained more control over more products through growing market shares. While China's exports grew rapidly in the past five years, most of the growth was contributed by FIEs rather than domestic firms. At the same time, the domestic value-added of the exports by FIEs has been small because such exports have basically consisted of processing or assembling. The trade surplus did not increase but instead fell since the growth of exports has been fueled by an equal amount of imports. Unlike popular views, a provocative counterclaim has emerged: the large absorption of FDI by China may not contribute to economic growth in the long run but may be a sign of some fundamental weaknesses in the Chinese economy. The debate on the role of FDI in the Chinese economy raises two groups of questions. First, what benefits and opportunities does FDI bring to China's development process, and what risks and dangers accompany it? When are the benefits and opportunities likely to predominate, and when are the risks and dangers likely to prevail? Second, can the Chinese government play a larger role in enhancing the use of FDI in the development process? If so, what policies should Chinese governments adopt to capture the benefits, avoid the dangers, and maximize the contributions of FDI? In sum, can China be a winner in the game with multinational corporations within the framework of the WTO?

Features of FDI Inflows After WTO Membership

China's membership in the WTO marks a new stage in the effect and volume of its FDI. Fulfillment of China's WTO obligations involves considerable investment liberalization, which will have a substantial impact on FDI inflows and operations of foreign investment enterprises. Table 2.1 summarizes the main commitments made by China to the WTO. Accession to the WTO has made the economy more attractive to foreign investors. For example, in services, in which FDI was largely restricted, China has committed to liberalizing a number of industries, including business services, communications, distribution, education, financial services, health and social services, and maritime and air transport services. The removal of foreign equity limitations will not only attract more new investors, but also enable foreign joint-venture partners to increase their equity shares in existing affiliates. Indeed, after the preliminary liberalization measures taken by China in the process of accession to the WTO FDI flows to the economy during 2000–2002 rose from $40 billion to $53 billion, mainly boosted by flows to the services sector. The share of the service sector in total inflows increased from an average of 8 percent during the 1979–1991 period to over 30 percent in 2002 (SSB 2003).

Unlike services, most manufacturing industries in China had been largely open to foreign investors and had already attracted a significant amount of FDI. Accession to the WTO may not, therefore, immediately have substantial

Table 2.1

Key Changes Promised by China upon WTO Accession

Agriculture
- Future farm subsidies will be capped at 8.5% of the value of domestic farm production
- Agricultural duties will fall from 22% to 17%

Automobiles
- Import tariffs on automobiles will drop to 25% by mid-2006 from the current 80–100%
- Restrictions will be lifted on category, type, and model of vehicles produced as joint ventures

Banking
- Foreign banks will be allowed to conduct domestic currency business with Chinese firms and individuals in phases
- All geographic restrictions on foreign banking business to be eliminated after five years

Distribution/Retail
- Restrictions on distribution services for most products will be phased out within three years

Energy/Oil
- Crude and refined oil sectors will be gradually opened to private traders
- Retail oil distribution will open in three years

Insurance
- Increased foreign ownership of life, property, and casualty insurance operations will be allowed*
- Foreign insurance companies will gradually enter the group, health, and pensions business

Securities
- Minority foreign-owned joint ventures will be allowed into the fund management industry
- Three years after accession, foreign firms will be allowed 49% stakes in joint ventures

Telecommunications
- Foreign companies can take increased stakes in mobile phone companies, in phases
- Tariffs on high-tech products will be eliminated by 2005**

Source: *Wall Street Journal*, September 17, 2001, p. 1.

* The level of foreign companies' ownership in insurance operations will not increase; rather, the number of cities in which they are permitted to operate will increase.

** The phase out in tariffs on high-tech products does not actually apply to telecommunications, rather, the phase out applies to semiconductors, computers, and other products associated with information technology–associated products.

FDI-generating effects. Indeed, the reduction of import restrictions and the elimination of trade-related investment measures in industries such as automobiles may reduce flows by eroding the incentive for "barrier-hopping" FDI. Nevertheless, over time, freer access to the import of inputs could help improve the cost-quality conditions of manufacturing and increase the attractiveness of the economy as a site for cheap labor-seeking manufacturing FDI.

Several new features of FDI flows have been emerging, which will have significant influences on China's benefits from and costs of FDI:

1. FDI from the United States, the European Union, and Japan grew fast, although Hong Kong and other Asian overseas-Chinese enterprises are still the largest source of China's FDI. In 1992, FDI from Hong Kong and Taiwan constituted 80 percent of total FDI flows into China, but the share dropped substantially a decade later, to 43 percent in 2001 (SSB 1993, 2002).

2. While small-scale and labor-intensive FDI projects have been dominant, large-scale and capital/technology-intensive FDI activities have increased substantially. According to UNCTAD (2003), about four hundred of the Fortune 500 firms have invested in over two thousand projects in China. The world's leading manufacturers of computers, electronics, telecommunications equipment, pharmaceuticals, petrochemicals, and power-generating equipment have extended their production networks to China. Inflows used to concentrate in labor-intensive industries until the early 1990s. Since then, capital/technology-intensive industries have been attracting more and more FDI. The production of FIEs in China is moving from the low level of the value chain to the high levels as technology-intensive activities of multinational corporations rise.

3. More FDI is market seeking rather than export oriented. With relaxation of export requirements and the Chinese government's WTO commitments, more products by foreign investment enterprises may be sold locally. This results in growing market shares for foreign firms in many industries.

4. Wholly foreign-owned enterprises (WFOE) have become the dominant entry model of FDI into China, and joint ventures are no longer favored by foreign investors. MNC's dominant entry mode into China used to be through joint ventures, but WFOE projects have risen since the mid-1990s and constituted 60 percent of total FDI in value received in 2001 (SSB 2002).

5. While the manufacturing sector receives a majority of FDI, growing investment flows now go to the service sector, for example telecommunications, banking, insurance, and retail. This is in large part due to the favorable FDI measures that have been introduced in the services sector, as well as in the manufacturing sector. For example, nearly all the big-name department stores and supermarkets such as Auchan, Carrefour, Dairy Farm, Ito Yokado,

Jusco, Makro, Metro, Pricesmart, 7–Eleven, and Wal-Mart have appeared in China (UNCTAD 2003). China will allow 100 percent foreign equity ownership in such industries as leasing, storage and warehousing, and in wholesale and retail trade by 2004, advertising and multimodal transport services by 2005, insurance brokerage by 2006, and transportation (railroad) by 2007. With more FDI in services, China's investment environment in turn may be further enhanced.

6. Many MNCs have chosen China as the location for regional operation centers and research-development (R&D) centers. Most recently, R&D activities have emerged as a bridge for FDI, with over one hundred R&D centers established by MNCs. Microsoft, Motorola, GM, GE, JVC, Lucent-Bell, Samsung, Nortel, IBM, Intel, DuPont, P&G, Ericsson, Nokia, Panasonic, Mitsubishi, AT&T, and Siemens, to name a few, all have R&D facilities in China.

7. Unlike FDI in many developing countries, almost all of the foreign affiliates that were established before 2001 took the form of greenfield investment (that is, setting up an entire new plant), rather than merger & acquisition (M&A). This has changed since China's entry into the WTO. In fact, China now encourages M&A as the investment form for multinational corporations, especially for China's large-scale, state-owned enterprises.

In sum, accession to the WTO will make China more attractive for FDI. The service sector will become more important as the engine of growth for inward flows of FDI. In the manufacturing sector, FDI will play a more prominent role in the process of restructuring and consolidation. As the FDI regime is gradually liberalized, inflows are likely to reach new and higher levels.

Conflicts Between MNEs and China

Few areas in economics arouse as much controversy as does the issue of the impact of FDI on its host economies. The on-going popular view suggests that FDI is likely to be an engine of host economic growth (UNCTAD 1992). The arguments this view is based upon include: (a) inward FDI may enhance capital formation and employment augmentation; (b) FDI may promote manufacturing exports; and (c) FDI may bring special resources into host economies, such as management know-how and international marketing networks. The recent literature emphasizes spillover effects of FDI in host economies that may be even more critical than the direct impacts mentioned above (UNCTAD 2003). The spillovers occur when advanced technologies embodied in FDI are transmitted to domestic plants simply because of the presence of MNCs. The technology and productivity of local firms may improve as

FDI creates backward and forward linkages and foreign firms provide technical assistance to their local suppliers and customers. The competitive pressure exerted by the foreign affiliates may also force local firms to operate more efficiently and to introduce new technologies earlier than what would otherwise have been the case.

At the other extreme, one could argue that inward FDI may be detrimental to the host economies for the following reasons: (a) FDI may lead to the shrinking of indigenous industries through intense competition due to the strong economic power of MNCs; (b) FDI may reduce a host country's welfare when MNCs manipulate the domestic market and transfer pricing; and (c) FDI may create enclave economies within a host country, widen the income gap, and bias the host economy toward an inappropriate technology and product mix (Ram and Zhang 2002).

The mixed effects of FDI on host economies reflect the fundamental conflicts between MNCs and host economies in many areas of interest. Table 2.2 summarizes the main points of such conflicts in the case of China. For example, China may desire large investments with an export orientation, but MNCs may prefer small investments aimed at the domestic market; China wants high-technology and high value-added projects, which may be the opposite of what MNCs are willing to offer; MNCs desire wholly owned affiliates, rather than the Chinese-majority joint venture structure preferred by China. While China's commitments as a WTO member (such as liberalized ownership structures and the opening of more sectors including services) may help to attract more FDI flows from Western MNCs, the benefits China can draw from the investment depend on China's bargaining power relative to MNCs. China may develop a regulatory system to manage and control MNC behavior within the WTO framework.

Given the potential for mixed effects of FDI, the outcome depends largely on a host country's capacity to influence and control MNC activities. Such capacity depends on the host country's bargaining power and the possibilities for increasing it. A country's bargaining power is determined by the nature of the host country and the attributes of the industries receiving FDI. If a host country is large and is seen as an important market for the multinational, if it would be costly for the multinational to relocate and the host government is well informed about those costs, then the country's bargaining position will be relatively strong. It may be able to get away with relatively high taxes on MNCs' profits and tight regulation of their behavior (e.g., their employment practices and their care for the environment). If, however, the country is economically weak and MNCs are footloose, then the deal it can negotiate is unlikely to be very favorable.

Table 2.2

Conflict Between MNCs and China in the Establishment Process of Foreign-Invested Enterprises (FIEs)

Host Government Preferences	MNC Preferences
To promote economic growth and maximize national welfare	To enhance global competitiveness and thus maximize profits
To obtain advanced and suitable technology	To transfer old and standard technology
To export more products by FIEs	To sell more in local markets
Joint venture or host majority joint venture	Wholly-foreign-owned enterprise structure
Large investment projects	Small or medium investment projects
Single market orientation	National market orientation
More local contents and intensive local linkages	More imports from parent factories
More profits from FIEs reinvested in host country	Increased repatriation of profits
More greenfield-investment projects	More projects through mergers and acquisitions
More FDI in desirable sectors in manufacturing, infrastructure, and agriculture	More FDI in profitable sectors such as finance, insurance, and other services
More "big bang" up-front capital injections	Gradually phased paid-in capital

Perceived Welfare from FDI to China

Desirable ◄─────────────────────────────► Undesirable

Source: Analysis by Kevin H. Zhang, based upon D.H. Rosen (1999).

The host's bargaining power is also influenced by features of the industrial structure. Three crucial aspects of the industrial structure have been identified: (a) the extent of competition in the industry; (b) the changeableness of the technology; and (c) the importance of marketing and product differentiation (Moran 1985). The bargaining power of a host country would be high relative to MNCs if competition is high, if technology is stable, and if marketing is of little importance.

To reduce dangers from FDI and to minimize the costs of using FDI, China has paid special attention to the following aspects: anticompetitive practices by foreign affiliates; volatile FDI flows and related payments deleterious to the balance of payments; tax avoidance and abusive transfer pricing by foreign affiliates; crowding out of local firms and suppression of domestic entrepreneurial development; crowding out of local products, technologies, networks, and business practices with harmful sociocultural effects; concessions to MNCs, especially in export processing zones, allowing them to skirt labor; excessive influence of MNCs on economic affairs and decisionmaking, with possible negative effects on industrial development and national security.

China's Advantages and FDI Policies

As the largest FDI recipient, China definitely has some unique advantages, including a huge domestic market and Hong Kong, Taiwan, and other wealthy overseas Chinese, and the liberalized FDI regime (Zhang 2000a, 2000b, 2001b, 2001c; Zhang and Markusen 1999). The large market along with the cheap labor makes China a highly desirable location for FDI and hence is an extremely strong, positive lure for MNCs. China has a special asset of overseas Chinese, particularly in Hong Kong and Taiwan, who provide most of the FDI received in China. Overseas Chinese not only share the same language, culture, and family tradition with China, but also have relatives, friends, and former business ties in China. Such "Chinese connections" make it much easier for them to negotiate and operate joint ventures in China than investors from elsewhere. China, perhaps, is the country with the friendliest FDI policy in the world. The attitude of the Chinese government toward MNCs is far more liberal than that of other developing countries, especially those in East Asia such as Japan, South Korea, and Taiwan.

These advantages along with China's rapid growth, improving infrastructures, and cheap resources largely enhance China's bargaining power and help to capture benefits from FDI. For example, the huge market has been the greatest strength China has used in bargaining with MNCs, particularly in industries in which international competition to enter that market is fierce (Zhang 1999). This strength especially provides China with the ability to utilize competition among the multinationals to play one off against another for better terms. Another advantage is the benefits to China from Hong Kong and Taiwan. These overseas Chinese investors contribute to the Chinese economy in various ways: their products are mainly for export, their labor-intensive technology is consistent with China's comparative advantages, their focus is primarily on cost reduction and price competitiveness, and the overall expense to the local economy is less.

China's competent central government lends credibility to its transactions and thus helps to maximize benefits and minimize costs of FDI. The government's monopoly over joint venture approvals allows it to determine the range of terms for FDI contracts. The central government also is positioned to supervise individual bargaining sessions at the firm level, and the state organs and personnel subject to central supervision can control the negotiating process (Zhang 2001d).

The benefits of FDI do not automatically accrue evenly across countries. It is possible for some countries to be worse, rather than better off with inward FDI flows. National policies matter when it comes to attracting FDI and for reaping the full benefits. In fact, well-designed host-government FDI policy is a sufficient condition for effective use of FDI. China singled out and encouraged export-oriented FDI and technologically advanced FDI, offering those investors many incentives. China's demands clustered around performance requirements in two categories: pressuring the multinationals to produce more value-added products domestically, providing more local content in their finished product, and expanding linkages in the indigenous economy; and pushing the multinationals to use their worldwide marketing networks to export more products and components out of China.

China's opening to FDI was symbolized by the promulgation of the "Chinese-Foreign Joint Venture Law" on July 1, 1979. While permitting entry of foreign firms, the law did not create a legal framework that allowed for currency convertibility and reduced red tape. In 1986, new provisions including preferential tax policies were established to encourage FDI. However, with the exception of offshore oil exploration and the real estate sector, FDI was invited exclusively for exports. Under the export-promotion FDI strategy, many export-processing and export-assembling plants (mainly from Hong Kong and Taiwan) were established in special economic zones, coastal cities, and economic and technological development zones. At the same time, the foreign investors that targeted domestic markets encountered many difficulties and, as a result, their investments were relatively small (Zhang 2000a).

The "export promotion" FDI strategy did not change much until 1992, when China began to gradually open its domestic market to multinational firms in certain sectors, including telecommunications, transportation, banking, and insurance. The gradual FDI strategy shift from export-promotion to technology-promotion was largely due to pressures from the United States and Western European countries that had increasing trade deficits with China due to its FDI export boom. Moreover, China realized that technology transfers from industrial countries might not be possible if market-oriented FDI was not allowed.

The Chinese government had been considering three objectives as key elements of its FDI strategy: attracting FDI, benefiting more from it, and reducing its dangers. The Chinese leaders understood that attracting FDI might not be enough to ensure they would derive its full economic benefits, since foreign investors might not transfer enough new technology or transfer it effectively and at the desired depth. Thus policies have been designed to induce investors to act in ways that enhance the development impact—by building local capacities, using local suppliers, and upgrading local skills, technological capabilities, and infrastructure.

The main policies and measures used by China to achieve its goal include:

1. Increasing the contribution of foreign affiliates to the host country through mandatory measures. The objective of this measure is to prescribe what foreign affiliates must do to raise exports, train local workers, or transfer technology. The key instrument here is the use of performance requirements.

2. Increasing the contribution of foreign affiliates to the host country by encouraging them to act in a desired way: The key issue here, as it is in attracting FDI, is using incentives to influence the behavior of foreign affiliates (incentives may be tied to performance requirements). Particularly important is enticing foreign affiliates to transfer technology to domestic firms and to create local R&D capacity. According to UNCTAD (2003), over four hundred centers for R&D have been established by MNCs in China, with $3 billion in R&D investment mainly in electronics, telecommunications, transportation, pharmaceuticals, chemical materials, and chemicals.

The Chinese government understood that benefits from FDI might increase as its capabilities to influence MNC activities strengthened over time. New technologies can be disbursed in China only if the skill base is adequate or if domestic suppliers and competitors can meet the MNCs' needs and learn from them. Export activities can grow only if the quality of the infrastructure so permits. Thus China worked diligently to adopt well-defined measures of investment promotion to attract the appropriate FDI projects. It designed realistic domestic-content requirements to upgrade domestic industries and set up optimal export-performance requirements to create advanced comparative advantages in global markets.

Challenges Following China's Entry into the WTO

While China's experience is impressive, challenges are severe, particularly following its accession to the WTO. China's FDI regime and relevant policies have to change or adjust to be consistent with the rules of the WTO. Large Western MNCs have great bargaining power relative to host countries, even to China. This power is greatly strengthened by their predominantly oligopolistic positions in worldwide product markets. With that power, MNCs enjoy the ability to manipulate prices and profits, to collude with other firms in determining areas of control, and generally to restrict the entry of potential competition.

FDI may be detrimental to the Chinese economy in the long run, since the negative effects of MNCs on host economies in general tend to show up ten to twenty years later. Rather than enhancing China's economic growth, FDI might actually slow down growth by making the Chinese economy dependent upon or controlled by large MNCs. A growing challenge facing China is displacement of indigenous production by foreign investment enterprises. MNCs could buy out existing import-competitive industries. More fundamentally, MNCs could use their competitive advantages in technology and management to drive local competitors out of business.

FDI may reduce China's foreign-exchange earnings on both current and capital accounts. The experiences of many developing countries with a long history of using FDI (Argentina, Brazil, and Mexico, for example) suggest that regular capital account deficits emerged as a result of MNCs' remitting excessive profits. The net negative impact on host economies' international balance of payments is associated with a reduction of host countries' welfare. After China hosts a certain amount of FDI, it is likely to experience similar problems of current and capital account deficits. Also, if mergers and acquisitions (M&A) become the dominant mode of investment, MNCs may bring little capital into China.

Contributions of foreign investment enterprises' public revenues may be considerably less than they should be as a result of transfer pricing and a variety of investment allowances provided by the Chinese government. Some evidence has showed that with transfer pricing, many foreign investment enterprises in China did not generate tax revenues that corresponded to their sales and profits. The role of MNCs in contributing public revenue has been insignificant.

The Chinese government has made great efforts to encourage transfers of technology and management skills, but the extent and content of such transfers have been unsatisfactory. MNCs are still keeping all R&D in their home countries so they are able to retain a monopoly on their technology. They are not willing to establish any linkages to local firms since such linkages may reduce their profits. Even with some transfers, the appropriateness of the technology transferred is still in question. MNCs may transfer some out-dated technologies, or not adapt the technology to local factor conditions or requirements.

The management know-how and technology provided by MNCs may in fact inhibit developing local sources of these scarce skills and resources due to the foreign dominance in Chinese markets.

The dangers from FDI could appear in other aspects of the long-term national welfare. MNC activities may reinforce China's dualistic economic structure and exacerbate income inequalities due to their uneven impact on development. Studies (for example, Zhang and Zhang 2003) have suggested that MNCs contribute to China's widening income gap, and exacerbate the urban bias and widen urban-rural differences. MNCs encourage inappropriate patterns of consumption through elite-oriented advertising and superior marketing techniques, and promote increasing consumption of their products at the expense of other (perhaps more critical) goods.

MNCs may influence government policies in unfavorable directions for China's development by gaining excessive protection, tax rebates, investment allowances, and cheap factory sites and social services. They may develop allied local groups through higher wages, hiring (displacing) the best of the local entrepreneurs, and fostering elite loyalty and socialization through pressures for conformity. MNCs may also foster alien values, images, and lifestyles incompatible with local customs and beliefs. Powerful MNCs may gain control over Chinese assets and jobs, allowing them to exert considerable influence on political as well as economic decisions at all levels in China.

A Final Overview

While FDI has been viewed as a catalyst to economic growth in developing countries, there have been no countries that have been successful in promoting growth through FDI in the long run. China's experience so far seems to be an exception. Evidence shows that the net effects of FDI on the Chinese economy are positive and, to certain extent, FDI has been the engine of China's economic growth.

China's success so far is associated with some unusual factors that are neither surprising nor accidental. China's special advantages come from three sources: the huge market, the large number of rich overseas Chinese investors, and the central government's effective FDI strategy and policy.

Challenges China has faced since joining the WTO derive from two areas: changes in China's FDI regime and policy under the WTO framework may undermine China's advantages and bargaining power and the net long-term effects of Western MNCs may be negative since they have strong market power and primarily target China's domestic market. With further opening of the domestic market to MNCs in almost all sectors, there are increasing opportunities for Western MNCs to gain at China's expense.

China still has a 50 percent chance to win the game with MNCs. From the Chinese perspectives, the outcome depends on how it balances technology transfers and domestic market protection. China should take full advantage of its large market to shape MNC activities. A strong and competent central government should continue to bargain with Western MNCs. FDI from overseas Chinese should be continuously encouraged with various incentives.

References

Hale, D., and L.H. Hale. 2003. "China Takes Off." *Foreign Affairs* 82, no. 6 (November/December): 36–53.

Huang, Y. 2003. *Selling China: Foreign Direct Investment During the Reform Era.* Cambridge: Cambridge University Press.

Lardy, Nicholas R. 1995. "The Role of Foreign Trade and Investment in China's Economic Transformation." *China Quarterly*, no. 144: 1065–82.

Moran, T.H. 1985. *Multinational Corporations: The Political Economy of Foreign Direct Investment.* Lexington, MA: Lexington Books.

National Bureau of Statistics. 1993, 2002, 2003. *China Statistical Yearbook.* Beijing: China Statistics Press.

Ram, Rati, and Kevin H. Zhang. 2002. "Foreign Direct Investment and Economic Growth: Evidence from Cross-Country Data for the 1990s." *Economic Development and Cultural Change* 51, no. 1: 205–15.

Rosen, Daniel H. 1999. *Behind the Open Door: Foreign Enterprises in the Chinese Marketplace.* Washington, DC: Institute for International Economics.

United Nations Conference on Trade and Development (UNCTAD). 1992, 2003. *World Investment Report.* New York: United Nations.

Zhang, Kevin H. 1999. "How Does FDI Interact with Economic Growth in a Large Developing Country? The Case of China." *Economic Systems* 23, no. 4: 291–303.

———. 2000a. "Human Capital, Country Size, and North-South Manufacturing Multinational Enterprises." *Economia Internazionale/International Economics* 53, no. 2 (May): 237–60.

———. 2000b. "Why Is US Direct Investment in China So Small?" *Contemporary Economic Policy* 18, no. 1: 82–94.

———. 2001a. "Roads to Prosperity: Assessing the Impact of FDI on Economic Growth in China." *Economia Internazionale/International Economics* 54, no. 1: 113–25.

———. 2001b. "What Explains the Boom of Foreign Direct Investment in China?" *Economia Internazionale/International Economics* 54, no. 2: 1–24.

———. 2001c. "What Attracts Multinational Corporations to Developing Countries? Evidence from China." *Contemporary Economic Policy* 19, no. 3: 336–46.

———. 2001d. "How Does FDI Affect Economic Growth in China?" *Economics of Transition* 9, no. 3: 679–93.

Zhang, Kevin H., and James Markusen. 1999. "Vertical Multinationals and Host-Country Characteristics." *Journal of Development Economics* 59: 233–52.

Zhang, Kevin H., and Shunfen Song. 2000. "Promoting Exports: The Role of Inward FDI in China." *China Economic Review* 11, no. 4: 385–96.

Zhang, Xiaobo, and Kevin H. Zhang. 2003. "How Does Globalization Affect Regional Inequality Within a Developing Country? Evidence from China." *Journal of Development Studies* 39, no. 4 (April): 47–67.

3

China's WTO Compliance

Commitment and Progress in the Initial Stage

Penelope B. Prime

China joined the World Trade Organization (WTO) in December 2001. This event—the culmination of years of difficult negotiations and compromise—was historic. China's membership meant the largest economy outside of the international trading system was brought into a regularized process of meeting timetables and following rules with respect to a vast array of trade, investment, and governance activity. The extent and interrelationships of these commitments, if successful, will result in a major liberalization of not only China's foreign trade regime, but of the economy overall.[1]

From the WTO members' point of view, negotiations with China over what was required for membership were especially difficult for two reasons. First, members were concerned that China's economy was not a market-based system. Since the development of certain sectors of China's economy were quite advanced but were often dominated by state-owned companies and state trading monopolies, members feared unfair competition in these areas. Second, members were not confident that China's central government would be able to enforce the terms agreed upon. Because of the strength of sector-based ministries, and weakened control of the central government over localities, members worried that the Chinese officials who made the commitments would not have sufficient power to ensure compliance.

One and a half years after joining, China's and the world's attention is indeed on compliance. Economic malaise, job loss, and trade imbalances in many parts of the world have caused analysts and politicians, in developing and developed countries alike, to look for reasons for these problems. Many economies are reluctantly adjusting to changes caused by China's impressive entry into international markets. At the same time people in China are dealing with the wrenching transition that has been going on for two decades, which received added impetus from WTO-induced liberalization.

The purpose of this chapter is to survey the commitments that China made for the first two years of WTO membership and evaluate broadly its progress toward meeting those commitments. This evaluation will take into account views on compliance from both inside and outside China, as well as develop the international and national economic contexts within which this process is unfolding.

China's WTO Commitments

While the negotiations for China's entry into the WTO were complex, implementation of the agreements will be even more so. The number of individual commitments and extent of market liberalizing goals are both vast. The U.S. General Accounting Office (GAO) has identified over seven hundred commitments for trade regime reform and over seven thousand goods and services for market access liberalization (GAO 2002). In addition, the GAO report emphasizes the interrelationships between many of the commitments.[2]

China's WTO agreement deals with eight areas: trade framework, import regulation, export regulation, trading rights and industrial policies, agriculture, services, intellectual property rights, and safeguards and other trade remedies. The agreements also vary by type, and include issues related to definitions, reporting, transparency, laws and regulations, guidance, adherence to WTO, and nondiscrimination. Further, some of the agreements have a phase-in timetable stretching to 2016. China's commitments regarding intellectual property rights and export regulation, however, were all due to be implemented upon accession, and the trade framework commitments were to be completed by the end of 2002. The commitments regarding the process of standardizing the technical barriers to trade as part of the import regulations were to be met by the end of 2003. Each of the other four categories has longer phase-in periods before being complete, but a substantial part of the commitments were to be accomplished upon becoming a member. A brief summary of the key elements of each category follows.

1. *Trade Framework:* This set of commitments deals with the nature and enforcement of laws and information regarding China's trade regime. Implementation has required changes, additions, or repeal of a large number of laws, and therefore has been a major impetus for development of the legal system generally. All of the changes were to be completed by accession in December 2001, except for some nondiscrimination aspects in pharmaceuticals, spirits, and chemicals, which were to be completed by December 2002.

Some of the commitments in this area went beyond what are normally expected of WTO members, such as allowing a period for public comment before a trade measure can be implemented.

2. *Import Regulation*: Because of the highly restrictive nature of China's trading system before trade liberalization began, many of the changes required to bring China into WTO compliance fell into this category. High tariff rates, quotas, and unnecessary technical standards and inspection procedures were in place to restrict trade, and many of these had to be lifted. The GAO estimates that about one-third of the commitments fall into this category (GAO 2002). Rules on the management of the system, such as how to issue licenses, what information needs to be published, how to classify country of origin, and how to value goods for custom purposes, were also part of the agreement.

The technical barriers to trade are also a major part of this category. These barriers cover packaging, marketing, labeling, and procedures for testing and sampling, which can create barriers to trade if not applied evenly or in a reasonable manner conforming to international standards. Implementation of the technical barriers commitments was to be phased in through June 2003.

3. *Export Regulation*: As part of its policy to build self-sufficiency under the pre-1978 system, China restricted exports of key agricultural and mining products. WTO allows such restrictions only in special cases such as times when there is a critical shortage of food. As of 1992, export-licensing requirements covered about half of China's exports. To become compliant, China agreed to end all export licenses except under exceptional circumstances, a stipulation that is allowed all member countries. China also agreed to bring export duties in line with WTO principles. All of these commitments were to be completed upon accession.

4. *Trading Rights and Industrial Policies*: A key element of China's formerly planned economy was state ownership of assets and state control of trading. This section of the WTO agreement can be viewed as the most relevant to domestic market liberalization. Containing over one hundred commitments, it deals with ending price controls, allowing competition with state companies in trading, investment and procurement, allowing state-owned enterprises to make their own buying and selling decisions, and separating investment and trade decisions from other potential goals such as domestic content, foreign exchange balancing, export promotion, and so on. The provisions to end general state trading rights will be phased in over three years (for silk it is four years), and the rules governing investment in the auto industry will be phased in over four years. Otherwise the commitments generally are applicable upon succession.

5. *Agriculture*: The agricultural sector in China has been one of the most

protected for many decades, with self-sufficiency in food as a national goal. The WTO commitments are a clear indication that this approach has ended, but the negotiations were particularly difficult in this area. In addition, many analysts in China worry about the effect more competition in agriculture will have on the livelihoods and options of millions of farmers.

One of the very last issues still being negotiated as the deadline approached for the WTO meeting in December 2001 was domestic support of agriculture prices. WTO sets a minimal level of support that is exempted from the total level of support allowed. Negotiators from China wanted China's support to be the same as developing countries, which is 10 percent, but other members argued this was too high. The compromise reached was 8.5 percent, which is lower than the developing country rate but higher than the developed country rate of 5 percent. Unlike many other situations, this was not a question of lowering support to meet the guideline, but rather setting a threshold for possible future support. Currently analysts estimate China's support of agriculture at only 2 percent.

6. *Services*: As a result of a bias toward heavy industrial production throughout the era of planning in China, the service sector is relatively underdeveloped. Hence Chinese negotiators argued for more time to prepare for liberalization in this sector as foreign providers of services are much more experienced and had been virtually barred from participating in the Chinese market. These concerns are reflected in the types of commitments that were agreed to, and the fact that most of them will be phased in over time rather than required at the time of joining. Nonetheless, over a period of three to five years China has committed to opening the business environment to areas such as insurance, distribution, banking, transport, and business services in major ways.

7. *Intellectual Property Rights (IPR)*: The main framework for IPR compliance falls under the WTO's agreement on Trade-Related Aspects of Intellectual Property Rights (TRIPS). All WTO members are required to comply with TRIPS and, accordingly, China's commitments were effective upon accession. The GAO has identified thirty-two commitments relating to IPR, with the majority focusing on enforcement. In principle, China had moved to support standard practice in complying with IPR protection laws before joining WTO. WTO members, however, were particularly concerned about enforcement in this category and therefore China's protocol deals with these concerns.

8. *Safeguards and Other Trade Remedies*: Uncertainty about China's ability to comply with its WTO agreements, combined with uncertainty about how China's liberalization and expected growth would affect individual economies, this last category of agreements allow member countries to use counter measures against Chinese imports under particular circumstances that they

deem to be detrimental to their economies. This category also includes a mandated review mechanism, which is much more involved and lasts a longer time than the regular reviews of other member countries. This mechanism will be discussed in more detail in the next section on monitoring China's compliance progress. In contrast to the other categories of agreements, these safeguards and trade remedies will be phased out over time.

Building Infrastructure to Monitor Compliance

One of the most important pieces of the adjustment process is for China to build an infrastructure to monitor progress and facilitate compliance. Commitments have been made, but to be able to comply, personnel need to be trained to understand the commitments, convey the new rules, collect information on what is actually happening in different sectors and parts of the country, and impose punitive measures where necessary. This in itself is a major commitment that will require resources. Estimates of the institutional and policy adjustment costs of WTO compliance reach millions of dollars for each area of implementation.[3]

As the previous section suggests, China's commitments are extensive and complicated. WTO member countries were concerned enough about compliance to build an unusual review process into the first ten years of China's membership. The WTO's Transitional Review Mechanism for China involves an annual review for the first eight years, with a final review in year ten. The protocol specifies what information China must provide for review, and requires responses to questions raised in the process of the review. The protocol further requires China to report on the development of trade with member countries and issues regarding the development of China's trade regime, not just progress in meeting commitments specific to WTO membership.[4]

Long before actual accession, different parts of the Chinese government began to study the changes that would be necessary for institutions and policy to be WTO compatible, and to begin training personnel to work on these issues. They also implemented some tariff, transparency, and other provisions ahead of accession. To prepare government to take on the tasks of compliance, the central government established a Department of the WTO within the Ministry of Foreign Trade and Economic Cooperation, later reorganized and re-named the Ministry of Commerce.[5] Other quasi-government or nongovernmental organizations were started as well. For example, a WTO Inquiry Center was set up under the China (Hainan) Institute of Reform and Development; the Shanghai WTO Affairs Consulting Center performs a variety of functions, including research about WTO implementation; the University of International Business and Economics in Beijing supports training and analysis at its WTO Research Center; and the China Society for WTO Studies is a national organization devoted to studying the WTO.

In addition, many organizations are training Chinese officials, business people, and other citizens to understand the changes their government agreed to and how to go about complying and enforcing the new rules. The U.S. government, primarily through the Commerce Department and the Foreign Commercial Service, has held many seminars and presentations on WTO basics as well as more specific topics. Governments of the European Union, Japan, and Australia have also made major efforts to help educate and facilitate the process, as have many nongovernmental organizations.[6] The EU, for example, has committed approximately 270 million euros to forty projects aimed at assisting with China's reforms and liberalization.[7] The Program for China's Accession to WTO and the EU-China Intellectual Property Rights Cooperation Program were two that were directly tied to WTO goals (Goldstein and Anderson 2002, 11).

U.S. government interest in China's compliance has been particularly high. During the negotiations for membership, the U.S.–China agreement was the linchpin that allowed the process to be completed. U.S. negotiators represented many concerns about China's membership, and the agreement passed Congress but with fierce debate and substantial opposition. Immediately upon China's accession, monitoring groups were formed. The Department of Agriculture set up a China Task Force; the International Trade Administration created a five-point compliance plan to be monitored through the Trade Compliance Center under the Market Access and Compliance Division of the U.S. Commerce Department; the Trade Policy Staff Committee held monthly meetings, chaired by the U.S. Trade Representative Office, for U.S. Government agencies that wanted to follow China's progress.

Since accession, U.S. government agencies have further extended their monitoring capabilities (GAO 2002). The U.S. Trade Representative and the Departments of Commerce, Agriculture, and State have increased staff and established or extended interagency teams. At least seventeen agencies are involved. The U.S. Trade Representative Office has also established an interagency group that works closely with the private sector to coordinate compliance information gathering and response activities.

The U.S. Congress has also been concerned with compliance. In 2000 when Congress authorized the president to grant Permanent Normal Trade Relations status to China, it also authorized resources for monitoring and enforcement efforts. Congress requested a series of studies to be done by the U.S. General Accounting Office, some of which are referenced here. The GAO has also developed an extensive, searchable database on China's commitments and their status.[8] The U.S. Trade Representative Office is required to submit a report to Congress by December 11 each year on the progress of China's compliance. In 2000, Congress established the U.S.–China Economic and Security Review Commission to study the national security implications of the U.S.–China bilateral relationship.[9] While the mandate of this Commission is not WTO compliance per se, it follows WTO developments closely and considers the implications in its on-going evaluations and formal reports submitted to Congress annually.

There are several key players focusing on monitoring China's compliance in the private sector as well. The National Association of Manufacturers (NAM) is keenly interested in developments in China since they see job losses as directly tied to policy in China. Although their concerns go beyond WTO, they maintain information and links for their members and the public on their website on WTO developments.[10] The American Chamber of Commerce in China and the U.S.–China Business Council (USCBC) both represent the interests of U.S. companies doing business with China and, as such, have an interest in balancing promotion of good relations with China while working to resolve issues on behalf of their members. Both organizations have helped their members keep abreast of developments as well as report their findings and perspectives to official U.S. government channels, and both have devoted resources to training people in China about WTO requirements.

WTO Adjustment: Compliance in the First Two Years

The first year of China's membership in WTO progressed relatively smoothly and did not generate serious criticism from domestic players or other WTO members. WTO members, including U.S. officials, generally congratulated China on its progress during year one (e.g., Xinhua 2002b). Many of the required tariff reductions had been met early and there was a flurry of activities related to the adjustment, including training and the passing of new laws and regulations. The China Society for WTO Studies, a nongovernmental academic institution, released a positive analysis of China's compliance. Its China WTO Report-2003 reportedly said that the intellectual property rights provisions had been "basically" met, and that China had strictly implemented its other obligations (Xinhua 2003b). Benefits of membership, such as inflows of foreign direct investment, were emphasized in the domestic press (e.g., Xinhua 2002a). The first annual review of the WTO Transition Review Mechanism went forward without major controversy, although the level of information sharing was apparently less than expected by some of the participants (USCBC 2003a, 5).

Foreign and domestic players expected year two to be more difficult, and they were right (Xinhua 2003a; Harmsen 2002). A confluence of circumstances came together to create widespread discontent globally concerning China's progress with meeting WTO commitments and the country's international economic strategy generally. Internally, the Chinese government was dealing with a major leadership transition from Jiang Zemin to Hu Jintao, and the outbreak of the SARS virus created a major health crisis for several months. Despite SARS, China's economy grew at an annual rate of about 8 percent in 2002 and 2003. This growth fueled increasing amounts of imports of inputs and raw materials, which was a stimulus for many countries, but simultaneously large inflows of foreign capital into manufacturing in China helped stoke fears of massive job losses elsewhere. China's pegged currency, which many analysts estimated was overvalued by at least 20 percent, and the large trade surplus with the United States, led to strident calls by U.S. interests for Chinese officials to revalue the renminbi.

Against this backdrop, the normally scheduled evaluations of China's WTO compliance progress went forward. Within China, the stance taken by the Chinese leadership was positive overall concerning China's compliance progress. After the leadership change at the sixteenth Party Congress in October 2002, press reports stressed that WTO commitments would be a high priority for President Hu Jintao and Premier Wen Jiabao (e.g., Morgan 2003). Lu Fuyuan, the commerce minister, was quoted as saying China has fulfilled its commitments in various ways, such as meeting the tariff reduction schedule on time or sometimes ahead of schedule (Xinhua 2003c). When information about new policy measures was announced, the fact that the measures were WTO compliant was often part of the press release (e.g., Xinhua 2003d). By fall 2003, however, in the face of serious criticism from numerous quarters in the United States, a Foreign Ministry spokesman stressed the seriousness with which China was taking its commitments, but also said that some "problems and unexpected difficulties" had been encountered (Xinhua 2003e).

Of the individual WTO member countries, by far the most serious evaluation of China's progress in meeting commitments has been undertaken by various public and private interests in the United States. The conclusions of these in-depth analyses, especially for the second year ending December 11, 2003, have been quite negative for the most part. Key criticisms focused on lack of transparency and enforcement of intellectual property rights, slow movement to open international trading rights and the domestic distribution system to foreign companies, missed deadlines on issuing rules for foreign offerings of finance in the automobile industry, improper non-tariff barriers on agricultural products, unreasonably high capital requirements for foreign companies setting up operations in banking, insurance, and telecom, and a whole list of commitments scheduled to be completed by December 2003, that appear far from the end goal.[11]

Beyond specific aspects of the WTO agreement that may be behind schedule, numerous interest groups within the United States have made serious public complaints against a wide range of trade and economic policies in China. For example, the U.S.–China Economic and Security Review Commission held hearings in September 2003 on China's industrial, investment, and exchange rate policies. On the basis of information collected during the hearings, the commission issued recommendations to Congress to address alleged currency manipulation, export subsidies, dumping practices, unfair industrial policies, and private sector transfer of technology and research and development centers from the United States to China. The commission interpreted these activities to be in conflict with WTO in principle if not specifically according to the letter of the Protocol (USCBC 2003a). The National Association of Manufacturers also testified in Congress and issued various reports on its analyses of the damage China's policies have had on manufacturing jobs in the United States (e.g., NAM 2003).

An obvious question arises from this comparison between Chinese and U.S. positions regarding China's WTO adjustment: Why are the assessments of progress from China and the U.S. so different? This gap is especially puzzling when some of the most serious U.S. criticism came from businesses with great interest in seeing China succeed, and that at times have bent over backwards to paint a positive picture of the business environment there.

Several possible reasons for this gap are proposed here. First, many substantial changes have been made in China to meet its commitments. This process involves a broad revamping of many aspects of China's economic, regulatory, legal, and governance systems. From the perspective of many in China, then, it may be difficult to perceive the distance to full compliance.

Second, there are at least three aspects of compliance. One is changing laws or rules to be in line with the letter of the agreement. A second is conveying those changes to the public, and laying out the ways that businesses could proceed to act on the changes. And a third is the enforcement of the new change, where everyone involved would know that the change had occurred and that new procedures or freedoms were to be allowed and even encouraged. In some of the identified problem areas, the first aspect of compliance has been met, but not necessarily the second and third. All three are necessary. As the process unfolds, however, it would be appropriate for Chinese government officials to announce that a particular rule had been changed to be WTO compliant before anyone had taken advantage of this change. In this sense, there might be a genuine belief that a particular aspect of WTO compliance had been completed when in fact much more work remained.

For example, levels of import quotas on industrial goods such as autos, tires, rubber, and crude or processed oil for 2003 met or exceeded what WTO required, and quotas on motorcycles were lifted one year ahead of schedule.[12] However, China still maintains a list of products that require registration or import permits, which directly violates the national treatment principle. In addition, the process of how industrial quotas are allocated, or who has received them, has not been made public. In this case, the initial aspect of WTO compliance has been met—and met early—but from a foreign company's perspective nothing has really changed yet in terms of how they would conduct business.

A third possible reason for the differences in perceptions of WTO compliance is lack of information. In some cases problems arise because of a lack of knowledge or understanding on the part of Chinese officials. The U.S.–China Business Council conducted a survey of their members in which many responded that problems in the area of customs and trade administration, and transparency, seemed in part due to lack of knowledge.[13] Some of the problem is no doubt due to the sheer number of changes. In customs, for example, the director of the General Administration of Customs, Mou Xinsheng, estimated that for 2002 the tariff rate on well over five thousand items was reduced to varying degrees (*Renmin Ribao* 2003). In addition, China's trade volumes increased substantially, adding to customs officials' workload.

Fourth, in some cases problems may exist because of insufficient resources. The U.S.–China Business survey identified enforcement of intellectual property rights (IPR) as an area where resources were severely lacking. China's laws have been carefully revised to meet the requirements for IPR protection in the WTO agreement, and Chinese officials are pleased with this progress (Feng 2003). However, this is another example of where process and enforcement make the laws virtually useless. When IPR protection conflicts with job creation at local levels, local officials are reluctant to enforce central government laws that would severely harm or even close the businesses involved.

Finally, conflicts of interests within bureaucracies are common, as is the related tendency to try to protect bureaucracy-specific resources. In China, competing interests between industries, regions, and the center and localities, have been well documented (Lieberthal 1995, 166–240; Yang 1997). In the U.S.–China Business Council's survey, government and industry protectionism was the overwhelming perceived reason given for the problems the participating U.S. companies were experiencing (USCBC 2003b, 3–5). Given the extent of adjustment that is expected to be necessary in agriculture and industries such as banking, foot-dragging is no surprise. However, this was one of the major concerns of member countries when they were negotiating China's entry into the WTO, and the apparent difficulties in this area could harm China's foreign relations.

China's Response and Context

Good international relations and an attractive business environment are important goals for China's central leadership. The success of China's economic reforms and growth are much too dependent on the global economy, and the U.S. economy in particular, for the situation to be otherwise. As deadlines for particulars in the WTO agreement to be met by the end of 2003 approached, and as international political pressure rose over currency and trade imbalance issues, some concessions were hastily made.

In late 2003, China's Ministry of Commerce and other governing bodies announced a number of decisions that addressed some of the WTO members' concerns. For example, in the automobile industry, during the lead-up to membership, Chinese negotiators wanted to cushion the entrance of foreign firms into this sector to give Chinese companies more time to prepare. One victory for foreign firms was that foreign non-bank financial entities could begin to offer financing for purchases of automobiles along with Chinese firms, and that this was agreed to as of the date of joining. The rules for car finance companies, however, were not issued and Chinese banks were able to profit from the rapid growth of this type of lending. Meanwhile, companies such as Ford, General Motors, and Volkswagen had prepared to take advantage of this market opening. Finally, in October 2003, the Central Banking Regulatory Commission issued rules covering local and foreign business participation, and indicated that the rules for implementation would be published soon after (McGregor 2003; Xinhua 2003f). The timing of this announcement might have been coincidental, but it nonetheless signaled some progress at a crucial time.

In response to pressure concerning China's large and growing trade surplus with the United States, in late 2003 Chinese officials announced several moves to mitigate possible protectionist measures by the U.S. Congress. During a visit to Beijing in late October by the U.S. commerce secretary, Donald Evans, China's premier Wen Jiabao promised to encourage Chinese companies to increase their imports from the United States (*People's Daily* 2003b). The proposed increase in purchases of U.S. goods came on top of the "Going Out" policy that was designed to encourage large Chinese companies to invest abroad, and new regulations allowing Chinese citizens to spend more foreign exchange to travel and study. Premier Wen met with a delegation of U.S. company representatives and the U.S.–China Business Council to discuss their concerns over market access. Chinese officials also announced that they would lower the value added tax rebate on exports beginning in January 2004, which would have a similar effect to raising the value of the Chinese currency by making exports more expensive.

Concessions on the currency issue were another matter. Officials indicated that floating the Chinese currency was premature given institutional and financial weaknesses in the banking system. While a flexible currency remains an explicit goal, the experiences of the Asian crisis made Chinese policymakers more cautious about opening the capital account and accepting the volatility and uncertainty of flexible exchange rates.

In line with these concerns, analysts and policymakers have been focusing on how to best restore the viability of the financial system and move ahead with reforms that would support financial strength in the future. The non-performing loan burden in the state banking system did not improve as much as had been hoped after moving bad debt to asset management companies in the late 1990s. Further reforms with respect to currency, interest rate determination, and privatization of financial services all hinge on a solution to non-performing loans and assets in the state sector. To this end the state banks may be recapitalized once again, and the State Council has decided to promote several dozen viable state companies to compete in international markets but to privatize much of the rest (Kynge 2003a, 2003b).

These moves to push reforms further are in line with the decisions announced as part of the Third Plenary Session of the Chinese Communist Party in October 2003 to complete China's transition to a market economy (*People's Daily* 2003a). The more progress that can be made to establish a sound market economy, the less of an issue the WTO commitments and trade imbalances will become. In addition, Chinese officials are pressing the United States to relax export restrictions on certain technology and information-related products, and to move toward granting China the status of a market economy, which would be beneficial to China within the U.S. anti-dumping framework. These moves would be almost routine if the state-based parts of China's economy were subject to market competition or were privatized completely.

Future Challenges for China

The commitments that China's leaders made in order to become a member of the WTO were vast and complex. Honoring those commitments will be challenging. In terms of the letter of the agreement, China has made substantial progress and has shown the intention to honor the accord. Compliance in terms of implementing and enforcing the new rules is also required, but has proven to be much more difficult. The complexities and competing interests within the Chinese bureaucracy create roadblocks in interpreting and instituting change. With each policy change there will be winners and losers, and the losers have an incentive to fight for more time or to dilute the effect in a myriad of ways.

In the current climate of intense global competition and shrinking manufacturing sectors, China faces tremendous pressure to meet its commitments on time and in full. The list of monitors is long, and transparency itself is increasing as part of the adjustment process. Ultimately, success in compliance will be tied closely to success in establishing a market economy. Those pushing for WTO membership from within China seemed to understand this. The next stage of realigning the public and private sectors in China will be an essential piece in increasing the probability of success within the WTO and in sustaining economic growth in the future.

Notes

1. For discussions of the process of China's entry into the WTO, see Lardy (2002) and Prime (2002).

2. This section draws from GAO 2002, and the Official Protocol, available at www.mac.doc.gov/China/ProtocolandDecision.pdf. The Protocol is provided by the U.S. Government through the Department of Commerce's Web site at www.export.gov.

3. These implementation costs are separate from the adjustment costs resulting from resource re-allocation due to price, tax, tariff, and other changes resulting from membership. See Finger and Schuler (1998) and the World Bank, cited in Bacchetta and Drabek (2002, 24–25, T8).

4. The full list of information required is available in Annex 1A in GAO 2002 and covers over five pages.

5. Waterman (2002, 14). Note that this section points out examples of organizations involved in monitoring China's compliance with WTO commitments and is not intended to be exhaustive.

6. For a sample of organizations and governments involved during China's bid and in the early stages of China's membership, see the table in Goldstein and Anderson (2002, 10–11).

7. See www.europa.eu.int/comm/external-relations/china/intro/.

8. This GAO database is accessible via www.gao.gov.

9. The Commission's charter, members, reports, etc. are available at www.uscc.gov.

10. The Association's China WTO Compliance Program can be accessed via their main Web site, www.nam.org.

11. See, for example, USCBC (2003a), Brilliant (2003), and USCIB (2003) for original testimony, and Hiebert and Murphy (2003) for a short summary.

12. This example is taken from USCBC (2003a, 2–3).

13. USCBC (2003b). In general, however, survey respondents did not emphasize lack of knowledge as the main reason for their difficulties.

References

Bacchetta, Marc, and Zdenek Drabek. 2002. "Effects of WTO Accession on Policy-Making in Sovereign States: Preliminary Lessons from the Recent Experience of Transition Countries." World Trade Organization, Development and Economic Research Division, Staff Working Paper DERD-2002–02 (April), World Trade Organization, Geneva.

Brilliant, Myron A. 2003. "China's WTO Record: A Two-Year Assessment." U.S. Chamber of Commerce testimony before the Trade Policy Staff Committee on September 18. Available at www.uschamber.com/press/testimony/030918wto.htm.

Feng, Jianhua. 2003. "Protecting Intellectual Property Rights." *Beijing Review* (April 24): 11–13.

Finger, J.M., and P. Schuler. 1998. *Implementation of the Uruguay Round Commitments: The Development Challenge.* Washington, DC: World Bank, Research Department, mimeo.

Goldstein, Brian L., and Stephen J. Anderson. 2002. "Foreign Contributions to China's WTO Capacity Building." *China Business Review* (January–February): 8–15.

Harmsen, Peter. 2002. "China Still Keeps Some Foreign Firms Waiting After One Year in WTO." Agence France-Presse (December 9), via *World News Connection*, December 10, Dialog accession No. 163251269.

Hiebert, Murray, and David Murphy. 2003. "Trade: The One-Two Punch." *Far Eastern Economic Review* (October 2): 26–28.

Kynge, James. 2003a. "China May Help Banks Again." *Financial Times* (October 29): 5.

———. 2003b. "China Plans Shake-up for State Enterprises." *Financial Times* (November 12): 5.

Lardy, Nicholas R. 2002. *Integrating China into the Global Economy.* Washington, DC: Brookings Institution Press.

Lieberthal, Kenneth. 1995. *Governing China: From Revolution Through Reform.* New York: W.W. Norton.

McGregor, Richard. 2003. "Beijing Opens Door to Foreign Car Loan Groups." *Financial Times* (October 6): 15.

Morgan, Benjamin. 2003. "China's WTO Pledges to Figure Prominently on New Leadership's Agenda." Agence France-Presse (March 2), via *World News Connection*, March 3, Dialog accession No. 167400116.

National Association of Manufacturers (NAM). 2003. "Testimony of Jay Bender, President, Falcon Plastics, Inc., on Behalf of the National Association of Manufacturers," June 25. Available at www.nam.org/s_nam/doc1.asp?CID=170&DID=226753/.

People's Daily Online. 2003a. "Party Decision to Press Forward Market Economy," October 21. Available at http://english.peopledaily.com.cn/200310/21/eng20031021_126546.shtml.

———. 2003b. "China to Expand Imports from U.S.: Premier Wen," October 29. Available at http://english.peopledaily.com.cn/200310/29/eng20031029_127075.shtml.

Prime, Penelope B. 2002. "China Joins the WTO: How, Why, and What Now?" *Business Economics* (April): 26–32.

Renmin Ribao. 2003. "PRC Customs Chief Interviewed on Work After WTO Entry," January 8, via *World News Connection*, February 6, Dialog accession No. 164751405.

U.S.–China Business Council (USCBC). 2003a. "China's WTO Implementation: An Assessment of China's Second Year of WTO Membership," written testimony by the U.S.–China Business Council for the U.S. Trade Representative Office, prepared on September 10. Available at www.uschina.org/public/documents/2003/09/ustryeartwoassessment.pdf.

———. 2003b. "Membership Priorities WTO Survey," September 10. Available at www.uschina.org.

U.S.–China Economic and Security Review Commission (USCC). 2003. "China's

Industrial, Investment and Exchange Rate Policies: Impact on the United States," September 25 Hearing. Available at www.uscc.gov.

U.S. Council for International Business (USCIB). 2003. Testimony by USCIB for the U.S. Trade Representative Office, September 10. Available at www.uscib.org.

U.S. General Accounting Office (GAO). 2002. "World Trade Organization: Analysis of China's Commitments to Other Members" (October) GAO-03–4. Available at www.gao.gov/new.items/d034.pdf.

———. 2003. "World Trade Organization: First-Year U.S. Efforts to Monitor China's Compliance" (March) GAO-03–461. Available at http://gao.gov/new.items/d03461.pdf.

Waterman, Jeremie. 2002. "Toward WTO: Highlights of PRC Implementation Efforts to Date, September 2001." *China Business Review* (January–February): 14.

Xinhua, Beijing Domestic Service in Chinese. 2002a. "Xinhua Examines Positive Aspects of PRC WTO Entry," December 10, via *World News Connection*, December 12, Dialog accession No. 163301298.

———. Beijing Xinhua in English. 2002b. "China's Performance Wins Wide Recognition Among WTO Members," December 10, via *World News Connection*, December 11, Dialog accession No. 163301351.

———. 2003a. "MOFTEC Minister Shi Guangsheng Warns of Adverse Impact of WTO Membership," March 7, via *World News Connection*, March 10, Dialog accession No. 167650525.

———. 2003b. "Report Summarizes China's Implementation of WTO Obligations," April 9, via *World News Connection*, April 10, Dialog accession No. 169300237.

———. 2003c. "Commerce Minister Lu Fuyuan Says PRC Not Worried by Double-Digit Imports Surge," July 24, via *World News Connection*, July 25, Dialog accession No. 174600313.

———. 2003d. "China to Continue Import Quotas on Agricultural Products," July 3, via *World News Connection*, August 1, Dialog accession No.174950296.

———. 2003e. "PRC FM Spokesman: China 'Seriously' Fulfills WTO Commitments," September 18, via *World News Connection*, September 22, Dialog accession No. 177400206.

———. 2003f. "China Issues Rules Governing Auto Financing Companies," October 4, via *World News Connection*, October 6, Dialog accession No. 178200140.

Yang, Dali L. 1997. *Beyond Beijing: Liberalization and the Regions in China*. London: Routledge.

4

After Accession to the WTO

Foreign Direct Investment Flows in Western China

Ying-Qiu Liu

Two important events have occurred in China in recent years. One was the decision of the Chinese central government to implement a development strategy for western China beginning in mid-1999. The second major event occurred when China joined the World Trade Organization (WTO) on December 11, 2001.

With China's accession to the WTO, not only have its foreign direct investment (FDI) flows increased more rapidly than before, but their growth rate in western China is higher than into eastern and central China. One reason for this is that the comparative advantage of an abundant low-cost labor supply in eastern and central China is diminishing. In recent years eastern China's average cost of labor has become almost three to four times higher than in western China. Since China's WTO accession this comparative advantage has moved from the eastern part of the country to the western part.

The Advantages of Western China

Western China has four major advantages that make it attractive to foreign investors.[1]

Vast, Underpopulated Territory

Western China has been defined in two ways. The earlier definition was primarily geographical. The current definition combines ecogeography with political policy.

Table 4.1

Comparison of Land Values in Various Regions of China in 2004 (RMB/sq.m.)

Prices in various regions	Land for multiple use	Land for business use	Land for residence	Land for industrial use
National Average	1,198	1,988	1,166	481
Northwest Region	777	1,167	732	457
North China Region	1,300	2,153	1,276	536
Pearl River Delta	1,129	2,160	1,058	436
Yangtze River Delta	1,450	2,344	1,540	521
Beijing and Tianjin Region	2,009	3,875	1,746	520

Source: Ministry of Land and Resources of People's Republic of China and China Institute of Land Surveying and Planning, *2004 Report on Monitoring the Land Values of Major Regions and Cities of China.* The above figures were calculated on the basis of monitoring the land values of fifty-one large or medium-size cities. See www.mlr.gov.cn/zt/djdtjcbg2004/index.htm.

Western China's geographic area comprises more than 66 percent of the country, but its population, only 311.3 million, is only about 24.7 percent of the country's total. As a result, the land values in western China are much lower than those in central and eastern China. For example, as shown in Table 4.1, land values in Beijing and Tianjin are much higher than those in other areas. There the cost of one square meter for business use in 2004 was more than US$460. But in the western region it was only US$140, and even in the northern region it was only about US$260. If you wanted to buy land on Wangfujing Street in Beijing, the cost might be more than US$1,500–2,000 per square meter. But in western China, in the provincial capitals, or the central cities, the cost per square meter might range from US$55.53 to US$141.80. In northwest China it would be even less expensive—around US$1.00–2.00, according to a survey of developing northwest China in 2000. And in some backlands the cost was close to zero.

Low Per Capita Income and Labor Costs

By the end of 2002, the gross domestic product (GDP) per capita for the country as a whole was RMB8,184.00 (i.e., roughly US$994.42), and for central and eastern China, including nineteen provinces and cities, it was about RMB13,179.47 (US$1,601.39). The GDP per capita for western China, including twelve provinces and numerous autonomous regions, was only RMB5,853.00 (US$711.18). It is more than 28.5 percent to 55.6 percent lower than the average for the country or the central and eastern regions.

Per capita income is lower in western China because labor costs are also very low. The monthly wage for an ordinary worker in western China is only RMB300–500, equivalent to US$500–800 a year, while in eastern China it would be at least RMB800–1,200, equivalent to US$1,150–1,750 a year. Western China's much lower than normal labor costs are a particular comparative advantage when it comes to attracting FDI.

Concentrations of Multiracial Minorities

Most members of China's fifty-five minority groups live and work in western China. They have different cultural traditions and customs. The diversity of ethnicity and lifestyles creates diverse demand in this area, which offers opportunities for more foreign investors to come and provide products or services tailored to the special features of the area.

Variations in Natural Resources and Development Levels

The twelve provinces and autonomous regions of western China can be divided between north and south. Each area consists of six provinces and autonomous regions. Southwestern China includes Yunnan, Guizhou, Sichuan, Chongqing, Tibet, and Guangxi. Northwestern China includes Shaanxi, Gansu, Qinghai, Ningxia, Xinjiang, and Inner Mongolia.

Resource conditions in the southwest are very different from those in the northwest. For example, in the southwest vegetation is more plentiful, rainfall is more abundant, and water resources are richer, while in the northwest the reverse holds true. In most provinces of the southwest the main problem is that the area is not only remote but also essentially undeveloped. In most provinces of the northwest the main problems are ecological—aridity and environmental imbalance.

In spite of the challenges of the area, potential abounds in its many special natural and anthropological resources. For example, there is abundant lithium in Qinghai and thulium in Inner Mongolia; richer, long-velvet cotton and colored cottons in Xinjiang; and extensive natural gas in Sichuan. Further natural resources exist in Yunnan, Guizhou, and Tibet, awaiting development. Historical and cultural resources throughout western China are also very rich, with Bodala (Potala) Temple, Ta'er Temple, Dunhuang Grottoes, Mount Emei and Jinding (Golden Summit) Temple, the Sichuan Buddha (Dafo), to name a few sites.

Current FDI Flows into Western China

A great deal of successful FDI has occurred in western China since China's economic system began to reform and open to trade. Guangxi Liuzhou

Heavy Machine, Xi'an Yangsen Pharmacy, and Inner Mongolia–Benz Heavy are examples of firms that have flourished. FDI success in western China revolves around the use of advanced technology, abundant capital, efficient management, and cheaper natural resources and labor forces. They profit from first-mover advantages. These absolute and comparative advantages allow those participating in foreign direct investment to make higher profit margins in China than in many other countries. According to statistics, in the developed market economy countries, including the United States, Japan, and Europe, most automobile companies experience profit margins of about 2.5 percent. The 2003 *China Industry Development Report* by the China Economic Information Network, State Information Center (China Economics Press, 2004), indicated that, in 2002, the average profit margin of China's automobile manufacture industry was 7.96 percent, while the rate for small passenger car manufacturers was 13.24 percent. In this field, Shanghai-Volkswagen, FAW-Volkswagen, Shanghai GM, and Guangzhou-Honda are the major successful foreign investors in China.

Another interesting example is Ford Motor Company. Ford had previously tried to invest in China's vehicle market. Subsequent to a meeting of Ford executives with Deng Xiaoping in June 1978, it sold 750 F-series trucks by mid-1979. This made Ford the first U.S. automotive manufacturer to pursue the Chinese market, and it was the first time any U.S.-built vehicles had been shipped to China since 1949. But until 1994 Ford did not have first-mover advantages. As an old Chinese saying goes, "Ford hasn't found the north" (*zhao bu zhao bei*, or "it hasn't found the right direction for making decisions" 找不着北). In August 1995, Ford spent US$40 million to buy a 20 percent equity stake in Jiangling Motors (JMC); in November 1998 it paid an additional US$54.5 million to increase its stake to 29.96 percent (according to the JMC public reports, reported at http://stock.sina.com.cn/stock/company/sz000550/4.html). It was not until 2001, as China's WTO accession promised to become a reality, that a 50/50 joint venture agreement between Ford and Chang'an Automobile Company in Chongqing was finally established, but its first product, a small passenger vehicle, did not appear until early 2003.

After the Chinese government initiated the Western China Great Development Strategy, including WTO membership, the door for FDI opened wider. There were strong expressions of interest from various countries. For example, during the Forum of Western China in Chengdu on October 21–22, 2000, sponsored by the State Council Office for Western China Development, in only two days foreign investors signed more than US$240 million in investment contracts with Chengdu.

Even though there is now strong interest in FDI in western China, the scale and proportion of FDI in western China are still very low compared with those in eastern or even central China. According to statistics on FDI flows in China between 2001 and 2003, FDI project numbers in western China increased slightly but the proportion in the area actually declined (see Table 4.2).

FDI patterns in western China are characterized as follows.

Small Investments

According to our research, the amounts of foreign direct investment in northwestern China are usually small or medium in size, about US$500,000. About 70 percent of investments fall into this category. Even an investment of US$700,000, although much lower than the average for the country as a whole, is considered a large investment in western China. An investment of more than US$1.8 million would be quite significant. In early 2002, Zhang Nianzu invested US$100 million in Xinjiang to develop the long-velvet cotton industry, which represented a substantial inflow of FDI.

Low-Technology Investment

In the past, FDI in western China has mostly focused on raw materials processing, high-waste energy products, and agricultural and livestock production. There are fewer investments in the high-technology and value-added segments. There has not yet been heavy investment in infrastructure, such as energy, public transportation, and communications services.

FDI Investment Profit Margins: The Need for Improvement

Most FDI has earned higher profit margins in eastern China over the past twenty years, as have many foreign investors in eastern China. By comparison to eastern China, the FDI profit margins are much lower in western China. According to our research in the northwestern provinces in 2000, the majority of FDI in the area was for small or medium-size projects, 70 percent of projects had investment amounting to less than US$500,000. The average investment amount per project in the area was only US$720,000, much less than the national average of US$1.8 million. The annual inspection in 1998 of foreign-invested enterprises in Gansu province showed that 326 of 601 foreign enterprises were in deficit, and fully funded projects comprised less than 47 percent (Chen Jiagui and Liu Yingqiu, *Development Report of the Northwest* [Chinese Social Science Press, 2000], p. 228).

Table 4.2

FDI Flows in Eastern, Central, and Western China, 2001–2003 (RMB 100 million)

	Regions	Project numbers	Percentage	Contracted Value	Percentage	Amount actually used	Percentage
2001	National Total	26,140	100.00	691.95	100.00	468.78	100.00
	Eastern China	22,492	86.04	603.51	87.22	408.54	87.15
	Central China	2,133	8.16	48.73	7.04	41.01	8.75
	Western China	1,515	5.80	39.71	5.74	19.22	4.10
2002	National Total	34,171	100.00	827.68	100.00	527.43	100.00
	Eastern China	30,001	87.80	731.78	88.41	457.29	86.70
	Central China	2,730	7.99	59.93	7.24	50.09	9.50
	Western China	1,440	4.21	35.97	4.35	20.05	3.80
2003	National Total	41,081	100.00	1,150.70	100.00	535.05	100.00
	Eastern China	36,159	88.02	1,005.30	87.36	459.51	85.88
	Central China	3,177	7.73	95.52	8.30	58.31	10.90
	Western China	1,745	4.25	49.88	4.33	17.23	3.22

Source: Chinese Academy of International Trade and Economic Cooperation, Ministry of Commerce, *China's White Paper on Foreign Trade and Economic Cooperation 2004* (Beijing: CITIC Publishing House, 2005), p. 107.

The Main Obstacles to FDI in Western China

Why has the amount of FDI in western China remained low until recently? Foreign investors who want to establish themselves in this area face many obstacles, most deriving from the traditional nature of the industries being launched. FDI is urgently needed in western China, but its business environment is challenging and unreliable. The following are five of the main obstacles for increasing conventional FDI in western China.

Geography

The main geographical features of western China are its higher elevation, remoteness, and distance from the sea. Beyond Guangxi, most of the western provinces are located far inland and their average elevation is more than 1,000 meters, in some areas more than 2,000 meters. Tibet is more than 3,600 meters above sea level. This drives transportation costs higher in western China than in eastern China. For example, it takes almost four hours to fly from Beijing to Urumqi; by train it could take more than fifty hours.

Educational Levels

There are three educational patterns in western China. First, the availability of higher education is unbalanced. There are many universities in western China—some of them famous not only in China but throughout the world (e.g., Communication University of Xian and the University of Lanzhou)—but most of them are clustered in the provincial capitals or large central cities. These universities are, therefore, not able to play more effective roles in pushing the local economy and society forward. Second, ordinary primary and middle schools are too few in number and too low in quality. Third, vocational and technological education do not serve the needs of local economic development, making it more difficult for foreign investment companies to secure a suitable labor supply.

Weak Industrial Infrastructure

In western China, not only does a traditional industry production structure dominate (mostly concentrated on raw materials processing and a conventional machining industry), but traditional technology dominates the entire production process. This has proved to be an economic barrier to the flow of FDI into the area.

Ideological Obstacle

In some areas of China, the concept of a market economy is still new. The benefits to be obtained from foreign companies investing in a particular area may still not be obvious. These are enormous changes in philosophy from earlier eras, and it can be a challenge on both sides to find understanding and mutual goals. These challenges can at times obstruct trade and investment.

Institutional Obstacles

There are three aspects of institutional obstacles. First is the non-state-owned economy, especially the non-public-owned economy, which still forms only a small part of the domestic national economy as a whole. Second is that government interference in economic activities is still excessive. Third, the domestic national economy is insufficiently dynamic, perhaps even more so in western China.

Strategies and Tactics for Successful FDI in Western China

How can foreign direct investment successfully enter western China? Here are six nonconventional strategies for FDI that should be considered.

First-Mover Advantages

Investing in western China is risky. But if the risks can be sufficiently off-set with strong revenues, those who do not let these opportunities slip through their fingers will have great success in western China. For example, Motorola took advantage of the opportunity to enter Tianjin before the end of the 1980s and ultimately achieved great success, but Siemens did not use this window of opportunity and failed to profit from China's huge communications market.

Motorola began to invest in Tianjin's Economic and Technological Development Zone before the end of the 1980s. During that period the conditions in this Special Economic Zone were difficult. But Motorola dared to move forward and finally established itself. Motorola had first-mover advantages. From the beginning of the 1990s, while they were introducing their first main product, Motorola Pagers, to the Chinese market, a communications revolution was taking place all over China. People at all levels of society were purchasing pagers, and their sounds could be heard everywhere in public—in markets and restaurants, university classes, and academic or government assembly halls, to name only a few. When pagers first appeared on the Chinese market, the retail price for one was more than RMB3,500, equivalent to almost US$450, a price affordable only by wealthy business-men or government officials. Within two years, Motorola dominated China's communications market. It is interesting to note that at the time Motorola was first entering the China market, one of China's top leaders had also invited Siemens to invest in China during his visit in Europe, but Siemens was unwilling to take the risk. Then, in the mid-1990s, when it saw Motorola's great success, it began to rethink the decision and to consider an entering strategy; but by that time, the pager market was saturated. At the same time Sony and Ericsson also were very interested in entering China. The result was that, after several competitive years, all of these newcomers together had taken only 20 percent of the pager and cellular phone market from Motorola. Clearly, being willing and able to meet the initial chal-lenges of entering a new market in western China, turning obstacles into opportunities, can offer great advantages to those first on the scene, as it did in the case of Motorola.

Combining Industrial Investment with Educational Investment

One lesson foreign investors have learned in western China is that to make industrial investments but not educational investments can frequently doom the enterprise to failure. Numerous situations have illustrated the importance of spending more money on education, especially on special skills training programs. This guarantees better profits. In western China labor costs are low, but the labor is unskilled. The greatest success derives from investing in education and labor training programs first.

High-Technology Development of Natural Resources

There are a large number of special natural resources in western China. For example, lithium is used to produce batteries. In western China lithium re-serves are rich. Qinghai province alone has almost 70 percent of the total world reserves. China's lithium resources could give it a natural monopoly in international markets. The mining and processing of lithium and related products present but one of many extremely promising competitive foreign investment opportunities in western China. At this time there are no foreign lithium production enterprises invested in the area.

An investor in western China that plans on using dated technology will likely fail. Of course, in China there are some FDI enterprises using second-hand technology, for example, Volkswagen, which has been profitable, but following China's WTO accession that is likely to change. Investors will be expected to utilize more advanced technology from the beginning.

Combining Technology-Intensive with Labor-Intensive Production

There is currently room for both technology-intensive and labor-intensive products in China. Most foreign investors use only one of these in their production. In western China the best choice is to combine the two in the production process. For example, the production of more electronic and communication products in western China is preferred over the more traditional manufacturing products, as the former combine high-technology production with higher labor intensity. These lightweight, low-volume, and higher value-added products are also easier and cheaper to transport.

Higher Value-Added Products

China seeks FDI in specialized productive processes that yield high-quality products. The type of goods to be produced is determined by western China's economic, geographic, and technical conditions.

Focus on Developing Expanded Market Products

The western interior of China is a center for manufacturing goods, but their market opportunities should be expanded geographically. FDI can make use of the region's cheaper natural resources and labor to produce special products or accessories for central and eastern China, or abroad. By doing so, they can take advantage of local production circumstances to be more competitive in the global marketplace, thereby increasing profits.

As premium investment areas become fewer in the world, western China has risen in its appeal for FDI since China joined the WTO. By utilizing new investment strategies, many of which have been described above, and by employing creative rather than conventional tactics, FDI enterprises will be able to realize greater success in western China.

Note

1. Since August 2000 the geographic area referred to as western China has been considered to consist of twelve provinces, autonomous regions, or municipalities: Chongqing, Sichuan, Guizhou, Yunnan, Tibet, Shaanxi, Gansu, Qinghai, Ningxia, Xinjiang, Inner Mongolia, and Guangxi.

Part II

The WTO and China's Economic Welfare

5

Foreign Direct Investment and Income Inequality

Xiaodong Wu

China has enjoyed rapid economic growth, at an average annual rate of over 9 percent, and low inflation rates, never in excess of 30 percent, since its economic reform began in 1978. During this period, China adopted a strategic economic policy to encourage foreign direct investment (FDI) so as to narrow its technology gap with developed countries and to boost economic growth. China's share of FDI in gross fixed capital was around 4 percent over the period from 1987 to 1992 and rose dramatically to 14.6 percent in the next five years (United Nations Conference on Trade and Development [UNCTAD] 1999; Zhang 2000). By 1997, China's share of total FDI stock in GDP reached 23.5 percent. Since 1993, China has become the second largest FDI recipient country after the United States (United Nations 1999). Firms with FDI have contributed to over 40 percent of China's total trade since the mid-1990s.

Meanwhile, income inequality in China is also rising. Fan Zhang and Jingping Zheng (1998) show that the Gini coefficient of the per capita wages in industrial sectors almost doubled between 1985 and 1995. The World Bank (1997) reports that the income inequality across all sectors has also increased dramatically and peaked in 1994 at around 40 percent. In 2003, the Gini coefficient reached 43.4 percent (World Bank 2003). Figure 5.1 shows China's Gini index estimated from two different sources but with similar trends, i.e., a peak around 1994 and another surge starting in the early 2000s. As rising income inequality can impede growth, undermine poverty alleviation programs, and contribute to social tension, the impact of FDI on economic pros-

Figure 5.1   **China's Gini Index of Income Distribution**

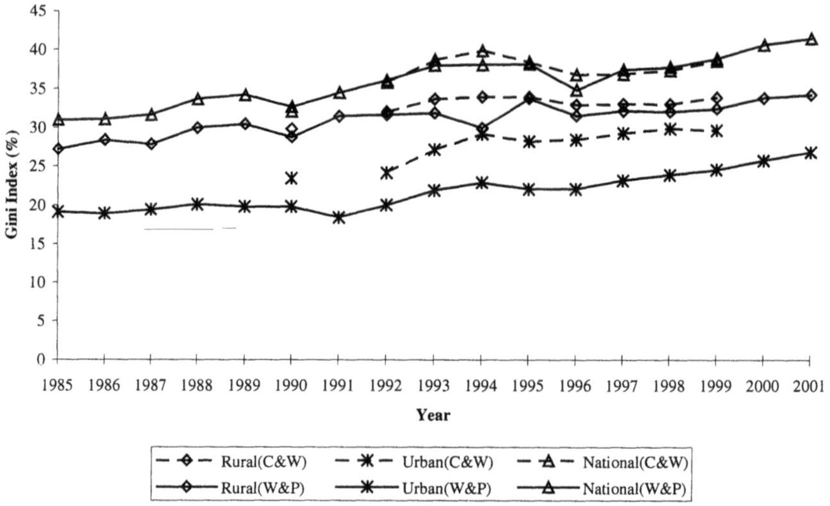

Sources: Chen and Wang (2001) and Wu and Perloff (2004).

perity and income inequality has significant policy implications, especially for China with its large volume of inward FDI.

As China embraces the world market through its membership in the World Trade Organization (WTO), FDI will penetrate further into the Chinese economy. The access to the Chinese market by foreign trade and investment under the WTO rules can bring dramatic changes to China's employment and division of labor. Notwithstanding the benefits FDI can bring, what potential risks can such influxes of FDI impose on the domestic economy? What policies can help a host country to reduce such risks and to maximize the benefits, especially with large FDI inflows as in China's case? The following analysis in this chapter will help policymakers to design policies to boost economic growth without aggravating income inequality.

The impact of inward FDI on economic growth, income distribution, and technology development, especially its important role in facilitating the transfer of advanced technologies from developed countries to less developed countries is well documented (Glass 2004; Glass and Saggi 2002b; Feenstra and Hanson 1997b). This chapter will contribute to this rich literature by deriving a rule-of-thumb prediction for the effect of inward FDI on a host country's relative wage of skilled versus unskilled labor when there is product differentiation.

Since a major source of income inequality is from wage disparities due to differences in education and training, or basically skills in general (Chen and Wang 2001), the focus here will be on the effect of FDI on China's relative wage of skilled and unskilled labor, and hence the impact of the huge FDI influx on China's income inequality. The chapter will then explore some policy implications for China's labor market reform so as to accommodate China's accession to the WTO in its ongoing fight against poverty.

There has not been a completely consistent explanation of how FDI can affect the relative wage of skilled to unskilled labor through technology transfer. Robert Feenstra and Gordon Hanson (1997a, 1999), Ronald Jones (1965, 2000), Edward Leamer (1998, 2000), Paul Krugman (2000), David Richardson (1995), and Xu Bin (2001) suggest that it is not clear whether factor- or sector-biased technical progress induced by FDI can change factor prices; it depends on a country's size and whether the technical progress is global or national. In general, sector bias matters as long as the technical progress is non-identical across countries, and factor bias is all that matters for a large economy if the technical progress is global and identical and the preferences are a Cobb-Douglas production function.

As shown in the discussion in the next section, many FDIs in China are in the differentiated sectors where quality as well as quantity matters. Thus, the following scrutiny will extend the existing analysis on the impact of technology on relative wages for homogeneous goods to study how FDI-induced technical progress can affect China's relative wages when there is product differentiation and when different levels of quality require different production skill intensity.

The key question addressed in this chapter is whether all FDI into China, a relatively labor abundant country, will indiscriminately lead to an increase in the relative return to skill, regardless of whether the FDI source country is a newly developed or a well developed country. If there are variations in how various types of foreign capital inflows affect the skill premium, then will the overall impact of FDI on the relative wage mainly be determined by which sector receives FDI or will this effect mainly be determined by whether FDI induces relatively skilled labor or unskilled labor biased technical progress? The following analysis will demonstrate that foreign direct investment into different industries can have different impacts on wage inequality. Thus, more foreign direct investment may not lead to more social inequality if it is directed into the appropriate industries.

Can Foreign Direct Investment Affect Wages?

The relatively small share of foreign funded enterprises (FFEs) in China's total employment may have concealed the significance of the impact of FDI

Figure 5.2   **Foreign Capital Invested in China**

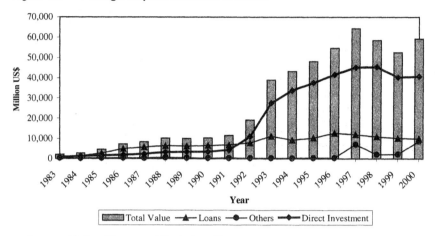

Sources: National Bureau of Statistics, *China Foreign Economic Statistical Yearbook, 2000*; National Bureau of Statistics, *China Statistical Abstract, 2001*.

on China's relative wage of skilled labor. However, wages like all other prices are set at the margin. FFEs can push up the wages even if their employment share is small.[1] Multinational firms may indeed have contributed to China's rising income inequality.

Zhang and Zheng (1998) show that the Gini coefficient of per capita wages in industrial sectors almost doubled between 1985 and 1995. Multinationals have been identified as one of the culprits responsible for this rise in income inequality. Moreover, Figure 5.2 shows that the inequality hike in 1994 coincided with the rise in FDI, and the more recent rise in the Gini index coincided with China's WTO membership, which has been drawing an increasing amount of foreign capital into China.

Moreover, the contribution to total employment of other ownership enterprises (including both domestic and foreign-owned or share holding corporations) has been growing rapidly and will continue to increase with China's accession to the WTO. Employment in these other ownership enterprises increased from only 0.36 percent of total long-term employees in 1985 to 17.18 percent at the end of 2000 (National Bureau of Statistics, *China Statistical Yearbook* 1985, 2001). In 1978, over 72 percent of newly employed persons in urban areas worked in state-owned enterprises (SOEs), and this rate fell to below 32 percent in 1997 (National Bureau of Statistics, *China Statistical Yearbook* 1998, 156).

Figure 5.3 reveals two significant turning points. One was in 1993 when China first became the second largest FDI recipient country after the United

Figure 5.3   **Annual Growth Rate of Long-Term Employees by Ownership**

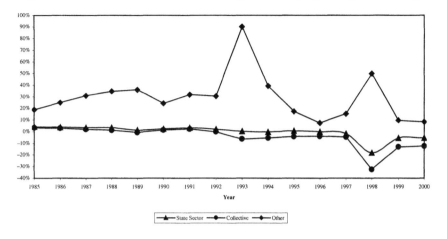

Sources: National Bureau of Statistics, *China Labor Statistical Yearbook, 2000;* National Bureau of Statistics, *China Statistical Abstract, 2000, 2001*.

Notes: From 1998 onward, the number of employees includes only on-post and staff workers. Other ownership enterprises include all domestically funded enterprises, cooperative units, joint-owned units, collective joint-owned units, limited liability corporations, state-funded corporations, and share holding corporations, but exclude private enterprises and township and village enterprises.

States (UNCTAD 1999). The annual growth rate of employees in the state sector fell from its stable more than 2 percent per year increase up until 1992 to only 0.28 percent in 1993, while the annual employment growth rate in the other ownership enterprises jumped from an average 25 percent increase between 1985 and 1992 to 90.07 percent increase in 1993. By 1994, the percentage of long-term employees in the other ownership enterprises had exceeded, for the first time, 5 percent of the total employment (National Bureau of Statistics, *China Statistical Yearbook* 1995). This coincided with rapid FDI growth from 1992 to 1993 and the correspondingly large increase in the total value of foreign capital invested in China as reflected in Figure 5.2.

The second turning point came between 1997 and 1998 when SOE reform was launched. Figure 5.2 shows that foreign capital inflow also reached its historic high during this period. Employment in the state sector fell dramatically and continued to fall in 2000, which clearly revealed the previously disguised unemployment problem resulting from China's command-and-control system. On the other hand, employment in the other ownership enterprises grew almost 50 percent in that year and showed plain signs of expansion in spite of the obvious contraction in the state sector (see Figure 5.3).

The collective-owned enterprises in the nonstate sector were squeezed by the other ownership enterprises as well as the state sector. Their numbers of employees kept falling throughout the 1990s. By 1999, the total number of employees in the other ownership enterprises surpassed that of collective-owned enterprises by over 1 million employees, although the latter was almost seventy-six times higher than the former back in 1985. One explanation is the many inherited disadvantages of the collective-owned enterprises under the command-and-control system ever since 1949 (see discussion in Wu 2003).

Although the exact causality cannot be determined without undertaking more rigorous econometrics analysis, these findings have confirmed that, empirically, we cannot rule out FDI as one of the factors that have caused the wage gap to increase and thus induced more labor migration between the state sector and the nonstate sector, especially between the SOEs and the other ownership enterprises.

Can the Effect of Foreign Direct Investment on Wages Be Uniform?

The relationship between the amount of FDI and the average wage in each sector is, however, not monotonic (Wu 2000). This suggests that not all types of FDI have the same effect on wages. To understand the variation, we can trace the sources and patterns of China's FDI. Figure 5.4 shows that, in the manufacturing sector, most FDI from the developing or newly developed countries are relatively labor-intensive while that from the developed countries are relatively capital or technology intensive. Overall, the developed countries invest mostly in technology or human capital-intensive (high-tech) sectors, such as electronics and machinery, while developing countries invest mostly in labor-intensive (low-tech) sectors, such as food and textiles (Chen 1997a, 1997b; Zhang and Zheng 1998).

Furthermore, Wu (2001) shows that China's foreign direct investment has come mainly from the newly developed countries or regions, a majority of which brings in relatively labor-intensive technologies as discussed above. However, there is a trend toward increasing percentages of FDI from developed countries such as the United States and Japan (Wu 2001). These types of FDI are likely to bring in more relatively skill-intensive technologies. This trend is likely to continue as China opens up sectors like telecommunications, information technology, and banking and financial services as required by its WTO agreements with the United States and the EU.

These differences give rise to the question in the introduction, that is, whether FDI in different sectors has varying impacts on the relative wages of skilled and unskilled labor. Since most FDI in China is export oriented providing a channel for foreign firms to exploit China's cheaper labor input, the

Figure 5.4   **Sectoral Composition of the Largest Foreign-Funded Enterprises in Manufacturing by Country Group**

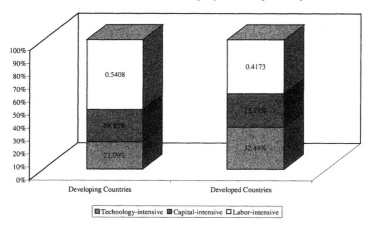

Source: Calculated from Huang, Xie, and Chen (1994).

traditional Heckscher-Ohlin-Samuelson model predicts that, as FDI induces more trade, the relative wage of unskilled labor to skilled labor in China (with a relatively abundant unskilled labor endowment) will increase. However, Figure 5.5 shows that the annual growth rate of real wages in those unskilled labor-intensive sectors is actually slower than the other skilled labor-intensive sectors with differentiated goods. Indeed, Robert Feenstra and Gordon Hanson (1997b), Wu (2000, 2001) and Zhang and Zheng (1998) all show that the entrance of multinationals can lead to an increase in the relative wage of skilled to unskilled labor if such inward FDI induces a relatively skill-intensive technical change.

By extending the existing analysis on homogeneous goods to include both horizontally (different varieties) and vertically (different quality) differentiated products, this chapter demonstrates that the above two types of foreign direct investment can push the relative wage in opposite directions. Thus, a balanced increase in varying types of FDI may have only a moderate overall effect on income distribution.

Why Is It Important to Consider Product Differentiation?

When consumers are willing to pay for higher quality goods, as reflected by the slogan "you get what you pay for," firms can charge a price above its average variable cost even when production shows constant returns to scale. This is consistent with the empirical findings in Ian Domowitz, R. Glenn Hubbard, and Bruce Petersen (1988), Robert Hall (1988), and Matthew

Figure 5.5   **Annual Growth of Real Average Wage**

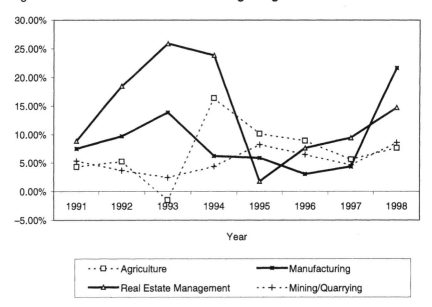

Source: Calculated from National Bureau of Statistics, *China Statistical Yearbook, 1998, 1999.*

Shapiro (1987), which reject the joint hypothesis of competition and constant returns to scale for many U.S. industries. Meanwhile, a higher quality is often produced with different skill intensities of production at a higher cost.[2]

If we simply think of different varieties of a product as different goods, then we still cannot explain why prices are above firms' average variable cost—and we may also have an empirical problem of how to define a product. Thus, it is important to develop a formal general equilibrium model incorporating product quality to reexamine the role of technology transfer on the relative return to skill in the presence of market power.

As discussed in the introduction, existing studies have focused on how technical progress affects the relative wage of skilled versus unskilled labor for an economy with homogeneous goods only. The effect can depend on whether technical progress occurs in a relatively skill-intensive or labor-intensive sector and whether it consists primarily of skilled labor or unskilled labor.

When there is vertical product differentiation, production of varying quality requires different skill levels. Skill intensity in a sector depends on both the relative wage and the endogenous choice of quality produced. Wu (2000) introduces both vertical and horizontal product differentiation, and focuses on the enforcement of intellectual property rights and the resultant impact on wages when FDI utilizes skilled labor technology in each differentiated sector. In her 2001 article, Wu extends her findings of 2000 by examining how vertical product differentiation and monopolistic pricing can affect the impact on wages of FDI utilizing either technologically skilled or unskilled labor in either the homogeneous or the differentiated sector.

To model the monopolistic competition among firms, Wu's papers adopt the Helpman-Krugman general equilibrium approach.[3] Elhanan Helpman (1981) and Helpman and Paul Krugman (1985) analyze the pattern of trade and the welfare effects of trade in a monopolistic competitive market by introducing horizontal product differentiation into a Heckscher-Ohlin framework. They focus on increasing returns to scale as the driving force of intra-industry trade rather than the pursuit of higher quality products produced with a higher skill intensity. Wu (2000, 2001) relaxes their assumption of identical technologies and identical cost structures to emphasize the cost difference of producing varying quality levels.

On the other hand, Harry Flam and Helpman (1987), Brian Copeland and Ashok Kotwal (1996) and Kevin Murphy and Andrei Shleifer (1997) allow firms to have different cost structures so as to endogenize a firm's choice of quality and to relate higher quality to increased labor inputs in production. Since their focus is the pattern of intra-industry trade as a result of population growth and technical progress, they use a Ricardian model with one factor (labor) of production.

To analyze the relative factor return, this chapter adopts the models developed in Wu (2000, 2001), which extend the one-factor Ricardian quality model to a two-factor Heckscher-Ohlin model. The model developed in Wu (2001) incorporates the approach in Massimo Motta (1992) and John Sutton (1991) in which consumers are allowed to consume more than one unit of a particular product. Wu (2001) also studies the relative wage impact of both skilled and unskilled labor biased technical progress induced by FDI, as well as FDI in both differentiated and homogeneous sectors.

What Are the Theoretical Predictions?

The major incentive for developing countries to encourage FDI inflow is to obtain the more advanced technologies owned by firms from developed countries. However, as shown in most of the empirical studies, due to this technological advantage, which leads to higher productivity, the wages of both skilled and unskilled labor are higher in the developed country than in the developing country. Thus, a firm in a developed country will find it profitable to take advantage of a developing country's lower labor costs (Brainard 1997;

Helpman 1992). By reallocating their production via foreign direct investment in a developing country, they can produce goods at a lower marginal cost by using less labor inputs than local firms. These multinational firms can charge a price above the product's average variable cost. These mutual benefits lead to a significant amount of FDI inflow from developed into developing countries.[4]

Through foreign direct investment either in the form of whole ownership or joint venture, firms in a small economy will be exposed to the more advanced technology used in the developed countries. This process of technology diffusion gives most developing countries a big incentive to promote foreign direct investment or even implement favorable FDI policies to compete with one another (see Glass and Saggi 2002a). This section will apply Wu's theoretical analysis (2000, 2001) to explain how foreign direct investment can affect the relative wages of skilled labor and on free trade and, also, how FDI in different sectors can have varying impacts on the relative return to skill by bringing in diverse types of technology transfer.

As discussed in Amy Glass and Kamal Saggi (2002a) and Wu (2000), the speed of this technology diffusion and hence the short- and long-run effects on relative wages depends on the intellectual property rights enforcement in a small economy. As in Wu (2001), this section will focus on the long-run effects and assume that technology transfer is inevitable so that all firms producing in the developing country will eventually use the new technology brought in by FDI. However, the new factor prices will still be different from those in the developed country because the developed country has different skilled and unskilled labor endowments and may have already developed more advanced technologies.

The standard Heckscher-Ohlin theorem suggests that, since the small open economy is endowed with less skilled labor, it does not have a comparative advantage in producing the high quality goods even with the same technology. Empirical results also show that multinational firms in the developing country will usually target lower quality brands rather than higher quality ones. Thus, this section assumes that the developing country still specializes in the lowest quality varieties and produces no high quality varieties even with foreign direct investment.

In the absence of FDI, quality and technology differentiation by itself still lead to results consistent with the Stolper-Samuelson theorem. Clearly, the Stolper-Samuelson theorem also holds if FDI is in the low-tech (unskilled labor-intensive) sectors with homogeneous goods, where FDI is purely induced by profits from the developing country's relatively cheaper unskilled labor. Thus, we are more likely to observe a decrease of the relative return to capital/skilled labor in a developing country, such as China, during the movement from autarky to free trade and investment with unskilled labor-intensive technologies, but before any FDI inflow with relatively skilled labor-intensive technologies.

In the presence of FDI with relatively skilled labor-intensive technologies, the induced technical progress tends to overturn the above Stolper-Samuelson effect. Wu (2000) focuses on the case where FDI is only in the differentiated sector and only induces relatively skilled labor-intensive technical progress. For tractability, each consumer buys only one variety and each firm charges a price equals to its marginal cost. In this case, trade in conjunction with multinationals increases the relative return to skilled labor, which cannot happen when there is only trade but no FDI.

Although Wu (2000) studies both horizontal and vertical product differentiation, his article did not discuss whether the rise in skill premium is because FDI induces a factor-biased or a sector-biased technical change, i.e., whether the rising skill premium is due to more FDI into the differentiated sector or due to more multinationals using relatively skilled labor-intensive technologies. Hence, the conclusion in Wu (2000) that FDI increases the relative return to skilled labor is actually a special case of Proposition 1, as discussed in Wu (2001).

Wu (2001) allows for FDI in both the differentiated sector and the homogeneous sector, as well as for the possibility of inducing both skilled labor and unskilled labor technical changes. Consumers can also buy more than one unit of the differentiated goods. Imperfect competition now leads to prices above marginal costs. Wu (2001) concludes that FDI will decrease the relative wage of skilled labor in the host economy, if the technical progress introduced by foreign direct investment is focused on unskilled labor by the Hicksian classification. However, if the FDI-induced technical progress is focused on skilled labor, then the relative wage of skilled labor increases regardless of whether FDI occurs in the homogeneous sector or in the differentiated sector.

Hence, unlike in the case of homogeneous goods studied in Jones (1965) and Xu (2001), when there is product differentiation, the effect of technical progress on the relative wage of skilled labor for a small country depends only on the factor bias. It no longer depends on sector bias, i.e., whether FDI induced technical progress occurs in a relatively skilled or unskilled labor-intensive sector. This is because the relative skill intensity between sectors can actually change depending on the endogenous choice of quality. Actually, there are several forces at work.

If a multinational firm uses a more skilled labor-intensive technology in a small open economy, then, first, this technology will increase the productivity of and the relative demand for skilled labor and hence its relative wage regardless of whether this multinational firm produces in the differentiated or the homogeneous sector. Second, as the relative wage of skilled labor increases, firms in both sectors will want to use less skilled and more unskilled labor. However, in the differentiated sector, this shift from skilled to unskilled labor will be limited as it will cause a decrease in quality and hence profit margin. Finally, there is a price effect according to the Stolper-Samuelson theorem. If the multinational firm operates in the differentiated sector, then the price will fall and so does the relative wage of skilled labor at equilibrium. The opposite will happen if the multinational firm operates in the homogeneous sector. Wu (2001) proves that all effects opposing the first effect dominate so that only factor bias matters in the end.

In sum, the wage gap between skilled and unskilled labor in a small labor abundant economy will decrease as it opens up more markets and attracts more FDI with advanced unskilled labor biased technology either into high-tech sectors or into low-tech sectors. On the other hand, FDI with advanced skilled labor biased technology will increase the wage gap as well as the host country's competitiveness in the high-end product markets. Although product differentiation makes the relative skill intensity between sectors endogenous, we can still consider an industry, such as electronics and autos, as a relatively skill-intensive industry even if it uses a large proportion of relatively labor-intensive inputs as long as quality upgrade requires more skilled labor relative to unskilled labor.

Applying the above theory to China, this section concludes that China's relative wage of skilled labor to unskilled labor will increase as China attracts more FDI into high-tech sectors using skilled biased labor technologies. This result is an extension to the standard Stolper-Samuelson theory with homogeneous products and technologies, which predicts that, in the absence of product differentiation, the relative wage of skilled labor to unskilled labor can only decrease. However, as more FDI flows into the Chinese economy, especially into sectors such as telecommunications, information technology, and banking and financial services as included in China's WTO agreements with the United States and the EU, the gap between skilled and unskilled labor is likely to increase in the future. To offset this negative impact of FDI on China's income inequality, China should also encourage foreign direct investments with more unskilled labor-intensive technologies although they may not have or use the top of the line technologies.

How Well Did Our Theory Explain China's Income Inequality?

Although comparable time series data on the average wage by occupation are not available, the following stylized facts can provide some support to our

Figure 5.6   **Annual Growth of Real Average Wage and FDI**

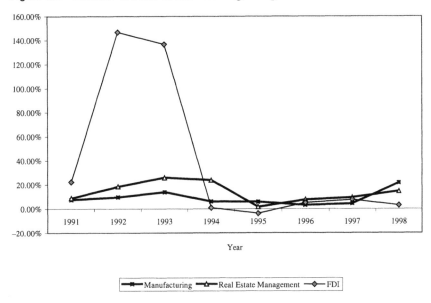

Source: Calculated from National Bureau of Statistics, *China Statistical Yearbook, 1998, 1999*.

theoretical results. Figure 5.6 shows that the growth rate of real wages is correlated with the growth rate of FDI in the 1990s after adjusting for inflation. Among the factors that contribute to real wage growth, FDI is clearly related to wage increases in FDI concentrated sectors, either capital/technology-intensive sectors (real estate management) or unskilled labor-intensive sectors (part of manufacturing). Such wage increases also appear to spread to other sectors (agriculture and mining). The upward pressure on overall wage growth brought about by FDI is evident.

More importantly, available data can show further that the wage increases of skilled labor outpace that of unskilled labor. Figure 5.7 clearly shows that the average nominal wage gap between the relatively differentiated or capital/skilled labor-intensive sectors (electric/gas and real estate) and the relatively homogeneous or unskilled labor-intensive sectors (agriculture and mining) widened over the years from 1990 to 1998. By 1998, foreign capital inflows into China reached a historical peak as shown in Figure 5.2. This implies that, while other factors may have affected wage inequality, large FDI inflows into the relatively differentiated sectors, using relatively more skilled labor-intensive technologies, have unmistakably contributed to the increase of the relative wage of skilled labor employed in these sectors.

Figure 5.7   **Average Nominal Wage by Sector**

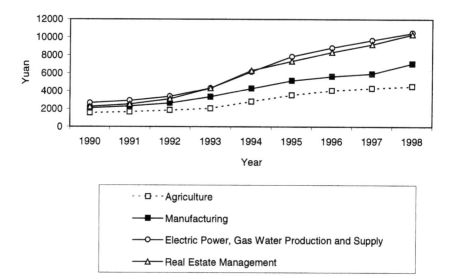

Source: Calculated from National Bureau of Statistics, *China Statistical Yearbook, 1998, 1999*.

Figure 5.7 also shows that the average nominal wage gap widened as well between the real estate management sector (a differentiated sector) with relatively higher skilled labor intensity and the manufacturing sector that has both differentiated and homogeneous products with relatively lower skilled labor intensity (as some manufacturing products are relatively unskilled labor intensive). All of these confirm that, as export oriented FDI flows to differentiated high-tech sectors with relatively high skilled labor intensities, the wage inequality of skilled to unskilled labor will increase rather than decrease under freer trade and investment.

Finally, Figure 5.1 and Figure 5.2 together indicate that the income inequality actually decreased after the first FDI surge in 1993 to 1994 (Chen and Wang 2001), when China started to encourage foreign capital inflow, but as FDI inflow continued to rise into the 2000s, the income inequality started to rise again (Wu and Perloff 2004). As studied in Wu (2001), the FDI inflow was mainly from the newly developed countries in the mid-to-late nineties. These FDIs brought in mainly unskilled labor-intensive technologies and employed a large amount of labor migrated from rural areas. From the theoretical analysis in the previous section, these FDI inflows should indeed help to reduce the wage gap between skilled and unskilled labor and hence income inequality.

Moreover, as poverty is positively related to income inequality (Chen and Wang 2001), this theoretical result can explain the empirical finding in Chen and Wang that although poverty incidence dropped significantly in the period of 1990 to 1999, poverty reduction was insignificant between 1990 and 1993, but was more significant in the period between 1993 and 1996, especially for rural poverty.

As China attracts more and more foreign capital from developed countries, such as Japan and the United States, FDI brings in more and more skilled labor-intensive technologies. Hence, the above trend has reversed. The wage gap is rising and so is income inequality, which has been gradually increasing since 1998 and has slightly passed its 1994 peak. Since most of these FDIs with skilled labor-intensive technologies are located in the urban sector, the theoretical prediction is consistent with the finding in Wu and Perloff (2004) that urban inequality is increasing faster than rural inequality and has played an increasingly important role in China's growing income inequality in recent years.

Although there are certainly other important reasons, such as economic growth or the Asian crisis analyzed in Chen and Wang (2001), that may have also contributed to China's growing income inequality over the past two decades, this chapter argues that the huge FDI inflow started in 1993 can be one of the driving forces and that the theoretical predictions in the previous section are consistent with empirical evidence. This view is shared by Chen and Wang (2001), who also conclude that human capital has contributed positively and significantly to economic growth, which is identified as their major factor accountable for the reduction in income inequality from 1990 to 1998. However, the development of human capital has evidently benefited from foreign capital inflows.

Implications and Conclusions

In China, attracting foreign direct investment has been a strategic economic policy adopted to upgrade technology and boost economic growth. The development of special economic zones and the tax break for joint ventures and wholly foreign-owned subsidiaries have made a significant contribution to the rapid increase of FDI inflows into China in the past three decades, especially in the 1990s. China's accession to the WTO in the early 2000s has further increased its FDI inflow.

Meanwhile, income inequality is becoming a more critically important issue for social stability as China experiences large layoffs of workers from the formerly state-owned enterprises during their restructuring toward a market economy. Indeed, multinational firms with relatively skill-intensive technologies contribute to China's rising income inequality as studied by Wu (2000, 2003). These FDIs have pushed up the relative wage of skilled labor and hence the wage in those relatively skill-intensive sectors, which is consistent with the sectoral wage data presented in Wu (2000). However, in his 2001 article, Wu shows that, although FDI from well-developed countries is increasing, a higher percentage of China's FDI is still from newly developed countries and regions with mostly relatively unskilled labor biased technologies, which can reduce the wage gap. Hence, FDI can have a neutral effect on the relative return to skilled labor in all sectors across the country. Based on the previous analysis, we can draw the following implications about China's FDI policy to promote economic growth and to minimize income inequality.

First, one type of foreign direct investment in China is aimed to take advantage of China's cheap unskilled labor and is mostly in China's export-oriented sectors. This type of FDI usually brings about relatively unskilled labor biased technology transfers in either the homogeneous or the differentiated sector. As a result, the relative wage of unskilled labor will increase and the income inequality between skilled and unskilled labor will decrease. Hence, it is beneficial, not only in terms of promoting economic growth but also in terms of reducing income inequality, to use favorable policies, such as tax breaks, to attract foreign direct investment with unskilled labor biased technology.

Indeed, Wu (2001) shows that almost 50 percent of China's inward foreign direct investment is from Hong Kong and Taiwan. Many multinational firms that originated in Hong Kong and Taiwan have set up factories in China and employ much of the unskilled labor displaced from farming. These foreign direct investments have definitely contributed to China's rapid income growth in the past two decades. Income per capita doubled in China from 1978 to 1994 (World Bank 1997) while income inequality fell slightly from 1994 to 1999 (Chen and Wang 2001). China has been very successful in utilizing its close social and cultural ties with Hong Kong and Taiwan to boost exports and growth in order to smooth the transition from a planned economy to a market economy.

Second, another type of foreign direct investment aims to profit from China's huge domestic market as well as through exporting. This type of FDI usually involves developing a new product to compete with the existing domestic products and hence inducing skilled labor biased technical progress mostly in the differentiated sector. This will certainly increase the relative return to skill. In China, most college graduates nowadays can earn a much higher wage than average if they work for foreign-funded enterprises (either wholly foreign-owned or joint venture), which usually use a relatively more skilled labor-intensive technology than local firms in China. This is the case studied in Wu (2000), where the wage gap between skilled and unskilled labor increases with inward FDI and the size of this increase depends on the enforcement of intellectual property rights in China. Hence, we can have the following trade-off between economic prosperity and income inequality.

On the one hand, such foreign direct investment introduces more advanced technology, increases China's competitiveness in the high-end product markets, especially in the high-tech sector, and facilitates China's gradual movement from exporting low value-added products to high value-added products and hence its potential economic growth, which will eventually help to reduce income inequality. On the other hand, however, such a technology transfer will, in the short run, intensify the social tension between skilled and unskilled labor in moving toward freer trade and foreign direct investment. This trade-off is also present if foreign direct investment is in the homogeneous sector as long as the induced technology transfer is focused on skilled labor biased technology.

Being aware of this trade-off, China can encourage small-scale foreign direct investment with relatively skilled labor biased technologies. For example, the computer software industry is skill intensive, but can operate on a relatively small scale with only a small number of employees. This can maximize gains from FDI in terms of upgrading China's technology and the profit margin of China's exports while minimizing the potential risk of rising income inequality between skilled and unskilled labor across the country.

After China's accession to the WTO, both types of FDI are expected to increase. Hence, as long as China maintains a balanced inward FDI with a focus on both skilled and unskilled labor biased technologies, inward FDI will facilitate China's technological development, increase its competitiveness in the world market with both low- and high-end products, and induce a balanced wage increase for both skilled and unskilled workers in China— eventually alleviating China's income inequality.

Notes

I thank Yingyi Qian, Kevin Honglin Zhang, and my colleagues Patrick Conway and Al Field for comments on my two earlier working papers leading to this chapter.

1. Leamer (1994, 1998, 2000) and Wood (1994, 1995) demonstrate that wages are linked to prices rather than to volumes. Their empirical results show that trade can be the main cause of growing wage inequality between skilled and unskilled labor regardless of the size of trade's contribution to total GDP.

2. For example, to build a higher-quality TV with a longer tube life or better picture quality requires much more research and more advanced or efficient production lines. Hence, the production of a higher quality TV requires a higher skilled to unskilled labor ratio in the production process than does the lower quality product.

3. A compendium of the trade models under monopolistic competition can be found in Grossman (1992).

4. However, a foreign firm's gain from foreign direct investment will be offset by its fixed cost of going multinational so that all multinational firms and local firms in both countries still can earn zero profits after taking into account their fixed cost.

References

Brainard, Lael S. 1997. "An Empirical Assessment of the Proximity-Concentration Trade-off Between Multinational Sales and Trade." *American Economic Review* 87, no. 4 (September): 520–44.

Chen, Chunlai. 1997a. "The Composition and Location Determinants of Foreign Direct Investment in China's Manufacturing." Working Paper 97/13. Australia: Chinese Economies Research Center, University of Adelaide.

———. 1997b. "Foreign Direct Investment and Trade: An Empirical Investigation of the Evidence from China." Working Paper 97/11. Australia: Chinese Economies Research Center, University of Adelaide.

Chen, Shaohua, and Yan Wang. 2001. "China's Growth and Poverty Reduction: Recent Trends Between 1990 and 1999." Working Paper. Washington DC: World Bank.

Copeland, Brian R., and Ashok Kotwal. 1996. "Product Quality and the Theory of Comparative Advantage." *European Economic Review* 40: 1745–60.

Domowitz, Ian, R. Glenn Hubbard, and Bruce Petersen. 1988. "Market Structure and Cyclical Fluctuations in U.S. Manufacturing." *Review of Economics and Statistics* 70 (February): 55–66.

Feenstra, Robert C., and Gordon Hanson. 1997a. "Productivity Measurement and the Impact of Trade and Technology on Wages: Estimates for the United States, 1972–1990." NBER Working Paper 6052 (June). Cambridge, MA: National Bureau of Economic Research.

———. 1997b. "Foreign Direct Investment and Relative Wages: Evidence from Mexico's Maquiladoras." *Journal of International Economics* 42, nos. 3–4 (May): 371–93.

———. 1999. "The Impact of Outsourcing and High-Technology Capital on Wages: Estimates for the United States, 1979–1990." *Quarterly Journal of Economics* 114, no. 3 (August): 907–40.

Flam, Harry, and Elhanan Helpman. 1987. "Vertical Product Differentiation and North-South Trade." *American Economic Review* 77, no. 5 (December): 810–22.

Glass, Amy J. 2004. "Imitation as a Stepping Stone to Innovation." Working Paper, Texas A&M University (February).

Glass, Amy J., and Kamal Saggi. 2002a. "Intellectual Property Rights and Foreign Direct Investment." *Journal of International Economics* 56 (March): 387–410.

———. 2002b. "Licensing Versus Direct Investment: Implications for Economic Growth." *Journal of International Economics* 56 (January): 131–53.

Grossman, Gene M., ed. 1992. *Imperfect Competition and International Trade*. Cambridge and London: MIT Press.

Hall, Robert E. 1988. "The Relation Between Price and Marginal Cost in U.S. Industry." *Journal of Political Economy* 96, no. 5 (October): 921–47.

Helpman, Elhanan. 1981. "International Trade in the Presence of Product Differentiation, Economies of Scale, and Monopolistic Competition: A Chamberlin-Heckscher-Ohlin Approach." *Journal of International Economics* 11 (August): 305–40.

———. 1992. "Multinational Corporations and Trade Structure." In *Imperfect Com-*

petition and International Trade, ed. Gene M. Grossman, 285–302. Cambridge and London: MIT Press.

Helpman, Elhanan, and Paul Krugman. 1985. *Market Structure and Foreign Trade: Increasing Returns, Imperfect Competition, and the International Economy*. Cambridge and London: MIT Press.

Huang, Zhengshen, Wenxia Xie, and Xianjing Chen. 1994. *China's 3000 Largest Foreign-Funded Enterprises 1994*. Beijing: China Reform Publishing House.

Jones, Ronald W. 1965. "The Structure of Simple General Equilibrium Models." *Journal of Political Economy* 73, no. 6 (December): 557–72.

———. 2000. "Technical Progress, Price Adjustments, and Wages." *Review of International Economics* 8, no. 3: 497–503.

Krugman, Paul. 2000. "Technology, Trade, and Factor Prices." *Journal of International Economics* 50, no. 1 (February): 51–71.

Leamer, Edward E. 1994. "Trade, Wages, and Revolving Door Ideas." NBER Working Paper 4716. Cambridge, MA: National Bureau of Economic Research.

———. 1998. "In Search of Stolper-Samuelson Effects on U.S. Wages." In *Imports, Exports and the American Worker*, ed. Susan M. Collins, 141–203. Washington, DC: Brookings Institution Press,.

———. 2000. "What's the Use of Factor Contents?" *Journal of International Economics* 50, no. 1 (February): 17–49.

Motta, Massimo. 1992. "Sunk Costs and Trade Liberalization." *Economic Journal* 102 (May): 578–87.

Murphy, Kevin M., and Andrei Shleifer. 1997. "Quality and Trade." *Journal of Development Economics* 53: 1–15.

National Bureau of Statistics. 2000. *China Foreign Economic Statistical Yearbook*. Beijing: China Statistics Press.

———. 2000. *China Labor Statistical Yearbook*. Beijing: China Statistics Press.

———. 2000–2001. *China Statistical Abstract*. Beijing: China Statistics Press.

———. 1985–2001. *China Statistical Yearbook*. Beijing: China Statistics Press.

Richardson, David J. 1995. "Income Inequality and Trade: How to Think, What to Conclude." *Journal of Economic Perspectives* 9, no. 3 (summer): 33–56.

Shapiro, Matthew D. 1987. "Measuring Market Power in U.S. Industry." NBER Working Paper 2212 (April). Cambridge, MA: National Bureau of Economic Research.

Sutton, John. 1991. *Sunk Costs and Market Structure: Price Competition, Advertising, and the Evolution of Concentration*. Cambridge and London: MIT Press.

United Nations. 1999. *World Investment Report 1999: Foreign Direct Investment and the Challenge of Development*. New York and Geneva: United Nations Publications.

United Nations Conference on Trade and Development (UNCTAD). 1999. *World Development Report 1999*. New York: United Nations.

Wood, Adrian. 1994. *North-South Trade, Employment and Inequality: Changing Fortunes in a Skill-Driven World*. Oxford: Clarendon Press.

———. 1995. "How Trade Hurts Unskilled Workers." *Journal of Economic Perspectives* 9, no. 3 (summer): 57–80.

World Bank. 1997. *Sharing Rising Incomes: Disparities in China*. Washington, DC: World Bank.

———. 2003. *World Development Indicators 2003*. CD-ROM. Washington, DC: World Bank.

Wu, Xiaodong. 2000. "Foreign Direct Investment, Intellectual Property Rights and China's Wage Inequality." *China Economic Review* 11, no. 4 (November): 361–84.

————. 2001. "The Impact of Foreign Direct Investment on the Relative Return to Skill." *Economics of Transition* 9, no. 3 (November): 695–715.

————. 2003. "Foreign Direct Investment and Dissemination of Job Opening Information in China." In *Improving Labor Market Opportunities and Security for Workers in Developing Countries*, ed. William T. Kosanovich, 141–70. Washington, DC: Bureau of International Affairs, U.S. Department of Labor.

Wu, Ximing, and Jeffrey M. Perloff. 2004. "China's Income Distribution over Time: Reasons for Rising Inequality." Working Paper (February), available at http://ssrn.com/abstract=506462/.

Xu, Bin. 2001. "Factor Bias, Sector Bias, and the Effects of Technical Progress on Relative Wages." *Journal of International Economics* 54, no. 1: 5–25.

Zhang, Fan, and Jingping Zheng. 1998. "The Impact of Multinational Enterprises on Economic Structure and Efficiency in China." Working Paper (August). Beijing: China Center for Economic Research.

Zhang, Kevin H. 2000. "Transition and Growth in China: The Role of Foreign Direct Investment." Working Paper, Illinois State University.

6

A New World Factory and China's Labor Force

Yan-Zhong Wang

The key to integration with the world economy is the liberalization of commodities, services, investment, and finance including high-technology staff to some extent, while not including the global liquidity of the general labor force (especially the low-skill labor in developing countries). For developing countries, one major issue is how to combine the great mobility of international capital with the great quantity, but weak liquidity, of international labor. China's accession to the WTO in 2001 becomes an important milestone in China's reform, an opportunity to enter a new stage, and an important event for integrating into the world economy. This means that China will further expand its opening to the outside world, while fully utilizing its plentiful and cheap labor resources.

Expansion of China's Industrial Production and Growth of the World Factory

China's Evolution from a Backward Agricultural Country into a Large Industrial Producer

China has built an independent and completely modern industrial system since the latter half of the twentieth century. Industry enjoys a more prominent position in the national economy. The percentage of industrial output in the GDP rose from 10 percent in 1952 to 44.3 percent in 2000. Industry has become the generator of China's economic growth and the most powerful economic sector. If the building industry is included, industrial output rises to 50.9 percent of the GDP for 2000. Industry has provided various sectors of the national economy with large amount of materials, technical equipment, and durable consumer goods needed by the people in their daily lives. China has become the world's largest home appliance producer, exporter, and consumer. The country has also built the world's largest fixed telephone and mobile telecommunication networks.

The output of China's major industrial products now ranks among the highest in the world. The output of China's major industrial products was noticeably small in 1949, only coal production ranked ninth in the world, while the output of all other industrial products was far below twenty-fifth place in the world. In 1978, the year China embarked on the road to reform and began opening to world markets, the output of coal, crude oil, electricity, cement, chemical fertilizer, chemical fibers, cotton cloth, sugar, and TV sets was the eighth in the world. In 1999, China led the world in the output of coal, iron and steel, cement, glass, home appliances, and textiles, and ranked second in the output of electricity, chemical fibers, and cotton cloth.

Industrial output has increased by a big margin, raising the supply of industrial products in China from shortages during the planned economic period to the present relatively surplus situation in which industrial production is now limited by market demands.

China's Journey from a Closed Economy to an Active Participant in Foreign Trade

From the 1950s to the end of the 1970s, China's industrialization was conducted basically within the confines of a closed economy. In 1978, the import and export trade had risen to RMB35.5 billion or US$20.6 billion. Since then, the speedy growth of industry and the reforms implemented in foreign trade policies have promoted rapid development and expansion in China. From 1979 to 2000, China's total foreign trade volume rose from US$20.6 billion to US$474.3 billion with an average annual growth rate of 15 percent. Specifically, exports rose from US$9.8 billion to US$249.2 billion with an annual increase of 15.7 percent, which was 6.5 percent higher than the increase of the GDP in the same period and nearly 10 percent higher than the average growth rate of trade in the world (6.3 percent) from 1981 to 1996. The increase in exports basically kept abreast of the rise in industrial output value, indicating that the speedy growth of industry was the main factor in promoting exports.

Along with the expansion of China's foreign trade, its industry has become increasingly dependent on exports. In 1978 the rate of dependence was 4.62

Table 6.1

Development of China's Foreign Trade and Changes in Export Dependence

Year	Total import and export volume (US$ billions)	Exports (US$ billions)	Export dependence (%)	Imports (US$ billions)	Import dependence (%)	Ratio of China's exports in world exports	China's ranking in world exports
1980	38.14	18.12	6	20.02	6.6	0.91	26
1985	69.6	27.35	9	42.25	14	1.42	17
1990	115.44	62.09	16.1	53.35	13.9	1.84	15
1995	280.86	148.78	21.3	132.08	18.9	3.28	11
1999	360.63	194.93	19.7	165.7	16.7	3.51	8
2000	474.31	249.21	23.4	225.1	20.8	3.98	7
2001	509.77	266.15	23.0	243.61	—	4.32	6

Source: National Bureau of Statistics, *China Statistical Yearbook* (2001, 150).

percent; in 1982, 7.82 percent; and in 1987, 12.3 percent. After the 1990s, the dependence of the Chinese economy on exports exceeded 20 percent, specifically 20.3 percent in 1997 and 23.4 percent in 2000 (see Table 6.1).

China's foreign trade has strengthened its position in the world economy. In 1978, China's exports ranked thirty-second in the world. In 1980, China's export volume was 0.9 percent of the world's total, placing the country in twenty-sixth place. This rose to 1.84 percent in 1990, which was twice as much as in 1980. In 2001, the percentage of China's exports rose further to 4.3 percent of the world's total, placing the country in sixth place.

Promotion of China's Industrial Competitive Advantages in World Markets Result in Its Rudimentary "World Factory"

Since 2001, there have been increasing comments at home and abroad with respect to China becoming a "world factory" or "world manufacturing center." However, Chinese scholars largely believe that development as a "world factory" means becoming the most important and largest production base of industrial products in the global marketplace, as well as a trading superpower that can influence or even determine price direction and future trends of the main industrial products in the world and could be strongly competitive in the entire industrial chain (e.g., production, research and development, technological innovation, quality, price, management, etc.). Based upon this comprehensive definition, China is obviously not yet a world factory. However, China possesses some important characteristics that give it the potential to achieve this goal.

Table 6.2

Development of the Exportation of Industrial Products

Year	Export volume of industrial products (US$ billions)	Percentage of total export volume (%)	Percentage of export of capital- and technology-intensive products in total export of industrial products (%)
1980	9.005	49.69	21.8
1981	11.759	53.43	20.66
1982	12.271	54.98	20.04
1983	12.606	56.72	19.61
1984	14.205	54.34	20.11
1985	13.522	49.44	15.75
1986	19.67	63.57	14.37
1987	16.206	66.45	15.17
1988	33.11	69.68	17.11
1989	37.46	71.3	18.89
1990	46.205	74.41	20.17
1991	55.698	77.53	19.69
1992	67.936	79.98	25.86
1993	75.078	81.83	26.51
1994	101.298	83.71	27.77
1995	127.295	85.56	31.82
1996	129.123	85.48	34.22
1997	158.839	86.9	33.96
1998	163.22	88.8	37.09
1999	174.99	89.77	39.55
2000	223.752	89.78	42.32
2001	—	—	44.63

Source: National Bureau of Statistics, *China Statistical Yearbook* (2001, 151).

First, Chinese industrial products have become competitive internationally. In its first, second, and third major industries, China has the most rapid growth and has opened those markets to the highest extent. Since the 1980s, China's industrial finished products have continued to rise, and in 2000 they constituted close to 90 percent of total Chinese exports (see Table 6.2). The industrial products exported by China are primarily labor-intensive, while the value of exported mechanical and electrical equipment, which are technology- and capital-intensive, has increased from 20 percent in 1990 to 42 percent in 2000 of China's total exports. The rise in China's exports to the outside world is mainly a result of the continual expansion of its finished products industry, demonstrating its importance in international markets.

Second, the role of foreign direct investment (FDI) in Chinese industrial production has become more important. Since the 1990s China has become

Table 6.3

The Changing Pace of Foreign Companies' Technology Transfers to China

Level of Technology	1997 (%)	2001 (%)
Advanced technologies of foreign companies	13	41
Relatively advanced technologies of foreign companies	54	45
Ordinary technologies of foreign companies	33	14

Source: Jiang (2002).

the developing country that attracts the largest FDI. By the end of 2001, China had attracted 390,484 foreign invested enterprises, and had actually utilized US$395.5 billion in foreign capital. Foreign invested enterprises have played an increasingly important role in China's economy, and the percentage of their contribution to China's total export value is continuously rising. In 2001, the value of their exports was US$147.5 billion, accounting for 55.4 percent of China's total exports. The exports of foreign invested enterprises have become an important force in impelling China to achieve rapid growth in the export of its industrial products. With China's membership in the WTO, it is expected that foreign invested enterprises will continue to expand their investment and speed up the transfer of advanced technologies to China (see Table 6.3). China has gradually become a key location for global research and development centers of the largest transnational companies.

Finally, China has the great potential to become the center of world manufacturing. On one side, China has a huge population and prospective mass market. The population of China is equivalent to the total current population of the developed industrial countries. At present, the developed countries have entered a post-industrialization stage, while China faces the task of industrializing 1.3 billion people simultaneously. On a positive note, decades of nurturing industrialization and rapid improvement in educational training levels have allowed a great majority of Chinese laborers to improve their skills. These efforts combined with the infusion of international capital bode well for China to become the manufacturing center of the Asian and Pacific region, or even of the world.

The Limitless Cheap Labor Supply Becomes the Engine for China's Growing Industrial Expansion

Currently, the rapid growth of China's economy mostly relies on large-scale inputs of capital and labor. According to the statistical data and some

Table 6.4

Increase of China's Labor Force and GDP Growth, 1952–2001

Year	1952	1978	1990	1997	1999	2001
GDP (billion RMB)	67.90	362.41	1,859.84	7,446.26	8,503.28	9,593.30
Employment (10 thousands)	20,729	40,152	63,909	69,600	70,586	73,025
In Urban Areas	2,486	95,14	16,616	20,207	21,014	23,940
In Public Sectors	1,603	9,499	13,895	13,927	—	—
Period	1953– 1978	1979– 1997	1979– 1990	1991– 1998	1999	2001
GDP Growth Rate (%)	6.1	9.8	8.8	10.8	7.1	7.3
Employment Growth Rate (%)	2.6	2.9	2.9	1.1	0.90	1.3
In Public Sectors (%)	7.1	2.3	3.3		—	—

Source: National Bureau of Statistics, *China Statistical Yearbook* (1998, 1999, 2001).

related researches and analyses, the continual growth in labor force input has apparently become one of the essential elements driving China's economic growth. Take, for example, the years from 1953 to 1978, when the annual employment growth rate in China was 2.6 percent, and the annual growth rate of GDP was 6.1 percent. From 1979 to 1997, the annual employment growth rate was 2.9 percent, and the annual GDP growth rate was 9.8 percent (see Table 6.4). Thanks to the development of education and healthcare, the quality of the Chinese labor force has been greatly improved. The annual longevity of Chinese people climbed from thirty-eight years in 1950 to sixty-nine years in 1997; people fifteen years old receiving education increased to 8.9 years in 1995 from 1.7 years in 1952. Owing to these and other improvements in conditions for the Chinese labor force, the annual growth rate for labor productivity (which was 1.78 percent during the period from 1952 to 1978) rose to 4.74 percent from 1978 to 1995. In respect to the structure of labor, large-scale industrialization has facilitated the labor transfer from the relatively low productivity of the agricultural sector to the secondary and tertiary industrial sectors and consequently boosted the allocation efficiency of employees. Employment transfers among Chinese sectors have had an influence upon the GDP—0.94 percent during the period from 1952 to 1978 and 1.44 percent during the period from 1978 to 1995 (Madison 1999). To sum up the above factors, it is very clear that labor growth is driving the growth of the Chinese economy. During the period from 1953 to 1997, labor contributed about 21 percent to GDP

Table 6.5

The Contribution of Increased Labor and Capital to GDP Growth, 1953–1997

Period	Total factor productivity (%)	Contribution of capital (%)	Contribution of labor (%)
1953–1997	15.32	63.71	20.73
1953–1978	–7.03	84.27	22.08
1979–1995	37.71	47.75	14.93

Source: Wang (2000).

growth, that is, about one-fifth of the economic growth in China derives directly from increased labor inputs (see Table 6.5).

Compared to the significant effect of capital inputs in the progress of industrialization in developed countries, the later industrialization progress of China mainly relies on availability of cheap labor. At the initial stage of industrialization, China has been confronted with shortages of capital and tremendous problems relating to resources, ecology, and environmental pressure that other industrialized countries have never met. In the planning stages of the new economy, China approved systems of "dual economy" and "dual society," utilized its administrative power to draw the initial capital for industrialization from the agricultural sector, and mobilized large-scale labor forces to construct industrial infrastructure. China's labor forces expand constantly, but more than two decades of wage freezes have allowed government to maintain low labor costs over a long period.

China has already created a basic framework of modernization, building a solid foundation for industrialization. Meanwhile, the development of village and township industries and economic reform has reduced the cost of labor for Chinese industry as a whole. From the onset of reform, labor prices in Chinese cities have increased continuously along with economic growth and the rise of the price of commodities. During the period from 1978 to 1990, the annual wage of employees in Chinese cities increased from RMB615 RMB2,140 and the annual wage of employees in state-owned enterprises increased from RMB644 to RMB2,284. During the period from 1990 to 1997, annual wages of employees in Chinese cities increased from RMB2,140 to RMB6,470 and the annual wage of the manufacturing employees has increased from RMB2,284 to RMB5,933 (see Table 6.6). A phenomenon worthy of attention is that the wage level of employees in manufacturing was highest before the reform, although it continued to rise slowly after the reform, but to a lower extent than that of the average employee in Chinese cities. The principal reason for this is that the surplus low wage labor force

Table 6.6

Labor Force and Wages in Urban Areas and in Township and Village Enterprises

Year	Average wage of labor in urban areas (RMB)	Average wage of labor in SOEs (RMB)	Average wage of labor in the manufacturing sector in urban areas (RMB)	Number of persons employed in the manufacturing sector in urban areas (10,000 persons)	Number of persons employed in the manufacturing sector in rural areas (10,000 persons)	Average wage of labor in township and village enterprises (RMB)
1957				1,528		
1978	615	644	676	2,115	1,734	
1980	762	803	752	3,595	1,942	
1985	1,148	1,213	1,112	3,947	4,136	
1990	2,140	2,284	2,073	4,620	5,572	1,380
1995	5,500	5,625	5,169	5,304	7,565	3,355
1996	6,210	6,280	5,642	5,439	7,860	4,195
1997	6,470	6,747	5,933	5,293	6,149	4,465
1998	7,479	7,668	7,064	5,083	7,334	—
1999	8,346	8,543	7,794	3,769	—	5,193
2000	9,371	9,552	8,750	3,496	7,467	5,507

Source: National Bureau of Statistics, *China Statistical Yearbook* (1998, 1999, 2001).

from the agricultural sector has edged out almost 50 million of the employees in state-owned and collective enterprises in the cities. Compared to the cities, labor prices in the countryside are lower. Since the middle of the 1990s, as competition became more intense for general industrial jobs, the growth rate of average employee wages in some industrial sectors remained stagnant, even decreasing slightly.

The manufacturing sector with international comparative preponderance becomes the principal support for China's incorporation into the world economic system. As China has become more open to the outside world, its participation has increased in the international marketplace. Its current comparative advantages include its low land and labor costs and its huge potential domestic market; its relative disadvantages lie in the areas of capital, technology, and management. The increasingly strong Chinese market is the foundation for the modernization of the Chinese economy and the basis for China's incorporation into the world economic system. Combining China's labor resources with domestic and overseas resources such as capital and technologies will develop an even greater Chinese market. The overall scale of the labor force in China is huge and without reserves at any time in the foreseeable future, thus it can guarantee a low-cost and high-quality supply for a

Table 6.7

Average Weekly Wages of Labor in the Manufacturing Sector in Some Asian Countries and Regions (US$)

Countries and regions	Average weekly wages	Ratio (China as 1)
China	30	1
Indonesia	31.7	1.07
Philippines	47.4	1.58
Thailand	58.3	1.94
Malaysia	77.9	2.6
Korea	243	8.12
Taiwan	328.9	10.96
Hong Kong	436.6	14.6

Source: Lu (2001).

comparatively long term. Since the 1990s, Chinese manufacturing employees have ranged from 90 million to 100 million, which surpasses the total of manufacturing employees of developed countries. In the meantime, a labor force of 200–250 million out of an estimated 330 million agricultural labor force in the countryside can be transferred to other economic sectors without decreasing agricultural output. At present, employment opportunities in both the cities and the countryside are scarce, consequently, pressure from surplus agricultural labor will cause the manufacturing labor force to maintain its advantage on price for a long period. The average wage of the manufacturing labor force in China is lower than that of developed countries, and also lower than that of the developing countries at the same development level (see Table 6.7), but the overall quality of the Chinese industrial labor force continues to increase. The quality of Chinese laborers is still low overall, but since China has a huge population, the total number of workers who have received a higher education and achieved a somewhat higher technical level is high. In 2000, the professional technical staff in Chinese cities reached 30.6 million, including 4.63 million technical workers in the manufacturing sector. In 2001 Chinese institutes of higher education recruited 2.68 million students, adult higher education recruited 1.96 million students, and postgraduate schools recruited 170,000. Students of all types of higher education reached 12 million. Each year there are 2–3 million students graduating from higher educational schools and more than 10 million students graduating from senior middle education schools; two-thirds of these students will enter the work force. Therefore, the substantial labor forces with good educations have contributed enormous human capital with which China attracts foreign capital and overseas enterprises and organizations to make China the base for their low–cost manufacturing production and research and development. This trend should continue for at least another twenty to thirty years.

China's WTO Membership and the Development of International Labor Cooperation

China's international labor cooperation in the narrow sense refers to the export of labor services. From 1979 to 2001, China signed contracts worth a total of US$121.8 billion for overseas contracting and labor services, completed projects worth US$88.46 billion, and dispatched labor service exports of more than 2.4 million man-hours. Since the mid-1990s, every year China has dispatched 400,000–500,000 laborers to foreign countries. Compared with the huge quantity of Chinese laborers, these numbers are small.

International labor cooperation is not limited to labor services; it also is comprised of all other types of Chinese labor resources related to international production, for example, those Chinese employees who work in foreign investment enterprises and Chinese export companies. Since the 1990s, the percentage of total employees in urban areas who were working in foreign investment enterprises achieved a noticeable increase from 0.97 percent in 1991 to 3.02 percent in 2000 (see Table 6.8). As a result of the rapid development of village and township industry, many village and township enterprises are the cooperative partners of foreign investors, especially investments originating in Hong Kong, Macao, and Taiwan. The statistical number of Chinese employees in foreign investment enterprises is only a part of the total Chinese employees in foreign enterprises. Among the 70 million emigrants who leave their hometowns, many are working in foreign investment enterprises in the coastal areas. In 2000 there were more than 25,600 joint ventures that were jointly founded or jointly funded by the village and township enterprises and foreign enterprises and enterprises from Hong Kong, Macao, and Taiwan. If estimated on the basis of the average employment scale of village and township enterprises and collective enterprises (55 persons per enterprise in the year 2000), these joint ventures have directly employed a labor force of over 1.4 million people. If all kinds of employment positions are included, the total Chinese labor force employed in foreign investment companies range from about 15–20 million.

Although the exportation of labor services and the employment of Chinese by foreign investment enterprises continue to grow, their percentage is too small when compared with China's huge labor resources. Even if the number of foreign investments maintains a continual and high rate of growth, the total employment opportunities they provide are limited. Therefore, international labor cooperation shall not be limited to the export of labor ser-

Table 6.8

Statistical Number of Employed Persons in Foreign Funded Units
(including Hong Kong, Taiwan, and Macao)

Year	Employed Persons (10,000 persons)	Percentage of Total Employees in Urban Areas (%)
1991	165	0.97
1992	221	1.28
1993	288	1.64
1994	406	2.2
1995	513	2.69
1996	540	2.73
1997	581	2.88
1998	587	2.89
1999	612	2.91
2000	642	3.02

Source: National Bureau of Statistics, *China Statistical Yearbook* (2001, 111).

vices and the attraction of foreign capital; it shall also include expansion of various other foreign-related trade and services. In 2001 China's total export of commodities reached US$266.2 billion (its total import of commodities was US$243.6 billion). Using a conversion rate of GDP US$910 per capita for the year 2001 means that livelihoods of about 290 million Chinese people (roughly 23 percent of the total population) are accounted for through exports. If you include the income generated through exports in the processing sector (US$147.5 billion), an even greater portion of the Chinese population relies upon exports. As is written in Jin Bei (2002), "The essence of the processing trade is the export of labor force." Similar to commodities exports, the export of Chinese services is also growing. Take international tourism for example. The employees of China International Travel Agency increased from about 53,000 in 1996 to almost 70,000 in the year 2000, and income from international tourism increased from US$10.2 billion to US$17.8 billion during the same period. Of course, even as China exports a growing amount of labor services, attracts foreign capital, and spreads the export of commodities and other services, it is also increasing investment in foreign countries, the importation of experts and labor services, and the importation of commodities and other services.

A broad estimate can be made of the total number of Chinese people from all walks of life who participate in international economic cooperation: labor services exports account for 0.3 percent of the total population; Chinese employees in foreign investment enterprises account for about 1–2 percent of the total population; people involved in foreign trade account for 23 percent of the total population, plus those employees participating in the export of services. The sum of these activities total about 25–30 percent of the total population of China. At present, China's participation in the international labor market is very small, and the country still is positioned at a low level in terms of the international economic system; that is to say, China is still peripheral to the world economic system and is still in the developmental stage involving mainly labor exports. After China's entrance to WTO, various forms of international cooperation, especially international labor service cooperation, will be developed and expanded further, accompanying China's steps to incorporate into the world economic system.

Prospects for China's Labor Cooperation in the International Market

The huge potential for China's participation in the labor sector of the international market has created the possibility of China becoming the processing center of world manufacturing. However, at present China is still in a secondary position. According to Japanese scholar Jin Bei's analysis (2002) of the market value of the Chinese garment industry (one of the most competitive Chinese industries in the international market), Chinese enterprises have only obtained the processing component of this market (19 percent) including 11 percent for wage and insurance parts, while other links of the value chain are controlled by foreign traders. After China enters WTO, the expansion of investment liberalization will speed up the progress for China to become the "world factory," and China will mainly put its investment in infrastructure, public services, land and labor, and its benefits are primarily to increase income, employment, and exports. Foreign investments mainly focus on capital, technology, management, marketing, and a few similar areas—and they receive the largest profits. As China progresses toward its goal of becoming the world's factory, it will stimulate the combination of world capital and a Chinese labor force. International capital has obtained the larger market share and has the greater choice of resource allocation around the globe. As China speeds up its progress, it will be able to incorporate its own economic resources into the world economic system and further expand its labor exports through the combination of its labor resources and world capital. It is a win-win situation even though there are some conflicts between various partners and competition among sectors. The continuing growth of the Chinese economy and the development of its participation in international labor markets will also result in the expansion of China's power and influence in the world economic system. China's membership in the WTO in 2001 is only the beginning.

References

Cheng Qiqian. 2002. "Analysis of a World Manufacture Center." *China's Industrial Economy* 4.

Editorial Group. 1998, 2001. *China Township and Village Enterprises Yearbook*. Beijing: China Agriculture Press.

Institute of Industrial Economics of the Academy of Social Sciences. 1999, 2000, 2001, 2002. Economic reports. Beijing: Economic Management Publishing House.

Jiang Xiaojuan. 2002. "Analysis on FDI to China in 2001 and Prospects in 2002." In *China Economic Prospects, 2002*, ed. Liu Guoguang et al. Beijing: Social Sciences Documentation Publishing House.

Jin Bei. 2002. "Some Main Features and Current Trends in China's Economy." *China's Industrial Economy* 1.

Lu Zheng. 2001. "Can China Be the Factory of the World?" *China Industrial Economy* 11.

Madison, M. 1999. *The Future of China's Economy*. Beijing: Xinhua Press.

National Bureau of Statistics. 1981, 1991, 2001. *China Statistical Yearbook*. Beijing: China Statistics Press.

Project Group for National Situation Studies of the Academy of Sciences. 1998. *Employment and Development*. Shenyang: Liaoning People's Press.

Wang Xiaolu, and Fan Gang, eds. 2000. *The Sustainable Development of China's Economy*. Beijing: Economic Sciences Press.

Wang Yanzhong. 2000. "China's Macro-Employment Management and Policies in the New Period." *Management World* 5.

———. 2002. "China's WTO Membership and Its Consequences for China's Industrial Employment." *China's Industrial Economy* 5.

7

China's WTO Membership

Commitments and Challenges

Nini Yang

This chapter investigates the complexity and ongoing debates about China's entry into the World Trade Organization (WTO) from three perspectives: major opportunities and challenges from China's perspective, the controversy from the United States' perspective, and the prospective impacts from the global perspective. Critical issues examined include China's fast growing economy and trade position in the world, the accelerating disparate distribution of welfare and associated problems within China, the emerging redistribution of worldwide foreign direct investment (FDI) under the WTO regime, and conflicting ideas about trade liberalization and the WTO raised by various interest groups from the West, particularly from the United States. Results indicate that China's WTO membership may dramatically reshape the landscape of world trade by engendering two major waves.

First, as the United States and the European Union normalize their trade relationships with China, China's exports will compete forcefully with other export-driven economies, intensifying low-cost commodity competition among developing nations in the Western marketplace. Second, as China lifts quotas and non-tariff mechanisms that have protected Chinese farmers and domestic industries, foreign capital will increasingly beat a path to enter the Chinese market, leading to accelerated foreign competition in various economic sectors within China, particularly in agriculture, financial services, and traditional industries, such as chemicals, petroleum, steel, machinery, and automobiles. Thus the China effect will not be uniform globally. Neither will it be equally beneficial to the Chinese. Suggestions for future research and implications to the practical world follow.

Table 7.1

China's Top Ten Trade Partners (Total Trade, US$ million)

Country	2003	Percent change	Rank
Japan	133,573.4	31.1	1
United States	126,334.4	30.0	2
Hong Kong	87,407.7	26.3	3
South Korea	63,231.1	43.4	4
Taiwan	58,367.0	30.7	5
Germany	41,876.3	50.7	6
Malaysia	20,127.8	41.0	7
Singapore	19,352.3	37.9	8
Russia	15,760.6	32.1	9
Netherlands	15,438.7	44.6	10

Source: PRC General Customs Administration, *China's Customs Statistics* (2004).

China's Economy and Its Trade Position in the World

Over the past decade, the world economy has been growing fastest in East Asia and the Pacific Rim, averaging 7.3 percent annually (World Bank 2004). Leading this growth is China's emerging market economy with an impressive annual growth rate of its gross domestic product (GDP) of around 8 percent and 9.1 percent for 2002 and 2003 respectively, while the world economy grew by 1.9 percent in 2002. With more than two decades of economic reform, China has built up a solid track record of shifting toward a more open and market-oriented economy. According to the World Bank (2001), China's annual economic growth has averaged around 8 percent for the past two decades, quadrupling her GDP since 1978. The *World Development Indicators* (World Bank 2001) have ranked China the seventh largest leading exporter (3.9 percent) and eighth largest leading importer (3.4 percent) of the world's merchandise trade. For commercial services, China has ranked as the twelfth leading exporter (2.1 percent) and the tenth leading importer (2.5 percent) around the world. Most recently, China has moved up to become the sixth largest economy in the world, with trade in goods accounting for 49 percent of her GDP (World Bank 2004). By the end of 2003, China's total foreign reserves reached US$410 billion and had further surged to US$440 billion by March 2004. Table 7.1 summarizes China's top ten trade partners in the global market in 2003.

It is estimated that the China effect will raise the world economic growth by a quarter percentage point in the next decade (Einhorn, Dawson, and Kunii 2001). China's WTO debut, however, is not uniformly good news to the world.

Table 7.2

China's FDI Growth (2001–2003)

Country	2001	2002	Percent change	2003	Percent change
Number of Projects Approved	26,139	34,171	30.7	41,081	20.22
Contracted Investment (US$ billions)	69.19	82.77	19.6	115.07	39.03
Utilized investment (US$ billions)	46.86	52.74	12.5	53.51	1.44

Source: PRC Ministry of Foreign Trade and Economic Cooperation, Beijing, 2004.

On the one hand, for example, Western farmers will win big from China's pledge to sharply limit import barriers on wheat, corn, rice, and other agricultural commodities, which could boost her food imports by US$73 billion over ten years. Already, prior to China's WTO membership, American farm and food exports to China had reached US$1.7 billion in 2000, making China the seventh-largest market for U.S. farmers and food industries (Baculinao 2001). On the other hand, as the United States and the European Union lift their last restraints on China's textile products, Mexico and the Caribbean markets could lose thousands of garment-industry jobs to China within seven years. At a time when most emerging markets are desperate for foreign capital, increased FDI is flowing to China. Multinational corporations such as Intel, Motorola, and Dell Computers are already moving production to China. Foreign carmakers such as General Motors, Ford, Volkswagen, Honda, and Toyota will launch new cars aimed at quality- and cost-conscious Chinese consumers, and set up nationwide dealerships and service networks (Roberts and Webb 2001). Table 7.2 highlights China's FDI growth after joining the WTO. China's strong FDI inflows reflect the increased market opening required by China's WTO membership, new opportunities related to preparations for the 2008 Beijing Olympics, and the government's push to build up the nation's infrastructure. Investors are shifting production facilities from other Asian counties to China while China is experiencing an influx of supplies of intermediary goods.

China's competitive advantages in the global economy include abundant cheap labor, millions of well-trained yet relatively low-paid engineers, and good infrastructure. Transportation from China to the key U.S. markets is faster than from some other markets in Asia. For example, shipment time from China to California takes fourteen days as compared to thirty days from

Table 7.3

Prospective Global Impacts of China's WTO Membership

Markets	Prospective China Effects
North America	Farmers will get a new market for agricultural and food products. Semiconductor, telecommunications equipment, and computer makers will get duty-free access to China.
United States	More trade and investment opportunities will be revealed in agriculture, semiconductor, telecommunications, pharmaceuticals, automobiles, and financial services, with growing trade deficits with China as China takes over some trade business from Japan, South Korea, and certain other economies.
Mexico	Garment and shoe industries will be hit hard as quotas limiting Chinese exports to the United States are lifted.
European Union	Imports of Chinese shoes, dishes, and kitchen utensils will rise as the EU phases out quotas. More FDI will flow from EU countries to China as China liberalizes the market under WTO.
Japan	Imports of a wide array of consumer goods will grow as more Japanese manufacturers shift production to China-based suppliers. Equipment, vehicle, and electronics exports will rise.
South Korea	Exports of fabrics to China's surging apparel industry could swell, as could outflow of industrial gear and high-grade steel.
Taiwan	US$16 billion trade surplus with mainland China will fall. More production will go to China, boosting competitiveness of Taiwan tech industries as well as reallocation of Asia-based FDI.
Southeast Asia	Thailand, the Philippines, Indonesia, and Malaysia will lose FDI to China. Pressure will grow to upgrade industries and workforces.

Source: Based on Einhorn and Kunii (2001); World Bank statistics (2004); and U.S.-China Business Council statistics (2004).

Sri Lanka. The total length of China's road transportation is ranked fourth in the world, about 1.7 million kilometers, including quality highway transportation for about 20,000 kilometers (Han 2002). Thus, China's arrival as a manufacturing superpower could reshape the landscape of world trade dramatically in a foreseeable future, but the China effects will not be uniform for all parties concerned. Table 7.3 highlights some prospective global impacts of China's WTO membership.

Since China's entry into the WTO in November 2001, it has been a loco-motive for the economic growth in Asia and the Pacific Rim. In 2003, China's open market accounted for 18 percent of South Korea's exports, 12 percent of Japanese exports, and about 6–7 percent of the total exports of the members of the Association of Southeast Asian Nations (ASEAN). Clearly, China's booming economy has significant impacts beyond its borders. China's current effort to engineer a soft landing in order to cool down the economy will generate significant repercussions to the rest of the world. For example, a 10 percent reduction in the growth of China's imports could result in a loss of about 1 percent GDP growth in South Korea and Taiwan (World Bank 2004). At the same time, China must balance the need to continue creating jobs and reforming the economy while keeping the economy stable and slowing down excessive investment. China's continued prosperity and economic stability will influence economic fortunes elsewhere. The effects of China's soft landing, however, remain to be seen.

A Historical Overview of China's Accession to the WTO

The World Trade Organization grew out of the General Agreement on Tariffs and Trade (GATT) signed by twenty-three nations in 1947. The most favored nation (MFN) clause calls for each member nation to grant every other member nation the most favorable treatment concerning imports and exports. However, GATT had no intention of becoming an enforcement mechanism, but virtually relied on moral suasion. With the increasingly large membership and the growing need for market discipline based on agreed upon rules and terms among the member nations, on January 1, 1995, GATT was supplanted by the WTO with three main purposes: (a) to help trade flow as freely as possible as long as there are no undesirable side effects, (b) to serve as a forum for trade negotiations, and (c) to settle disputes through neutral procedures based on an agreed legal foundation.

Retrospectively, China was an original signatory of GATT, but the Nationalist government on Taiwan withdrew China's membership in 1949. The People's Republic of China applied to resume China's status as a contracting party of GATT in 1986. As GATT turned into the WTO, China requested conversion of its status from that of a Working Party to full membership. On November 10, 2001, the WTO members unanimously voted to admit China, and on the following day, Taiwan joined the WTO as well. Yongtu Long, head of the Chinese delegation, described the negotiation, which took fifteen years to conclude, as "long," "painstaking," and with "numerous difficulties and frustrations" (Long 2001).

From GATT to WTO, the international body today has grown to include

Table 7.4

The United States' Top Ten Trading Partners (2003, US$ million)

Country	U.S. Exports	U.S. Imports	Subtotal	Balance	Rank
Canada	169,769.0	224,165.3	393.65	−54,396.3	1
Mexico	87,457.3	138,073.5	235.53	−40,616.2	2
China	28,418.5	152,379.1	180.80	−123,960.6	3
Japan	52,063.7	118,029.0	170.07	−65,965.3	4
Germany	28,847.9	68,074.1	96.89	−39,199.2	5
United Kingdom	33,895.7	42,666.9	76.56	−8,771.2	6
South Korea	24,098.6	36,963.3	61.06	−12,864.7	7
Taiwan	17,487.9	31,599.9	49.09	−14,112.0	8
France	17,068.2	29,221.2	46.29	−12,153.0	9
Italy	10,596.9	2,5463.6	36.01	−14,866.7	10

Source: Based on U.S. Census Bureau statistics in 2004.

147 members. Mike Moore, WTO director-general, maintains that with China's accession, the near universal acceptance of the WTO rules-based system will serve a pivotal role in underpinning global economic cooperation (Moore 2001).

Counterpoints from the U.S. Perspective

Despite China's continuous efforts to open up to the outside world and her growing penetration into the global marketplace, China's accession to the WTO has caused heated debates in the West as well as within China. Many, at least from the Chinese perspective, consider the negotiations with the United States as extremely difficult and frustrating. From the U.S. perspective, major issues of high controversy include the growing trade deficits between the two countries, human rights and environmental concerns within China, and job losses in the United States. Table 7.4 lists the world's top trading partners with the United States. According to the U.S. Census Bureau statistics in 2004, these trading partners represent 68.47 percent of U.S. imports, and 65.89 percent of U.S. exports in goods. While each of these top ten trade partners has contributed to the U.S. overall trade deficit, notably China has exceeded Japan to represent the largest portion of the U.S. trade deficit since 2000. Until November 2001, China and Taiwan were the only two major U.S. trade partners not in the WTO. Tables 7.5 and 7.6 list the world's top exporters and importers with the United States. According to the 2004 U.S. Census Bureau statistics, China is ranked the second-largest exporter and the fifth-largest importer for the United States.

Table 7.5

The World's Top Fifteen Exporters to the United States
(Goods, Fiscal Year-to-Date, February 2004)

Country	Exports (US$ billions)	Percent of Total	Rank
Canada	38.0	18.2	1
China	25.4	12.2	2
Mexico	22.8	10.9	3
Japan	19.4	9.3	4
Germany	11.1	5.3	5
United Kingdom	6.7	3.2	6
South Korea	6.4	3.1	7
Taiwan	4.9	2.4	8
France	4.5	2.2	9
Italy	4.1	2.0	10
Ireland	4.1	1.9	11
Malaysia	4.0	1.9	12
Venezuela	3.4	1.7	13
Saudi Arabia	2.8	1.0	14
Brazil	2.6	1.3	15
Subtotal: Top 15 Countries	160.2	76.9	—
Total: All Countries	208.5	100.0	—

Source: Based on U.S. Census Bureau statistics in 2004.

Table 7.6

The World's Top Fifteen Importers from the United States
(Goods, Fiscal Year-to-Date, February 2004)

Country	Imports (US$ billions)	Percent of Total	Rank
Canada	27.7	22.6	1
Mexico	16.3	13.2	2
Japan	8.1	6.6	3
United Kingdom	5.7	4.6	4
China	5.6	4.6	5
Germany	4.8	3.9	6
South Korea	4.1	3.3	7
Netherlands	3.7	3.0	8
Taiwan	3.1	2.6	9
France	3.1	2.5	10
Singapore	2.6	2.1	11
Belgium	2.5	2.1	12
Brazil	2.4	1.9	13
Hong Kong	2.3	1.9	14
Australia	2.1	1.7	15
Subtotal: Top 15 Countries	94.1	76.7	—
Total: All Countries	122.7	100.0	—

Source: Based on U.S. Census Bureau statistics in 2004.

Table 7.7

Recent History of the U.S. Trade Balance with China (US$ billions)*

U.S.	1999	2000	2001	2002	2003	February 2004 year-to-date
Exports	13.1	16.2	19.2	22.1	28.4	5.6
Imports	81.8	100.2	102.3	125.2	152.4	25.3
Balance	−68.7	−83.8	−83.1	−103.1	−124.0	−19.8

*Total may not add up exactly due to rounding.
Source: Adapted from U.S. Census Bureau statistics in 2004.

Among the U.S. opponents are the labor unions such as AFL-CIO (American Federation of Labor and Congress of Industrial Organizations) and numerous NGOs (nongovernmental organizations) for human rights, fair trade, and environmental protection (Nolt 1999). The U.S. trade deficit with China often assumes center stage in debates about the trade relationship between the two countries. Table 7.7 summarizes the U.S. trade balance with China between 1999 and 2004.

Although the U.S. International Trade Commission estimated in 1999 that China's accession to the WTO could increase U.S. exports by 10.1 percent and imports from China by 6.9 percent, critics maintained that the absolute deficits would continue to grow. Major concerns over the China-WTO deal suggest spiraling trade deficits, job losses, and deepening income inequality in the United States (Scott 2000). Recent trade statistics can be used to argue for either side.

Advocates champion the belief that China's accession to the WTO will benefit many major U.S. industries, and U.S. consumers will win ultimately from the low-cost commodities made in China. Among those likely to gain the most are U.S. farmers, financial companies, and high-tech industries. China's concessions in the financial sector are the most profound, because they benefit not only U.S. banks and insurance companies but also other U.S. exporters and investors as U.S. financial service companies assist them and their Chinese customers. As new sectors of the Chinese economy are opened, the U.S. export opportunities will increase work for Americans in industries such as aerospace, chemicals, entertainment, computers, waste treatment, biotechnology, telecommunications equipment, medical equipment, and other high tech products. Tables 7.8 and 7.9 list the top U.S. exports to and imports from China respectively, indicating significant merchandise trade increases in both directions.

Table 7.8

Top U.S. Exports to China (US$ million)

Commodity Description	2002	2003	Percent change
Electrical machinery and equipment	3,950.1	4,782.6	21.1
Power generation equipment	4,109.1	4,639.6	12.9
Oil seeds and oleaginous fruits	917.9	2,877.4	213.5
Air and spacecraft	3,428.8	2,451.2	−28.5
Medical equipment	1,258.6	1,594.0	26.6
Plastics and plastic products	995.2	1,247.5	25.4
Iron and steel	591.1	1,213.9	105.4
Organic chemicals	619.9	1,105.3	78.3
Cotton	153.4	769.3	401.6
Copper	319.6	652.3	104.1

Source: U.S. International Trade Commission, U.S. Department of Commerce.

Table 7.9

Top U.S. Imports from China (US$ million)

Commodity Description	2002	2003	Percent change
Power generation equipment	21,070	31,039.8	47.3
Electrical machinery and equipment	25,408	30,043.1	18.2
Toys and games	15,491	17,399.9	12.3
Furniture	11,225.6	13,670.4	21.8
Footwear and parts thereof	10,763.1	11,144.8	3.5
Apparel	7,473.5	9,156.8	22.5
Leather and travel goods	4,782.8	5,440.6	13.8
Plastics and articles thereof	4,144.3	4,779.9	15.3
Iron and steel	3,094.4	3,855.5	24.6
Medical instruments	2,874.0	3,386.9	17.8

Source: U.S. International Trade Commission, U.S. Department of Commerce.

Opportunities and Challenges from the Chinese Perspective

Although China's gross national income is one of the largest in the world, ranked sixth, its per capita income is among the lowest, ranked 136th in 2002 (World Bank 2004), which, however, was significant progress from its 142nd position in 2001. Concerns over China's WTO membership are not just its prospective economic and trade-related impacts globally but also the increasing disparate distribution of welfare and the lack of workers' protections within China. While many Chinese have benefited from the economic reform, and about 100 million have joined the middle class, which means earning at least US$2,500 a year, millions more are slipping into a new underclass of displaced peasants, unemployed or underemployed factory workers, and low-level laborers whose wages barely sustain them (Einhorn, Dawson, and Kunii 2001). Agricultural sectors, heavy industries, and small-scale producers of fertilizers, steel, cement, motorcycles, and farm machines, in which China is not a competitive producer, will suffer in two ways: directly from increased foreign competition, and indirectly from losing capital to more lucrative sectors.

In the case of China, about 90 percent of the poor live in the rural areas (World Bank 2004), while China's WTO accession could easily mean a 3 percent reduction in per capita farm income (Baculinao 2001). Some 70–100 million poorly educated villagers are roaming the cities for job opportunities. About 60 percent of those farmers fail to find city jobs and have to return home. Alarmingly, there has been a steady drop in farm acreage across the country due to non-farming commercial use and some weather-related events, resulting in a 5.8 percent drop in grain output. In 2003 alone, total arable land shrank by 4.3 percent, providing a lightning rod for the government's new announcements regarding the safeguarding of land for grain production (World Bank 2004). On the one hand, China's entry into the WTO would mean an increase of US$2 billion in U.S. agricultural exports to China. The U.S. Department of Agriculture has estimated that China's WTO membership would potentially add US$1.6 billion by 2005 to the annual total of the U.S. export of grains, oilseed products, and cotton (Baculinao 2001). On the other hand, given that China's urban unemployment has been rising due to the ongoing reform and downsizing of state-owned enterprises, the massive numbers of surplus laborers from the rural areas remain a big challenge to China's long-term socioeconomic stability.

As rural poverty remains high and rural-urban income and non-income disparities continue to widen, a stronger emphasis on growth with equity has become increasingly critical. Industrial sectors that will gain directly from China's accession to WTO include textiles, clothing, toys, food processing, and other simple consumer products, but they only constitute a small fraction of the total economy. The growth of jobs in those sectors may not be rapid enough to counteract the fall of employment in the less competitive sectors. Meanwhile, under pressure from international competition that pushes the urban economy to shift toward more capital- and technologically intensive sectors, the number of jobs created by a given economic growth will decline. This pressure could be exacerbated under the WTO regime.

Underlining China's current strategic efforts for long-term prosperity and socioeconomic changes are three key dimensions—modernization, urbanization, and globalization—all of which are forces driving toward both convergence and divergence in the distribution of the nation's wealth and economic opportunities.

Future Global Implications

Integrating China into the global economy is a major policy challenge for both China and the rest of the world. With continuous economic transformation and rapid economic growth, China is becoming a major international trading power, but the prospective impacts of China's WTO membership will not be uniform globally. Neither will it be equally beneficial to the Chinese.

In a comparative study on the impact of globalization of the world economy, Sassen (1991) illustrates that the process of globalization has led to a division of the workforce into specialized high-salary work and low-wage support services across cultures. Similarly across cultures, large segments of urban populations have been pushed to marginal employment. Policymakers as well as business organizations should be aware of the major challenges associated with rapid socioeconomic changes in China. For example, the increasingly unequal distribution of power and welfare will force such critical issues as pension reform, housing, health care, and unemployment compensation. The market discipline required by the WTO rules will deepen reform of both industries and bureaucracies. FDI and accelerated foreign competition will create pressure for effective organizational change and human resource development. Western management practices entering China will have to adapt to the Chinese cultural environment in addition to the Chinese economic, political, and legal conditions. In this regard, foreign organizations, investors, and policymakers will have much to learn from China and about China. As well, China will have much to learn about the WTO rules and mechanisms for effective management of emerging trade-related conflicts and resolutions. Chinese organizations also have much to learn about effective development and uses of China's natural resources, physical and financial resources and capacities, and human resources.

References

Baculinao, E. 2001. "Beijing Faces Serious Challenges: WTO Membership Could Lead to Rural Upheaval." CNBC and *Wall Street Journal*, International News, November 10.

Einhorn, B., C. Dawson, and I.M. Kunii. 2001. "Asia's Future: China." *Business Week* (October 29): 48–52.

Han, J. 2002. "China's Road Transportation Ranked the 4th in the World." *People's Daily*, Overseas Edition (March 18): N 5364.

Long, Y.T. 2001. "Statement at the 18th Session of the Working Party on the Accession of China." *WTO News* (September 17).

Moore, M. 2001. "Statement at the Conclusion of the Meeting of the Working Party on China's Accession." *WTO News* (September 12).

Nolt, J.H. 1999. "China in the WTO: The Debate." *Foreign Policy in Focus* 4, no. 38.

PRC General Customs Administration. 2001. *China's Customs Statistics.* Beijing.

————. 2004. *China's Customs Statistics.* Beijing.

Roberts, D., and A. Webb. 2001. "China's Carmakers: Flattened by Falling Tariffs: WTO Membership Means Stiffer Competition from Imports." *Business Week* (December 3): 51.

Sassen, S. 1991. *The Global City: New York, London, and Tokyo.* Princeton: Princeton University Press.

Scott, R.E. 2000. "The High Cost of the China-WTO Deal." Economic Policy Institute, *Issue Brief* 137, February 16.

World Bank. 2001. *World Development Indicators.* Washington, DC.

————. 2004. *World Development Indicators.* Washington, DC.

8

Corporatism

Rebuilding the Framework of China's Welfare Regime

Bing-Wen Zheng

This chapter reviews the history of corporatist welfare regimes and focuses on the relationship between the welfare regime and its economic system. It is the nature of a welfare regime that determines the type of economic system; any such administration today contains certain corporatist factors, and the type of welfare regime is embodied in the state's choice of values. The chapter further explores China's Trade Union Law Amendment (adopted September 26, 2003), in which, for the first time, legislation has defined the legal role and status of trade unions in "collective bargaining."

Corporatism in Western Welfare States at Present

The welfare state systems of developed countries, established after World War II, were based on cooperation among three parties—the employees' organization, the employers' organization, and the state. The welfare systems of those countries shared several basic features. First, the three parties to the systems served as a buffer to lessen class contradictions and social conflicts, to control interest blocs, and to maintain social stability, thus bringing about a necessary sociohistoric stage.

Second, among the three parties, the employees' association is a public organization that has a relatively independent legal status and takes as its goal the signing of social contracts for employee benefit.

Third, to ensure that this institutional arrangement is capable of allowing both economic development and social justice, the employees' organization must be a legal entity recognized by the state, an organization with lawful standing and full capacity within the framework of the law.

Among some scholars in the West, the term "corporatism" is used to define and analyze the contemporary Western welfare state—and the welfare state is even deemed a manifestation of corporatism (Keane 1984, 14).

In the past decade or so, some scholars in the West used the quantitative method to gauge the elements of corporatism among major developed countries. J. B. Williamson and F. C. Pampel (1993) have done some pioneering work in this respect. In their studies of public pensions, they selected 396 groups of statistics for eighteen countries over a period of twenty-two years (1959–1980) from data provided by the International Labor Organization (ILO), and worked out a group of coefficients that gave them a method of measurement. Each nation was ordered based upon its corporatist factor scores (Williamson and Pampel 1993, 194).

Within this spectrum, at one end are the Nordic European countries, which have the largest number of corporatist factors, and at the other end are the English-speaking countries that have the least number of corporatist factors. Japan, Australia, and some West European countries are in the middle. Williamson and Pampel, gerontologists and experts in pension benefits, introduced the variables of pensions, aging populations, and GDP into the assessment process. They argued there were elements of the equation that affected the payment of pensions and revealed the importance of the senior population as an interest bloc (real or potential) in the political structure of a country and in its public policies. In their view, those variables are important in gauging and assessing corporatist factors.

Gosta Esping-Andersen (1990) deepened the study of the corporatist welfare system in his "decommodification" research into labor power and social welfare in capitalist societies. He found the decommodification tendency is higher in the Nordic European countries and lower in the Anglo-Saxon nations. The regimes of the former show more signs of corporatist factors, while there are fewer in the latter. He selected eighteen typical countries for assessment of their corporatist factors. But his approach differed from that of Williamson and Pampel—the variables he introduced covered a broader scope. He included the three additional factors of "means-tested poor relief" (as a percentage of total public social expenditure), private pensions (as a percentage of total pensions), and private health spending (as a percentage of total health expenditures). Based on the relevant coefficients he defined, he ranked the eighteen countries according to their corporatist factors and their degree of corporatism—and his findings were similar to those of Williamson and Pampel. The six English-speaking countries (the United States, Canada, Britain, Ireland, New Zealand, and Australia) were given lower corporatist factor scores, each having one or two points, while the other twelve nations (including Japan but excluding Switzerland, Denmark, and Holland) each had more than four points. The highest scores went to Italy (12), France (10), Japan and Austria (each 7), Germany (6) (Esping-Andersen 1990, 70, table 3.1).

In order to prove his assertion (i.e., to show the potential variations for decommodification of the welfare states), Esping-Anderson added unemployment insurance to such variables as pension insurance premiums and medical insurance premiums. After making weighted calculations of the population ratio in the eighteen countries of his study, he proceeded to calculate decommodification fractions and found marked differences in the three social insurance items on the question of their decommodification potential within those countries, thus revealing qualitative differences among them in the degree of decommodification of social welfare.

On the basis of the different scores regarding the degree of decommodification of social welfare, those eighteen countries were placed in three different groups (Gosta Esping-Andersen 1990, 52). In the first group are the Anglo-Saxon countries (Australia, the United States, New Zealand, Canada, Ireland, and Britain), which basically are liberal regimes with a very low degree of decommodification. The second group includes Italy, Japan, France, Germany, Finland, and Switzerland, each with varying higher degrees of decommodification. The third group includes the Scandinavian countries (Austria, Belgium, the Netherlands, Denmark, Norway, and Sweden), which have the highest decommodification scores, almost all of which are social democracies. For them, a high degree of decommodification and a corporatist regime can be synonymous. This is no coincidence, but an indication of the fact that the higher the degree of decommodification, the more corporatist factors among the three groups, and the higher the degree of corporatism. An important feature of corporatism may boil down to higher decommodification in the form of social welfare, for those countries of the first group where liberalism had a predominant historical position in their regimes the inverse appears to be true.

The Welfare Regime and the Economic System

The choice and formulation of a social security system essentially means that the choice and formulation of a corresponding economic system in a sense embodies the nature of a country's social economic system. First, the volume of public expenditure and the supply of public goods, the differences in the social security system and the social welfare regime, are important indicators of the economic system of a country. This includes not only those separate social security systems such as arrangements for the elderly, the unemployed, the handicapped, and medical care programs, but also those systems of investment and production vital to the personal interests of the members of a society such as education, housing, and public health, and issues related to the operation of the national economy such as banking (the operation of pension funds), banks (the financial and banking system), finance (the social insurance budget), and the labor market, as well as the degree of commodification of the social welfare services and the redistribution of the national income (i.e., the mode of economic system).

In China, for example, subsidies in kind in the form of distributing free residential housing as part of the social welfare system during its planned economic phase was, in fact, a component of a highly centralized economic system. In another example, prior to China's implementation of economic reform and more liberal trade policies, when jobs were assigned 100 percent by the state, there was no free movement of the labor force and there was no unemployment. That situation was perfectly in keeping with the highly centralized economic system.

Second, if we view the relationship between the welfare regime and the economic system from the perspective of public choice, we may say that making a decision for the public good is a process of public choice. In this case, then, the choices of a welfare regime correlate somewhat with public choice. Following this logic, we may conclude that the amount of corporatist factors in the welfare regime of a country may directly or indirectly affect the process of public choice. The tripartite cooperation, that is, the consensus among the three parties to a negotiation in the corporatist regimes of many developed countries, is a perfect manifestation of this. That is why, in a sense, corporatism or the welfare state, in the eyes of some scholars, has been seen as an institutional response to market failures and public domain failures (Barr 1998, 81, 97–98, 196, 410–11; Crouch and Dore 1990, 4–7).

Third, like other economic functions of the government, government intervention in the provision of social security and social welfare also has a "boundary" problem and, in this sense, the social welfare and social security systems of a country may be deemed a replica of its economic system. The width of the boundary between government intervention and government regulation in other fields of economic management similarly reflects the width of the boundary for social security. The point is that in the half century since World War II, the retrenchment and expansion of social welfare services in the Western countries show time and again that government responsibilities are often automatically met by private charity institutions.

A Measure of Corporatist Factors Exists in All Regimes Today

The corporatist factor, or the degree of cooperation among the tripartite partnership, is a question of size, not of existence, in the economic and welfare systems of any developed country today. Since their emergence toward the end of the nineteenth century, more particularly since the beginning of the twentieth century, corporatist factors have co-existed like the two sides of a coin with the social security system of almost all of the developed nations. This historical phenomenon is an indisputable stage in the course of the development of modern civilized countries, an indispensable element in today's social security and social welfare systems.

First, throughout the industrialized world today, a social security system without elements of corporatism is almost nonexistent. As mentioned previously, those countries with the least number of corporatist factors, that is, atypical corporatist welfare states, are the United States and some other English-speaking countries. But even in the United States, collective negotiation at the micro level (i.e., the level of the business) is institutional in nature. Of the 14 million employees of the state and local governments, seven million, or 50 percent, have the right of collective bargaining and 13 percent of these workers are trade unionists.

Second, the introduction of the corporatist regime has been a historical stage in the development of the modern civilized society. The vigorous development of the workers' movement in Europe more than a century ago, as a direct result of Marx's analyses and writings, served as a catalyst to the birth of a social security system in the modern sense, and even the U.S. Social Security Act of 1935 was the product of the fight waged by the American workers (Zinn 1997).[1] We may even go so far as to say that the working class played and is still playing a leading role in the big machinery of industrialized society or post-industrialized society and has helped promote the modern welfare state. As many Western scholars point out, without the early workers' movement, there would have been no social democratic parties; the workers' movement, trade unions, and succeeding political parties have furnished the necessary conditions for the emergence and survival of corporatism (Lash and Urry 1987, 304–5). Among those countries at the same level of economic development, the number of corporatist factors undoubtedly is closely related to the strength of social democratic thinking and the power of the trade unions. Destruction of this objectivity, therefore, obviously amounts to the destruction of the structure of the capitalist system and modern capitalist civilization.

Third, the future of the evolution of the social economic system and the social welfare system essentially is not a question of where it will go, but where it has come from. The industrial revolution and the workers' movements brought about the modern social security system and corporatist factors will not vanish overnight. Institutional evolution must take this path, although the conditions within each country may differ.[2]

A Welfare Regime Embodies the Choice of Values

There are quite a number of so-called objective indices when we appraise the merits and demerits of a corporatist regime or the quantity of corporatist factors in a country. In the heated debates between the middle-left that strongly defends corporatism and the role of trade unions and neo-liberalism that vehemently attacks those things in developed countries, they all base their positions upon statistics to prove their point and to show their role in the competitiveness of enterprises and in economic development. But in reality the appraisal and choice of a social security mode involve another important issue, that is, the question of values. In the two principal modes of providing social security, neo-liberalism tends to emphasize the role of the market and individuals whereas corporatism leans toward the role of government guidance and collectivism. Between these two extremes are "mixtures" selected by many countries to achieve balance and choice in the realization of efficiency and justice. This kind of integration and choice embodies the leading values and the balance of interests of different social strata in a country.

The leading values of a country are derived from its cultural and historical heritage, its concrete ideological choice, religious beliefs, and the goals of its values. When examined in this manner, the selection and creation of a social security system is not merely a technical issue, an issue of "good" or "bad," but a question of choice.

In designing a social security framework, foresight and an understanding of that country's past as well as its present are essential. Understanding a country's past means to be conscious of how these issues have evolved in its history, what has been its traditional course in the areas of corporatism and the political and social participation of trade unions and other communal organizations. Understanding the present requires an analysis of the ongoing changes in economic power and social strata.

To outline and design a social safety net necessitates noting the features of the present state of society, primarily the development of various social strata and interest blocs, and then proceeding to regulate the social mechanisms through the institutional mechanisms. Since social security is a means of national income redistribution—"public goods" to be consumed by the entire society—its distribution determines to a great degree the "stability" of society. Not to consider "distribution" and "stability" means no simultaneous attention to the issue of "justice and efficiency," because with attention to the minimization of costs of the institution, a simple principle of institutional choice may lead to a certain "idealization."[3] Historical experience shows that a conflict of interests between interest blocs, social strata, districts, and even cities and countryside may lead to social conflicts that can result in maximum social and institutional costs, reflecting a lack of forethought in the planning process. Potential social instability is the greatest potential cost to the system.

Feasibility of a Corporatist Welfare Regime in China and the New Trade Union Law

Some years ago a number of scholars in the West used the idea of "local corporatism" to analyze changes taking place in social life in China, and the emerging concept of a "citizen society" (Oi 1992, 99–126). Other Western scholars mentioned in passing the term "corporatism" in their discussions of local Chinese social organizations and citizen society (White 1996). Those Western scholars proceeding from the perspective of a citizen society with social changes in the regime came to believe that the corporatist theory of nationalization provided a more accurate definition of the changes taking place in China (Unger and Chan 2001, 52–60).

Western scholars concentrated on two major issues: the relationship between economic organizations and the state and the organizational forms of the social interest blocs (Zhang 1998, 147–66). In recent years, Western scholars have gradually focused on corporatism as a means for designing the regimes of countries in transition. For example, when discussing the issue of social stability in the former East European socialist countries, public opinion in the West included views that "multiparty democracy is not suitable for these countries, which must have stable structures to mediate various interests, to channel and contain social conflicts. Liberal corporatism appears to be the best way of mediating extra-party interests, because it involves a higher degree of stability than pluralism" (Schwarz 2000). Chinese scholars, in reviewing the framework of the Chinese social security system, have also mentioned the concept of corporatism. They believe "for China today, in view of its socialist values, welfare philosophy, and ideals, and in view of history, the present, and the future, and in the interest of the individual, the state, and the well being of the entire society, the corporatist social welfare regime is worth seeking" (Chang 2001).

So long as European corporatist welfare is an unavoidable historical stage in the process of human civilization (although it has its share of problems), we should pay attention to and study it. So long as the choice of certain corporatist social security systems may affect the choice of a corresponding economic system in the future, we should have a reasonable expectation when designing a social security system that it fully represents our pursuit of specific values. We should proceed from our present national situation, gain from our "late-comer" status and our unique political advantage, so as to avoid those problems already confronted by other welfare states. We can learn from their experiences. Since a welfare regime and an economic system are so closely linked and co-exist, neglecting the evolution of the welfare system in the course of economic transition could lead to failure of our economic and market reform goals.

A number of the pressing technical problems that have surfaced in the course of establishing a social security system in China have attracted the concentration and attention of Chinese academics and policy research departments. These problems include nominal transfers between private banking accounts, recessive debts, and deficits in the budget of social security. In view of China's choice of values, efficiency, and justice, and from the perspective of maintaining political advantage and social stability, we should undoubtedly reconsider the institutional design and goals of our social security and welfare systems. It is not only of great importance for the present, but also of historical significance to reexamine and assess our social security and welfare framework. It directly affects China's overall social stability. Historically, it will ultimately affect the economic structure—a vital lifeline of the country.

Judging by the present state of our social welfare and social security systems, it appears that the institutional problem to be resolved is that of legalizing workers' participation in collective bargaining. Collective bargaining in businesses is the most fundamental prerequisite of tripartite cooperation in the modern welfare system. And, in fact, the "Resolution on Revising the Trade Union Law of the People's Republic of China," promulgated in October 2001, has provided the long-sought legal solution for employees' organizations.

The Experiment with Tripartite Partnership in Chinese Business Enterprises

In the history of social security, the tripartite partnership began at the micro level in a single business enterprise and gradually spread to the entire trade, even to the national and multinational level; it is the most fundamental unit of a modern welfare regime. We may say that in the early days when China was shifting from a central planned economy to a market economy, it had already begun experiments on collective negotiation in enterprises, but only to a limited degree within foreign-funded business as a necessary means of attracting foreign investment.

The Ministry of Labor and the Ministry of Foreign Trade and Economic Cooperation jointly promulgated on August 11, 1994, the "Provisions for Labor Management in Foreign-Funded Enterprises," which is the first Chinese official document granting trade unions in foreign-funded enterprises the right to sign collective contracts through negotiation. Article 8 of the document stipulates: "The trade union (representatives from workers shall be elected if there is no trade union) shall represent the workers in signing collective contracts with management through negotiation on labor remuneration, working hours and holidays, labor safety and health, insurance and welfare." The Chinese Ministry of Labor in 1997 circulated a document entitled "Some Points Regarding Collective Negotiations on Wages in Foreign-Funded Enterprises," which stipulates that local governments and departments across the country should follow this policy. Following this, the provinces, autonomous regions, and municipalities directly under the State Council worked out local regulations and decrees within specific local conditions. For example, Hebei province in its "Rules on the Management of Foreign-Funded Enterprises" allows the wage level of the workers to be fixed by business enterprises through collective negotiation in accordance with the wage guideline announced by the local people's governments or local labor administrative departments, and provided that the minimum wage of the workers within legal working hours should not be lower than the local minimum wage standard.[4]

Besides foreign-funded enterprises, with the urging of local Chinese governments Chinese enterprises have made much progress in this area in recent years. It is estimated that a collective contract system based on negotiations has been introduced in more than 400,000 Chinese enterprises, involving 76 million workers. Virtually all state-owned, collective, and foreign-funded enterprises in cities and towns have adopted labor contracts with management signed by over 95 percent of the workers. And over 60 percent of the employees of private enterprises and individually owned businesses have signed labor contracts with their employers. Nearly 30 million workers in township enterprises have signed labor contracts. In the past few years, thirteen provinces, autonomous regions, and municipalities directly under the State Council have promulgated regulations and decrees regarding collective contracts and twenty-eight provinces, autonomous regions, and municipalities directly under the State Council have continued the task of encouraging the signing of collective regional and trade contracts (Ministry of Labor and Social Security 2002). Although China has virtually instituted a system for the coordination of labor relations, maintained stable labor relationships, and accumulated valuable experience, there does not yet appear to be sufficient appreciation of the significance and importance of collective negotiations in a social security system and social welfare regime. It has been treated as merely a matter of "protecting workers' rights" as a part of the reform of enterprise insurance and management.

New Trade Union Law—the First Pillar of a Modern Welfare Regime

From an objective point of view, the promulgation of the new Trade Union Law has created the first supporting pillar of the legal framework for the institution of a modern social security system and social welfare regime. After many years of deliberation and discussion, the Standing Committee of the National People's Congress passed the "Resolution on the Revision of the Trade Union Law of the People's Republic of China" at its 24th meeting on October 27, 2001, thereby making major amendments to the 1992 Trade Union Law (henceforth this resolution will be referred to as "the new Trade Union Law").

Public opinion, more or less in consensus, summed up the new Trade Union Law thus: The promulgation of the new Trade Union Law undoubtedly is very timely and will play an important positive role in protecting the legitimate rights and interests of workers in enterprises at a time when workers' rights and interests are time and again being hurt seriously and sometimes shockingly in some foreign-funded enterprises, private enterprises, and township enterprises. However, if we view it in greater depth, i.e., in view of the building of a new framework of a social welfare regime, the new Trade Union Law definitely will play a much greater role.

First, the new Trade Union Law stipulates that "labor relations shall be coordinated through negotiations on an equal footing and a collective contract system" and that a "tripartite negotiation system" be instituted for handling labor relations (see new Trade Union Law 2001, Articles 6, 20, and 34). The term collective negotiation refers to agreements to be reached between representatives of the employer and representatives of the employees by which labor remuneration and working conditions will be resolved. Collective negotiation has been deemed a great social invention for the normalization of labor-capital conflict resolution, a specific right every laborer is entitled to or should be entitled to in a modern democratic society (Yang and Li 2000, 297). The new Trade Union Law shall go down in the annals of New China as the first legislation on the role and status of the trade unions in collective negotiations. It is an effective mechanism for the coordination of labor relations, the emancipation and development of productive forces, and a major institutional innovation in the building of a modern enterprise system, modern social welfare regime, social security system, and even economic institutions at the time of China joining the WTO and merging into the global economic tide.

Second, if we say the corporatist welfare regime and social security system, with its varying features and degrees of maturity within each country, may be considered an inescapable stage of human history, then the promulgation of the new Trade Union Law should be deemed China's entrance into this stage, the first pillar to support the building of a modern welfare regime and social security system. A modern social security system requires an employees' organization, practicing corporatism, with the status of a corporate body and a lawful monopoly within an industry or a department, rather than a situation (as in Russia) where a number of mutually independent or competing trade union organizations may exist within one enterprise or trade and it is impossible to identify their legal status as representative of the employees as a group. In that case the prerequisites for tripartite cooperation are lacking. The new Trade Union Law, for the first time in history, stipulates: "The All-China Federation of Trade Unions, local trade union federations and industrial trade unions have the status of a legal person. Local trade unions at the grassroots level which are qualified by the general rules of legislation to have the status of legal persons should be granted the status of a legal person (Article 14)," and "the All-China Federation of Trade Unions and the trade union organizations represent the interests of the workers" (Article 2). These provisions have, in fact, established a fine prerequisite for the implementation of a modern social welfare system while its provisions on the appointment and dismissal of trade union chairpersons, trade union fees, the main tasks of trade unions, and penalties attending violations of the new Trade Union Law have legally ensured the status and function of trade unions.

Third, the promulgation of the new Trade Union Law actually lays a legal foundation for the structure of a "micro-corporatist" social security system. In some academic writings, the corporatist regime is classified into micro-, meso-, and macro-corporatism (Crouch and Dore 1990, 5). The provisions of the new Trade Union Law on "the signing of collective contracts" (i.e., collective negotiation and settlement through consultation) are limited in the main within enterprises and the content of negotiation mainly covers "wages, labor safety and health, and social insurance" (Article 30) and, more specifically, covers "convening discussions regarding wages, welfare, labor safety and health, social insurance and other matters of vital importance to the personal interests of workers and the discussions should be attended by representatives of trade unions" (Article 38). Objectively speaking, the rights granted to trade unions by the new Trade Union Law belong to micro-corporatist welfare. It has ushered China's social security system over the threshold of the framework of the modern welfare regime. The diversity of the modern welfare regime and social security system will evolve continuously in the course of practice, with some concepts eventually discarded and others added.

Time and practice will answer such questions as what degree corporatism should reach, in what arenas the tripartite partnership should be conducted, and what forms of corporatism best fit China's circumstances. What is important is that the first step has been taken. China will blaze a new path in creating social security and social welfare systems that comply with the needs of the country and yet retain the features of China's socialist market economy.

Notes

1. This information reinforces that the New Deal and Social Security Act of 1935 were the products of the workers' movement in the United States.

2. For example, compared with European, especially Nordic European, countries, the United States has many fewer corporatist factors. They have been growing relatively slowly since World War II; the trade unions play a fairly insignificant role in collective negotiations at the national level and there are more social aids than social insurance, and so on. This probably has something to do with some of the unique national characteristics of the United States, such as the scattered trade unions, a larger portion of residents living in the suburbs, a greater percentage of managerial personnel, among others.

3. Some Chinese scholars favor individual negotiations instead of collective negotiation. They say there is no cultural tradition that advocates collective negotiation and that it may involve greater institutional costs.

4. Available at http://china-window.com/Hebei_w/gywm/indexc.html

References

Albert, Michel. 1998. *Capitalisme contre capitalisme.* Paris: Editions du Seuil.

Barr, Nicholas. 1998. *The Economics of the Welfare State.* Oxford: Oxford University Press.

Chang Zonghu. 2001. "Academic Review: A Useful Probe of Restructuring China's Social Security System—An Overview of the National Symposium on Social Welfare Theories and Policies." *Social Sciences in China* 3, no. 127. As quoted by Chen Tao in his speech.

Crouch, Colin, and Ronald Dore. 1990. "Whatever Happened to Corporatism?" In *Corporatism and Accountability: Organized Interests in British Public Life*, ed. Colin Crouch and Ronald Dore. Oxford: Clarendon Press.

Esping-Andersen, G. 1990. *The Three Worlds of Welfare Capitalism.* Cambridge: Polity Press.

Lash, Scott, and John Urry. 1987. *The End of Organized Capitalism.* Cambridge: Polity Press.

Keane, John. 1984. *Public Life and Late Capitalism: Toward a Socialist Theory of Democracy.* Cambridge: Cambridge University Press.

Ministry of Labor and Social Security. 2002. *Special Issue of Laws and Policies* 1, no. 157.

Mishra, R. 1990. *The Welfare State in Capitalist Society.* Hertfordshire: Harvester Wheatsheaf.

New Trade Union Law. 2001. *Journal of Shenzhen Special Economic Zone* (October 29): A4.

Oi, Jean. 1992. "Fiscal Reform and the Economic Foundation of Local State Corporatism in China." *World Politics* 45: 99–126.

Schmitter, P.C. 1974. "Still the Century of Corporatism?" *Review of Politics* 36: 85–131.

Schwarz, Peter. 2000. "Chirac's European Vision Unleashes Controversy in France." Available at www.wsws.org/articles/2000/jul2000/chir-j11.shtml.

Unger, Jonathan, and Anita Chan. 2001. "China, Corporatism and East Asian Models." *Strategy & Management,* no. 1: 52–60.

White, G. 1996. *In Search of Civil Society: Market Reform and Social Change in Contemporary China.* Oxford: Clarendon Press.

Williamson, J.B., and F.C. Pampel. 1993. *Old-Age Security in Comparative Perspective.* New York: Oxford University Press.

Williamson, P.J. 1989. *Corporatism in Perspective.* London: Sage.

Yang Tiren, and Li Lilin. 2000. *The Labour Relationship in Market Economies—Theory, Institution and Policies.* Beijing: China Labour & Social Security Publishing House.

Zhang Jing. 1998. *Corporatism.* Beijing: Chinese Social Science Publishing House.

Zinn, Howard. 1997. *A People's History of the United States, 1492–Present.* New York: Harper Perennial.

9

China's Trade-Related Investment Measures and Their Development Following WTO Accession

Jian Zhang

China has initiated a series of investment laws and regulations since late 1978 when it began to open its markets to the outside world. These investment policies cover a wide range of issues, such as tax and labor laws, environmental regulations, land administration, profit repatriations, and other related policies that have become more and more specific and detailed. As a member of the WTO, China will continue to improve its legal framework for foreign investors in order to boost overseas investment in agriculture, high-tech sectors, and other fields. Defining Trade Related Investment Measures (TRIMs) is new for China, although some related policies were already in place.

From the Uruguay Round to Doha

The TRIMs agreement came into effect on January 1, 1995, and a Working Party was established in 1996 to conduct analytical work on the relationship between trade and investment. When provisions of the WTO agreement came into effect, members had a transitional period in which to eliminate the TRIMs. The WTO recognized that some TRIMs might lead to trade distortions and violate the principles of the General Agreement on Tariff and Trade (GATT). Therefore, WTO members negotiated a multilateral agreement on TRIMs in the Uruguay Round (UR). The agreement requires countries to phase out TRIMs that have been identified as being inconsistent with GATT rules.

TRIMs are established by the host country governments for foreign investors in order to ensure the positive impacts of foreign direct investment (FDI) on the FDI-receiving countries' employment and export performance. The domestic sectors can be protected under TRIMs from the increasing competition after the injection of foreign investment. TRIMs are used by developing countries more commonly than by developed countries. It is because most infant industries in developing countries are not competitive compared to those in developed countries. Therefore, it is necessary to use TRIMs to protect their local industries during the transitional period.

TRIMs were one of the new issues addressed in the UR negotiations in 1986. The United States and other major industrialized countries were seeking to reduce the trade impacts of restrictions and requirements host developing countries had imposed, especially in the area of FDI. TRIMs had not been addressed directly in previous GATT negotiations. Investment policies also raise questions of national sovereignty. It is not surprising that industrialized countries might view issues surrounding TRIMs rather differently than developing countries. Developing countries considered performance requirements necessary to channel FDI according to their national development policy objectives, to offset preferential treatment or incentives, and to offset or preempt the anticompetitive practices of multinational enterprises (MNEs) (McDonald 1998).

The UR started with a discussion about whether a more ambitious approach should be adopted in order to include more general investment incentives. This did not succeed due to considerable opposition from developing countries. In the end, the only thing the round managed to achieve in this respect was to confirm the interpretation of certain GATT provisions contained in the Canada-Foreign Investment Review Act (FIRA) panel case, that is, only some narrow trade-related measures were covered. There was a list of fourteen measures initially; the eight measures proposed by the United States were whittled down to three categories in the final agreement, and these were only partly covered.

The unsuccessful result of TRIMs in the UR led to developed partners trying other equivocal approaches to the issues of concern. Many MNEs were probably quite comfortable with performance requirements accompanied by incentives, whether in the form of subsidies or protected markets. The United States began to move away from a position of net investor abroad and toward the status of host country for substantial investment from others. The EU and the United States were also concerned about some of the possible negative effects of inward investment, such as a lack of local content and the specter of investments that were no more than assembly operations of imports made abroad.

The results in the UR were limited. They confirmed that GATT Articles

III (national treatment) and XI (prohibition of quots) apply to local content and trade balancing requirements. Local content requirements (LCRs) are forbidden by the TRIMs agreement. The agreement that resulted from the UR did deal with some very obvious abuses, but avoided some equally obvious ones because they could not be fitted into Articles III and XI of the GATT. For example, export performance requirements were still generally allowed. An export performance requirement will not fall under Article III if it is not linked to local purchases or production, or under Article XI if it is not couched in terms of a prohibition on imports or exports. Finally, the TRIMs agreement only covers goods.

Two basic issues separated the participants in the TRIMs negotiations and they were as follows: (1) whether the disciplines developed in this area should be limited by existing GATT articles or expanded to develop an investment regime, and (2) whether some or all TRIMs should be prohibited or should be dealt with on a case-by-case basis. The two issues demonstrated the direct and significant restrictive and adverse effects on trade.

The United States and Japan were in favor of an international investment regime that would establish rights for foreign investors and reduce constraints on MNEs. They believed that TRIMs had adverse trade effects and that this was a sufficient reason to make the case for applying general principles and disciplines to control them. The EU focused on measures that had a considerable restrictive impact on trade. They believed that direct and indirect trade effects of investment measures should be evaluated separately. Indirect trade effects caused by TRIMs, in their view, were related to licensing, local equity and technology transfer requirements, remittances and exchange restrictions, and investment incentives. They proposed that TRIMs with indirect effects would be subject to consultation and dispute settlement procedures. Developing countries insisted upon mandating and limiting the negotiating exercise to the effects of investment measures or regulations with a direct and significant negative impact on trade. They wanted to ensure that there could be no priority presumption that investment measures were inherently trade restrictive or distorting. They also argued that they used TRIMs to offset the anticompetitive practices of the MNEs. The United States and the EU considered such measures outside the scope of the negotiating mandate.

The results were not much more than a clarification of some policies in the 1947 GATT text. The resulting agreement only used an illustrative list to identify policies that conflicted with GATT Articles III:4 and XI:1. Some developing countries strongly suggested that this five-page text regarding TRIMs should not be extended into the next round. They further argued the length of the transition period for developing country members should be extended. Four major reasons supported their argument: (1) only developing countries have yet to phase out notified TRIMs; (2) many developing countries have a perception that the agreement is against their development interests; (3) the five-year transition period was not enough time for the countries to benefit from those policies; and (4) the ninety-day notification period was too short for WTO members to examine their regimes for compatibility.

The Doha Ministerial Conference in Qatar in November 2001 pushed the trade talks between developed and developing countries to a new round. There were three contending forces in Doha:

1. Developing countries were unable to force either a development round or gain concrete commitments to address their concerns with implementation issues, although they won some language on trade-related aspects of intellectual property rights (TRIPs), and placed agricultural export subsidies and anti-dumping rules on the table.

2. Organization for Economic Cooperation and Development (OECD) countries wanted to launch a round that would include the four so-called new issues—investment, competition policy, government procurement, and trade facilitation. They were only able to achieve a commitment for negotiations on these issues after the fifth ministerial in 2003 and only with "written consensus" from member countries. The EU won some language on the environment, and succeeded in qualifying the scope of the agricultural negotiations.

3. Developing countries created a new negotiating dynamic at the ministerial conference by demanding and playing an important role in shaping its outcome. The "Doha Development Agenda" set a "work program" for the WTO and its various working groups and committees until the next ministerial meeting in 2003. The Doha agenda was the last gasp for effective efforts by the so-called Quad (Canada, the United States, the EU, and Japan) to dominate trade talks. Developing countries, like India, fought harder than ever before to prevent this.

In short, it was quite difficult to say who the winners and who the losers were at Doha. It "succeeded" by conventional measures if the metric is having a declaration that everyone signed, irrespective of the internal contradictions and qualifications within it. Doha failed to address effectively the ongoing development concerns of developing countries and failed to resolve the WTO's crisis of legitimacy that dates to the 1999 Seattle ministerial.

Definition of TRIMs

The narrow definition of TRIMs would be the measures designed to influence trade volume or trade patterns. Such measures include export performance requirements mandating that a minimum level of output be exported and local content regulations stipulating that a minimum amount of inputs be sourced domestically. However, the broad definition of TRIMs should include any governmental policies affecting the issues, such as macroeconomic, regional, employment, and industrial regulations.

The following is the content provided by the U.S. delegation for the extensive list of TRIMs in the UR negotiations in 1992 (Maskus and Konan 1990):

1. Local content requirements specify that a minimum volume or value of inputs or percentage of the value of local production be produced from sources in the host country.

2. Export performance requirements mandate that a minimum volume or value of output or percentage of output be exported.

3. Trade balancing requirements link an investing firm's exports of outputs to its imports of inputs in some way, say by requiring that the firm sustain a minimum trade surplus.

4. Product mandating requirements demand that a firm supply specified markets, typically in the host country but also in other countries, with outputs produced only in designated local facilities.

5. Domestic sales requirements specify that an investor produce certain goods for the local market.

6. Manufacturing limitations place restrictions on the amount and types of products that can be produced in local affiliates in order to reserve the market for locally owned firms.

7. Technology transfer and licensing requirements compel the investor to transfer specified technologies on noncommercial terms, perform particular levels or types of research and development locally, or license production in the host country, often with limitation on royalties paid.

8. Remittance limitations restrict the ability of investors to repatriate earnings from an investment and may also control foreign exchange allocations for this and other purposes.

9. Local equity requirements specify that a minimum percentage of a firm's equity must be owned by local investors.

Investment incentives provide financial advantages, such as tax limitations, duty remissions, and subsidies, or inducements for foreign investors to locate facilities in the host country. In general, such incentives are offered to offset the negative effects of the various performance requirements imposed.

This list is apparently the widest categorization of TRIMs to date that has been advanced for potential discipline. The major questions concern the trade distortions caused by these measures. It is obvious that all of them may distort international trade. The first three measures may be considered to directly distort trade in the sense that such distortion is their primary intent. The possible trade distortions emerging from the other TRIMs on this list are less direct but self-evident. For example, manufacturing requirements can affect decisions on production location and therefore have an impact on trade patterns. While licensing and equity requirements can change the firm's perceived tradeoff between the net benefits of licensing and exports, remittance limitations may affect a firm's decision to enter or withdraw from a specific market and result in a suboptimal global distribution of production and trade.

The distinction between direct trade impacts and indirect trade impacts of TRIMs is central to the multilateral negotiations. Some consensus has emerged that the GATT has competence over those policies with direct trade-distorting intent. The remaining question is whether such policies are to be prohibited. There is seldom agreement about the GATT's potential role in disciplining the broader, indirect measure.

Whether TRIMs distort trade is still a question. The empirical evidence that existing measures have resulted in significant distortions is limited. This is due to difficulties in measuring the relation of TRIMs to investment decisions and subsequent trade flows. TRIMs requirements tend to be focused on specific industries, with the automotive, chemical and petrochemical, and computer/information industries leading the list. The characteristics of trade-related investment measures are more likely to exist in the developing countries than the developed countries. The extent of investment covered by TRIMs regulations is heavily weighted toward the developed countries.

Local content TRIMs are more frequent than export TRIMs in the automotive industry, with the reverse being true in the computer/information industries. In chemicals and petrochemicals, both domestic content and export performance TRIMs are prominent.

The data on coverage of investors suggest that developed country regulations cover more breadth of investment. For example, the amount of U.S. investments in the countries with the most extensive presence of TRIMs regulations is US$30 billion in the top twenty "middle income developing countries," versus US$230 billion in the top twenty "developed countries."

The negotiating mandate on TRIMs, as adopted at Punta Del Este, states:

> Following an examination of the operation of the GATT articles related to the trade restrictive and distorting effects of investment measures, negotiations should elaborate, as appropriate, further provisions that may be necessary to avoid such adverse effects on trade.

Several proposals for TRIMs have been analyzed. First, it is hoped that by allowing limited exceptions and by imposing rigorous standards of demonstration on complainants, the developing countries will be induced to join the agreement. Second, an attempt must be made to convince major capital-importing developing countries that joining the agreement will provide them with net benefits. However, this is a difficult task, but some arguments may be made in its favor. First, the point must be made that the use of highly restrictive TRIMs are counterproductive to development efforts. Gradual liberalization of TRIMs may be expected in most cases to attract more FDI and technology as firms react to more open and less opaque policy regimes. Furthermore, such investment would likely provide greater efficiency gains than current flows may through the combination of protected markets, incentives, and performance requirements. This possibility would be enhanced by more general liberalization of surrounding trade and industrial policies in host countries.

The Impact of TRIMs on the Economy: Theory and Evidence

According to economic theory, using TRIMs has advantages and disadvantages. Generally speaking, TRIMs will benefit the host countries while hurting the FDI-sending countries. Neoclassical economic theory assumes perfect competition, and any government intervention in the market is regarded as inefficient and welfare-reducing. In light of the neoclassical economic theory, TRIMs are not a first-best solution. On the other hand, new trade theory, called strategic trade theory, assumes imperfect competition and economies of scale. It advocates that the government intervene in the market to address market failure and improve social welfare.

TRIMs in Neoclassical Analysis

There are two principal frameworks for analyzing the impact of TRIMs (Mutti 1994): the neoclassical framework of perfect competition and the newer "strategic trade" framework of oligopoly and imperfect competition. The TRIMs' debate demonstrates how important the choice of an appropriate theoretical framework is for designing policy responses.

In the neoclassical analysis, we often assume a perfect competition market structure, where there are many firms and every firm is a price taker, and the firms charge the price equal to marginal cost. Government intervention in this case would lead to negative welfare and distortion. The conventional case against TRIMs comes from extending the neoclassical presumption against public intervention to international markets, asserting that protection and promotion create distortions in the pattern of both trade and development.

Let us look closely at the criticism of the most visible forms of TRIMs intervention, LCRs and investment incentives within the neoclassical framework. A TRIMs requirement which mandates a certain amount of domestic content on the part of foreign investors, like any other form of import protection, raises the cost of production to the subsidiaries upon which it is imposed, reducing consumption and withdrawing resources that could be more productively used elsewhere in the economy.

A TRIMs requirement to export is also problematic. Within the neoclassical model, output costs in the local market must by definition be higher than world prices or else domestic subsidiaries of foreign corporations would be exporting on their own. Consequently, the export requirement becomes a government subsidy to induce the firm to respond. This will reduce consumption further and draw more resources into the inefficient sector.

For these reasons, it is not difficult to understand why the neoclassical economic tradition is critical of LCRs and export-promotion TRIMs. It is obvious that it is undesirable from the perspectives of the host country, the home country, and globally.

TRIMs in New Trade/Strategic Trade Theory

Strategic trade analysis centers on industries in which there are market imperfections and barriers to the entry of competitors. It concentrates on public policy in second-best contexts where only a relatively small number of firms exist, with oligopolistic interactions among them.

In contrast to neoclassical analysis, the strategic trade framework assumes imperfect competition, with barriers to entry into the industry that include increasing returns to scale and that generate rents for the participants (Krugman 1986; Spencer and Brander 1983). Such rents may sometimes emerge in the form of higher than normal profits, but more often they show up in terms of high wages and benefits and research and development (R&D) expenditure (Katz and Summers 1989).

The strategic trade theory calls into question traditional concepts about comparative advantage. In developed countries, strategic trade theory has been used to nurture domestic firms in such industries as semiconductors, supercomputers, and aerospace. However, there is considerable concern in the economics community that strategic trade theory may be used to justify an epidemic of special pleading for protection and promotion that runs contrary to market-based competition. Paul Krugman has argued that there is a risk that interest groups that have a stake in trade policy will use this framework to advocate policies that are not likely to benefit the nation as a whole.

There are two arguments of particular relevance to developing countries for strategic trade posits. First is that properly constructed public intervention on the part of the host country can shift rents from parent corporations to host country tax authorities and/or host country consumers. The second is that properly constructed public intervention on the part of host country authorities can transfer production from home country or third country locales to equivalent locales in the host country, improving host country welfare. On the other hand, improperly constructed public policies can produce a disproportionately harmful impact on trade and development. Thus, strategic trade theory leaves public policy analysts with a more difficult task than neoclassical trade theory. Using an imperfect competition framework, the impact of public intervention cannot be assumed to be automatically undesirable or distortionary, but neither can it be assumed to be beneficial or welfare enhancing. The dangers of misusing strategic trade analysis can easily be used by special interests seeking protection (Moran 1998).

TRIMs in China After Joining the WTO

China signed the bilateral agreements with the United States upon China's accession to the World Trade Organization (WTO) on November 15, 1999, and with the EU on May 19, 2000, respectively. By September 13, 2001, China had also completed bilateral negotiations with all other WTO members. China gained approval to join the WTO on November 11, 2001, in Doha, Qatar, and officially become a member on December 11, 2001.

After its accession to the WTO, China amended policies for foreign investment in a comprehensive manner, consistent with its commitments. First, as China promised under the Sino-U.S. bilateral agreement, China abolished requirements on foreign exchange balance, trade balance, local content, and export performance. Second, the newly amended Industrial Guideline Catalogue for foreign investment expanded the extent of opening up and took encouraging foreign investment as a general policy. The industries falling under the "encouraged" category increased from 186 to 262, and the number of "restricted" industries was reduced to 75 from 112. Finally, China further loosened equity limits on foreign investment, for example, the requirement of majority equity holding by the Chinese side in the public dock facilities of ports was relaxed. On the other hand, China cautiously implemented its TRIMs policies without immediately opening up all of its domestic market. For example, upon its accession to the WTO, China made no promise to open up the ten currently prohibited types of projects to foreign investment. Agriculture, forestry, and fishery were three types of projects closed to foreign investment.

Under the Sino-EU bilateral agreement, China has also made substantial market access commitments in the fields of telecommunications, insurance, foreign trade, automobiles, and agricultural products, as well as in other services sectors. Regarding the removal of nontariff barriers, China will ease anti-free trade economic policies, including export licenses, requirements for local content, and export subsidies of manufactured goods, privileges enjoyed by local firms in pharmaceuticals, chemical products, cigarettes, and alcohol.

From the above agreements between China and the United States and the European Union, we can conclude that the United States has higher expectations on the subject of TRIMs than does the EU. China is just beginning to implement TRIMs. There are still many improved measures needed.

After access to the WTO, most industries such as agriculture, finance, manufacturing industry, logistics and transportation, telecommunications, textiles, and tourism face fierce competition with foreign industries in terms of price and market share. In the agricultural sector, the Chinese government has revised scores of rules and regulations to implement WTO commitments. Some changes have been made at the cost of sacrificing the interests of rural areas. With lower tariff rates, China has imported more edible oils than previously—in July 2002, 300,000 tons of edible oils were imported, which put heavy pressure on the Chinese domestic oil producers. In addition, some unpredictable technical barriers that hurt the interests of Chinese farmers have prevented Chinese agricultural products from entering world markets due to varying regulatory rules. Furthermore, if foreign countries subsidize their agriculture sectors, and their products enter the Chinese market at a lower price, Chinese farmers will not be able to compete with foreign firms and will suffer losses.

Reform in the finance sector is also challenging. The Chinese government tends toward a middle path between opening up too fast and not opening up fast enough. Foreign banks have been allowed to conduct RMB business in China. The difficult task for policymakers is to balance the salutary effects of introducing foreign competition into its domestic banking market and the danger that the gigantic foreign companies will overpower China's financial institutions.

In the transportation and logistics industry, several Chinese provinces, such as Jiangsu, Zhejiang, and Guangdong, and the cities of Beijing, Tianjin, Chongqing, Shanghai, and Shenzhen have been chosen for joint venture pilot programs. The firms will integrate transport, storage, loading, processing, packaging, delivery, information handling, and imports and exports as a complete supply chain with one-stop logistics services. Chinese domestic express delivery services have developed very rapidly in the past few years but in the area of quality of services still have difficulty in competing with the foreign firms if this market is truly open. The logistics industry is a newly developing industry in China and faces severe competition from foreign firms.

The information and telecommunications industry is also facing the most severe challenges since the new technological revolution. China now is the biggest telecommunications market in the world and is growing rapidly. After joining the WTO, the prices of the phone industry dropped dramatically due to the strong competition between domestic and foreign firms. However, China lacks the legal and regulatory framework required to implement interconnection agreements and prevent anticompetitive behavior. China's main telecom infrastructure provider, MPT, and its provincial PTAs, are too close to the government to freely and impartially provide information about their systems to competitors.

China is the world's largest textile producer. The Chinese government will encourage big textile manufacturers to develop into giant companies with international competence over the next five years. When China entered the WTO, problems such as low efficiency and structural imbalances prevailed, which prevented the full development of the textile industry in the global marketplace. The growth rate of China's textile industry has averaged 6.5 percent per year for the past ten years. In 2000, China exported US$52.1 billion in raw textiles and garments, which accounted for 20.9 percent of the country's overall exports and 13 percent of the world's textile trade volume respectively. With low import quotas on cotton, China's textile and apparel sector is one of the few sectors that will see an obvious and immediate benefit from WTO membership with the lifting of import quotas by other countries. Quotas on Chinese textile imports will formally end in 2005 according to a WTO-wide agreement. China will benefit greatly from access to a much larger international textile market.

Three years after China's accession to the WTO, many disputes remained in various sectors between China, the United States, the EU, and other trading partners. In the past decade, China's economy has experienced rapid growth, making China into a factory for the world. However, the gap between rich and poor has dramatically increased and unemployment has risen as well. How to achieve a balance between maintaining rapid domestic economic development and complying with WTO commitments is still a challenge for the Chinese government.

The Road Ahead

An activist trade policy involving protection-cum-domestic content like TRIMs becomes an acceptable means of reducing the impact of the oligopolistic power enjoyed by international investors and correcting for their distortions of local markets. Under neoclassical assumptions of perfect competition, the imposition of TRIMs (LCRs and investment incentives) on foreign firms hurts the prospects of the host country. Under strategic trade theory, with imperfect competition, the implementation of TRIMs may enhance the welfare of host countries.

The failure of the Uruguay Round regarding TRIMs occurred because the different interest groups had different focuses and expectations. The United States wanted to have general disciplines to restrict TRIMs, while the EU was concerned about the direct and indirect effects of the investment policy and proposed to separate these effects and to set up specific rules. The developing countries were more concerned regarding the a priori presumption that investment measures were inherently trade restrictive or distorting, and therefore they did not have much incentive to sign on to the TRIMs.

In the 2001 Doha Round, the United States proposed a narrow agenda, which included the liberalization of trade in agriculture and services, plus some commitments to cut remaining tariffs on industrial goods and a few relatively easy things, such as streamlining customs procedures. This was not supported by Japan and the EU. The United States made every effort to accelerate the textile liberalization and was loath to renegotiate the antidumping rules. The United States also worked to address the TRIPS, which were originally discussed in the Uruguay Round.

The EU proposed a broad agenda, which was considered to be "new issues" in the Doha Round. This included investment policy, competition policy, and the environment. However, the EU's emphasis on the environment may have been an excuse for reintroducing agricultural protection. Poor countries that felt unfairly treated in the Uruguay Round hoped to gain at the Doha meeting, but they doubted that the policies would be implemented and concluded that no essential progress on TRIMs had been made in Doha.

With membership in the WTO, China has more opportunity in most industries to access global markets, but this access also challenges the existing Chinese political and economic system. China promised to follow the bilateral agreements and WTO rules, TRIMs have been implemented, and membership will benefit both investors and the development of the Chinese economy. In addition, China may become a good role model for the benefits of implementing TRIMs in developing countries. Theoretically, developing countries would be better off agreeing to TRIMs, as gains will outweigh losses.

Acknowledgment

The author thanks Hung-Gay Fung and Denise Eby Konan for helpful comments on an earlier draft.

References

Katz, L.F., and L.H. Summers. 1989. "Industry Rents: Evidence and Implications." *Brookings Papers on Economic Activity* (Special Issue): 209–75.

Krugman, P. 1986. *Strategic Trade Policy and New International Economics.* Cambridge, MA: MIT Press.

Maskus, Keith E., and E. Denise Konan. 1990. "Developing New Rules and Disciplines on Trade-Related Investment Measures." *World Economy* 13, no. 4 (December 1990): 523–40.

McDonald, Brian. 1998. *The World Trading System, the Uruguay Round and Beyond.* London: Macmillan; New York: St. Martin's Press.

Moran, Theodore H. 1998. *Foreign Direct Investment and Development: The New Policy Agenda for Developing Countries and Economies in Transition.* Washington, DC: Institute for International Economics.

Mutti, John. 1994. "TRIMs, Policy Change, and the Role of the GATT." In *Analytical and Negotiating Issues in the Global Trading System*, ed. Allan Deardorff and Robert Stern. Ann Arbor, MI: University of Michigan Press.

Spencer, B.J., and J.A. Brander. 1983. "International R&D Rivalry and Industrial Strategy." *Review of Economic Studies* 50, no. 4 (October): 707–22.

10

China's Employment and WTO Accession

Ju-Wei Zhang

Challenges to Employment

China is now facing severe problems of employment, which is clearly reflected in a steady decrease of the employed in formal urban sectors. In 2000, around 116.13 million people were employed in formal urban sectors, 5.18 million less than in the previous year. Statistics from the National Bureau of Statistics indicate that the total employed in formal urban sectors was 113.67 million by the third quarter of 2001, 4.85 million less than in the same period of 2000. The rate of decrease was 4.09 percent. The National Urban Labor Monitoring Network in sixty-two cities showed that labor demand was still far behind labor supply in the last quarter of 2001, and the ratio of supply to demand was around 75 percent. Furthermore, the severe situation in employment will not be alleviated in the short run, but will continue to deteriorate for a relatively long period for several reasons.

First, the total labor supply is still growing. Population expansion in China will continue, and it is estimated that the working-age population between fifteen and sixty-five will grow annually by 8 million from the year 2000 to 2015.

Second, the rural-urban segmentation of the labor market has aggravated the conflict between labor supply and demand. The division between agriculture and nonagriculture in household registration and administration (the *hukou* system) has raised serious institutional barriers to migration from rural to urban areas. As a result, a large number of rural laborers are forced to become a floating population looking for jobs from year to year. A survey by the National Bureau of Statistics and the Ministry of Labor and Social Security reveals that the number of rural laborers seeking jobs outside their own townships was around 52 million in 1999, an increase of 2.68 million compared with that in 1998, of which the number of those seeking jobs outside their own provinces was estimated at around 21 million (Mo 2002). In 2000, the rural laborers seeking jobs outside their own townships reached 61 million, an increase of 9.3 million compared with that in 1999, of which around 28.24 million sought jobs outside their own provinces (Zhang 2001).

Third, the problems of layoffs and unemployment are still severe in urban areas. From 1998 to 2000, approximately 23 million workers in state-owned enterprises were laid off. Although many policies were formulated to encourage reemployment of the laid-off workers, there is still a very large proportion not being reemployed. In 2000, there were around 3.61 million workers who had been laid-off from state-owned enterprises who had successfully found a job, but the rate of reemployment was only 35.4 percent. In 2001, the total laid-off workers who had found jobs was 2.27 million, which was 1.33 million less than in the previous year. This represents a 30.6 percent rate of reemployment, that is, a decrease of 4.8 percent from the previous year (National Bureau of Statistics and Ministry of Labor and Social Security 2002).

Fourth, the contribution of economic growth to employment has declined continuously. For a long time, China maintained a rapid economic growth rate. However, the growth of employment has not paralleled economic growth, but has exhibited a reduction in its rate of growth. In 1997, GDP grew by 8.8 percent and employment grew by 1.1 percent; in 1998, a 7.8 percent growth rate in GDP corresponded to a growth rate of 0.5 percent in employment; in 1999, the growth rates of GDP and employment were 7.1 percent and 0.9 percent respectively; in 2000, GDP grew by 8.0 percent, but employment only grew by 0.8 percent (National Bureau of Statistics 2002).

These figures suggest that the elasticity of employment with respect to economic growth has fallen. Two factors might be responsible. First, business enterprises have generally taken two measures to improve their efficiency and competitive ability, one is to lay off workers and the other is to increase capital intensity. Obviously, both measures would undermine their capability to absorb new labor. Second, in the adjustment of the economic structure, some labor-intensive enterprises have gone bankrupt, and new ones have not taken their place. It is true that employment opportunities rely on economic growth, but economic growth does not necessarily mean more employment opportunities unless favorable policies are developed.

Figure 10.1   **Economic Growth, Employment Growth, and Employment Elasticity**

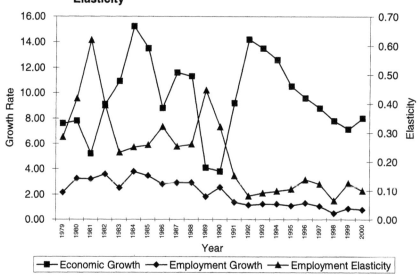

Source: National Bureau of Statistics, *China Statistical Year Book.* Beijing: China Statistics, Press, 2002.

Economic Growth and Employment

China's sustained economic growth over a long period has brought tremendous new employment opportunities. In the early stages of economic reform, such as in 1979–1981, 1 percent growth in the economy corresponded to 0.44 percent growth in employment, resulting in 1.8 million new jobs each year (see Figure 10.1). With economic development, economic growth's contribution to employment has gradually declined.

Observing employment elasticity with respect to economic growth by industry, we can see the following trends and characteristics (see Table 10.1).

At first, the overall employment elasticity tends to decrease. The overall employment elasticity decreased from 0.44 in 1979 to around 0.11 in 2000. The decline of elasticity suggests a change in the factors contributing to economic growth: the contribution of labor (excluding human capital) has decreased, the contribution of capital (including physical capital and human capital) has increased, and the intensity of capital in the economy is increasing.

Second, the capabilities of the primary, secondary, and tertiary industries to absorb labor vary. In 1979–2000, the average employment elasticity of primary industry (agriculture and related enterprise) was 0.06, followed by 0.34 in secondary industry (manufacturing), and 0.57 in the tertiary (service)

Table 10.1

Change of Employment Elasticity, 1979–2000

Year	Primary industry	Secondary industry	Tertiary industry	Overall	3 Year moving average of overall
1979	0.18	0.47	0.75	0.29	—
1980	−1.14	0.50	1.16	0.42	—
1981	0.32	2.02	0.72	0.62	0.44
1982	0.32	0.77	0.19	0.39	0.48
1983	0.11	0.38	0.56	0.23	0.41
1984	−0.07	0.72	0.88	0.25	0.29
1985	0.47	0.45	0.44	0.26	0.25
1986	0.12	0.79	0.45	0.32	0.28
1987	0.28	0.33	0.46	0.25	0.28
1988	0.74	0.25	0.43	0.26	0.28
1989	0.98	−0.38	0.37	0.45	0.32
1990	N.A.	N.A.	N.A.	N.A.	N.A.
1991	0.28	0.11	0.40	0.15	0.29
1992	−0.18	0.12	0.48	0.08	0.23
1993	−0.51	0.23	0.79	0.09	0.11
1994	−0.63	0.14	1.03	0.10	0.09
1995	−0.56	0.18	1.07	0.11	0.10
1996	−0.39	0.29	0.79	0.14	0.11
1997	−0.03	0.19	0.29	0.12	0.12
1998	0.09	−0.04	0.20	0.07	0.11
1999	0.54	−0.15	0.21	0.13	0.11
2000	0.25	−0.15	0.39	0.10	0.10

Source: National Bureau of Statistics, *China Statistical Yearbook.* Beijing: China Statistics Press, 2001.

sector. The figures indicate that the economic growth in primary industry has the lowest ability to absorb labor. Secondary industry has a better ability to do so. With a great potential to absorb labor, the economic growth in the tertiary industry is contributing the most to employment.

The contribution of economic growth to employment in primary industry resulted in a pool of surplus labor. Coupled with strong fluctuation, the employment elasticity of primary industry is very low. Taking into consideration its role in the economy, it is not difficult to figure out that the characteristic of its employment elasticity is actually reflecting the role that primary industry played in employment, functioning like a "pool." Since its employment elasticity does not necessarily represent the change in real employment in agriculture, its fluctuation is more reflective of the change of employment in the other two industries rather than of its own. When employment faces difficult times in the secondary and tertiary industries simultaneously, the employment elasticity of primary industry will be increasing. In

Figure 10.2 **Ratio of Employment Share to GDP Share by Industry**

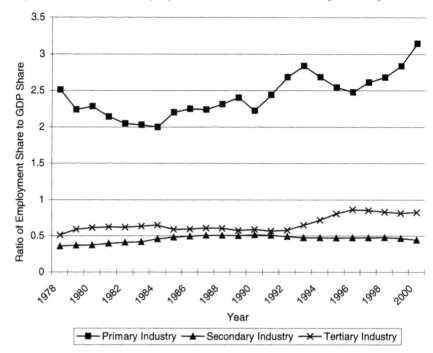

Source: National Bureau of Statistics, *China Statistical Year Book*. Beijing: China Statistics Press, 2002.

other words, decreasing employment elasticity within primary industry corresponds to increased employment in the other industries (Zhang 2002).

Changes in employment elasticity within secondary industry are characterized by the effects of labor cuts. The employment elasticity of secondary industry tends to be decreasing to a relatively low level. Since 1998, it has been negative. This is the same period when reform in state-owned enterprises was taking place. This negative employment elasticity is a reflection of improved efficiency through workforce reduction.

Increases in employment opportunities come mainly within tertiary industry. Although its employment elasticity appears to be declining, the extent of the decrease is much smaller than in the primary and secondary industries. Moreover, the employment elasticity of tertiary industry has remained at a relatively high level. Generally, tertiary industry tends to be labor intensive, which corresponds with higher employment elasticity. Any decrease of elasticity is more closely related to structural changes within this industry. The tertiary industry includes not only the traditional sectors like retail, food, and living services, but also the emerging sectors such as housing, finance and insurance, and consultancies, among others. The traditional sectors tend to be more labor intensive, and the emerging sectors tend to be more capital intensive. As a result, employment elasticity will decrease as the emerging sectors grow faster than the traditional sectors.

The Impact of China's WTO Membership on Employment

What prospects will employment have in China following its entry into the WTO? Generally speaking, China's accession into the WTO will not be able to reverse the trends of economic development that have taken place in the last decades, but will provide a clearer agenda for continuous economic reform and provide a much expanded external environment for its market-oriented economy. The evolving employment structure and the developing labor market will continue within the WTO framework.

After WTO entry, China's comparative advantage in labor-intensive industries will be further intensified and its economic transition will be accelerated. This means that employment elasticity will be increasing. Given an employment elasticity of 0.1 at present, its 10 percent growth suggests an increase of employment opportunities for more than 500,000 people per year. A doubling of the current employment elasticity, say reaching an employment elasticity of 0.2, means an annual increase of more than 5 million employment opportunities given a constant rate of economic growth.

The most significant comparative advantage in China lies in its huge labor force and lower labor costs. With China's entry into the WTO, the optimum allocation of resources worldwide could make China a center of manufacturing in the world, providing a very sound foundation for China's sustainable economic growth over a relatively long period. So, it seems, there is no net negative effect of WTO membership on employment in China in the long run. But, in the short run, WTO membership will have a relatively strong structural impact on employment, and the extent of those impacts will be different depending on the characteristics of each market segment. The frequency of job switching will increase, and the conflicts between employment and unemployment will become even more severe.

In China, agriculture is the largest industry or sector in terms of employment opportunities. Out of total employment, agriculture makes up 50 percent. Agriculture is also the most inefficient industry in terms of productivity. The low labor productivity in agriculture is not a state of equilibrium but a structural distortion: a huge number of rural surplus laborers are forced to stay in agriculture. Because of the so-called surplus labor in agriculture, the loss of agricultural employment due to the import of cereals associated with

WTO membership seems insignificant. It is estimated that there are around 150–200 million redundant laborers in agriculture, and WTO membership will cause a loss of 1.5 million agricultural employment opportunities—that is, 0.7–1.0 percent of the total surplus labor, a negligible amount. The impact on agriculture of China joining the WTO is more significant in terms of income rather than in terms of employment.

According to the rules of the WTO, opening either factor markets or product markets will have the strongest impact on secondary industry. It is the ongoing structural adjustment in secondary industry that led to negative employment elasticity for the period from 1998 to 2002. This implies that the economic growth is associated with a net reduction of employment opportunities in secondary industry. Even so, there are still some sectors in which new labor is absorbed. In general, it seems that the total opportunities for employment will not change much in secondary industry as a result of WTO participation.

The sectors with increasing opportunities for employment include textiles and wearing apparel; furniture and fixtures; electronics and communication equipment and apparatus; electricity, gas, and water provision services; wood and cork products; leather and leather products; cultural, educational, and sports products; tap water production and supply; black metals mining; plastic products, electronic machinery and equipment. The number of employed in those sectors grew in 2000, and their share of employment in thirty-seven sectors of secondary industry is 24.19 percent. It is expected that employment in those sectors will continue to grow. On the other hand, the sectors incurring the strongest impacts on employment are those that are more capital and technology intensive. The employment in those sectors is shrinking, which will continue with China's WTO membership. Those sectors include metallurgy, automobiles, mechanics, food processing, and electronic and communications equipment, among others.

The tertiary industry, services sectors, can be classified as tradable and non-tradable services. Tradable services mainly include capital- and knowledge-intensive sectors like financial and insurance services. Nontradable services include labor-intensive sectors such as wholesale, retail trade, and catering. With more market opening after entry into the WTO, imports of tradable services such as those in finance and insurance will be growing. But this does not necessarily mean a reduction of employment opportunities in this industry because the imported services must be matched with local labor. As we know, even within the framework of the WTO, labor is still not allowed to move freely across borders. Of course, the increase in service imports will affect domestic sectors involved in the same service businesses. At the same time, WTO membership will encourage the development of sectors in non-tradable services, and the employment in those sectors will certainly be increasing since they will not encounter any international competition.

In short, we do not see any negative effect on employment from joining the WTO, either in the short or long run. The impact of the WTO on employment is more structural. Job switching will accelerate and the problems of unemployment will become even more severe. Therefore, employment must be addressed as a priority in the social and economic policies in China.

References

Mo Rong. 2002. *Report on China's Employment in 2002*. Beijing: China Labor and Social Security Press.

National Bureau of Statistics. 2002. *China Statistical Year Book*. Beijing: China Statistics Press.

National Bureau of Statistics and Ministry of Labor and Social Security. 2002. *China Labor Statistical Year Book 2002*. Beijing: China Statistics Press.

Zhang Hongyu. 2001. "A Report on Rural Migrant Laborers." Paper presented at the International Seminar on the Labor Market in Transitional China, Beijing.

Zhang Juwei. 2002. "A Study of Employment Elasticity." *China Industrial Economy*, no. 5.

Part III

Financial Reforms and Capital Markets

11

China's Financial Reform in Banking and Securities Markets

Hung-Gay Fung and Qingfeng "Wilson" Liu

Since the economic reforms in 1978, China has experienced substantial economic growth of about 9 percent before and 7 percent after the 1997 Asian financial crisis. Clearly, the impressive growth of the Chinese economy was attributable to a number of factors such as restructuring the state-owned enterprises (SOEs), setting up various economic zones to attract foreign investments, and drastically changing trade policies to promote international trade. It is apparent that reforms in China's financial system have contributed to its economic success. The purpose of this chapter is to document the recent changes and discuss the challenges facing the financial system in China.

China's financial system, particularly the banking sector and securities markets, has been viewed by many as the last bastion of the decades-old planned economy (*China Daily*, October 24, 2003) and plagued by perennial problems that include mountains of non-performing loans, corporate malfeasance, poor quality of publicly listed firms, corruption, fraud, and inefficiency as a result of decades of state monopolization and government-mandated financing.

Overall, China's financial system is better characterized as a bank-based system in comparison to the financial-markets–based system in the United States. That is, the banks play a more important role than the securities markets (Allen, Qian, and Qian 2002). The ongoing banking reforms have to address the non-performing loans, moral hazards, and capital inadequacy problems that have posed serious challenges for policymakers. In addition, how to boost the competitiveness and efficiency of local Chinese banks has become a pressing issue because China will allow open and free competition from foreign banks after 2006 in line with its World Trade Organization (WTO) accession agreements signed in 2001.

The development of the securities markets, on the other hand, is critical in allowing Chinese firms to raise capital and attract foreign firms to invest in the Chinese economy. The Chinese stock market has experienced dramatic growth over the past two decades from a purely domestic A-share market to a B-share market for foreign investors, and then to the implementation of the Qualified Financial Institutional Investor (QFII) program allowing foreign financial institutions to invest in domestic financial markets. These developments have reshaped and transformed the Chinese financial system. The banking sector and securities markets together play a pivotal role in economic activities and will determine whether the Chinese economy can achieve healthy, stable, and sustainable growth in the coming years. As a result, the government has to transform both the banking sector and securities markets in such a way that they become competitive and viable in a market-oriented setting, and within a relatively short time frame. In this chapter, we will discuss a number of recent measures and steps taken by the Chinese government in restructuring the financial infrastructure in order to improve the transparency and efficiency of the banking system and securities markets.

Banking Reforms

Since the WTO accession, China's banking sector has been facing growing competition from foreign banks.[1] The four major state-owned Chinese banks— Bank of China (BOC), Industrial and Commercial Bank of China (ICBC), Agricultural Bank of China (ABC), and China Construction Bank (CCB)— or the "Big Four," are expected to lose a third of their most qualified staff to foreign rivals, which offer better pay, bonuses, and training opportunities. To slow down foreign competition, the authorities and domestic banks have resorted to some restrictive regulations and exceptional measures. First, foreign banks are required to have at least US$72.3 million in operating capital to conduct full services. Second, foreign banks can only open one branch each year. Third, the People's Bank of China (PBOC), China's central bank, requires foreign banks to maintain 60 percent registered capital in local currency and "demonstrate a need" for opening an office or branch, thereby forcing them to disperse capital to individual branches rather than concentrating it at headquarters to reduce operating costs. In addition, some domestic banks tried to price out foreign banks by offering loans with interest rates lower than LIBOR (London Interbank Offered Rate, the most widely used benchmark or reference rate for short-term interest rates) and waiving the commonly required standby letter of credit from a foreign bank.

These protective regulations and measures cannot, however, last forever because China has promised in its WTO accession agreement to allow foreign banks similar access (to that of domestic banks) to Chinese individuals and businesses by December 2006. This deadline has created tremendous pressures for the government to take steps to prepare Chinese banks for the upcoming competition. So far, these steps include restructuring the four major commercial banks, loosening the restrictions on foreign investment in domestic banks, privatizing banks, and liberalizing the interbank market. These moves, along with the recent establishment of the Closer Economic Partnership Arrangement (CEPA) between mainland China and Hong Kong/ Macao, have provided early opportunities for foreign banks to enter China's banking markets and gain a competitive edge right away without waiting until 2006.

The "Big Four" and the Non-performing Loan Issue

The big four control approximately 70 percent of the banking business. The most serious problem facing the banks is the mountain of non-performing loans inherited from the policy loans in the earlier regime. The Agricultural Bank of China had the worst non-performing loan (NPL) ratio at 30.07 percent at the end of 2002. The NPL ratio was 12.91 percent for the China Construction Bank, 19.16 percent for the Bank of China, 22 percent for the Industrial and Commercial Bank of China, and 26.54 percent for the Agricultural Bank of China as of June 2003, while the overall ratio for the Big Four was 22.9 percent, with bad debt amounting to US$375 billion. Standard and Poor's in June 2003 estimated the ratio to be much higher, at approximately 50 percent with a worth of over US$500 billion or nearly half of China's GDP ("China Is Booming; Bubble, Anyone?" People Net, March 9, 2004; Yahoo! Finance, December 9, 2004). And some analysts put the figure as high as US$700 billion (*China Daily*, October 24, 2003).

The Chinese government mainly uses capital injection and debt-for-equity swaps to reduce the NPL (Fung 1999, 2003). It has taken several significant measures in recent years. First, the government in 1998 issued RMB270 billion (or US$33 billion) in bonds to inject capital into the Big Four. In late 2003, China again injected US$45 billion from the country's foreign-exchange reserves into the Bank of China and China Construction Bank. The amount was split evenly between the banks (*Wall Street Journal*, January 7, 2004, A3). The move was intended to put these two first in line among the country's Big Four banks to make stock offerings overseas that could attract billions of dollars more in investment. The ICBC was expected to be the next bank to

Table 11.1

The Four Asset Management Companies

Asset Management Company	Affiliated bank	Bad loans transferred/ disposed/cash recovered (US$ billion)	Examples of companies affected
Oriental (Dongfang)	Bank of China	$32.30/10.44/1.98	Jiangxi Phoenix Optical Appliance
Cinda	China Construction Bank	$45.06/14.63/4.55	Beijing Cement Plant
Huarong	Industrial and Commercial Bank of China	$49.17/16.39/3.54	Market NPL overseas with Ernst & Young
Great Wall	Agricultural Bank of China	$42.86/19.91/1.9	Hualu Electronic

Source: *Wall Street Journal*, November 8, 1999, February 21, 2001, and March 9, 2004.

receive foreign reserves, at an estimated amount of US$40 billion. And reportedly there would be a total of US$120 billion, including the US$45 billion already designated for the CCB and BOC, to be used for the transformation of the Big Four to publicly listed groups or corporations (*Financial Times,* January 11, 2004 [Chinese ed.]).

Second, four government asset management companies (AMCs)—Oriental (Dongfang), Cinda, Huarong, and Great Wall—were established in 1999 to manage bad debt. Table 11.1 shows the four AMCs, mainly financed through government bonds and affiliated with the Big Four. Most of the NPLs (US$170 billion) will be transferred to government asset management companies, while the remainder of the funding requirement will be dealt with through capital infusions. The government has taken numerous moves to tackle the NPL problems by issuing RMB1.4 trillion of government bonds to fund these initiatives. So far, the AMCs have disposed of about 30 percent of the total loans in their portfolios, while the cash recovery rate from the loan disposal ranges from about 10 percent (Great Wall) to 31 percent (Cinda). Third, the China Banking Regulatory Commission and its local branches have been set up since late 2002 to strengthen lending oversight. Fourth, the government issued new banking rules for the Big Four to reduce NPLs, such as a 3–4 percent decrease in the NPL ratio and a RMB70 to RMB80 billion drop in NPL amounts. The government has also mandated a five-level loan classification system to increase the transparency of bank operations. Last, the Law on Banking Regulation and Supervision, passed on December 27, 2003, provided a legal framework to govern bank lending activities. The banks have also made their own efforts to address this problem. They have established strict credit and lending management rules, installed new procedures for lending, and set their own quotas for NPL reduction.

These measures appeared to be working, at least on the books. As of June 2003, the NPL balance for the Big Four was 22.9 percent, a decline of 4.02 percent from the beginning of the year; the balance of other state-owned banks was 9.34 percent, a decrease of 3.51 percent. But critics argue that this progress with the NPL ratio was not due to the improvement of the operating system or governance structure, but to the drastically increasing size of outstanding loans (*People's Daily,* September 17, 2003). That is, the NPL ratio's numerator decreased far less than the increase in the denominator. At the end of August 2003, the total outstanding loans reached RMB16.31 trillion, a 23.9 percent rise from the previous year, leading some to argue that the economy is overly hot. To exacerbate the situation, close to 60 percent of these loans are either intermediate- or long-term loans (*Sina,* October 21, 2003, http://finance.sina .com), which is similar to the situation in the Thai banking system before the 1997 Asian financial crisis and may conceal the actual NPL problem.[2] Mortgage loan balances, in particular, grew from RMB310.6 billion at the end of 1998 to RMB2.13 trillion as of November 2003, jumping almost sevenfold within five years. The banks doled out RMB426.4 billion in mortgage loans in the first three quarters of 2003 alone, which may fuel an overheating real estate sector. On the deposit side, only 43 percent of all deposits are in fixed-term savings accounts, and the majority of these savings have a one-year term or shorter (*Deutsche Welle,* November 12, 2003 [in Chinese]). This is also reminiscent of the situation before the savings and loan debacle in the United States in the 1980s. As a matter of fact, most of the current NPL balance emerged after the transfer of RMB1.4 trillion NPLs to AMCs in 1999. And the government will not be able to afford another such massive transfer.

Among the fundamental causes of the NPL problem are government-mandated lending, corruption, and malfeasance (*Wall Street Journal,* October 23, 2003). A large number of managers and officers in the banks are party officials with inadequate banking expertise and training to evaluate risk and return tradeoffs. They have to report to all levels of governments instead of to boards of directors or shareholders. Many bad lending decisions are actually made by government officials for political or other reasons and carried out by the banks. In a move to address this moral hazard problem, the Big Four have planned to issue initial public offerings (IPOs) to become equity-based banks. Three out of the Big Four had submitted IPO proposals to the State Council as of the end of 2004.

As a first step, two of the Big Four have hired internationally renowned accounting firms in preparation for IPO issuance. The Bank of China, deemed as one of the best among the Big Four in terms of financial performance, continues to use PricewaterhouseCoopers as its auditor. The Industrial and Commercial Bank of China has retained Ernst & Young to review its branch network. Hiring American accounting firms will help the banks adapt to the international accounting and settlement systems necessary for IPO issuance. The Bank of China has set a goal of listing its stock in 2005 and the ICBC in 2006 or 2007. The China Construction Bank has indicated that it would strive to be the first among the Big Four to go public. Only the Agricultural Bank of China has not announced any clear goal for being listed, possibly because it has the worst NPL situation among the four.

In January 2004, the top officials in the Chinese government reportedly decided on a timetable for the Big Four to go public. According to the timetable, the CCB, BOC, ICBC, and ABC would go public in 2004, 2005, 2006, and 2007 respectively. The CCB would be the first to issue an IPO by the end of 2004, possibly in the Hong Kong Stock Market, to obtain about US$6 billion in new financing. The BOC would likely choose New York for its IPO (*Financial Times*, January 11, 2004 [Chinese ed.]). However, because of corruption scandals, accounting problems, and governance issues, the listing plans of both the CCB and the BOC had not materialized by the end of January 2005, and sources close to the banks believed it would be unlikely that these plans would be initiated in 2005 (*Yahoo! News*, January 30, 2005).

The high NPL ratios are the major obstacle to stock listing. The ICBC has adopted a "securitization" plan with the assistance of Credit Suisse First Boston (*Wall Street Journal*, October 22, 2003). In the plan, several bad loans would be packaged into junk bonds and then auctioned off in pieces. Buyers of these bonds are entitled to interest payments and can trade these securities on a secondary market, like the newly established China Technology and Equity Exchange (CTEE) in Zhongguancun, Beijing (see below for details). Another more popular approach being considered is to restructure the banks into a two-layer corporate entity—a holding group and an equity-based banking corporation. The equity-based corporation would transfer most of the bad loans to the holding group and thereby achieve an NPL ratio below 6 percent to meet the criteria for going public. Some analysts, however, suggest that taking this shortcut might not be the ideal way to address the governance problem because the original management still retains control of the equity-based banking corporation through the holding group, which (based on the proposals) would keep 80 percent of the shares (*People's Daily*, September 17, 2003).

Table 11.2

Mid-Year Report Summary for the Five Listed Banks in 2003

Bank name	Earnings per share (RMB)	Net assets per share (RMB)	Net profits (RMB 1000s)
Shenzhen Development Bank	0.139	2.225	270,340.7
Huaxia Bank	0.158	1.599	395,190.0
Pudong Development Bank	0.168	2.836	656,834.6
Minsheng Bank	0.190	1.975	638,050.0
China Merchants Bank	0.194	3.003	1,108,029.0

Source: http://rich.online.sh.cn, October 23, 2003.
Note: The exchange rate for RMB/US$ was approximately 8.28 in 2003.

Bank Privatization

Several banks have listed their shares on the stock exchanges—a step consistent with the government's intention to privatize part of the banking sector. Shenzhen Development Bank was the first bank to list shares through initial public offerings on the Shenzhen Stock Exchange. Shanghai Pudong Development Bank, established in 1993, became the second bank to be listed on the Shanghai Stock Exchange (SSE) on September 23, 1999. On December 19, 2000, China's only private bank, the Minsheng Bank, was also allowed to list on the SSE. Two other banks, Beijing-based Huaxia Bank and Shenzhen-based China Merchants Bank, have also gone public. Table 11.2 shows the five listed banks and the recorded sizable net profits in their 2003 mid-year reports. Minsheng Bank has the second best earnings per share among the five, only marginally below that of China Merchants Bank.

Established on January 12, 1996, the sixteen-branch Minsheng Bank's three biggest shareholders are all private companies—Sichuan New Hope Investment Co. Ltd., the Oriental Group, and China Fanhai Holdings. Minsheng Bank's total asset growth rate has been among the highest in China's banks and its NPL ratio among the lowest.[3] In October 2003, the China Banking Regulatory Commission (CRBC) granted approval for the World Bank's private sector unit, the International Finance Corporation (IFC), to take a 1.6 percent stake in Minsheng Bank (*Financial Times*, October 27, 2003). This was the first time the Chinese government approved a foreign entity to buy into a privately owned bank. The IFC will have a board seat at Minsheng, which may help improve the bank's governance structure, boost its international image, and promote an expected Minsheng Bank stock offering in New York and Hong Kong early in 2005 (the investment bankers are Goldman Sachs, Citibank, and the Deutsche Bank). The government has also in recent years approved minority stakes for foreign financial institutions like the Hong Kong & Shanghai Banking Corporation (HSBC), Citibank, and IFC in several regional state-owned commercial banks including the Bank of Shanghai, Xiamen International Bank, Pudong Development Bank, and Nanjing City Commercial Bank. So far, Minsheng Bank has remained China's only private bank. Another private bank—Nanhua Bank—in the southern Guangdong province has been proposed and has been in the works for several years, but it was still awaiting PBOC approval as of November 2003. On the other hand, there have been numerous cases in which private enterprises wanted to take over the control of state-owned urban commercial banks, but none of these moves were successful, mainly due to the government's deep-rooted distrust of private businesses.[4] Recent comments by high-ranking PBOC officials may signal a positive shift in the regulators' attitude toward the establishment of more private banks (*China Entrepreneurs,* November 11, 2003), but there remain obstacles, both operational and political, despite the growing pressures from the WTO agreements as the 2006 deadline approaches.

The Interbank Market

The Chinese interbank market was initially for underground lending and borrowing by townships and village enterprises. The PBOC formally allowed its establishment in 1985 as part of the economic reform. The fact that the interbank market was mainly a short-term market contributed to the speculative bubble economy in the early 1990s as funds from it were invested in securities and real estate markets. Starting in 1996, the interbank market became more transparent because more explicit rules (such as the maturity of the loans) were imposed and stricter regulations (such as the type of loans for liquidity deficiency) were enforced. In the meantime, the PBOC has gradually loosened the interbank market membership restrictions. Urban commercial banks, urban and rural credit cooperatives, insurance companies, fund management companies, securities companies (brokerages), and later foreign banks, financial leasing companies, and foreign insurance companies, have all received permission to participate in the interbank market.

On October 24, 2002, a new regulation announced by the PBOC even allowed any legal entity, not just financial institutions, to trade in the interbank market, which some analysts believed was a step to merge the interbank market and the exchange-based securities markets (*Shanghai Securities,* November 30, 2002). The number of members increased from sixteen in 1997 to 733 at the end of 2002, and total trading volume jumped 26.5 times from RMB446.3 billion to RMB11.84 trillion during the same period.

Out of the total trading volume in 2002, RMB1.21 trillion, or 10.23 percent, was attributed to the national interbank lending and borrowing market with a tendency toward shorter maturity.[5] The interbank government bond repurchase market accounted for US$10.19 trillion, or 86.05 percent. The remaining 3.72 percent came from current securities and foreign exchange transactions. The interbank repurchase market of Chinese government treasury bonds experienced exceptional growth since it started trading in 1997. This increased participation further strengthens the important role the interbank market plays in liquidity adjustment for the banking sector.

Historically, foreign banks had difficulty in raising renminbi to fund their loans. Approval from the Chinese government is required to obtain these funds. For any foreign bank that operates in China, having renminbi funds at hand would give it an edge in the Chinese market because it would have more money to lend to corporate customers operating in China than its competitors, who likewise have difficulties raising renminbi funds. The Administrative Rules for RMB Inter-bank Transactions (Draft), released on November 26, 2002, initiated the process of opening up the interbank market for all Chinese banks and overseas banks that offer renminbi services. Some foreign banks have been able to raise RMB loans with fixed maturity terms from their Chinese counterparts in the interbank market. The contractual parties were able to freely determine the interest rates. This development is one of the key components of the market reform of the banking sector that provides potential opportunities for foreign banks to expand their RMB-denominated banking services (People's Bank of China 2002).

Closer Economic Partnership Arrangements (CEPA) with Hong Kong and Macao

Mainland China signed the Closer Economic Partnership Agreements (CEPA) with Hong Kong on June 29, 2003, and with Macao on October 17, 2003. Both agreements, which took effect on January 1, 2004, cover three areas: trade in services, trade in goods, and trade facilitation. They are China's first free trade pacts since joining the WTO (*Dawn*, June 30, 2003; *Sina*, October 20, 2003).[6]

Based on the CEPA, the minimum asset requirement for a Hong Kong or Macao bank to establish a branch in China will be reduced to US$6 billion from US$20 billion; the one branch per year restriction will be removed; and the branch will be allowed to conduct RMB deposits, exchange, credit cards, remittances, and other services with the PBOC as the settlement bank (*Markov Processes International News,* November 18, 2003). This agreement provides Hong Kong and Macao banks a head start in the race to establish a footing in the immense Chinese market, while other foreign banks have to wait until 2006 to receive similar treatment.

Foreign banks can still take advantage of this arrangement by establishing a branch or acquiring a local bank in Hong Kong or Macao. CEPA requires that a branch be registered in Hong Kong/Macao for three years and that a local bank be owned for one year. To meet and take advantage of this requirement, Taiwan Fubon Financial Holding spent HK$20 billion (US$2.56 billion) to acquire the Hong Kong–based International Bank of Asia, a majority-owned unit of Arab Banking in October 2003 (*Southern Metropolitan,* October 26, 2003 [in Chinese]). For the numerous foreign banks that have long had a Hong Kong branch, the one-year requirement may not pose an issue at all. So far, many Hong Kong–based and eligible foreign banks have indicated that they will soon set up new branches and/or offices in China.

Securities Market Reforms

The Shanghai Stock Exchange and the Shenzhen Stock Exchange, the two main stock exchanges in China, were founded on December 19, 1990 and July 3, 1991, respectively. Stocks traded on these two exchanges are divided into A- and B-shares. A-shares were restricted to domestic investors while B-shares targeted international investors. Most listed companies are state-owned enterprises while some are private firms. In terms of the significance to the economy, the stock markets are playing a much less important role in the economy than is the banking system. Table 11.3 shows the total bank credit in 1999 was 111.30 percent of GDP, the highest among all the countries in the sample,[7] whereas the total traded market value was only 10 percent of the GDP, lower than many countries.[8] Therefore, it is natural for the authorities to encourage the growth of these markets to alleviate the excessive burden on the banking system in supporting corporate financing and economic expansion.

The Shanghai and Shenzhen stock markets witnessed significant growth for the past decade. Table 11.4 displays the number of listed firms, A- and B-share market values, and total market value as a percentage of GDP. The total market capitalization of the two stock markets grew by an average 80.03 percent between 1992 and 2000.[9] The stock markets, however, took a sharp turn with the arrival of the new millennium. The total stock market capitalization decreased by 10.12 percent in 2001 and 11.94 percent in 2002. The price drop was uncharacteristic of an economy that has been growing at one of the world's fastest rates.[10]

There are numerous possible causes for this setback in China's stock market development. First, the division into A- and B-shares is a double-edged

Table 11.3

The Weights of Banks and Securities Markets: China vs. Other Countries

Country	Bank credit as a percentage of GDP	Total traded market value as a percentage of GDP	Total market capitalization as a percentage of GDP
China	111.30 (24.2*)	10.0	32.5
English-Origin Countries	40.8	14.4	42.8
French-Origin Countries	34.1	4.5	15.4
German-Origin Countries	100.0	61.8	43.8
Scandinavian-Origin Countries	50.2	7.5	23.2

*Refers to bank credit issued only to the private sector.
Source: The data is for year-end 1999 and compiled from *China Statistical Yearbook* (2000); Allen et al. (2002); Levine (2000); and *Taiwan Economic Journal*, available at www.tei.com.tw.

sword. The policy did help ensure that control of major businesses remained domestic. But at the same time it creates a significant barrier that prevents foreign investment from taking a more active role in the transition and modernization process of domestic companies, particularly those huge and inefficient state-owned enterprises that were allowed to be listed. Lack of participation by foreign capital also kept demand for domestic financial securities at a relatively low level.

Second, the unique stock structure of China's listed companies creates a source of stress and pressures for shareholders. A listed firm typically has only one-third of its shares publicly traded, causing a dramatically high price to earnings ratio (P/E). The remaining two-thirds non-circulating shares are mostly held by government entities (*guoyougu,* or state-owned shares), or corporate entities (*farengu,* or legal entity shares). From time to time, rumors that this vast majority of non-circulating shares held by the government would soon be allowed to flood the markets exerted a serious negative impact on market sentiment. The attitude of the authorities to this vital issue has mostly been vague and ambiguous so far, increasing market uncertainties.

Third, in recent years there have been several high-profile corporate scandals involving top management in embezzlement, cooking the books, and illegal investments. Many such incidents are due to poor transparency in

Table 11.4

Summary Data of the Shanghai and Shenzhen Stock Exchanges

Year	Number of listed firms in Shanghai Stock Exchange	Number of listed firms in Shenzhen Stock Exchange	Shanghai A-share market value (billion RMB)	Shenzhen A-share market value (billion RMB)	Shanghai B-share market value (billion US$)	Shenzhen B-share market value (billion HK$)	Total market value as a percentage of concurrent GDP*
2002	713	507	2,500.53	1,263.44	5.70	34.00	37.03
2001	643	506	2,713.35	1,536.19	8.22	48.57	45.23
2000	568	506	2,690.42	2,109.55	4.13	25.38	54.37
1999	480	455	1,450.30	1,188.78	1.74	15.38	32.52
1998	434	403	1,060.31	878.67	1.22	10.20	25.02
1997	379	351	912.30	812.59	2.25	17.67	23.67
1996	289	226	533.96	413.36	1.95	20.83	14.52
1995	185	130	244.56	87.08	1.11	6.40	5.94
1994	168	115	248.73	102.59	1.38	5.45	7.88
1993	104	74	208.84	124.81	1.47	7.55	10.22
1992	29	22	47.88	45.75	0.49	3.23	3.80

*The B-share market values are converted from RMB using prevailing exchange rates obtained from the U.S. Federal Reserve Bank online at www.federalreserve.gov/.

Source: Data are compiled from the Taiwan Economic Journal (2003) and Financial Times (2003).

	1992	1993	1994	1995	1996	1997	1998	1999	2000	2001	2002
RMB/US$	5.7662	5.8145	8.4462	8.3174	8.2982	8.2796	8.2789	8.2803	8.2782	8.2867	8.2871
RMB/HK$	0.7447	0.7527	1.0917	1.0757	1.0729	1.0687	1.0687	1.0655	1.0614	1.0628	1.0628

The RMB/US$ exchange rate made a sudden jump from 5.8145 to 8.69 on January 7, 1994, and has stayed above 8.0 ever since.

corporate decisionmaking processes, loophole-laden accounting regulations and practices, and lack of external scrutiny and monitoring. These problems have seriously weakened investor confidence in China's securities markets.

Fourth, China's stock markets, still quite immature, are mostly driven by capital flows and speculation rather than fundamental factors such as corporate earnings (*Shanghai Securities,* December 11, 2002). News and rumors thus have a larger impact than in many other countries.

In view of these issues, the Chinese government has taken some steps recently. The establishment of the QFII program, a new equity exchange, and the policy changes for the fund management industry and foreign joint ventures mark a positive development in the authorities' attitude toward modernizing the securities markets and opening the door wider to foreign investment.

The Qualified Foreign Institutional Investor Program

When the Chinese stock markets were established in the early 1990s, the stocks were divided into A- and B-shares, with A-shares restricted to domestic investors and B- shares to foreign investors. Beginning June 1, 2001, B-shares were opened to domestic individual investors with foreign currencies (still not open to domestic institutional investors as of the end of 2004). The A-share market was no longer off limits to foreign investors with the establishment of the QFII program by the Securities Regulatory Commission and the PBOC, along with the State Administration of Foreign Exchange, on December 1, 2002.

The QFII program is a type of transitional arrangement for emerging markets with foreign exchange control and incomplete currency convertibility in the capital account to open their domestic financial markets (in China's case, the A-share and bond markets) to foreign institutional investors. QFIIs can convert an approved amount (investment quota) of foreign currency into local currency within specially controlled accounts and invest in local securities markets. Interests, dividends, and capital gains from these investments can, with approval, be converted back to foreign currency and remitted out of the country. As a result, foreign investors can invest in domestic markets through QFIIs and the local government can maintain macroeconomic and foreign exchange control to avoid the undesirable impact of free capital flows on the domestic economy and markets.

Foreign institutions are required to apply for QFII status through a custodian bank, which should meet the requirements of having (1) a specific fund custody department, (2) paid in capital of more than RMB8 billion, (3) sufficient professionals familiar with custody, (4) the ability to manage the entire assets of the fund safely, (5) qualifications to conduct foreign exchange and

RMB business, and finally (6) no material breach of foreign exchange regulations in the preceding three years. The Chinese government has approved nine custodian banks: six mainland banks (the Big Four, plus the Bank of Communications and China Merchants Bank), and three foreign banks (Citbank, HSBC, and Standard Chartered).

In May 2003, the first five QFIIs (UBS, Nomura, Citibank, Morgan Stanley, and Goldman Sachs) were approved within two weeks after the SARS (severe acute respiratory syndrome) situation stabilized. The approved investment quota for UBS is US$300 million, Nomura is US$50 million, Citibank is US$75 million, Morgan Stanley is US$300 million, and Goldman Sachs is US$50 million. One of the reasons for the approval of QFIIs is the varying performance of the stock indices. During the first eight months of 2003, the Hong Kong H-share index rose by over 50 percent, and other stock indices, including the Hang Seng, also increased by about 10 percent. In contrast, the Shanghai and Shenzhen A- and B-share indices dropped during the same period. The SARS outbreak in the spring of 2003 exacerbated the bear market.

On July 9, 2003, Swiss-based financial group UBS AG announced the first trade in China's A-share market. UBS purchased the RMB-denominated shares of Baoshan Iron & Steel Co., Shanghai Port Container Co., Sinotrans Air Transportion Development Co., and ZTE Corp. The size or value of the transactions were not disclosed. As of October 13, 2003, there were nine QFIIs.

The market entry of QFIIs was delayed for more than a month (*Securities Markets Weekly,* July 28, 2003 [in Chinese]), mainly because the trade date (T+0) settlement system in China allowed little time for the parties in a transaction to compare records. If errors occurred in the transaction, it was nearly impossible for the custodian banks to notify the China Securities Depository and Clearing Corporation (CSDCC) of an incorrect instruction before market close on trade day (T) to transfer the settlement obligation to the broker (*Finance Asia,* March 14, 2003). Then cash payment would be halted altogether due to the restrictions set by the Banking Law and the Securities Law. This problem would not exist in the T+1 (trade date plus one day) settlement system, which has been adopted by most other countries. In June 2003, UBS signed agreements with the brokerage companies, the CSDCC, and custodian banks under the arrangements of the Securities Regulatory Commission to change the settlement system from T+0 to T+1 to solve the problem.[11] Only after that did UBS execute its first trades. This issue was actually raised in late 2002, when QFII arrangements were announced, but it took more than seven months for this simple technical issue to be resolved, illustrating the inefficiencies of the bureaucracies that foreign investors need to be aware of. By October 2003, three months after the first trade, UBS had used up its investment quota of US$300 million. It immediately applied for an additional investment quota of US$500 million on October 15, 2003. HSBC has invested 60 percent of its investment quota of US$100 million in the stocks of state-owned enterprises.

Due to the limited capital approved so far, the QFIIs may not be able to exert decisive influence on the market, but they have made positive impacts in some sectors. The four companies in which UBS purchased A-shares outperformed the market in the following months. By mid-October 2003, the prices of A-shares of the four had changed by approximately +5 percent, +0.2 percent, –0.5 percent, and –7 percent respectively, while the Shanghai A-share Index had dropped by over 9 percent.

The QFII program has far-reaching ramifications. First, it can help decrease the pricing segmentation between the A- and B-share markets as foreign capital now has access to both. The fact that A-share prices are generally higher than B-share prices for the same Chinese company has been widely documented in Fung, Lee, and Leung (2000), Sun and Tong (2000), Yeh, Lee, and Pen (2002), Bergstrom and Tang (2001), Chen et al. (2001). Second, QFIIs bring advanced investment practices and concepts to the domestic A-share market, which could help make Chinese financial markets more mature, efficient, and compatible with international standards. These concepts include the emphasis on the transparency of corporate governance, the protection of the interests of small investors, and advanced and rational investment valuation techniques. Third, the involvement of QFIIs would push the A-share companies (many of them are SOEs) to adopt international rules for accounting, auditing, risk assessment and management, and credit ratings. Finally, the QFIIs' rich experience with financial derivatives would help the research and establishment of such markets in China.

Securities Funds

Securities funds debuted in October 1991 with the establishment of the Wuhan Securities Investment Fund and Shenzhen Nanshan Risk Investment Fund. The Securities Investment Fund Provisional Regulations that took effect in November 1997 brought about rapid development in securities funds in terms of their number, types, and value. The first Western-style open-end fund, Hua'an Innovation Fund, was launched with the assistance of JP Morgan on September 11, 2001. Since then, many open-end funds have emerged and taken over the mainstream in the industry. Bond funds, index funds, fund series, and joint-venture fund management companies have all been initiated in recent years. Table 11.5 provides a snapshot of the fund management industry as of September 2003.

Table 11.5

**A Summary of China's Fund-Management Industry
in September 2003**

Number of fund management firms	Number of securities funds	Money under management	Value as a percentage of A-share market	Value as a percentage of GDP
32	87	RMB155.3 billion	13	2.17

Source: Shanghai Securities (2003).

The securities funds have actually been negatively affected by the stock market decline in recent years. As of November 2003, their total asset value was 2.17 percent of China's GDP, far lower than those in the United States (approximately 60 percent) (*Shanghai Securities,* November 17, 2003). This may suggest there exists considerable room for growth and potentially lucrative opportunities for foreign financial institutions. The Securities Investment Fund Law, which took effect on June 1, 2004, followed many international fund management principles and practices regarding fund governance, the qualifications and responsibilities of fund trustees and managers, information disclosure, as well as the types of securities that could be invested. It provides a legal groundwork for the industry's foreign investment and future development.

A New Equity Exchange

China had only two stock exchanges in Shanghai and Shenzhen until March 2003 when China Technology and Equity Exchange (CTEE) was founded in Zhongguancun, Beijing. CTEE was founded by nine state-owned and private companies with a total investment of RMB65 million. Although CTEE is still in an embryonic form, it has the potential to develop into a future over-the-counter market for high-tech firms since Zhongguancun is the location of thousands of technology companies and is termed "China's Silicon Valley." CTEE allows domestic and foreign financial institutions to trade Zhongguancun's corporate equity shares.

CTEE has reached agreements with several investment brokerage firms in Shanghai to help list CTEE's projects in other exchanges (*China Daily,* November 27, 2003). It is negotiating with over twenty property trading centers in other cities, and conducting road shows in Zhejiang, Jiangsu, and Guangdong provinces to introduce listed projects to potential investors and partners.

In October 2003, CTEE created a "virtual financial supermarket" specializing in trading NPL assets (*China Daily*, November 27, 2003). CTEE has signed agreements with two of the four asset management companies—Huarong and Oriental—and is negotiating with the other two—Cinda and Great Wall. As of October 15, 2003, about RMB20 billion of NPL assets had been listed on CTEE, with another billion renminbi expected by the end of the year. The NPL assets cover industries such as the high-tech sector, building materials, copper, and real estate.

A-Shares for Foreign-Controlled Companies

Joint-venture companies with foreign minority ownership have actually been allowed to issue A-shares since the early stages of the stock markets. Lianhua Synthetic Fiber became the first joint-venture firm to be listed in 1992. As of September 2003, there were nearly eighty joint-venture firms listed on the Shanghai or Shenzhen Stock Exchanges, or about 6 percent of the total number of public companies (*Securities Times*, September 15, 2003). Foreign holdings in these firms ranged mostly from 10 percent to 45 percent. Foreign-controlled firms have had difficulty in obtaining approval to issue A-shares.

Since 2001, several executive orders and stipulations have been issued to loosen listing restrictions. On September 15, 2003, Beijing-based Sanyuan Foods Co. Ltd. was among the first foreign-controlled joint-venture firms to issue A-shares. Foreign equity ownership in Sanyuan was 73 percent before the issue and 55.76 percent afterward (*Securities Times*, September 15, 2003). It remains unclear if the authorities would continue to allow foreign joint-venture firms to be listed due to concerns about the high P/Es for the current circulating shares, the impact of foreign investment on domestic shares, and pressures from an increasing number of domestic state-owned and private firms that have been trying to get listed.

Summary and Future Outlook

There have been significant changes and developments in China's pivotal banking system and securities markets since China joined the WTO in 2001. But China's financial system remains dominated by the banking sector, mostly state-owned banks, to provide financial services to businesses. The significant decline in China's stock market capitalization since 2000 further exacerbates this imbalance between financial markets and the banking sector.

The heavy dependence on a banking system that has long been plagued by many structural and political problems prevents the optimization of investment and financing structures, increases systemic financial risks, and may create formidable roadblocks for China's economic performance in the years ahead. In response to this, the Chinese government has undertaken gradual deregulation and loosened restrictions in many areas in the financial system in line with China's WTO commitments. For foreign financial institutions and investors, these moves and changes may offer early opportunities for them to enter and compete in this potentially lucrative market. For policymakers of developing countries that intend to restructure their financial systems, these reforms may also provide valuable experiences and lessons. So far, these reforms in China have been found useful and productive. Of course, more in-depth reforms are needed to address the numerous deep-rooted internal structural problems, which still pose serious challenges for the Chinese government in its quest to establish a healthy, vibrant, and sustainable market-oriented economy.

China's banking regulator, China Banking Regulatory Commission, has recently issued a set of rules allowing both locals and foreigners to trade futures, options, and other instruments beginning March 2004 (*Financial Times* 2004, 25). It is expected the change in regulatory stance allowing derivatives trading will have a substantial impact on the development of the financial markets. It seems clear that the new rules acknowledge the need for derivatives in a well-functioning financial market, and give further momentum to its ongoing changes in China.

Notes

1. As the *Financial Times* (March 28, 2002) reported, the Swedish-invested, Nanjing-based Ericsson joint venture dumped its Chinese banks in favor of Citibank for better banking services.

2. In Thailand's case, the capital market was open to foreign investment and the Thai baht was partially convertible. The reckless lending in the banking system and the bubble in the real estate market were among the many facets of the 1997 financial crisis. This experience may influence the reluctance of Chinese authorities to liberalize the capital account.

3. By the end of September 2003, Minsheng's total assets had grown to RMB359 billion from RMB36 billion in 1999. Its NPL ratio was 1.74 percent at the end of the second quarter of 2003. For more details, see http://finance.sina.com.cn (November 7, 2003).

4. A main concern of the authorities is that these private businesses might use the private bank as their "ATM" if they gain control of it.

5. See the People's Bank of China, *Quarterly Statistical Bulletin*, 1997–2002, and *Shanghai Securities*, January 14, 2003, available at www.cnstock.cn.

6. The sovereignty of Hong Kong and Macao was returned to China in 1997 and 1999 respectively but they remain separate customs areas.

7. The bank credit to the private sector is only 24.2 percent of the GDP, sug-

gesting the vast majority of the bank loans, or 78.26 percent, go to state-owned enterprises.

8. As Allen et al. (2002) point out, total traded market value is a more accurate measure for China's stock markets because the majority of the shares of many listed state-owned enterprises are held by the government and not circulated in the secondary market.

9. The B-share market values are calculated using concurrent exchange rates.

10. Some believe the decline is temporary and transitional in nature because of the size of the annual GDP (over RMB10 trillion), resident deposits (over RMB10 trillion), insured assets (over RMB1 trillion), and postal savings (over RMB0.9 trillion), which are still fast growing. Savings interest rates at the banks alone are not able to meet the investment demand of this immense capital. See www.homeway.com.cn (November 22, 2003).

11. Now the A-share markets have adopted the T+1 system.

References

Allen, Franklin, Jun Qian, and Meijun Qian. 2002. "Comparing China's Financial System." Working paper, University of Pennsylvania.

Bergstrom, Clas, and Ellen Tang. 2001. "Price Differentials Between Different Classes of Stocks: An Empirical Study on Chinese Stock Markets." *Journal of Multinational Financial Management* 11, nos. 4–5 (October–December): 407–26.

Chen, G.M., Bong-Soo Lee, and Oliver M. Rui. 2001. "Foreign Ownership Restrictions and Market Segmentation in China's Stock Markets." *Journal of Financial Research* 24, no. 1 (Spring): 133–55.

Fung, Hung-Gay. 1999. "Chinese Banking: Challenges and Opportunities in the New Millennium." *Business Forum* 24, no. 3, 4: 2–6.

———. 2003. "Rise of Capitalism in China." *China Business Review* 2, no. 1 (August): 1–7.

Fung, Hung-Gay, Wai Lee, and Wai Kin Leung. 2000. "Segmentation of the A- and B-share Chinese Equity Markets." *Journal of Financial Research* 23, no. 2 (Summer): 179–95.

Homeway Info Tech Company. 2003. November 22. Available at www.homeway.com.cn.

Levine, Ross. 2000. "Bank-Based or Market-Based Financial Systems: Which Is Better?" Working paper, University of Minnesota.

People's Bank of China (PBOC). 1997–2002. *Quarterly Statistical Bulletin*. Available at www.pbc.gov.cn.

———. 2002. "Draft for Renminbi Interbank Lending Administrative Measures, issued on November 26. Available at www.pbc.gov.cn.

Sun, Qian, and Wilson H.S. Tong. 2000. "The Effect of Market Segmentation on Stock Prices: The China Syndrome." *Journal of Banking and Finance* 24, no. 12 (December): 1875–1902.

Yeh, Yin-Hua, Tsun-siou Lee, and Jen-fu Pen. 2002 "Stock Returns and Volatility Under Market Segmentation: The Case of Chinese A and B Shares." *Review of Quantitative Finance and Accounting* 18, no. 3 (May): 239–57.

12

How Do Chinese Firms Raise Capital?

An International Comparison

Hung-Gay Fung, Wai Kin Leung, and Stanley J. Zhu

Modigliani and Miller (1958) show that the mix of different securities within firms, that is, their capital structure (or financing choices), does not affect their value in a perfect market, because the real assets, not the mix of securities, determine a firm's value. In an imperfect market, the capital structure does matter. There are two traditional approaches to capital structure in an imperfect market—the static tradeoff theory and the pecking order theory. According to the static tradeoff concept, the firm sets a target debt-to-equity ratio and gradually moves toward it, while in the pecking order concept in the U.S. market, firms prefer internal to external financing, and debt-to-equity financing if they issue securities. Myers (1984) suggests that firms prefer internal financing. If external financing is necessary, firms start with debt, then possibly hybrid securities like convertible bonds, then equity issues as a last resort.

The financial structure of firms may differ between developing and developed countries. The International Finance Corporation (IFC), the private sector investment arm of the World Bank Group (IFC 1991) found that internal finance ratios in developing countries are well below the levels of those in developed countries, that is, they rely more heavily on external sources. Glen and Pinto (1994), in a study of seven developing countries, argue that the government plays an important role in capital structure decisions because regulation controls the innovation of instruments and impacts the issue and pricing of those approved. They found that (1) the use of capital markets as a source of external financing soared during the1990s, and (2) significant differences in the capital structures among sample countries reflected the diversity of financial markets, tax codes, and investor preferences.

In China, state bank loans have been the most important source of financing for firms prior to the share system reforms and the opening of the two stock exchanges. State-owned banks were often not operating on commercial principles, and loan policies were often guided by personal connections. As a result of the economic reforms since 1978, China has implemented bank policies to improve their capital adequacy and their efficiency through adoption of the risk-return principle of granting loans. In addition, the stock market reforms enable Chinese firms to raise external capital by issuing shares and debts, rather than through bank loans.

Our analysis indicates that bank loans are still the major source of funding for Chinese enterprises despite their ability to issue equities in the financial markets. Besides bank loans, Chinese enterprises raise funds primarily through equity financing in terms of initial public offerings and seasonal offerings. The preference for issuing equities as compared to other financing mechanisms can be attributed to a number of factors: policy constraints (given the quota for equity issues), cost of equity considerations, market impediments, and bias in the preferences of major shareholders who control the firm.

Empirical Results on Corporate Financing

Singh (1995) examined financing patterns in the top listed manufacturing companies in ten developing countries and found that these firms depended heavily on external funds, especially new issues of shares. This result is at odds with the pecking order concept in the U.S. market and also with Mayer's findings concerning the financing patterns in developed countries (Mayer 1989, 1990). Table 12.1 shows the financing patterns in these ten developing countries, where equity financing is most important, followed by internal financing. Debt financing is the least important, with some exceptions such as in Korea, India, and Turkey.

It is also important to compare the financing choices between developing and developed countries. Table 12.2 compares the financing patterns between developed and developing countries. It illustrates two points. First, emerging market firms have a lower level of debts than firms in developed countries for 1994–2000. That is, the use of external equity financing among firms in developing countries is higher than that of developed market firms. Second, the use of current liabilities is similar in the two groups of countries; current

Table 12.1

Financing Patterns in Developing Countries (percentage of total)

	Mean			Median		
	Internal	Equity	Debt	Internal	Equity	Debt
Rep. of Korea	19.5	49.6	30.9	15.8	46.9	30.4
Pakistan	74.0	1.7	24.3	67.5	5.2	23.9
Jordan	66.3	22.1	11.6	54.8	25.5	6.8
Thailand	27.7	n/a	n/a	14.7	n/a	n/a
Mexico	24.4	66.6	9.0	23.1	64.7	1.0
India	40.5	19.6	39.9	38.1	16.3	38.9
Turkey	15.3	65.1	19.6	13.4	66.6	16.9
Malaysia	35.6	46.6	17.8	29.7	48.0	12.0
Zimbabwe	58.0	38.8	3.2	57.0	43.5	0.0
Brazil	56.4	36.0	7.7	46.0	37.2	5.6

Source: Singh (1995).

Table 12.2

Comparison of Financing Patterns Between Developed and Developing Countries

	1994	1995	1996	1997	1998	1999	2000
Total liabilities/total assets (%)							
Developed markets	59	56	56	56	56	55	56
Emerging markets	50	52	50	52	52	52	52
Non-current liabilities/ total assets (%)							
Developed markets	22	20	20	19	18	18	19
Emerging markets	17	17	17	17	16	15	17

Source: Glen and Singh (2003).

liabilities appear to fund a larger portion of total assets than long-term liabilities do in both groups.

The U.S. market represents the most advanced equity-based financial market. Table 12.3 shows financing patterns in the United States from 1980 through 1999 and demonstrates several key features of the U.S. capital structure. First, internally generated cash flow is the dominant source of financing, that is, about 70–90 percent of long-term financing comes from cash flow from operations. Second, borrowing or issuing new equity covers financial deficit, but the latter seems to be unimportant. Third, retained earn-

Table 12.3

Financing Patterns in the United States (percentage of total)

	1980	1985	1990	1995	1996	1997	1998	1999
Internal financing	65	83	77	67	87	79	81	70
External financing	35	17	23	33	13	21	19	30
New borrowing	31	36	36	42	23	35	51	47
New stock	4	−19	−13	−9	−10	−14	−32	−17

Source: Ross, Westerfield, and Jaffe (2002).

Table 12.4

Financing Patterns in Developed Countries (percentage of total)

Panel A: 1991–1996 Financing Patterns Across Developed Countries

	USA	Japan	UK	Germany	Canada	France
Internal financing	82.8	49.3	68.3	65.5	58.3	54.0
External financing	17.2	50.8	31.7	34.5	41.7	46.0

Source: Ross, Westerfield, and Jaffe (2002).

Panel B: Percentage of Financing Sources in Developed Countries

(% of total)	Canada	Finland	France	Germany	Italy	Japan	UK	USA
Retentions	76.4	64.4	61.4	70.9	51.9	57.9	102.4	85.9
Loans	15.2	28.1	37.3	12.1	27.7	50.4	7.6	24.4
Bonds	8.5	2.8	1.6	−1.0	1.6	2.1	−1.1	11.6
Shares	2.5	−0.1	6.3	0.6	8.2	4.6	−3.3	1.1
Others*	−2.6	4.8	−6.6	17.4	10.6	−15	−5.6	−23.0

*Others includes capital transfers, short-term securities, trade credits, and statistical adjustments.
Source: Mayer (1990).

ings increase faster than capital spending and the financial deficit is usually low. Finally, U.S. firms generate more internal financing sources than firms in other countries. Firms in other countries rely to a greater extent than U.S. firms on external equity.

Table 12.4 displays the financing patterns for several developed countries. The results reveal several interesting points. First, retained earnings or internal financing are the dominant source of financing in developed countries, especially in the U.K. and the United States. In the U.K., retentions are almost the only source of funds for investment. Second, the contribution of the securities market is very weak. In the United States, companies raised about 12.7 percent (Panel B, Table 12.4), a substantial amount compared to other countries, of financing from the securities market. Third, the stock markets in the U.K. and the United States have the lowest net funding contribution despite their well-developed capital markets. Finally, banks are an important source of external financing in all countries, especially in continental Europe and Japan, which are primarily bank-based economies.

Financing Activities in China

Sources of financing in China come in various forms: (1) Short-term financing obtained through cash management and credit management; (2) internal financing through retained earnings plus depreciation; and (3) external financing from such sources as debt financing like term loans and bonds, and equity financing like initial public offerings (IPOs), rights offerings, and public offerings

There are tradeoffs for each option of financing in terms of costs and benefits. For term loans, there is no China Securities Regulatory Commission (CSRC) registration requirement, but they are subject to inspection by banks along with restrictive clauses, collateral, guarantee, terms, size, monitoring, and governmental involvement. For bonds (corporate bonds or enterprise bonds, and convertible bonds), market timing, floatation terms, and interest rate risk are critical. With IPOs (A-shares, B-shares, H-shares, etc.), there are the benefits of flexibility of issue size, depending on the market, free usage, plus other advantages of going public, but these require a special approval process, high floating fees, information disclosure, ownership dilution, and reorganization prior to listing. For seasoned equity offerings (SEOs), a firm has to satisfy strict requirements, market sentiment, and receive approval from the CSRC. There are others financing options such as venture capital and leasing, and so on, but they are not the major sources for the time being.

Figure 12.1 shows the debt-to-asset ratios for five thousand large Chinese industrial firms over time. The total debt-to-asset ratios show a downward trend with about 57 percent in 2002, which is more in line with other developing countries in recent years (see Table 12.2) but is, of course, larger than that of developed countries.

Table 12.5 shows the capital structure in the financial statements of listed Chinese firms. The results indicate that leverage ratios are quite stable over years, and the debt ratio is about 45 percent, much lower than the percentage in Table 12.4, despite different study periods, implying listed firms are less burdened with debts. Through IPO and SEOs, equity financing is important.

Figure 12.1 **Liability to Asset Ratio: Change of Liability to Asset Ratio for 5,000 Large-Scale Industrial Enterprises in China**

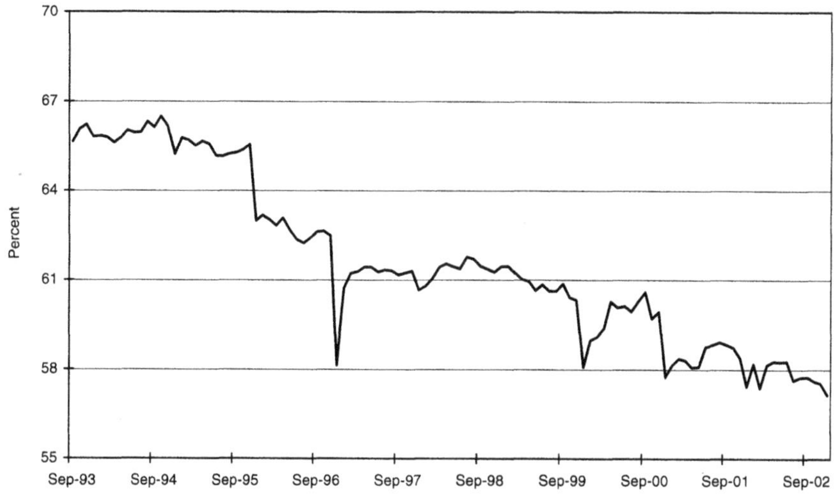

Source: CEIC, a Hong Kong–based data service provided by CEIC Data Company Ltd.

Table 12.5

Capital Structure of Listed Chinese Companies

	1998	1999	2000	2001	2002
Number of observations	1,130	1,289	1,330	1,340	1,331
Debt ratio (%)	43.83	45.87	44.53	45.13	45.71
Interest-bearing debt / total assets (%)	22.45	23.53	22.23	23.99	23.85
Bank loans / total assets (%)	22.39	23.31	22.09	23.99	23.67
Long-term liabilities / total assets (%)	3.09	2.72	2.86	2.94	2.77
Bank loans / total liabilities (%)	51.19	52.83	52.73	55.66	54.21
Long-term liabilities / total liabilities (%)	8.02	6.32	6.82	6.42	6.48
Trade credit / total liabilities (%)	7.30	7.00	6.41	6.52	7.71

Source: Genius Securities Information System, China, company data.
Note: The values presented are all medians; trade credit includes accounts payable and prepaid sales receipts.

The interest-bearing liabilities are almost exclusively bank loans. The long-term liabilities are only a trivial part of total assets (about 3 percent) or total liabilities (7 percent). Finally, bank loans account for more than half of total liabilities, implying that short-term accounts payables are important components of short-term liabilities.

Table 12.6 shows how the fixed asset investments of Chinese firms were

Table 12.6

Sources of Fixed Asset Investment in China, 1996–2002
(percentage of total)

	1996	1997	1998	1999	2000	2001	2002
State Budgetary Appropriation	2.68	2.76	4.17	6.22	6.37	6.70	7.02
Domestic Loans	19.58	18.93	19.30	19.24	20.32	19.06	19.67
Foreign Investment	11.76	10.63	9.11	6.74	5.12	4.56	4.63
Open Market Fundraising	53.15	54.95	51.76	53.39	52.16	52.39	50.64
Others	12.83	12.74	15.65	14.40	16.03	17.29	18.04

Source: CEIC, a Hong Kong–based data service provided by CEIC Data Company Ltd.

financed from 1996 through 2002. Fund-raising activities included retained earnings, stock offerings and bonds, and also due from related companies/parent company/government, among others. In this category, internal financing is critical. It seems clear that short-term bank loans, which make up about 20 percent of the fixed asset investment of Chinese firms, are used to finance long-term capital projects.

Table 12.7 shows a detailed analysis of the sources for financing fixed asset acquisitions in different types of enterprises in 2002. Individual enterprises relative to other enterprises rely much less on bank loans, reflecting the difficulty of obtaining these loans in China, while state-owned enterprises can get bank loans relatively easily. Collective enterprises and jointly owned enterprises rely more heavily on internal and external equity financing than do other types of firms.

Table 12.8 shows financing choices of Chinese firms according to the 2003 Monetary Policy Report (Q2) released by People's Bank of China. The results reveal several interesting points on the nature of external financing for Chinese enterprises from 2000 through 2003. First, bank loans were the dominant sources of external financing for non-financial enterprises and institutions (including enterprises and government bodies), and accounted for 70–80 percent of the total financing. Second, issuing government bonds was a major financing method for government bodies and accounted for about 15 percent of total financing. Third, financing through corporate bonds was minimal at about 1 percent. Finally, equity was an important yet erratic source of financing for enterprises after bank loans. In the year 2000 bull market, equity financing accounted for 12.25 percent of total financing, but in 2002, it accounted for only 4 percent.

Internal financing relies on earnings plus depreciation. Since People's Bank

Table 12.7

Sources of Fixed Asset Investment by Firm Type in 2002 (percentage of total)

	State-owned enterprises	Collective enterprises	Individual enterprises	Jointly owned enterprises	Share limited companies	Foreign invested enterprises	Special investment companies*	Others
State Budgetary Appropriations	14.24	6.87	0.02	0.34	1.01	0.23	0.12	1.94
Domestic Loans	24.39	10.56	9.96	15.93	23.81	16.99	21.18	11.80
Foreign Investment	2.20	4.46	0.23	0.60	2.15	37.51	22.05	3.02
Fundraising (Outside or Open Market?)	47.81	68.53	56.96	57.60	48.08	32.84	30.03	59.27
Others	11.37	9.58	32.83	25.53	24.94	12.43	26.62	23.97

*Special investment companies are foreign invested companies by investors from Hong Kong, Macao, and Taiwan.
Source: CEIC, a Hong Kong–based data service provided by CEIC Data Company Ltd.

Table 12.8

Capital Raised by Non-Financial Enterprises and Institutions

	2000	2001	2002	1st Half 2002	1st Half 2003
Capital raised (RMB billion)					
Total	1,716.3	1,655.5	2,397.6	1,073.4	2,127.2
Loans	1,249.9	1,255.8	1,922.8	866.7	1,903.3
Gov. Bonds	247.8	259.8	346.1	157.5	182.4
Corp. Bonds	8.3	14.7	32.5	7.5	6.5
Equity	210.3	125.2	96.2	41.7	35.0
Percentage of total					
Loans	72.83	75.86	80.20	80.74	89.47
Gov. Bonds	14.44	15.69	14.44	14.67	8.57
Corp. Bonds	0.48	0.89	1.36	0.70	0.31
Equity	12.25	7.56	4.01	3.88	1.65

Source: People's Bank of China publications, various issues.

Table 12.9

Capital Raised by Listed Chinese Companies (percentage of total)

	1998	1999	2000	2001	2002
Internal	19.61	20.93	17.08	15.89	11.42
External	80.39	79.07	82.92	84.11	88.58
Equity	14.80	11.70	14.96	9.40	5.82
Bond	0.29	0.44	0.08	0	0
Bank loans	64.15	64.82	60.94	73.69	81.13
Others	1.07	1.49	1.44	1.02	1.58

Source: Genius Securities Information System, company data, and *Taiwan Economic Journal* (TEJ), available at www.tei.com.tw

of China does not provide this information, we use information provided by *Taiwan Economic Journal* (TEJ). Table 12.9 shows the internal and external capital raised by listed Chinese companies. Note that the percentage is measured as capital raised through a specific method divided by the total funds raised during the year. Several points are noteworthy. First, the fraction of funds raised through internal sources decreased from 19.61 percent in 1998 to 11.42 percent in 2002. Two reasons contributed to the decrease: worsening operational performance and higher payout ratios. Second, the financing ability of the stock market fluctuated with the market status. Third, bank loans were the dominant source of financing, especially when the stock market could not function well. The corporate bond is practically zero in all years.

Table 12.10

**Capital Raised by Listed and Non-Listed Chinese
Companies** (RMB billion)

	1998	1999	2000	2001	2002
A-share IPOs	44.53	55.75	97.89	66.73	68.17
B-share IPOs	2.58	0.38	1.40	0	0
Rights issues	37.60	32.90	51.95	43.06	5.66
Public issues	4.92	5.59	27.49	13.47	18.92
H shares	3.82	4.71	56.20	7.03	18.19
Corporate bonds	14.79	15.82	8.3	14.7	32.5

Source: China Securities Regulatory Commission publications, various years.

Note: Corporate bonds include also convertible bonds and enterprise bonds issued by non-listed companies. Public offerings refer to seasoned equity offerings. H-share values include those shares traded in the U.S. market in the form of American Depository Receipts (ADRs).

Chinese Capital Markets

Equity Market

The equity market stands out as an important source of financing for businesses since 1990. The earliest stock issuance dates back to 1984, when Beijing Tianqiao and Shanghai Feile made an equity offering for the first time. By the end of 1990, the number of share companies increased substantially to over one hundred, and total capital raised approached RMB4.59 billion. In the late 1980s, trading centers came out in some large cities. To unify the markets, the authorities closed down these trading centers and established Shanghai Stock Exchange in December 1990 and Shenzhen Stock Exchange in July 1991. Table 12.10 shows the types and amounts of equity financings from 1998 through 2002. IPOs are the most important equity raising activity. Rights offerings were important before 2002 but the SEOs became more important in 2002. This is due to the change in regulatory stance of the Chinese government, which initially promoted rights offerings but later offered SEOs.

The equity market in China is purposely separated into tradable and nontradable shares. The tradable shares are those offered in the public marketplace through IPOs or SEOs at a premium over the net asset value, or offerings specially approved by the authorities. The nontradable shares are those held by promoters that are often government or government-authorized institutions and enterprises, and are sold to mutual funds and strategic investors. Tradable shares are further divided into tradable A-shares, B-shares,

Figure 12.2 **Shenzhen and Shanghai Composite Indices, 1991–2002**

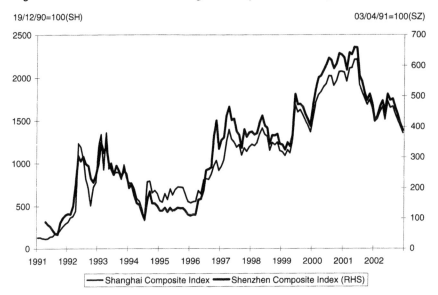

Source: Genius Securities Information System, company data, and *Taiwan Economic Journal* (TEJ), available at www.tei.com.tw

and H-shares. A-shares are priced in domestic currency (RMB), and traded in Shanghai or Shenzhen. B-shares are priced in foreign currency (U.S. or H.K. dollars) and also traded in Shanghai or Shenzhen. H-shares are offered to overseas investors and traded in Hong Kong, and many of them are also packed into American Depository Receipts and traded on the New York Stock Exchange (NYSE) or Global Depository Receipts (GDRs) to be traded in other markets. Figure 12.2 shows the trends of the Shanghai and Shenzhen composite indices.

A-Share Market

The capital-raising ability of the equity market has relied heavily on the performance of the secondary market. The peak years of the Chinese stock market were 1993, 1997, and 2000, and they also were the most active IPO periods. Table 12.11 reports the number and amount of the A- and B-shares issued from 1992 to 2002. In recent years, both types of shares issues have reduced substantially.

Table 12.12 reports the number and amount of rights issues along with seasoned equity offerings. Rights issues were prominent in 1997, 1998, 1999, 2000, and 2001, while public issues became noticeable starting in 2001 be-

Table 12.11

IPO Issues in China, 1992–2002

	A-share IPOs		B-share IPOs	
	Number	Capital raised (RMB bn)	Number	Capital raised (RMB bn)
1992	39	3.90	18	4.71
1993	125	17.36	23	5.03
1994	110	18.19	14	3.24
1995	24	2.28	13	2.83
1996	203	21.40	15	4.54
1997	206	59.85	18	8.24
1998	106	39.32	5	0.93
1999	98	49.12	2	0.38
2000	137	86.92	6	1.26
2001	79	59.73	0	0
2002	71	48.35	0	0

Source: Genius Securities Information System, company data.
Note: We compute the number and capital raised as the sum of firms listed in the year, and thus, they may be smaller than the CRSC reports in Table 12.9.

Table 12.12

Seasoned Equity Offerings in China, 1993–2002

	Rights issues		Public issues	
	Number	Capital raised (RMB bn)	Number	Capital raised (RMB bn)
1993	55	4.95	0	0
1994	61	4.58	1	1.08
1995	63	4.92	0	0
1996	46	7.10	0	0
1997	108	23.69	0	0
1998	152	36.47	8	3.05
1999	121	28.71	6	6.45
2000	168	53.36	25	22.70
2001	84	43.06	16	20.61
2002	19	5.63	32	21.89

Source: The data of 1993–2000 are from Fung, Leung, and Zhu (2002); the data of 2001–2002 are from Genius Securities Information System.

cause of relaxed restrictions by the Chinese government. The data in Table 12.10 and Table 12.12 are somewhat different because of the differences in sources and calculation methods.

Figure 12.3 **Capital Raised in the B- and H-Share Markets**

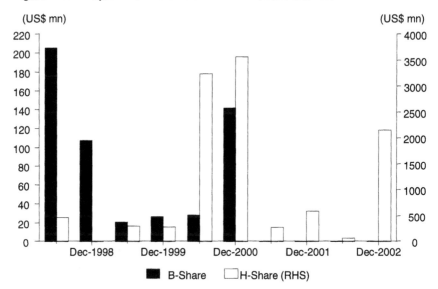

Source: Genius Securities Information System, company data, and *Taiwan Economic Journal* (TEJ), available at www.tei.com.tw

B-Share Market

The B-share market launched in 1992 provides a way for foreign investors to share in the growth of the Chinese economy in the form of equity ownership in the Chinese stock market. The B-share market was too narrow to meet the increasing financing needs of large SOEs. Since the successful IPO of Tsingtao Beer in the Hong Kong and New York markets in 1993, B-shares have had a depressed secondary market due to a lack of clear policies and funds inflow, and this has hampered the IPO activities in return. In February 2001, Beijing opened its B-share market to domestic investors to reactivate it. The new policy resulted in a threefold rally, but the market has headed down again along with the A-share market since June 2001.

Figure 12.3 shows that the capital raising ability of the B-share market is very weak compared to the Hong Kong and international markets. Equity offering activity has terminated since 2001. Low liquidity and low levels of transparency make B-shares a less favored investment vehicle.

Bond Market

Government bonds dominate the bond market, while corporate bonds account for only a very small proportion. Although the Chinese government

Table 12.13

Bond Market Summary, 1998–2002

	1998	1999	2000	2001	2002
Panel A: Number of bonds issues					
Treasury bonds	n.a.	15	15	16	16
Financial bonds (State Development Bank)	5	13	13	21	20
Financial bonds (Import & Export Bank)	3	3	4	7	7
CITIC bonds	0	0	0	1	1
Corporate bonds	29	29	5	5	n.a.
Total	37	60	36	48	44
Panel B: Value of bonds issued (RMB billion)					
New Issues					
Treasury bonds	380.88	401.50	465.70	488.40	593.40
Financial bonds*	195.02	180.09	164.50	259.00	307.50
Corporate bonds	14.79	15.82	8.30	14.70	32.50
Outstanding					
Treasury bonds	776.57	1054.20	1302.00	1561.80	1930.00
Financial bonds*	512.11	644.75	738.33	853.45	1005.40
Corporate bonds	67.69	77.86	86.16	100.86	133.36

*Financial bonds include bonds issued by the State Development Bank and Import & Export Bank.
Source: www.chinabond.com.cn (Panel A); CEIC Data Company Ltd. (Panel B).

tries to foster the bond market, there are many obstacles. They include: (1) regulations that give preferential treatment to T-bonds and privileged issuers, (2) investors' lack of understanding of risks and concern about fund flows in the market, and (3) the reluctance of firms to issue bonds for lack of independent rating agencies. The issuer may be allowed to decide the interest rate according to the covenants of the bond. Generally, coupon rates of corporate bonds have a cap of 140 percent of the deposit savings rate of the same maturity.

Table 12.13 shows the bond market statistics from 1998 through 2002. Panels A and B indicate that most of the bonds issued are government bonds. Corporate bonds play a minor and insignificant role in the bond market in terms of number of issues and values.

Table 12.14 shows the trading volume of bonds and common shares in

Table 12.14

Trading Volume of Securities in China, 1998–2002 (RMB billion)

	1998	1999	2000	2001	2002
A-shares	2,341.77	3,104.97	6,027.87	3,324.20	2,714.20
B-shares	12.85	27.00	54.80	506.31	84.80
Corporate Bonds*	6.10	9.91	22.80	10.29	12.12
Total bond market	2166.18	1829.05	1911.92	2040.62	3324.95

*Corporate bonds are those traded in the exchange market, while the total bond market includes treasury bonds (spot and repurchase) and corporate bonds in both the interbank bonds market and the exchange market.

Source: Genius Securities Information System, company data, and *Taiwan Economic Journal* (TEJ), available at www.tei.com.tw

Figure 12.4 **Lending Rates in China**

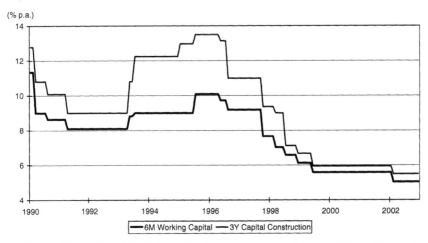

Source: Genius Securities Information System, company data, and *Taiwan Economic Journal* (TEJ), available at www.tei.com.tw

China. Clearly, government bond trading was the most important in 2002, while shares trading, which used to be the most important before 2000, has become less important because of the general market decline in share values.

Cost of Capital

Lending rates by banks have declined over time as shown in Figure 12.4. The rates include short-term as well as longer-term rates, indicating that the cost of business financing for Chinese business has decreased.

Table 12.15

The Mean and Median Values of ROE for the Listed Firms in China, 1997–2002

	1997	1998	1999	2000	2001	2002
Number of firms	511	708	812	909	1,040	1,101
Mean ROE (%)	6.96	5.38	5.53	4.13	2.52	1.41
Median ROE (%)	10.23	10.26	9.14	7.4	6.19	5.55

Source: Genius Securities Information System, company data.

Table 12.16

P/E Ratios in China, 1997–2002

	1997	1998	1999	2000	2001	2002
Shanghai A-shares	43.43	34.36	38.14	59.14	37.59	34.50
Shenzhen A-shares	42.66	32.31	37.56	58.74	40.76	38.21
Shanghai B-shares	11.99	6.04	10.05	25.23	43.39	30.61
Shenzhen B-shares	10.66	5.71	10.37	13.23	25.30	17.51

Source: Genius Securities Information System, company data, and *Taiwan Economic Journal* (TEJ), available at www.tei.com.tw

Assuming constant dividend growth, the cost of capital, k, is related to the price-earnings ratio (PER) according to the formula:

$$k = \frac{1 - RR}{PER} + g$$

where RR is the retention ratio and g is the growth rate of the dividend.

Firms in China are reluctant to pay cash dividends; therefore they have less cash burdens when funded through equity. Table 12.16 shows the gradual decline of price-earnings ratios for stocks in the two stock exchanges. Because of low dividend payout ratios and high P/E ratios, the first term in the above equation is almost negligible.[1] Table 12.15 shows the return on equity (ROE) and Table 12.16 shows the price-earning (P/E) ratios for 1997–2002. Because the growth rate of earnings theoretically equals the retention rate (RR) times return on equity (ROE), the worsening of ROE over time (as shown in Table 12.15) implies the cost of equity is decreasing. The decline of equity financing further motivates Chinese firms to fund their projects through equity issues.

Figure 12.5 **Stock Indices for Various Markets**

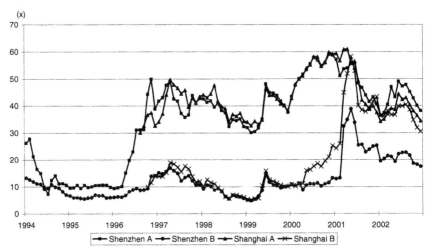

Source: Genius Securities Information System, company data, and *Taiwan Economic Journal* (TEJ), available at www.tei.com.tw

These results indicate that Chinese firms tend to raise capital through the equity market because they are less bound to cash payments and are subject to less restrictive monitoring, compared with bank loans and corporate bonds. The imbalance between equity supply and demand and separate share structure pushed stock prices in the secondary market high. The corporate bonds market is still far from developed due to a lack of legal framework and institutional structure.

In addition, the major shareholders in listed Chinese companies are nonfloatable shareholders, and they control the firms' operations. These shares can be traded by bilateral negotiations, typically at book values, but there is a huge discount of the book value relative to the market value of the traded shares. The major stockholders with nonfloatable shares can thus maximize their book values by issuing more outstanding shares in funding projects. That is, their goal can be accomplished by exploiting the liquidity premium (the price differential between floatable and nonfloatable shares). The conflict between major shareholders and minority shareholders has led to a bias toward continued equity financing (Huang and Fung 2004).

Conclusion

China appears to acquire equity over time and its total debt-to-asset ratios show a downward trend to about 57 percent in 2002 from the previous year, which is more in line with developing countries in recent years but is, of course, larger than theirs. In terms of external financing, bank loans are the dominant source, which accounts for 70–80 percent of all financing, followed by equity financing. Thus, China is, in fact, a bank-based financial system despite the economic changes that have taken place over the past twenty plus years.

The role of the stock market provides an important financing source for Chinese companies. IPOs are the most important equity-raising activity. Rights offerings were important before 2002, but SEOs became relatively more important in 2002. This is due to the change in regulatory stance of the Chinese government, which initially promoted rights offerings but later favored SEOs. In addition, because of the market segmentation of tradable and nontradable shares, the controlling shareholders of the nontradable shares prefer to issue tradable shares to increase the book value of their nontradable shares. This bias will favor equity issues over other financing options. Chinese firms do not typically give out cash dividends to shareholders because of cash constraints, implying a lower cost of equity. The bias in equity financing in China for the past many years, which resulted from financial reforms, is due to a number of factors, including declining equity costs, regulatory restrictions, and market segmentation between tradable and nontradable shares with price differentials. Of course, the regulatory policy changes have also affected the pattern of financing for Chinese firms.

Note

1. Chinese companies pay high stock dividends.

References

Fung, H.G., W.K. Leung, and Jiang Zhu. 2002. "Rights Issues in China: Development, Regulation, and Announcement Effects." Paper presented at the Midwest Finance Association Conference, Chicago.

Glen, Jack, and Brian Pinto. 1994. "Debt or Equity? How Firms in Developing Countries Choose." IFC discussion paper, no. 22, World Bank, Washington, DC.

Glen, Jack, and Ajit Singh. 2003. "Capital Structure, Rates of Return and Financing Corporate Growth: Comparing Developed and Emerging Markets, 1994–2000." Working paper, International Finance Corporation.

Huang, A.G., and H.G. Fung. 2004. "Stock Ownership Segmentation, Floatability, and Constraints on Investment Banking in China." *China and World Economy* 12, no. 2 (March–April): 66–78.

International Finance Corporation (IFC). 1991. "Financing Corporate Growth in the Developing World." IFC discussion paper, no. 12, World Bank, Washington, DC.

Mayer, Colin. 1989. "Myths of the West: Lessons from Developed Countries for Development Finance." World Bank working paper, no. 301, Washington, DC.

———. 1990. "Financial Systems, Corporate Finance and Economic Development." In *Asymmetric Information, Corporate Finance and Investment,* ed. R. Glen Hubbard. Chicago: University of Chicago Press.

Modigliani, F., and M. Miller. 1958. "The Cost of Capital, Corporation Finance, and the Theory of Investment." *American Economic Review* 48: 261–97.

Myers, S.C. 1984. "The Capital Structure Puzzle." *Journal of Finance* 39: 575–92.

Ross, Stephen A., Randolph W. Westerfield, and Jeffrey Jaffe. 2002. *Corporate Finance.* Homewood, IL: McGraw-Hill/Irwin.

Singh, Ajit. 1995. "Corporate Financial Patterns in Industrializing Countries: A Comparative International Study." IFC technical paper, no. 2, World Bank, Washington, DC.

13

The Debt Financing Gap for Small Business in China

Changwen Zhao and Kun Li

The development of small- and medium-sized enterprises (SMEs) is an issue attracting global attention. Since the 1980s, there has been a growing recognition that they play a key long-term role in creating jobs, initiating technological innovations, and enhancing competitiveness. In recent years, the Chinese government has paid more and more attention to start-ups and SMEs. The SMEs in China have become an important driving force for job creation and technological progress. However, their development in China is greatly held back by the disadvantageous position of SMEs in accessing financial resources.

Broadly speaking, there are two major financing resources for an enterprise: internal and external. Internal financing includes the initial equity investment, depreciation, and the capitalization of profits, while external financing is provided by the financial institutions and the capital market. The two resources have different implications with respect to capital cost, extent of risk, tax-shields, and corporate governance. Businesses should choose the optimal financing instrument and capital structure to maximize their market value.

The problem with SMEs is that external financing is often unavailable or only available in very limited ways. At the start-up stage, the problems of asymmetric information are most keenly felt by SMEs since they have no track record or credit history and little or no collateral (excluding that of the entrepreneur). Financing at this stage then is largely informal, either through personal financing (including that obtained from banks as personal debt) or private equity investment by outsiders. For a small portion of SMEs, in particular those with expected market potential, venture capital might be a possible alternative for funding. Over time, an improved credit history will allow them—assuming their continued viability—to borrow from banks and make larger lump-sum investments. Finally, for some very successful SMEs, the possibility of public equity financing will arise in the form of an initial public offering (IPO)—the favored exit strategy of venture capitalists. For the majority of SMEs, financial resources are very limited and growth is severely constrained by the financial gap. Basically, the financial gap is the shortage of capital supply compared with capital demand. The Macmillan Report that identified a chronic shortage of long-term capital for the smaller company was the first to use the financial gap concept (Macmillan 1931). It pointed out that the threshold for obtaining financing from financial institutions and the public capital market made it inaccessible to SMEs. Moreover, information asymmetry weakened the limited funds supply and widened the financing gap. Because business can finance either through debt instruments or equity instruments, if an SME has a "debt financing gap," it can make up for it with "equity financing," and the "equity financing gap" can be also covered by "debt financing." However, if the debt financing gap and the equity financing gap coexist, the SME will have great difficulty financing its operations. Unfortunately, this is the situation in China.

Literature Review

A large amount of research has been done on small business financing and, broadly speaking, it approaches the problem from the following perspectives:

Technological Innovation and External Financing from Financial institutions

Many studies show that external financing is the key for the development of SMEs, especially those involved in high-tech ventures. Financial innovation could greatly promote technological innovation and high-tech industrialization. Austrian economist Joseph A. Schumpeter emphasizes the close relationship between financing and innovation. He points out that the entrepreneur is not a capitalist. The entrepreneur's innovation efforts are unlikely to be actualized without external financing support. At the same time, the entrepreneur's failure to innovate could also put the financial institutions in a difficult position, even to the brink of bankruptcy (Schumpeter 1949). Morton Kamien and Nancy L. Schwartz provide some evidence for this argument (Kamien and Schwartz 1983). Entrepreneurial financing begins with the efforts of start-ups to utilize self-financing, for example, the personal savings of the entrepreneurs' friends and family. As firms grow up, they turn to financial institutions, especially banks, for their financing needs. John Bonin and Paul Wachtel (2003),

Amarnath Bhide (1999), and David G. Blanchflower, Andrew Oswald, and Alois Stutzer (2001) find that at certain critical stages in the development of high-tech start-ups, access to external sources of capital is necessary for both the firms' survival and growth.

Debt Financing and Equity Financing of SMEs

The existing research shows that SMEs at different stages of their life cycle have varying optimal financing choices. While private equity financing dominates the early stage investment, the increasing use of bank loans will become possible as the SMEs have established their credit history and consolidated their banking relationships (Cobham 1999).

Myers thinks that there are two types of corporate assets, that is, "assets already in place," and "growth opportunities." Growth opportunities can be viewed as call options. The value of such "real options" depends on discretionary future investment by the firm. Issuing risky debt reduces the present market value of a firm holding real options by inducing a suboptimal investment strategy or by forcing the firm and its creditors to bear the costs of avoiding the suboptimal strategy. Corporate borrowing is inversely related to the proportion of market value accounted for by real options (Myers 1977). Armen Hovakimian, Tim Opler, and Sheridan Titman find that due to the negative relationship between growth opportunities and target leverage predicted by tradeoff theories, high market-to-book firms have low target debt ratios and, therefore, are more likely to issue equity and less likely to issue debt (Hovakimian, Opler, and Titman 2001).

The Causes of the Debt Financing Gap for SMEs

Latimer Asch thinks that SMEs, especially high-tech SMEs, are always neglected by the banks and other financial institutions. Compared with large companies, the small loan volume for SMEs makes the marginal costs of the financial institutions higher, even reducing marginal profit to zero. In addition, the high failure rate of SMEs makes banks reluctant to make loans to them (Asch 2000). Loans to small businesses have historically been very costly because of the paucity of information about small firms and the high personnel costs required to obtain the information (Petersen and Rajan 2002). Small banks are a primary source of credit for small businesses. Unlike large, publicly traded firms, which have access to capital markets, small businesses rely heavily on bank loans. These small businesses often borrow from financial institutions with which they have established long-term relationships that prove mutually beneficial. This long relationship enables banks to assess the borrower's ability to repay at a lower cost, reducing the cost of information collection. Borrowers, in turn, enjoy better access to credit and lower borrowing costs. Small banks make more of these "relationship" loans than do large banks (Strahan and Weston 1998). Thus, there is a very strong correlation between bank size and loans to small business (Strahan and Weston 1998). In addition, the consolidation of banks can hurt small businesses and young firms by reducing the incentive for banks to forge long-term relationships with SMEs (Strahan and Weston 1998). Finally, it is more difficult for small businesses to acquire loans in areas of high bank concentration than in other regions (Myers 1984).

Akerlof uses the "lemons" market for used cars to illustrate how sellers of good quality cars can use a warranty to signal quality to buyers who cannot otherwise distinguish between good cars and lemons (Akerlof 1970). Zhong and Qian have shown that due to the high risk of SMEs, banks usually lack incentives to make loans if the interest rate is controlled. If the interest rate is not controlled, it will drive out some high-quality customers and the loan market could get into a "lemon market" when banks set the interest rate too high. So, the best choice for SME financing is equity financing (Zhong and Qian 2001).

How to Ease the Financing Gap of SMEs

Many studies emphasize the importance of developing small banks and other financial institutions with information advantages in making loans to small businesses. Becattini (1990) analyzed the role of local banks in easing access to credit. Local banks have more information about local people, local projects, and local firms because of their long-term relationships with the community. Actually, "being local" could help banks in carrying out lending activity, particularly in the evaluation of borrowers' risk factors beforehand and in the monitoring of borrowers retroactively to prevent moral hazard (Stiglitz and Weiss 1981). Banks operating in a local community can easily gather more information on borrowers, thus reducing problems of adverse selection. Besides, long-term interaction and peer monitoring hypotheses believe that a long-term relationship between small businesses and banks will reduce the loan risks through peer monitoring (Banerjee, Besley, and Guinnane 1994). One of the reasons for SMEs' debt financing difficulties in China is the mismatch of size between financial institutions and SMEs, that is, because there are very few small banks in China. Thus, the best way to resolve SME financing difficulties in China is by developing non-state-owned financial institutions (Lin and Li 2001).

The Debt Financing Gap of SMEs in China

The experience of many countries demonstrates that access to credit is vital for the survival of small businesses. Basically, China is a bank-based finan-

Table 13.1

Distribution of Financial Resources in China's Financial Institutions and Capital Market

Year	Number of listed companies	Total market capitalization as a eercentage of GDP	Total loans by financial institutions	The ratio of total loans to GDP
1990	10	0.07	17,680.7	89.98
1991	14	0.50	21,337.8	92.64
1992	53	4.40	26,322.9	91.97
1993	183	9.40	32,943.1	100.51
1994	291	8.00	40,810.1	92.18
1995	323	6.00	50,538.0	91.20
1996	530	14.30	61,152.8	97.83
1997	745	24.37	74,914.1	106.77
1998	851	24.50	86,524.1	121.80
1999	949	32.26	93,734.3	130.60
2000	1088	53.79	99,371.1	127.36
2001	1160	45.37	112,314.70	136.34
2002	1224	37.43	128,627.75	125.62

Source: Based on data from *China Financial Yearbook* (2002), *China Statistical Yearbook* (2002), and People's Bank of China.

cial system and its capital market is still in a primitive stage of development. The share of market capitalization, that is, capitalization through issuance of bonds and stocks, is only 37.4 percent of GDP—a very low level compared with developed countries. By contrast, the ratio of total loans to GDP in 2002 was 125.6 percent, so clearly banks and other financial institutions are the main financing channels for SMEs.

However, given their leading role in SMEs' external financing, banks rarely meet the fund demands of SMEs. Many of these businesses cannot get bank loans even if they can provide collateral or are willing to accept higher interest rates. The International Finance Corporation (IFC) shows that SMEs are disadvantaged in debt financing compared with big enterprises. The failure rate of their loan applications is 23 percent, while only 12 percent for big enterprises. According to the government report, the loans to SMEs represents only 8 percent of the total loan amount, which mismatches the role of SMEs in the Chinese economy (one-third of the GNP, two-thirds of the added value of industry, 38 percent of exports, and one-fourth of the national fiscal income). We can also see the difficulties in obtaining financing for SMEs in the sample survey shown in Table 13.2.

Table 13.2 reports that the main financing channel for a sample survey of enterprises is internal financing and commercial credit, while bank loans only

Table 13.2

The Capital Structure of Enterprises in China, October 1999–October 2000 (%)

Size*	Equity	Earnings retained	Informal equity	Bank loans	Credit cooperative loans	Consumption credit	Informal credit	Listed stocks	Bonds
≤50	36.7	21.3	2.3	13.5	6.8	12.4	6.2	0.8	0
51–100	42.3	13.9	6.2	5.4	8.3	15.4	8.5	0	0
100–500	32.2	11.8	4.4	20.6	7	18.5	4.8	0.7	0
≤501	27.7	10.3	0.8	22.6	6.6	27.8	2.7	0.9	0.6
	19.3	15.2	0.4	47.1	2	13.5	0	1.4	1.1

Source: Survey from managers of 352 companies in Beijing, Tianjin, Hebei, and Zhejiang (Li, Wang, and He 2000).
*The size of the enterprise, in RMB10,000, using US$1 = RMB8.2.

Table 13.3

**Rejected Business Loan Applications in China,
October 1999–October 2000** (percent)

Size*	Cases of application	Number of applications	Cases of applications rejected	RC/AC	Number of applications rejected	RN/AN
≤50	736	1,537	478	64.95	1,213	78.92
50–100	360	648	203	56.39	375	57.87
101–500	159	507	65	40.48	224	44.18
≥501	46	152	12	26.09	37	24.34
Total	1,301	2,844	758	58.26	1,849	65.01

Source: Survey from managers of 352 companies in Beijing, Tianjin, Hebei, and Zhejiang (Li, Wang, and He 2000).
*The size of the enterprise, in RMB10,000, using US$1 = RMB8.2.

account for a very small portion. Moreover, Table 13.3 shows that the failure rate for loan applications of SMEs is higher than that of larger companies.

Table 13.4 reports the survey results of successful loan applications. The success rate of small business is roughly 77 percent, while the success rate of the big enterprise is 88 percent. Meanwhile, SMEs make fewer loan applications because they know banks seldom lend money to small businesses. The IFC reported a similar situation: the success rate for loan applications is negatively correlated with firm size.

The financing difficulties for SMEs in China are attributed to many causes, some of which are the same as in other countries and some of which are specific to China. In the following sections we discuss the major factors involved.

Information Asymmetry, Moral Hazard, and Adverse Selection

Information asymmetry and moral hazard are common problems banks face when making loans to firms. However, these problems are particularly serious when making loans to SMEs. While there are usually many public sources for information on large firms, reliable information on SMEs is essentially internal and unavailable to outsiders, including external creditors. Due to an underdeveloped credit system, the problems of information asymmetry and moral hazard in China are more serious than in other countries. It is almost impossible for banks to make loans to SMEs based only on audited financial statements they have submitted, because the SMEs will only provide favorable information and try to hide facts which would not be favorable for borrowing. To get loans, they may even cheat the banks. Banks usually lack a

Table 13.4

Business Applications for Bank Loans in China, October 1999–October 2000

Enterprise size	Number of enterprises	Application rate (percentage)	Number of applications	Number of approvals	Success rate (percentage)	Loan size*
≤50	235	0.17	209	159	0.76	1048.1
51–100	72	0.46	274	214	0.78	478.8
101–500	82	0.63	449	391	0.87	634.5
≥501	29	0.83	227	199	0.88	2282.6

Source: Survey from managers of 352 companies in Beijing, Tianjin, Hebei, and Zhejiang (Li, Wang, and He 2000).
*In RMB10,000, using US$1 = RMB8.2.

long-term relationship with and/or reliable information resources for small businesses. Thus, they are very reluctant to make loans to SMEs.

To compensate for the higher risk involved in SME loans, banks may charge higher interest rates. Because banks cannot differentiate between good projects and bad projects, the uniform high interest on SME loans will cause the projects with lower risks to pull out of the loan market, and the remaining loan applications are usually projects with higher risks. Thus, at high interest rates, banks are aware that borrowers with low-risk projects will not apply for loans, and that the borrowers who do apply are always at risk of default. A high interest rate results in adverse selection. Consequently, banks reduce the number of loans to SMEs; the result is that they may still not be able to get loans from banks even if they are willing to accept a higher interest rate.

In China, the SMEs usually are classified at the D level in credit assessment by the Bank of China (BOC), one of the "big four" state commercial banks, no matter what the enterprise's innovation ability and market competitiveness are. So it is not a fair playing field for SMEs. In the words of Zingales: "Empirically, the emphasis on large companies has led us to ignore the rest of the universe: the young and small firms, who do not have access to public markets" (Zingales 2000).

Return and Cost Asymmetry of Banks

The high cost of SME lending is the main barrier to reducing the financing gap for SMEs. For instance, U.S. banks apply the same procedures and criteria they use in lending to big businesses to SME loan applications. Studies by lending associations have shown that the so-called "Manual Underwriting"—collecting and checking the financial statements and other labor-intensive work—takes at least twelve hours and costs between US$500 to $1,800. As a result, SME lending is not viewed as a profitable business (Asch 2000). In China, the failure rate of loans to high-tech SMEs is above 80 percent and the ratio of partial failure to complete failure is 6:2 (Qian 2001). Given these figures, we estimate that banks can make a profit only if the net difference between the banks' lending rate to high-tech SMEs and the banks' cost of capital is at least 7 percent, but the difference is only 4 percent in China now. Thus, if banks make loans to high-tech SMEs, the banks will average a negative return.

From a sample survey, SMEs' frequency of applying for loans is five times higher than big firms, while the average amount of loans to SMEs is only 0.5 percent of that to big companies. The information and management costs for banks on SME loans is 5–8 times as large as that on loans to big businesses. In China, the interest rates are tightly controlled by the government. Although banks are allowed to fluctuate their loan rates within a small range, they are not allowed to raise them high enough to cover their costs in the case of SME lending. This severely discourages banks from making the loans.

Lack of Guarantees and Collateral for Loans

Loan guarantees can be used as an alternative to collateral to secure bank loans. The providers of loan guarantees may include governments, other companies, and guarantee agencies. To promote the development of SMEs, governments in many countries offer loan guarantees to SMEs that have market potential but fail to meet the criteria for collateral loans. The 7(a) plan of the United States, the Loan Guarantee Scheme (LGS) of the United Kingdom, and SOFARIS of France are all credit guarantee projects sponsored by governments.

In fact, in addition to the above-mentioned countries, nearly 50 percent of the countries and regions in the world have also established systems of credit guarantees to provide capital support for SMEs. The U.S. Small Business Administration offered guarantees for US$31 billion in SME loans through the 7(a) plan during the ten years from 1980 to 1991. During the ten years from 1991 to 2000, the SBA helped 435,000 SMEs obtain US$94.6 billion in guaranteed loans (SBA 2001). Although the number of cases and total sum of the LGS in the United Kingdom are smaller than those in America, still credit guarantees were provided for £206 million in loans to 4,279 SMEs from 1999 to 2000. It has been proven that the system of credit guarantees can effectively lessen the debt financing gap for SMEs.

As a transition economy, China is trying hard to separate government functions from market functions. Thus, government guarantees for business loans are not encouraged. Private guarantees are limited to SMEs with special relationships. These include guarantees provided by large shareholders or private venture investors. Some intermediary credit guarantee agencies have been recently established, but they have relatively fewer resources and little experience, and need more time before they can really play a significant role. By 2000, there were twenty-eight provinces in China where small business credit guarantee agencies had developed, and seventy cities where small business credit guarantee agencies were set up, through which over RMB4 billion devoted to SME guarantees was collected (Chen and Guo 2000). However, the total number of SME loans through credit guarantee agencies is still considerably small, and most small businesses still cannot find guarantee providers. Therefore, the ratio of credit guarantee loans of big commercial banks in China continues to decline and the ratio of collateral loans keeps rising.

In China, collateral is the major form of loan security. However, many companies do not have the ability to provide enough collateral for loans, especially SMEs at the expansion stage. In an unpublished survey conducted by the Bank of Shanghai in 2001, about two-thirds of the responding companies considered collateral the main obstacle to obtaining bank loans. This problem is even more serious for high-tech enterprises because their working capital and intangible assets make up a large part of the total assets. When making loan decisions, banks often emphasize the value of collaterals over the borrower's prospects for making profits. Banks accept different kinds of collaterals, including land and buildings and housing and saving certificates convertible to cash, but the discount rate of collaterals is fairly high. The collateral rate of land and real estate is about 70 percent, 50 percent for machinery, and 10 percent for special equipment. In addition, collateral appraisal services are not well regulated and the value of collaterals is highly affected by the subjectivity of the people who perform the appraisal.

Financial Depression Effect

Interest Rate Effect

Fundamentally, the financial gap existing in SMEs in China is due to financial depression. Because the interest rate is controlled below the equilibrium level, it cannot reflect the real status of capital supply and demand, and this results in excessive demand and capital supply shortages. It is reasonable for financial institutions to charge higher interest rates or fees when they offer loans to SMEs to compensate for the higher loan cost and the higher risk involved. In the United States, the interest rate charged by middle and small banks for SME loans is about 1–1.5 percentage points higher than that charged by big banks to big enterprises. At equilibrium, the interest rate of SME loans is higher than the average market rate. However, the regulations on interest rates and fees do not allow banks in China to provide loans to SMEs at an equilibrium market interest rate. The controlled interest rate is always lower than the equilibrium market interest rate. A survey conducted by the IFC in 2000 shows that the average interest rate in the non-official financial market in China is 100 to 200 percent higher than the official interest rate. To some extent, this explains why most financial institutions are unwilling to offer loans to SMEs. The controlled loan rate fails to reflect the difference of credit level between the big and small companies.

In China, interest rates on deposits and loans are fixed by the government and commercial banks do not have the right to charge different loan rates to different customers. The only thing the commercial banks can do is to reduce the number of loans approved (i.e., credit rationing) to avoid possible losses, and this leads to difficult SME financing. From the above analysis, we can see that interest rates do not function well to bridge the demand and supply of capital in the credit loan markets for Chinese SMEs. Besides, the risk of adverse selection makes banks unwilling to make loans solely based on interest rate considerations, even if borrowers are willing to accept higher interest rates and banks have loan-making capacity.

Institutional Effect

Compared to developed countries, indirect financing for Chinese businesses has its own unique feature: the four state-owned commercial banks control most of the financial resources in China, while the small and medium financial institutions remain less developed. Although the proportion of the assets of state-owned banks in the Chinese banking industry has decreased from 83.6 percent in 1995 to 67.9 percent in 2001, they still monopolize the banking sector. The remaining twelve commercial banks account for 9.4 percent, 4,500 rural credit cooperatives 9.4 percent, 90 urban credit cooperatives 4.4 percent, and other financial institutions 8.9 percent. Moreover, the four state commercial banks also monopolize the business in settlement and foreign exchange. As a result, the behaviors of the major state commercial banks have a direct impact on SME financing.

Chinese state commercial banks have begun their reform. However, because the ownership of state banks and state-owned enterprises is essentially the same, and the government has not established an effective state-owned assets management system, the state-owned banks behave differently when they make loans to state-owned businesses and non-state-owned businesses. When the state-owned banks make loans to state-owned enterprises, they do not consider the risks much because they expect that the government will bail them out if these loans end up with losses and that the risks will be transferred ultimately to central finance. This is shown clearly in the bankruptcy policies of state-owned enterprises (SOEs). However, when state-owned banks are deciding whether or not to make loans to private SMEs, they tend to be too cautious because they cannot transfer the risks to the government (according to the current law, non-performing loans to private companies and foreign companies cannot be written off). Meanwhile, since 1999, the state commercial banks began to establish a responsibility system and loan makers are required to be responsible for the consequences of their loan-making decisions. This will inevitably make lenders more cautious when making loan decisions—and thus increase the difficulties of SME financing.

If we look at the organization of banks, the United States has a long history

Table 13.5

Distribution of Assets, Deposits, and Loans by Type of Financial Institution in 2001 (%)

Type of financial institution	Assets	Loans	Deposits
Banks	77.30	80.63	78.89
State banks	67.90	69.55	66.80
Other banks	9.40	11.08	12.09
Non-banks	23.70	19.37	21.11
Urban credit cooperatives	9.40	5.29	5.95
Rural credit cooperatives	4.40	12.26	13.16
Others	8.90	1.82	2.00
Total	100.00	100.00	100.00

Source: Based on *China Financial Yearbook* (2002) and data from People's Bank of China.

of a unit banking system and several dozen large banks coexist with more than 3,000 small banks. U.S. small banks are more willing to make loans to SMEs than large banks because, on the one hand, they do not have enough capital for making loans to big businesses, and, on the other hand, they have advantages of information collection for SME financing. Chinese banks follow the branch system, and every state-owned bank has from 3,000 to 5,000 branches and the number of independent small local banks is very limited. None of the big national banks regard SMEs as their main customers. Moreover, they do not have advantages of information in making loans to SMEs.

The Effects of Bank Reconstruction on SME Financing

Although the reconstruction of Chinese state banks just began, it has already shown important effects on business financing and economic development. After the 1997 Asian financial crisis, China speeded up the progress of reforming its banking system. In early 1998, the People's Bank of China (PBOC), the central bank, canceled the quota controls for bank loans and replaced them with asset/liability management. In 1998, with the help of the United States, the Chinese government adopted a new credit classification system that is based on the likelihood of default. The new system classifies the bank loans into five categories: Normal, Needing Special Attention, Abnormal, Doubtful, and Loss. Following the practice of the Federal Reserve System of the United States, China merged the provincial branches of the PBOC into nine regional branches in 1999 so as to reduce local government intervention on loan decisions.

At the same time, the government adopted several measures to lower the proportion of state banks' non-performing loans (NPLs) and to control the growth of new NPLs. For example, in 1998 the Chinese government issued RMB270 billion in special government bonds to increase the state banks' capital. The recapitalization increased the core capital ratio of the Big Four by 4.7 percent on average and made them meet the criteria of the Basel Accord. In 1999, in order to help the Big Four, the Chinese government set up four asset management companies (AMCs) to deal with the NPLs. Each AMC took care of one bank. By the middle of 2000, the transfer of NPLs was completed and a total volume of NPLs worth RMB1.4 trillion had been transferred to the four AMCs. According to the statistics of the PBOC, by the end of 2002 the four AMCs had disposed of a total of RMB301 billion NPLs (not including the policy-oriented shares converted from debt), reclaimed assets of RMB101 billion, including RMB67 billion in cash. The proportion of reclaimed assets and reclaimed cash are 33.6 percent and 22.4 percent (PBOC 2003) respectively. The proportion of NPLs in the portfolio of the four state commercial banks was 25.4 percent by the end of 2002, reaching RMB2.2 trillion.

Based on historical experiences, during the bank reconstruction period the loans to businesses will decrease sharply. For instance, from 1989 to 1992, U.S. domestic commercial loans decreased by 23 percent (Berger, Kyle, and Scalise 1999). This was also what happened during the Asian Financial Crisis as shown in Table 13.6. There are two factors that cause banks to reduce their loans during reconstruction: the high ratios of NPLs in the reconstructed banks and tight government regulations on their loans. As China just began the reconstruction of its banking system, the difficulties for SMEs in obtaining loans will last for some years to come.

Several Possible Choices to Reduce and Eliminate the Debt Financing Gap

Chinese SMEs face both serious equity financing gaps and debt financing gaps at the same time. Thus, it is impossible for SMEs to shift to equity financing when debt financing fails to meet their capital needs. Besides the separation between the money market and the capital market, the underdevelopment of the capital market also determines that measures to eliminate the debt financing gap for SMEs are limited.

Theoretically, there are three ways to reduce the gap of debt financing for the SMEs. First would be to increase interest rates to balance the capital supply and demand. However, in practice, this would not necessarily push financial institutions to make loans to the SMEs due to the possibility of adverse selection. The second way would be to reduce the capital demands

Table 13.6

The Growth Rate of Bank Loans in Some Asian Countries and Areas (%)

	1990–1995	1996	1997	1998
Indonesia	19	12	20	−26
Hong Kong	6	7	17	−8
Korea	11	12	15	−7
Malaysia	14	24	21	−1
Philippines	13	40	27	−12
Singapore	13	15	11	0
Thailand	20	12	9	−12
Japan	2	1	−1	−1

Source: Hawkins and Turner (1999).

of SMEs at the present interest rate level through measures such as more restrictive loan criteria, but this would constrain the innovation and development of SMEs. A third possibility would be to increase the effective supply of capital to buffer the financing gap. At present, the last is the most feasible choice and it can be done in the following ways.

Reducing and Eliminating the Gap by the Government

The debt financing gap for SMEs indicates that they are facing a problem of market failure. Therefore the government may take some actions to correct the failure. In fact, the experiences of many countries show that the government may play an active role in the development of SMEs.

Policy-Oriented Banks and Public Investment Funds

It is very common for governments to build purported financial institutions to provide low-interest loans to SMEs. For instance, in Japan, there are financial institutions such as the Japanese SMEs financial pool, the national financial pool, the merchant and industry financial pool, the environmental financial pool, and so forth, most of which are wholly financed by the government and make medium- and long-term loans to SMEs at a favorable interest rate two or three percentage points below the market level. German banks also provide long-term fixed rate loans through a venture capital support plan. Canadian Federal Commercial Development Banks, South Korean SMEs Banks, and Singapore Pacific Financial Company are all these types of institutions. Although there are three policy-oriented banks in China, that is, the National Development Bank, the Chinese Import and Export Bank, and the Chinese Agricultural Development Bank, they all have their special mission and none have a direct relationship with SME financing.

In many cases, government support takes the form of venture capital. The British government set up its regional venture fund and high-tech fund in 1998. The former finances the SMEs directly through equity investment, and the latter invests in special funds or venture funds, which, in turn, invest in SMEs. By 1999, the high-tech fund had invested over £20 million and attracted another £77 million. In China, there are two types of government-sponsored funds targeting SMEs. The first takes the form of development funds and provides loan support to SMEs, the most important of these being the Innovation Fund for Small Technology-based Firms (IFSTF). The second type takes the form of venture funds. The development funds tend to provide support to the less developed regions, while the venture funds provide commercial investment. At present, the size of these funds is still small and their operations often lack efficiency.

From Tables 13.7 and 13.8, we can see that there are two problems with government-sponsored funds. First, the total investment of government funds and the number of supported projects are still small. Second, most of the investments take the form of interest-free loans, which often result in the low efficiency of the projects and rent-seeking behavior by government officials.

Government Guarantee Plans

In some countries, the government has established special institutions to facilitate SME financing. These institutions cooperate with banks and nongovernmental investors to provide loan guarantees for the SMEs. The Small Business Administration (SBA), established in 1953 by the U.S. government, is an example. The SBA has ninety-six branches and cooperates with 7,000 commercial banks to provide 75–80 percent of the guarantees of the total loan amounts for SME loans, and the length of maturity is up to twenty-five years. For the British small company loan plan, the length of maturity can be as long as ten years, the amount up to £250,000, and the guarantee ratio 85 percent. The "SMEs development plan," the "SMEs investment capital plan," and the "SMEs current capital plan" by the Indonesian government since 1973 are all plans of this nature.

The Chinese government may learn from the experiences of other countries and invest more in governmental funds to provide loan support for SMEs. The funds can be invested in high-tech start-ups as seed capital, or used to provide loan guarantees for the SMEs. The support from the government will effectively reduce the transaction cost between the SMEs and the banks, making banks more willing to provide these loans. In addition, in selected

Table 13.7

The Size of the Innovation Fund for Small Technology-Based Firms

	Year 1999				Year 2000			Total
	1st Qtr	2nd Qtr	3rd Qtr	4th Qtr	1st Qtr	2nd Qtr	3rd Qtr	
Total investment (RMB million)*	102.22	140.78	213.48	359.04	141.31	172.29	153.01	1282.13
The number of projects	125	205	277	481	188	230	198	1703
Average investment in one project (RMB million)*	0.8178	0.6867	0.7707	0.7464	0.7516	0.7491	0.7732	0.7529

Source: Innovation Fund for Small Technology-Based Firms, Management Center, Ministry of Science and Technology, Beijing.
*US$1 = RMB8.2.

Table 13.8

Investments of Innovation Funds for Small Technology-Based Firms

	Year 1999				Year 2000			Total
	1st Qtr	2nd Qtr	3rd Qtr	4th Qtr	1st Qtr	2nd Qtr	3rd Qtr	
Discounted loans								
Number of projects	54	71	84	122	33	32	42	438
Investment (RMB million)*	47.85	53.28	65.25	98.51	27.50	27.70	34.81	354.90
Interest-free loans								
Number of projects	71	134	193	359	155	198	156	1,266
Investment (RMB million)*	54.37	87.50	148.23	260.53	113.81	144.59	118.20	927.23
Proportion of interest-free loans								
Project(%)	54.80	65.37	69.68	74.64	82.45	86.09	78.79	74.34
Investment (%)	53.19	62.15	69.44	72.56	80.54	83.92	77.25	72.32

Source: Innovation Fund for Small Technology-Based Firms, Management Center, Ministry of Science and Technology, Beijing.
*US$1 = RMB8.2.

cities the government has established an SMEs Financing Company (SMFC), which is financed partly by the government and partly by bank loans. SMFC invests in selected SMEs, playing an intermediary role between them and the commercial banks. The government provides guarantees to bank loans borrowed by SMFC, but not on loans made by SMFC to SMEs.

Developing the Non-State-Owned Small Banks and Non-Bank Financial Institutions

The traditional commercial bank is very careful about lending to SMEs due to the high risk involved. Based on international experiences, small banks are more prone to lend to SMEs. However, small banks and small and medium non-bank financial institutions (SMNFI) are rare in China. There are about eighty urban commercial banks, urban credit cooperatives, and rural credit cooperatives providing certain financial support to the local SMEs. But even for this small number of banks, many of them do not focus their business on SME loans, and problems like unclear ownership, inefficient corporate governance, and interference from the local government harm their operation efficiency. The Chinese Minsheng Bank, which is positioned as a bank serving the local SMEs, is too small to fill in the huge gap between capital demand and supply. The existing small and medium financial institutions in China are far from meeting the capital needs of SMEs. To ease up the difficult situation of SME financing, more small banks and SMNFI targeting SMEs should be established as soon as possible to provide financial services to this business segment.

For the time being, Chinese small banks and SMNFI are under integration and many of them are eager to get rid of historical NPLs and improve their liquidity. This may make them reluctant to make loans to SMEs. However, the experience of the United States shows that the integration of small banks and SMNFI will improve lending to SMEs in the long run. So by accelerating the integration process, small banks and SMNFI would be able to play a more active role in reducing the SME financing gap.

The Reform and Innovation of the State-Owned Commercial Banks

The reform of the state banks should target improvement of corporate governance and gradually phase out interest rate control. At the present time, the PBOC fixes the uniform interest rate that all banks must follow, only allowing fluctuations within a very small range. Thus, the official bank loan rate is often much lower than the rate prevailing in the non-official capital market. The basic solution to the problem of SME financing is to let the market decide the interest rate.

Only when banks can decide interest rates and service fees by themselves can they increase lending to SMEs and optimize financial resource allocations.

The innovation of debt financing is another possible choice for increasing bank loans to SMEs. Innovation can be applied in the following areas:

1. Innovation of guarantees and collateral. The bank can control the risk of loans made to SMEs by developing new forms of collateral and guarantees or making more flexible use of existing forms of guarantees and collateral.
2. The half-floor investment. Banks may introduce some mechanisms of venture fund investment, for example, the half-floor strategy. The half-floor investment targets customers at the expansion stage, that is, customers who need capital to expand their production but still need some time for realizing profit. With the risk properly controlled, the half-floor investment may significantly expand bank business and provide substantial support to SMEs.
3. Financial leasing. Studies show that leasing is a very important external financing channel for SMEs. One study by City University Business School in the U.K showed that, in the UK, 19 percent of the total liabilities in the balance sheet in half of the SMEs was in the form of financial leasing. Another study by the UK SMEs Commercial Investigation Center disclosed that 36 percent of the SMEs made use of financial leasing in 1999. Financial leasing is still a new instrument for most Chinese SMEs and, according to international experiences, there should be room for expansion for this form of financing.
4. The credit rating system. Commercial banks should improve their present credit rating mechanism and decentralize their loan-making decisions. More specifically, they should establish a separate credit rating system for SMEs. The existing credit rating system, which focuses on the present status of the business and ignores potential future cash flow, treats all businesses with the same criteria. This puts the SMEs, especially those involved in high-tech operations, at a disadvantage because innovation takes a long time and during this process they cannot be as profitable as mature companies.

The World Trade Organization and Its Impact on SME Financing

China's entry into the World Trade Organization (WTO) shows its determination to build a market economy and further open up to the outside world.

This will undoubtedly bring great changes to Chinese society and have important implications for SME financing. There are major challenges as well as opportunities. Accession to the WTO has led China to open its potentially huge domestic market. The SMEs in China are facing competition not only from domestic producers, but also from producers all over the world. The pressure of fiercer competition will force the SMEs to improve and upgrade their production to better meet the demands of consumers. This will increase their financing needs.

But the major changes emanating from the WTO agreement will be conducive to the mitigation of the SME financing difficulties. The improvement of the legal and institutional framework of the financial sector and the increasing competition resulting from the entrance of foreign banks and the establishment of more domestic private banks will lead to the application of market-oriented financing instruments, the linking of the small enterprise sector to the formal capital markets, the introduction of innovative financing techniques such as leasing, factoring, and securitization, and the introduction of new and variable techniques for securing loans. These will hopefully open up more channels for SME financing and reduce the debt financing gap.

Conclusion

1. SMEs will continue to be a strong force in technological innovation. However, financing services in China constrain their innovation capacity and impede the restructuring and sustainable development of the Chinese economy.
2. The co-existence of a debt financing gap and an equity financing gap make it even more difficult for SMEs to obtain financing.
3. The key reason for the debt financing gap in China is the monopoly in the banking industry. The state-owned banks are in transition from "plan" to "market"; the non-state-owned small banks and SMNFI are still young in the market. Meanwhile, the credit rating system is far from being established.
4. International experience indicates that the government should lend support and credit guarantees to SMEs when the market cannot bridge the financing gap. At the same time, the reform of the financial system should be accelerated in China.
5. No individual solution or policy can solve the problem of the debt financing gap for SMEs. A systematic solution needs to take the stakeholders' interests into consideration and gradually ease the conflict between the demand for and the supply of funds.

References

Akerlof, G. 1970. "The Market for Lemons: Quality Uncertainty and the Market Mechanism." *Quarterly Journal of Economics* 84: 488–500.

Asch, L. 2000. "Credit Scoring: A Tool for More Efficient SME Lending." *SME Issues* 1, no. 2.

Banerjee, Abhijit, Timothy Besley, and Timothy Guinnane. 1994. "Thy Neighbor's Keeper: The Design of a Credit Cooperative with Theory and a Test." *Quarterly Journal of Economics* 109, no. 2: 491–515.

Becattini, G. 1990. "The Marshallian Industrial District as a Socio-economic Concept." In *Industrial District and Inter-firms Co-operation in Italy*, ed. F. Pyke, G. Becattini, and W. Sengenbergen. Genoa: International Institute for Labour Studies.

Berger, Alan N., Margaret K. Kyle, and Joseph M. Scalise. 1999. "Did U.S. Bank Supervisors Get Tougher During the Credit Crunch? Did It Get Easier During the Bank Boom? Did It Matter to Bank Lending?" Working Paper of the Federal Reserve Bank. Available at www.federalreserve.gov/pubs/feds/2000/200039/200039pap.pdf.

Bhide, A.V. 1999. *The Origin and Evolution of New Businesses*. Oxford: Oxford University Press.

Black, Bernard S., and Ronald J. Gilson. 1999. "Does Venture Capital Require an Active Stock Market?" *Journal of Applied Corporate Finance* (Winter): 36–48.

Blanchflower, David G., Andrew Oswald, and Alois Stutzer. 2001. "Latent Entrepreneurship Across Nations." *European Economic Review* 45, no. 4: 680–91. Available at http://ideas.repec.org/a/eee/eecrev/v45y2001i4–6p680–691.html.

Bonin, John, and Paul Wachtel. 2003. "Financial Sector Development in Transition Economies: Lessons from the First Decade." *Financial Markets, Institutions & Instruments* 12, no. 1: 1–66.

Chen Xiaohong, and Guo Kunsheng, eds. 2000. *SMEs Financing (Zhongxiao qiye rongzi)*. Beijing: Economics Publishing House.

Cobham, Alexander. 1999. "The Financing and Technology Decisions of SMEs." Technology and Policy Working Paper, Finance and Trade Policy Research Centre. Queen Elizabeth House Working Paper Series no. 24, Oxford University.

Dai Xianglong. 2003. Speech delivered before the China Development Summit Forum, Beijing, March 24.

Deng, Leping, and Sun Conghai. 2001. "Technology Innovation and Capital Markets: Observations of Theory and Experience." *Journal of Financial Analysis* 9 (in Chinese).

Dixit, A.K., and R.S. Pindyck. 1994. *Investments Under Uncertainty*. Princeton: Princeton University Press.

Donaldson, G.G. 1961. *Corporate Debt Capacity: A Study of Corporate Debt Policy and Determination of Corporate Debt Capacity*. Boston: Division of Research, Graduate School of Business Administration, Harvard University.

Hawkins, John, and Philip Turner. 1999. "Bank Restructuring in Practice: An Overview." Policy paper no. 6 (August), Bank of International Settlements, Basle.

Hayes, Elizabeth. 2000. "Market Conditions Are Key to Venture Decisions." *Los Angeles Business Journal* (March 20).

Hovakimian, A., T. Opler, and S. Titman. 2001. "The Debt-Equity Choice." *Journal of Financial and Quantitative Analysis* 36: 1–24.

International Finance Corporation. 2000. IFC research report, unpublished.

Kamien, Morton I., and Nancy L. Schwartz. 1981. *Dynamic Optimization: The Calcu-*

lus of Variations and Optimal Control in Economics and Management. Amsterdam: North-Holland.

Kaplan, S.N., and P. Strömberg. 2001. "Venture Capitalists as Principals: Contracting, Screening, and Monitoring." *AEA Papers and Proceedings* 91, no. 2: 426–30.

Lander, D.M., and G.E. Pinches. 1998. "Challenges to the Practical Implementation of Modeling Valuing Real Options." *Quarterly Review of Economics and Finance* 38 (Special issue): 537–67.

Li Yang, Wang Guogang, and He Dexu. 2000. *The Frontier of Chinese Financial Theory.* Beijing: Social Science Literature (in Chinese).

Liao Li. 2000. "The Life Cycle of High-Tech Enterprises." *Journal of Finance and Economics* 3 (in Chinese).

Lin Yifu, and Li Yongjun. 2001. "The Development of Small- and Medium-Sized Financial Institutions and the Financing of Small- and Medium-Sized Businesses" (*Zhongxiao jinrong jigou fazhan yu zhongxiao qiye rongzi*). *Economic Analysis* 1, no. 1.

Macmillan, H. 1931. *Report of the Committee on Finance and Industry.* CMD 3897. London: HMSO.

Myers, S.C. 1984. "Finance Theory and Financial Strategy." *Interfaces* 14: 12–137.

———. 1977. "Determinants of Corporate Borrowing." *Journal of Financial Economics* 5 (November): 147–75.

Pennings, E., and O. Lint. 1997. "The Option Value of Advanced R&D." *European Journal of Operational Research* 103: 83–94.

People's Bank of China (PBOC). 2003. *People's Bank of China 2003 Yearbook.*

Petersen, Mitchell A., and Raghuram G. Rajan. 2002. "Does Distance Still Matter? The Information Revolution in Small Business Lending." *Journal of Finance* 57, no. 6: 2533–70.

Pindyck, R.S. 1993. "Investment of Uncertainty Cost." *Journal of Financial Economics* 34: 53–76.

Qian Yinyi. 2001. *The Reform of Chinese Corporate Construction and Finance* (*Zhongguo de gongsi zhili jiegou gaige yu rongzi gaige*). Beijing: Chinese Economics Press.

Qiu Huarui. 2001. *Theory About SMBs Financing.* Beijing: Chinese Economics Press (in Chinese).

Schumpeter, J.A. 1949. *The Theory of Economic Development.* Oxford: Oxford University Press.

Schwartz, E.S., ed. 2001. *Real Options and Investments Under Uncertainty.* Cambridge, MA: MIT Press.

Schwartz, Eduardo S., and Carlos Zozaya-Gorostiza. 2000. "Valuation of Information Technology Investments as Real Options." Available at www.anderson.ucla.edu/documents/areas/fac/finance/6–00.pdf.

Sogorb-Mira, Francisco. 2000. "On Capital Structure in the Small and Medium Enterprises: The Spanish Case." December. Available at http://papers.ssrn.com/sol3/papers.cfm?abstract_id=277090/.

Stiglitz, J., and A. Weiss. 1981. "Credit Rationing in Markets with Imperfect Information." *American Economics Review* 71, no. 3: 393–410.

Strahan, Philip E., and James P. Weston. 1998. "Small Business Lending and the Changing Structure of the Banking Industry." *Journal of Banking and Finance* 122: 821–45.

Trester, Jeffery, J. 1998. "Venture Capital Contracting Under Asymmetric Information." *Journal of Banking and Finance* 22: 675–99.

U.S. Small Business Administration (SBA) 2001. *Small Business Lending in the United States, 2001 Edition: A Directory of Small Business Lending Reported by Commercial Banks in June 2001.* Available at www.sba.gov/advo/stats/lending/2001/sbl_study.pdf.

Willner, R. 1995. "Valuing Start-up Venture Growth Options." In *Real Options in Capital Investment—Modes, Strategies, and Applications,* ed. L. Trigeorgis, 221–39. Westport, CT: Praeger.

Xu Lan. 2000. "The Life Cycle of High-Tech Enterprises and Financial Resource Rationing." *Journal of World Economy* 6 (in Chinese).

Yu Ziyou, and Song Tao. 2001. *Theory and Practice of Venture Investment (Fengxian touzi lilun yu shijian).* Shanghai: Shanghai University of Finance and Economics Press.

Zhang Shuzhong. 2001. *A Systems Analysis of the American Venture Capital Market.* Beijing: Chinese Social Science Press (in Chinese).

Zhao Changwen. 2002. "The Innovation and Selection of the SMBS Financing System." *Journal of Sichuan University* 2 (in Chinese).

Zhong Jiakun, and Qian Yanying. 2001. "Difficulties in Financing: The Case of Private High-Tech Enterprises" *(Zhongguo minying keji qiye rongzi zhangai fenxi). Journal of Guangdong Business College* 5: 29–32.

Zingales, Luigi. 2000. "In Search of New Foundations." *Journal of Finance* 55, no. 4: 1623–53.

14

Institutional Reform in the Chinese Banking System and China's Implementation of Commitments to the WTO

Mei Liao

In the process of China's accession to the World Trade Organization (WTO), the United States assumed a leading role in the negotiations over the past fourteen years. The two countries reached tentative agreement in November 1999 through the U.S.-China Market Access Agreement. Following this, China and the United States reached an agreement on major outstanding issues in June 2001, which signaled the end of the second phase of the accession process. Both sides claimed that the completion of the talks was a win-win result. Peter Davidson, the general counsel of the United States Trade Representative, admitted that the U.S.-China agreement was "a set of comprehensive, verifiable, one-way trade concessions that substantially open China's market across the spectrum to U.S. goods, services and agriculture. . . . It is not a favor to China. Indeed, it contains the most rigorous and broad-ranging commitments ever required of a new member to the GATT [General Agreement on Tariffs and Trade] or WTO."[1]

There have been concerns about the capacity of China to implement its commitments. To this there are two opposing views: positive versus negative. With respect to the financial sector, the negative view is that China will succumb to foreign competition because of its financially weak banks and immature financial market mechanism. The positive view is that since there are many barriers permissible within the WTO framework, for example, opaque and cumbersome regulatory guidelines on leverage, loan to deposit ratios, and foreign exchange, the competitive ability of foreign banks could still be limited, and China may well navigate through the hard times in the phase-out periods.

To identify the capacity and prospects for China to implement its General Agreement on Trade in Services (GATS) commitments, this chapter first assesses the performance of China's domestic banking system as background information, and then focuses on analyzing the discretion that China may have in its choice of possible measures to ensure the stability and development of its domestic banks in line with the principles contained in the GATS of the WTO. The inherent defects of China's banking system are such that it will not be by any standard strong enough to resist the competition from the foreign banks, and the sequencing of China's GATS commitments seems to disadvantageously position the domestic banks. However, some flexible interpretations of GATS rules seem to be able to provide certain leeway for China to remedy its loopholes in the commitments and its evolving financial system.

An Assessment of China's Banking System

The Structure of China's Banking System

The contemporary banking system in China has developed from the initial one-bank system that dominated China's pre-reform era before 1978. The People's Bank of China (PBOC) served both as the central bank and a commercial bank with a limited role in providing working capital to enterprises. Most long-term investment financing was channeled to enterprises through the state budget and all investment projects were financed with budgetary grants. Under such a system, the M2 money supply was only 32 percent of GNP (M2/GNP). The quantity of loans in relation to GNP was 52.2 percent (L/GNP), and the supply of securities in relation to GNP was barely 0.04 percent of GNP (S/GNP) (Li 2001).

Since 1978, the Chinese financial sector has undergone gradual changes to meet the requirements of a transition economy through a process of decentralizing the existing financial institutions and creating new financial institutions, instruments, and markets. The reform has been targeted at building the functions of the financial sector in capital mobilization and allocation and enforcing the role of the central bank in macroeconomic management. The institutional changes from 1979 to 1997 were the establishment of a two-tier banking system, consisting of a central bank and the commercial banking institutions, including state-owned banks, state policy banks,[2] stockholding banks, and foreign banks. At the same time, a batch of nonfinancial institutions was also created. By the end of 2001, there were four state-owned banks, three state policy banks, ten stock-holding commercial banks with either regional or national coverage, and eighteen urban cooperative banks. By early 1999, there were already 146 branch offices of foreign banks, thirteen joint ventures and private banks registered in China. Compared to 1978, the M2/GNP in 1996 tripled to 108.6 percent, the Loan/GNP ratio increased to 90.2 percent, and the Securities/ GNP ratio grew to 28.02 percent (Li 2001).

The four state-owned commercial banks were created initially as specialized banks for separate sectors of the economy under an economic planning mechanism. Of the four, the Agricultural Bank of China was set up to take over the PBOC's rural banking business. Under its supervision there is a network of sixty thousand rural credit cooperatives[3] to provide small-scale banking services. The Bank of China (BOC) and the China's Construction Bank (CCB) were separated from the PBOC in a similar way. As independent specialized banks, (BOC) handles international financial and trade transactions and (CCB) deals with financial services for the construction sector. The Industrial and Commercial Bank of China deals mainly with urban banking services. Since the promulgation of the Commercial Banking Law in 1995, these business constraints among the four banks have been diluted. The development of stock-holding commercial banks started in the 1980s. By the end of 1999, they had total assets of US$2,453.2 billion, accounting for 16.3 percent of all financial assets in China.

The growth of the ten national stock-holding banks was mainly the result of the regional development policy. As local governments and some large state-owned enterprises, especially in the special economic zones and coastal regions, gained more decision-making power and financial flexibility in their regional business development, they began to set up their own banks to support continued growth. With ownership restructuring, these banks underwent a transformation from quasi-state ownership to stock-holding banks. Some have listed on the stock market. In most of the banks, either state-owned banks or state enterprises hold the major stakes. For example, China Construction Bank, one of the four state-owned commercial banks, holds 51 percent of the stock of China Investment Bank, while the stock of China Minsheng Bank is held solely by 172 private companies. Figure 14.1 shows the structure of the Chinese banking system.

The urban cooperative banks, which evolved from the former urban credit cooperatives (UCCS), a quasi-bank form, first emerged in 1984 to provide banking services to medium and small private enterprises. By the end of

Figure 14.1 **Structure of the Chinese Banking System**

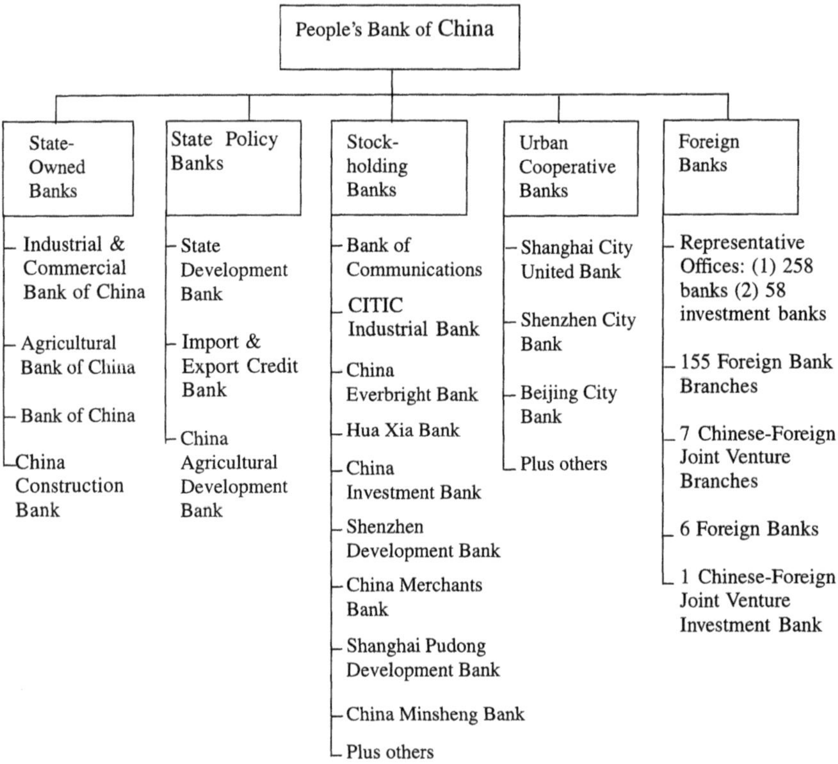

People's Bank of China

State-Owned Banks	State Policy Banks	Stock-holding Banks	Urban Cooperative Banks	Foreign Banks
– Industrial & Commercial Bank of China	– State Development Bank	– Bank of Communications	– Shanghai City United Bank	– Representative Offices: (1) 258 banks (2) 58 investment banks
– Agricultural Bank of China	– Import & Export Credit Bank	– CITIC Industrial Bank	– Shenzhen City Bank	– 155 Foreign Bank Branches
– Bank of China	– China Agricultural Development Bank	– China Everbright Bank	– Beijing City Bank	– 7 Chinese-Foreign Joint Venture Branches
– China Construction Bank		– Hua Xia Bank	– Plus others	
		– China Investment Bank		– 6 Foreign Banks
		– Shenzhen Development Bank		– 1 Chinese-Foreign Joint Venture Investment Bank
		– China Merchants Bank		
		– Shanghai Pudong Development Bank		
		– China Minsheng Bank		
		– Plus others		

Source: People's Bank of China, www.pbc.gov.cn

1996, the assets of the eighteen urban cooperative banks totaled about US$25.9 billion, with savings of US$15.2 billion and loans of US$9.4 billion.

In 1979, China started to open its financial market. From 1979 to 1982, only representative offices of foreign banks were permitted. After 1982, a number of pilot business branches of foreign banks were allowed to set up in the special economic zones. In 1985, the promulgation of "Regulations on Foreign Banks and Joint Venture Banks in Special Economic Zones" allowed foreign bank branches in five coastal cities.[4] In 1996, foreign financial institutions were allowed to do local currency business in savings and deposits, clearing and settlement, national bonds and other securities business. In 1998, Shenzhen became the second pilot city to allow foreign banks to do local currency business, and at the same time new regulations for expanding local currency resources for foreign banks were also promulgated. By the end of June 1998, the total assets of foreign financial institutions was 2.6 percent of the total assets of Chinese domestic financial institutions and 16.4 percent of total foreign exchange assets in China. By 1999, the number of foreign bank branches totaled 155, the number of registered banks was thirteen, including seven joint venture banks and six solely-owned foreign banks.

The Functions of the Central Bank

China's central bank, the People's Bank of China (PBOC) has evolved through-out three different historical stages: at the first stage from 1949 to 1984, the PBOC operated as an overarching financial institution under the central planning mechanism responsible for both currency policymaking and credit operation. At the second stage from 1984 to 2003, the omnibus responsibilities were pruned, and the PBOC began to take monopoly responsibility for making and enforcing monetary policies, issuing banknotes, supervising not only the banking system, but also the securities and insurance markets. Its functions were legalized in March 1995 by the enforcement of the Law of the People's Bank of China—also called the "Central Bank Law." Since then the PBOC had undergone a series of changes in its functions, organizational structure, policy framework, and monetary instruments. According to the Central Bank Law, the PBOC assumed the functions of (1) the monetary authority, (2) the bank of banks, (3) the bank of the government, and (4) banking supervision authority (Feng 1999; Dai 1997). At this stage, China was in transition from a central planning economy to a market economy, and the government maintained the power and authority to control economic development. The financial market in China was still in a preliminary stage of development. The central bank in China had its own unique features compared with the functions of central banks in industrialized countries.[5]

First, there was a low level of independence. According to the Central-Bank Law, the PBOC will operate according to instructions from the State Council in formulating monetary policies and conducting supervision and administration over the financial sector in China (Article 2). Apart from the functions that a central bank was generally required to perform, it was also stipulated that the PBOC should perform "other functions" designated by the State Council (Article 4). With regard to policies for annual money supply, interest rates, exchange rates, and other important issues designated by the State Council, all must be submitted to the State Council for a final decision before their enforcement (Article 5). The State Council also had the right to decide what monetary instruments the PBOC will apply (Article 22). With regard to human resource management within the PBOC, it was stipulated that the governor of the PBOC should be nominated by the State Council, approved by the National People's Congress, and appointed by China's president. The term of office should not be limited by law. The removal of the president of the PBOC followed the same procedure (Article 9). With respect to the bank's business scope, the State Council had the right to decide about loans to some specified nonfinancial institutions (Article 29).

Second, credit planning and interest rate control were the PBOC's two major direct monetary instruments for conducting monetary policy (Article 4). The credit planning was the administrative tool adopted by the PBOC to control money supply. It was in conjunction with the budget plan of the government, which was one important governmental policy tool for influencing the level and pattern of investment in the economy and controlling industrial development. By means of the credit plan, the PBOC determines the state-owned commercial banks' credit volume directly in aggregate and by sectors and regions. The interest rate policy was used since 1979 by the PBOC to adjust credit conditions and hence to conduct macroeconomic control. The PBOC had direct authority over interest rates on bank deposits from non-bank units and over bank loans to business firms, as well as the interest margin charged by the banking sector. In the determination of interest rates, the PBOC followed governmental industrial and regional policies and did not tie them closely to risk, maturity, inflationary expectations, or the opportunity cost of alternative investments on the financial market.

Limited open market operation was another important feature of the PBOC before 2003. Though the PBOC started to introduce open market operation practices in 1996 (Feng 1999), the traded volumes of government bonds had not yet been significant and they had little impact on banks' lending behavior. This was mainly caused by three factors: (1) There was a lack of short-term government securities. Currently, government bonds mainly offer maturities of medium- and long-terms (i.e., 3–year, 5–year, and 10–year bonds). The volume of short-term bonds was very small. (2) Bank interest rates were not market-determined. Although the controls on the interbank interest rates had been removed since early 1996, the transmission of monetary policy to the real economic sector, especially with regard to the investments of enterprises, was ineffective. (3) There was a gap between international banking supervision standards and those currently in use by the PBOC.

The third stage that the further institutional reform the PBOC has embarked on came after 2003, when the amended Central Bank Law was ratified by the National People's Congress. The major changes are the shift of the supervision responsibilities for the banking system, securities, and insurance sectors from the PBOC to three newly set-up independent regulatory institutions (i.e., China Security Regulation Commission, China Insurance Regulation Commission, and China Banking Regulation Commission). The macro-control of the financial market became the major role of the PBOC, which enforced the position of the PBOC as the arm of the central government in market control.

Domestic Commercial Banks

The establishment of commercial banks in China is not by registration but by the approval of the PBOC in accordance with the regulations in "The Company Law of the People's Republic of China" (The Company Law) and "The Commercial Banking Law."[6] There are also "Provisional Regulations on Senior Financial Professionals Management" to govern the appointment of administrative personnel in the banking system.

Though China is pushing forward its reform of the commercial banking system toward efficiency to meet the challenge from the foreign banks upon joining the WTO, questions arising from an assessment of its current banking mechanisms and performance have cast doubt on the efficiency of the reform at its present pace. The hurdles existing in its capital organization structure, corporate control structure, and operation management mechanism suggest that the whole system will face cruel competition with foreign banks during the first five years. The survival and development of the domestic banks will depend largely on the protective measures the Chinese government takes in line with the rules of the WTO, especially the policies concerning market access, national treatment, and most-favored nations.

Capital Property Structure

State-owned capital property and stock-holding capital property are the two major types of capital property found in China's commercial banking system. Of the two, state-owned capital property holds the major share of commercial banking capital properties. Its total assets in 1998 accounted for 88.9 percent of domestic commercial banking capital properties. With the financial support of the government, the state-owned banks have much stronger market power than non-state-owned commercial banks, yet they have inherent deficiencies in their capital property management structure caused by:

1. Unclear capital property rights between the state and the banks that has resulted, for banks, in a lack of guarantee of autonomous management and self-regulation, and the neglect of cost in debt management and of risk in asset management.

2. Unclear debtor and debt liability rights. The effects of unclear property rights directly induce the lack of incentives and inefficient asset management, especially bad debt management, since in theory and by law the state holds unlimited liability for the liability banks produce.
3. Lack of asset replenishment ability. Under the current capital organization system, every decision made must be submitted to the State Council for approval. The four state-owned banks can only rely on the state's financial budget to replenish their assets.
4. Lack of efficient business management mechanisms. For the state-owned banks, unclear business ownership has made it difficult to set up a sound trust relationship between the principal and business agents concerning decision-making, implementation of policies, and supervisory mechanisms. The stock-holding banks are constrained by the tight lending policy of the PBOC. Their limited capital stocks and comparatively higher credit risk make them unable to compete and break the monopoly of the state-owned banks.

Corporate Control System

The corporate control system refers to the measures that the property owner uses to control his business. In China's commercial banking system, the corporate control mechanism does not have much influence because of deficiencies in the fiduciary relationships between stockholder and the board of directors, between principal and agent, and deficiencies in the supervisory functions. For the state-owned commercial banks, the establishment of boards of directors, boards of supervisors, and executive bodies are under the control of the government. The control of the boards of directors and boards of supervisors over the executive body is superficial. For stock-holding commercial banks, legal corporate control is also deficient. As the major stockholders of the commercial banks are either state-owned enterprises or governmental institutions, the inherent unclear ownership relationships impair the functions of the boards of directors and it is always in question whether or not the board can safeguard the rights of stockholders. As the directors are designated, not elected, by the stockholders, the importance of the role of directors is greatly weakened.

The inner supervisory mechanisms remain by far one of the hottest issues for discussions on banking system reform (Li 2000; Tang 2000; Wang 2001). At present, much talk has been directed at setting up a system in compliance with the Basel core principles for effective banking supervision. It is still not clear when an effective working system can be put into operation.

Organizational Structure

The structure of China's commercial banking system was developed by setting up branches or sub-branches either within the boundaries of China or within designated regions. The creation of new branches is under the strict control of the PBOC. Their approval is the first step in the process. Second, it is required that the total volume of the working capital that the headquarters bank is supposed to allocate to its branches cannot exceed 60 percent of its total capital assets and, third, the asset/liability ratios have to meet the requirements set by the PBOC.

The branch system is based on one single legal entity represented by the head office (the legal entity at the first tier); the branch and sub-branch offices do not have legal entity status. Interbranch transactions are not allowed. In practice, because of the excessive autonomy of the branch offices, especially those state-owned commercial banks, interbranch market transactions do occur.

Such an arrangement has brought unavoidable management hurdles (Wang 2000), including: (1) The multi-layered administrative structure obstructs information transparency, which has made it difficult for the implementation of instructions from head offices and increased the cost of management. (2) Unclear segregation of duties between administration and operations; there is no independent management division. The mixed structure weakens independent management. (3) Segregation of business by products, not by target customers, leads to low efficiency and wasted resources. (4) Finally, there is a loose monitoring and supervision system.

Practices in other countries have proven that an efficient monitoring and supervisory system should be structured and operated as a highly centralized, independent, and authoritative body. However in China, as the Commercial Banking Law applies directly to corporate entities represented by the head offices of commercial banks, the branches and sub-branches only function as subordinates to the unitary control of their head offices. This structural mechanism has resulted in the Central Bank's external monitoring and supervision extending only to the head offices. The internal monitoring and supervision system is under the control of each bank's head office. Internal supervision is subject to the control of parallel administrative sectors. They tend to work together in order to transmit the supervision from the organs above them.

Low Efficiency

The deficiencies in structural and operational mechanisms have resulted in low performance for China's commercial banking services, as reflected by the following indexes:

1. Operational efficiency indexes. There are three sets of data used to reflect the operation capacity and profit-making potential of a bank (Zhao 2001):

- The net income after taxes to asset (NIT/AS) ratio reflects a bank's asset capacity for making profit. In America, the ratio ranges from 1–2 percent. In 1997, France, Germany, Italy, Spain, the UK, and Belgium were respectively at 0.04 percent, 0.53 percent, 0.73 percent, 0.33 percent, 0.72 percent, and 0.47 percent (Molyneux 1997). Table 14.1 shows that there is a gap in performance between the four state-owned banks and the foreign banks. Their general average level of NIT/AS ratios in 1997 and 1998 were 0.12 percent and 0.075 percent. The four major banks have a rather weak position for profit making in competition with foreign banks. However, the newly developed stock-holding banks are closer to the levels of the foreign banks.
- The ratio of net income to operation income (NI/OI) is an indicator of a bank's dynamic potential. This ratio indicates the range of profits retained by the bank for expansion. The higher it is, the lower its operation costs will be, and vice versa. In 1997, this ratio for Citibank (United States), Chase Manhattan (United States), ABN AMRO Bank (Netherlands), and HSBC (UK) were respectively 21.3 percent, 19.2 percent, 15.75 percent, and 24.7 percent. Comparatively, the data in Table 14.1 shows that the four state-owned banks had a much lower level than the foreign banks, while the stock-holding banks reached or even surpassed the levels of the foreign banks.
- The ratio of profit to staff (P/S) is an important index for measuring the productivity of banking services and the capacity of working staff to make profits. In this regard, the level of foreign banks is above 69 percent, while the general level of both the state-owned and stock-holding banks in China is between 0.16 percent and 35 percent. The level of the Big Four hovers around 0.16–6.0 percent. One of the explanations for this low level is the over-staffed bureaucratic institutional structure, which induces high costs and causes low efficiency.

2. The cost and efficiency indexes. Changes in banking costs are among the important objective factors that decide the level of a bank's productivity. The level of operation costs reflects the level of a bank's operational cost management. The best operational management efficiency is achieved with the least possible manpower and physical materials. As interest rates are not yet allowed to float in China, it is therefore important to treat operational expenditures as inputs for a bank and to assess the bank's efficiency by analyzing the ratio between inputs and outputs.

Table 14.1

Operational Efficiencies of Major Commercial Banks in China, 1997–1998

Bank	NP/NGO		NIT/AS		P/S	
	1997	1998	1997	1998	1997	1998
ICBC	0.08	0.09	0.38	1.91	0.55	0.61
ABC	0.03	0.05	0.64	2.54	0.16	0.17
BOC	0.17	0.10	4.16	1.20	3.49	5.57
CCB	0.28	0.06	1.54	1.29	0.56	0.29
BC	0.63	0.30	18.19	10.44	11.49	2.9
CITIC	1.09	1.11	13.55	32.16	37.89	35.15
CEB	1.8	1.83	33.22	17.6	64.00	28.31

Source: China Finance Yearbook (1998, 1999).
Note: Acronyms are ICBC (Industrial & Commercial Bank of China), ABC (Agricultural Bank of China), BOC (Bank of China), CCB (China Construction Bank), BC (Bank of Communication), CITIC (CITIC Industrial Bank),CEB (China Everbright Bank).

Three indexes reflect these considerations.

- The operational cost ratio (OPR) is the ratio of operation expenditure to total income. It reflects expenditures to achieve gains. The lower the ratio is, the stronger control a bank has over its operational expenditures, and the higher its operational efficiency.
- The cost expenditure–asset ratio (CEAR) is the ratio of operational expenditures to total assets. It reflects the cost expenditure level of a bank's asset maintenance.
- The average personnel cost (APC) is an indicator of manpower capacity. It is decided by salary level, infrastructure, and maintenance costs, and other costs of running an office.

On average the operational cost ratio for the Chinese commercial banks is around 13 percent, while in countries such as Germany, France, Italy, Spain, and the UK, this ratio is kept around 49–67 percent. The general average level of cost expenditure/assets as well as average personnel costs of the Chinese banks is also lower than those of these countries.

Table 14.2 shows the operational efficiency of the Chinese commercial banks. This set of indexes raises at least two concerns. From the aspect of working resources input, a proportional arrangement between cost and assets is a condition for maximizing profit-making potential. The low levels of operational cost ratios and cost expenditure to assets indicate low levels of both human resource management and working facilities. Low levels of inputs will hamper efficiency.

Table 14.2

Operational Efficiencies of Major Commercial Banks in China

Bank	OPR (%)	CEAR (%)	APC ($1,000)
ICBC	3.70	0.73	6.36
ABC	17.2	1.34	5.00
BOC	16.0	1.02	16.2
CCB	14.2	2.25	1.37
BC	14.7	0.94	1.21
CITIC	14.2	1.00	2.88
CEB	8.37	0.67	1.94

Source: China Finance Yearbook (1998).
Note: For acronyms see Table 14.1.

From the aspect of potential dynamics for competition, this low level may indicate that there is a need for the Chinese banks to increase their inputs of working resources in order to upgrade their management competitiveness.

3. The capital assets arrangement index refers to the apportionment of assets according to profit ratings and lending terms based on the nature of assets, their structure, and requirements of liquidity for liabilities, the prioritization of the total assets for the liquidity, and profit maximization. The ratio of loans to savings is a major index, which reflects not only the efficiency of the assets management of a bank, but also the strength of its asset liquidity. In 1997, Citibank maintained a level of 104 percent for its loans to savings ratio, while that of HSBC was 92.6 percent, Chase Manhattan 88 percent, and ABN AMRO Bank 106.8 percent. Table 14.3 shows the ratio of lending to saving in Chinese banks. The results indicate that the average level of the ratios of Chinese banks is lower than those of foreign banks. The table indicates that there exists excessive savings in the performance of Chinese commercial banks. The possible direct causes for this could be (1) the fear of credit risk that leads to repression of loaning, and (2) a passive strategy on asset liquidity management, which hampers the effective liquid asset arrangement.

The high ratio of non-performing loans is another symptom affecting the performance of Chinese commercial banks. Especially the four big state-owned banks, whose non-performing loans accounted for 27.3 percent of GDP in 1998 (Song and Wu 2001). Although the state adopted measures to support the four state-owned banks by (1) injection of RMB270 million in capital in 1998 and (2) creating four asset management companies[7] in 1999 to save the banks from insolvency, the deficiencies in the banking system as previously discussed still risk producing non-performing loans.

To address the problems summarized above, the authorities have embarked on a far-reaching financial program. Its key elements are enhanced central

Table 14.3

Commercial Banks: The Ratio of Lending to Saving, 1997–1998

Year	ICBC	ABC	BOC	CCB	BC	CITIC	CEB
1997	88.63	89.39	82.66	84.3	67.11	NA	73.56
1998	86.30	NA	82.43	82.9	65.12	NA	73.56

Source: China Finance Yearbook (1998, 1999).
Note: NA = not available.

bank regulation and supervision, plus the adoption of incentives to encourage business-like behavior by large state-owned banks.

The Open Market and Government Policies

The accession to the WTO will undoubtedly continue to induce drastic reform in China's banking system. In the past twenty or more years, China's banking system has operated under monopoly within a comparatively closed market situation and has been protected by the government. This section gives an overview of current government policies concerning the banking industry. Until 2001, the policies on foreign banking services in China can be classified into two categories: inferior national treatment and supranational treatment.

Inferior National Treatment Policies

These are the restrictions on foreigners' market access:

1. Requirements for qualified establishment. First, to set up a bank or a branch, the applicant must have an established representative office in China for more than two years. Second, for setting up a bank, the total capital assets required should be no lees than US$10 billion at the end of the year prior to filing the application; for a branch, it should be no less than US$20 billion.
2. Restrictions on the business scope. The foreign banks are only allowed to do foreign exchange business with foreigners, joint-venture enterprises, and state-owned enterprises.
3. Restrictions on the volume of local currency business. It is stipulated by the People's Bank of China that the capital assets in local currency (RMB) should not exceed 50 percent of its foreign exchange liabilities. If any foreign bank intends to expand

its local currency business, it has to expand its foreign exchange capital assets by increasing loans in foreign exchange to Chinese enterprises.

4. Geographic restrictions on business locations. Foreign banks are only allowed to set up one branch office in each major city in China. Only a couple of cities in the special economic zones are permitted to have foreign banks do local currency businesses.

5. Restriction on nonconvertible capital items. As the foreign exchange lending business falls into the category of capital items, any enterprises in China that intend to borrow foreign exchange from a foreign bank have to be assessed by the State Foreign Exchange Bureau.

Supranational Treatment Policies

Compared with the policies for domestic banks, foreign banks enjoy certain privileges.

1. The capital deposit required by the People's Bank of China is only 3–5 percent, compared to 13 percent required of domestic banks.

2. The tax rate levied on foreign exchange businesses by foreign banks is much lower than that on corresponding domestic banks. The income tax rate for most foreign banks in China is set at 15 percent, while for the domestic banks it is kept at 33 percent (Qian 2000). At the same time, foreign banks are either exempted from operations taxes or are liable for a lower rate.

3. Foreign exchange rate control is another important instrument the Chinese government uses to protect its domestic market. By far, China's central bank controls interest rates on all deposits in domestic currency by using the renminbi (RMB)/dollar exchange as the basic rate and sets cross rates against other currencies by referring to international markets. In September 2000, the authorities lifted controls on interest rates on all foreign currency loans and on foreign currency deposits in excess of US$3 million.

Starting from 2001 after the accession to the WTO, the restrictions on the foreign banking industry have been gradually loosened to conform with the commitments. As of the end of 2004, there were 62 foreign banks from 19 countries to set up 204 business institutions in 18 cities throughout China, of which 105 had acquired the authority to do local currency business. The total capital assets of foreign financial institutions in China reached RMB31,929 billion, an increase of 13.6 percent over the same period of the previous year. Though equal national treatment means foreign banks will eventually compete with domestic banks on an equal footing, the different income taxation mechanism applied to foreign banks and domestic banks still operates. According to a survey from the Finance Ministry (Finance Ministry Information Office 2004), the actual taxation level for foreign banks is only at 10.35 percent to 13.09 percent, which dampens the domestic banks' competitiveness, especially those middle and small financial ventures.

The GATS and China's Commitments

The GATS consists of a set of general rules that apply across the board to measures affecting trade in services, and sector-specific commitments on market access and national treatment. Apart from these, there are also several GATS provisions that apply mainly or exclusively to sectors where specific commitments are undertaken. Furthermore, the GATS also includes a set of attachments: annexes that take into account sectoral specifics and ministerial decisions relating to the implementation of the GATS (WTO 1993).

Specific GATS Provisions

Banking, insurance, and other financial services is the largest service sector under the classifications of the GATS. The GATS speaks to trade in services through certain supply modes (as defined in Article I), to include the following four.

1. *Cross-border*: services supplied from the territory of one member into the territory of another; for example, a consumer from a financial institution located abroad taking out a loan or purchasing insurance coverage.
2. *Consumption abroad*: services supplied in the territory of one member to the consumers of another; for example, the purchase of financial services by consumers while traveling abroad.
3. *Commercial presence*: services supplied through any type of business or professional establishment of one member in the territory of another; for example, when a foreign bank or other financial institution establishes a branch or subsidiary in the territory of another country and supplies financial services.
4. *Presence of natural persons*: services supplied by nationals of one member in the territory of another. This mode includes both independent service suppliers and employees of the services supplier of another member; for example, independent financial con-

sultants or bank managers of one member in the territory of another member.

Two general rules that apply to government policies affecting trade in services are most-favored-nation (MFN) treatment and transparency. Article II on MFN treatment requires each member to "accord immediately and unconditionally to services and services suppliers of any other Member treatment no less favorable than that it accords to like services and services suppliers of any other country." Departures from the MFN principle are permitted for the measures listed in, and meeting the conditions of, the Annex on Article II Exemptions.[8] Article III on transparency requires each member to publish all measures of general application affecting trade in services, and to inform each member promptly of any changes in measures affecting trade in services covered by its specific commitments.

The specific commitments on market access and national treatment are the core of the GATS, and the impact of the agreement depends to a large extent on the commitments made by members. Both the market access and national treatment provided for in the schedules must be extended to all foreign services suppliers on a nondiscriminatory basis, irrespective of whether a country has listed any MFN exemptions.

GATS' Article XVI (the market access provision) stipulates that measures restrictive of market access that a WTO member cannot maintain or adopt, unless specified in its schedule, include six limitations on: (1) the number of service suppliers; (2) the total value of services transactions or assets; (3) the total number of service operations or the total quantity of service output; (4) the total number of natural persons that may be employed in a particular sector; (5) specific types of legal entity through which a service can be supplied; and (6) foreign entity participation (e.g., maximum equity participation). With the exception of (5), the measures covered by Article XVI all take the form of quantitative restrictions. In scheduled sectors, the existence of any of these limitations has to be indicated with respect to each of the four modes of supply, as described above.

A member's specific commitments can be seen as the outcome of a two-step decision. Each member first decides which service sector will be subject to the GATS market access and national treatment disciplines. It then decides what measures will be kept in place for that sector that violate market access and/or national treatment respectively.

Though GATS provides a framework of rules that WTO members follow, these rules apply only where a country makes a specific commitment to grant access to foreign services, and exemptions are allowed. Individual WTO members each have specific commitments in individual sectors and have granted market access subject to specified limitations, such as those on the number or scope of business that is permitted. Thus there is no general requirement that WTO members open their services market to foreigners and grant them national treatment.

China's Commitments to the WTO

The multilateral negotiations between China and the working party of WTO members were conducted with the understanding that nothing is definitively agreed until everything is agreed. The seven areas under negotiation cover trade framework, intellectual property rights, standards and regulatory measures, compliance and monitoring mechanisms, trade-distorting industrial policies, foreign currency reserve–related restraints on trade, and other.

Commitments to Liberalization of the Banking Sector

China has made the following commitments on market access and national treatment:

1. Licensing. The condition for setting up a subsidiary of a foreign bank or a foreign financial company in China requires total assets of more than US$20 billion at the end of the year prior to filing the application. Setting up a Chinese-foreign joint bank or a Chinese-foreign joint finance company requires total assets of more than US$10 billion at the end of the year prior to filing the application. It is required that foreign financial institutions wishing to engage in local currency business must have three years of business operation experience in China, with profit-making performance for two consecutive years prior to the application. All economic-needs tests or quantitative limits on licenses will be eliminated. Five years after accession any existing nonprudential measures restricting ownership, operation, and juridical form of foreign financial institutions shall be eliminated.

2. Business scope. Upon accession foreign financial institutions will be permitted to do foreign exchange currency business in China without restriction as to clients. For local currency business, two years after accession, foreign banks are to be permitted to provide services to Chinese enterprises; five years after accession, foreign banks are to be permitted to provide services to all Chinese clients.

3. Geographic limitations on local currency business. During the first year of WTO membership, China will open two additional cities to foreign banks conducting renminbi (RMB) transactions.[9] Every year thereafter it will open four new cities to foreign banks. Five years after accession, all geographic restrictions will be removed.

To implement these commitments, changes in China's trade framework, compliance and protection mechanisms, trade-distorting industrial policies, and foreign currency reserve–related constraints on trade are crucial.

Another issue that may cause concern from other WTO members is how China will implement WTO provisions on balance of payments measures and foreign exchange controls to regulate its imports and provide protection for specific domestic industries. By Article XII of GATS, members may temporarily impose restrictions on imports or access to foreign currency when faced with a deterioration of their holdings of foreign currency reserves. These provisions are available for all members facing a serious decline in their monetary reserves to reduce the demand for foreign currency and to allow reserves to accumulate. China may use the provisions to regulate its imports and provide protection for specific domestic industries. By far there is no clear agreement on this issue.

The Implications of China's Financial Commitments and Some Uncertainties in Interpreting GATS Regulations

The essence of the WTO regulations is to standardize border measures and internal measures for application to trade by member countries. In the case of services, as the classification of the four modes indicates, internal measures are the major sources of restrictions. It is therefore crucial for GATS to discipline those restrictive policies adopted by member countries in relation to market access and national treatment.

According to the "Schedule of Specific Commitments on Services" (WTO 2001b), entries in the schedule of commitments in a given sector with respect to a particular mode of supply fall into one of four categories: (1) Full commitment: "none" or "no limitations," which implies that the member does not seek in any way to limit market access or national treatment through measures inconsistent with Articles XVI or XVII; (2) Commitment with limitations: the member describes in detail the measures maintained which are inconsistent with market access or national treatment, and implicitly commits itself to take no other inconsistent measures; (3) No commitment: "unbound" indicates that the member remains free to maintain or introduce measures inconsistent with market access or national treatment; (4) No commitment technically feasible: "unbound" indicates that for the sector in question, a particular mode of supply cannot be used, for instance cross-border supply of hairdressing services. Financial services are provided mainly in two ways: cross-border (mode 1) and through the presence of a foreign establishment (mode 3).[10] In the case of China, the commitments made in the banking sector are progressive across the two modes of supply in the phase-out period.

Before 2001, there existed in China's banking industry at least six types of limitations on foreign banks, these are: (1) limitations on the number of suppliers; (2) limitations on the participation of foreign capital, which require a qualified working capital and assets; (3) limitations on the total number of service operations; (4) limitations on the right to establishment; (5) limitations on business scope; and (6) limitations on geographic location, of which there are four types that are explicitly prohibited by the market access provision of Article XVI. In the commitments for phase-out periods, China only retains limitations on geographic location and "some scope of business" while removing other restrictions on the four modes of supply. This will allow a progressive inflow and outflow of capital under mode 1 and mode 3.

Two questions arise in interpreting the scheduling of China's commitments to market access and the relationship between GATS Article XVI and Article XVII. First, to what extent do China's commitments reflect actual access conditions in the banking sector? Second, what domains of national treatment can be identified and applied in relation to safeguard measures, prudential measures, and other protection measures China may possibly use to maintain the stability of its domestic banking industry?

Six possible problems may crop up in China's banking sector upon accession to the WTO. Domestic banks will confront foreign banks in competition for a share of (1) foreign currency deposits, (2) local currency business, (3) international settlement services, (4) loaning services, (5) retail business, and (6) personal consumption credit business. Given the poor performance of Chinese domestic commercial banks in past years, it is doubtful they can survive the competition. It is therefore possible that the Chinese government will wish to avail itself of GATS rules and apply necessary measures to protect its weak banking system.

Capital Account Convertibility

China retains control on capital account convertibility, which can serve as a hedge against the entry of foreign banks and may well give some leeway for the domestic banks to speed up reform and find remedies for their operational deficiencies. Though in the scheduling of China's commitments in the banking sector, cross-border supply (mode 1) is basically unbound, the policy of capital account convertibility implicitly limits the availability of cross-border capital mobility to foreign banks. The priority given to commercial presence (mode 3) instead may also serve to have some form of control on short-term capital movement.

An empirical study (Mattoo 2000) has shown that the liberalization of mode 3 in the phase-out period can result in less distorted and less volatile capital flows and more stable financial sectors. This is because mode 3 has certain advantages that a country needs to strengthen its financial capacity: (1) it may have a positive effect on institutional capacity and enhance the stability of the financial system in the long run; (2) a country can benefit from the institution-building effect of commercial presence with only limited commitments to capital account liberalization; and (3) it is more likely to help the development of a strong domestic service sector as domestic institutions tend to learn more from the practice of foreign institutions' commercial presence.

When a regulatory and supervisory framework has not been completed and with reliable ratings not yet likely to be developed so soon after accession, the effect of the liberalization of the capital account at this premature stage is likely to induce foreign investors to engage in short-term commitments. The large capital inflows this causes can undermine monetary policies and, coupled with lax regulatory policies, can stimulate reckless lending and asset bubbles. Volatile capital flows can undermine macroeconomic and exchange rate management, and worsen the liquidity or solvency problems of banks. This can exacerbate financial sector difficulties and, furthermore, provoke a balance of payments crisis. In China, with its underdeveloped financial systems, maintaining control on capital account convertibility will help to evade the GATS rules on market access and national treatment.

Protection Evasion Measures Under the GATS

Protection evasion measures under the GATS are mainly related to the interpretation of the relationship between Article XVI and Article XVII. For example:

1. Taxation. One of the weaknesses detected by Matoo (1996) is that the list under Article XVI does not include all measures that could restrict market access. GATS Article XX:2 states:

> Measures inconsistent with both Article XVI and XVII shall be inscribed in the column relating to Article XVI. In this case the inscription will be considered to provide a condition or qualification to Article XVII as well.

The market access column in the schedules of commitments contains measures that are inconsistent with Article XVI only, as well as those that are inconsistent with both Articles XVI and XVII. In China's case, the government might adopt certain measures as a remedy for its commitments. Take taxation for example. Before accession, China levied a lower tax rate on foreign enterprises than on domestic enterprises. Starting from 2001, China could raise the tax rate by adopting a high nondiscriminatory tax on foreign currency business, since it is the only business that foreign banks are permitted upon accession, and this would not affect the domestic banks significantly because they have been limited by the state. Raising the tax rate may well serve to limit market access, without being obliged to the schedule since fiscal measures are not covered. Secondly, the limitations must be read as "minimum guarantees" rather than "maximum quotas," that is, China, which has promised to liberalize all quantitative limitations after five years, may be able to prolong the period allowed for this step until later.

2. Different treatment for services and suppliers. There is another uncertainty raised by a difference between the text of Article XVI and XVII and the manner in which commitments on national treatment are scheduled. As Matoo (1996) pointed out: "when a Member has bound itself to provide national treatment under all four modes . . . the question is whether nominally identical commitments translate into effective equality of treatment."

In the case of China's banking system, the four state-owned banks are under the umbrella of the government's credit plan and interest control, which implies that they may have priority over other suppliers in taking deposits and granting loans. Given the national obligation, who else could claim a right to be included in the priority list? Paragraph 10 of the Explanatory Note states that: "There is no obligation in the GATS which requires a Member to take measures outside its territorial jurisdiction. It therefore follows that the national treatment obligation in Article XVII does not require a Member to extend such treatment to a service supplier located in the territory of another Member."

China is not obliged to extend its credit plan or other measures provided to domestic banks to suppliers located outside its territory. Especially, it is the treatment of suppliers that the Explanation Note addresses, not the treatment of services. That is to say, China is not obliged to extend its governmental credit plan to suppliers located outside the territory even though their service is supplied within it.

3. Government support. Arising from the argument about services and suppliers is the question of government support, normally in the form of certain governmental instructions or guidance. In China, this business practice is maintained owing to inherent deficiencies caused by the nonmarket mechanism. According to Article IX of GATS, when certain business practices of service suppliers may restrain competition and thereby restrict trade in services they are subject to consultation between the involved parties. According to the "Report of the Working Party on the Accession of China" (WTO 2001a), China has confirmed:

> China would ensure that all state-owned and state-invested enterprises will make purchases and sales based solely on commercial considerations, e.g., price, quality, marketability, availability, and that the enterprises of other WTO members will have an adequate opportunity to compete for sales to and purchases from these enterprises on nondiscriminatory terms and conditions.

It is not identified, however, in this statement what role the government is to play in the decision-making process of the state enterprises, which is not necessarily by means of regulations or certain policy guidance. It is rather difficult to determine in China's situation whether or not a purchase and sale are based on commercial considerations. It can be assumed therefore that the Chinese government can still influence its state enterprises without violation of GATS.

Furthermore, an uncertainty about intent in Article XVI and XVII is raised when attempting to interpret Article VI, which deals with domestic regulations. It is stipulated in Article VI:5:

> The Member should not apply licensing and qualification requirements and technical standards that nullify or impair such specific commitments in a manner which:
>
> (i) does not comply with the criteria outlined in subparagraphs 4(a)[objectivity and transparency], 4(b) [not more burdensome than necessary to ensure the quality of the service], and 4(c) [in the case of licensing procedures, of not being in themselves a restriction on the supply of the service]; and
>
> (ii) could not reasonably have been expected of that Member at the time the specific commitments in those sectors were made (Article VI).

The content of (ii) above could be read as "grandfathering" all existing restrictive requirements. If China requires a certain qualification for the establishment of a subsidiary or tax measure out of prudential reasons for the purpose of limiting the competition from foreign banks, it could, therefore, "reasonably have been expected" when the specific commitments were made.

4. Product-specific safeguard commitments and prudential measures of GATS. In the Annex on Financial Services of GATS there is a "prudential carve-out" for domestic regulations to ensure that the opening of markets that the agreement is intended to achieve will not jeopardize prudential regulation and supervision. It permits a country to take prudential measures " for the protection of investors, depositors, policy holders or persons to whom a fiduciary duty is owed" or "to ensure the integrity and stability

of the financial system" regardless of any other provisions of the GATS (WTO 1993). This provision may not, however, be used to avoid a country's obligation and commitments under the agreement. Disagreement over whether a particular measure falls within prudential carve-out is subject to WTO dispute settlement procedures and thus potentially to be determination by a dispute settlement panel. The key issue involved here is how to draw a line between prudential measures and discriminative measures. Especially in China's case, when its overall financial system is underdeveloped, certain nonprudential measures under otherwise market conditions may be taken as prudential. Since the United States can lock in a supra-GATT article on "product-specific safeguard measures" to deter the importation of Chinese products, China may well use a similar method, for example, in the name of market disruption, to take certain measures to protect its financial market.

The uncertainties in interpreting the above GATS rules suggest from one point the complexity of defining services trade. From another point, these gray areas seem to provide a clue for members to avoid a potential crisis. The whole analysis on China's commitments and applicability of GATS rules has come to suggest that if China's market conditions can accommodate the competition of foreign banks, there will be no reason to question if China can live up to its commitments. However, China may avail itself of the WTO rules to effectively protect its under-construction financial system.

Institutional Track Reliance and Reform

In the first two years following China's entry into the WTO, the Chinese banking system has steered itself prudently toward an opening market system. Though its regulatory body, the China Banking Regulatory Commission, has operated since April 2003, the topic of reforming the banking mechanism remains untouched. Understandably, it takes time for China to nurture the proper environment for institutional change in the banking system, especially when this involves a drastic shift of governmental responsibility from commercial banking activities. If China is to perform its financial commitments to the WTO, the four state-financed commercial banks must undergo reform, otherwise they will not be able survive in the competition with foreign banks.

Conclusion

This chapter assesses the asymmetry between China's banking system and its financial commitments to the WTO and problems in interpreting the national treatment obligation in the GATS. As the banking sector becomes market oriented and all of the banking infrastructures demanded by a market economy are still developing, China's compliance relies largely on the governmental policy and trade framework. All the arguments on the capability of China's compliance are induced by concerns about its weak financial system and mechanisms to prevent financial crisis in an open market. Though GATS regulations are directed at modes of supply, the intention of negotiators is to extract the largest number of possibilities for capital mobility from each other.

Since the WTO functions as a contractual trade institution where all countries are supposed to have the opportunity to participate on an equal basis in the negotiation process, it can be envisaged that China may also improve its commitments, and thus achieve a progressively higher level of liberalization, by participating in the periodic negotiating rounds.

Notes

1. A statement by General Counsel Davidson to the U.S.-China Security Review Commission, August 2, 2001. Available at www.usembassy.it/file2001_08/alia/a1080503.htm.

2. State policy banks are state-owned, nonprofit financial institutions that are in charge of fiscal allocation and government bond issues. They finance state development projects that are normally of significance to the national economy and require heavy investment and long-term returns that commercial banks are not willing and not capable of handling. They do not have branches and their business is conducted through an agency of commercial banks. At present, there are three policy banks: the China Development Bank, the China Import & Export Bank, and the China Agriculture Development Bank, each responsible for specific functions (Dai 1997, 6–10).

3. A credit cooperative is an economic organization formed by craftsmen based on free membership, equality, and mutual benefit. They have existed in China for more than one hundred years. As a form of property rights, a credit cooperative is different from stockholding in some respects. First, they have a different share-buying mechanism, not based on holding control but on equal ownership. Second, there is a different business aim. It is to provide services for its members, not for maximizing dividends. Third, there is a different management philosophy. They have a principle of "one share holder one vote" not "one share one vote"; all share holders enjoy equal rights. Finally, they may have a different dividend distribution. Profits are mainly for capital accumulation and belong to the entire membership (Dai 1997, 32).

4. These include Shenzhen, Zhuhai, Xiamen, Shantou, and Hainan province.

5. In September 1983, the Chinese State Council passed a resolution to reform the PBOC by separating central banking from commercial banking functions. The PBOC was made the country's central bank (PBOC 1984a). See www.pbc.gov.cn/jinrongfaguizhengce/guifanxingwenjian.asp (in Chinese).

6. This was adopted in May 1995 and came into effect in July 1995.

7. These four companies, financed by issuing government-backed bonds, purchase non-performing loans at face value from the banks in exchange for equity positions in the borrowing firms. They seek to recover as much as possible through a

combination of liquidation, auction, securitization, sale of equity, mergers and acquisitions, and private placements of the assets they acquire.

8. The possibility of taking MFN exemptions under the GATS ended when the WTO agreement entered into force, except in maritime, financial, and basic telecommunications services, three sectors where negotiations have not yet been definitively concluded. Any new exemptions can only be obtained by seeking a waiver under paragraph 3 of the WTO agreement.

9. Quoted from "Foreign Trade Barriers—China" at www.usconsulate.org.hk/uscn/2001.htm.

10. Arranging a loan with a foreign bank abroad via telephone would fall under mode 1, whereas the same loan arranged through the domestic subsidiary or branch of a foreign bank would fall under mode 3.

References

Dai, Xianglong, ed. 1997. *Finance Know-How for Cadres (Ganbu jinrong zhishi duben)*. Beijing: China Finance Publisher.

Feng, Wei. 1999. *China's Financial Sector Reform in the Transition to a Market Economy*. New Brunswick, NJ: Transaction.

Finance Ministry Information Office. 2004. "In Response to Super-National Treatment."

He, Chengying. 2001. "The Impact of WTO Accession on Financial Industry and Listed Companies." *Finance and Insurance* 2: 105–7.

Kono, Masamichi, and Ludger Schuknecht. 1998. "Financial Services Trade, Capital Flows, and Financial Stability." WTO Staff Working Paper ERAD, 98–12.

Li, Jijian. 2001. "The Divergence of Financial Development and China's Financial System Reform" (*Jinrong fazhan yu Zhongguo de jinrong tixi gaige*). *Finance and Insurance* 2.

Li, Shixiang. 2000. "On Authorized Management Within the State-Owned Commercial Banks" (*Lun guoyou shangye yinhang neibu de shouqun guanli*). *Finance and Insurance* 8: 67–70.

Mattoo, Aaditya. 1996. "National Treatment in the GATS: Cornerstone or Pandora's Box?" WTO Working Paper (January). Available at www.wto.org/english/res_e/reser_e/wpaps_e.htm.

———. 2000. "Financial Services and the WTO: Liberalization Commitments of the Developing and Transition Economies." *World Economy* 23.

Molyneux, Philip. 1997. *Efficiency in European Banking*. New York and London: Garland.

National People's Congress. 1995. *Law of the People's Bank of China, PRC (Zhongguo renmin yinhang fa)*. Available at www.pbc.gov.cn/jinrongfaguizhengce/jinrongfalv.asp.

People's Bank of China. 1984a. *The Resolution of the State Council on the Function of the People's Bank of China (Guowuyuan guanyu Zhongguo renmin yinhang zhineng de jueding)*. Beijing. Available at www.pbc.gov.cn/jinrongfaguizhengce/jinrongfalv.asp.

———. 1984b. *The Role and Functions of the Central Bank (Zhongguo renmin yinhang de zuoyong yu zhineng)*. Available at www.pbc.gov.cn/jinrongfaguizhengce/guifanxingwenjian.asp.

Qian, Xiaoan. 2000. "The Impact of WTO Accession on China's Banking Industry and Strategies" (*Jia ru shimao zuzhi dui Zhongguo yinhangye de yingxiang ji duice*). *Finance and Insurance* 5: 39.

Shen, Yuliang. 2003. *Multilateral Trading System & China's Economic Institutional Transition (Duo bian maoyi tizhi yu woguo jingji zhidu bianqian)*. Shanghai: Shanghai Social Science Academy Printing House.

Song, Qinghua. 2001. "Banking Crisis: The Reality China Is Doomed to Confront" (*Yinhang weiji: Zhongguo jijiang mianlin de xianshi*). *Finance and Insurance* 2: 48–52.

Song, Xinguo, and Wu Jingjie. 2001. "The Development Trend of the Chinese Banking Industry After Accession to the WTO" (*Ru shi hou Zhongguo yinhangye de fazhan qushi*). *Finance and Insurance* 3: 137, 24.

Tang, Xiaoguang. 2000. "On Restructuring China's Commercial Banking System" (*Lun Zhongguo yinhangye de chongzu*). *Finance and Insurance* 2: 68–69.

U.S. Consulate General, Hong Kong. 2001. "USTR General Counsel on China's 'Imminent' WTO Accession" (August 2). Available at www.usconsulate.org.hk/uscn/2001.htm.

United States General Accounting Office (GAO). 2000. *World Trade Organization: China's Membership Status and Normal Trade Relations Issues* (GAO/HSIAD-00–94). Available at http://usinfo.state.gov/regional/ea/uschina/ns00094.pdf.

United States Trade Representative Office (USTR). 1999. *China's Draft Services Schedule, The U.S.–China Agreement*. Available at www.ustr.gov/assets/Document_Library/.

Wang, Kang. 2000. "On the Deficiencies in China's Commercial Banking System" (*Lun Zhongguo shangye yinhang de quexian*). *Finance and Insurance* 4: 42–44.

Wang, Zhaoxing. 2001. "The Market Infrastructure for Effective Banking Supervision" (*Yinhang you xiao jianguan de shichang jichu*). *China Finance* 7.

William, John. 1999. "Whether and When to Liberalize Capital Account and Financial Services." WTO Staff Working Paper, ERAD-99–03 (September) Available at www.wto.org/english/res_e/reser_e/erad-99–03.doc.

World Trade Organization. 1993. *General Agreement on Trade in Services*, MTN.GNS/W/164,3. Available at www.wto.org/english/docs_e/legal_e/legal_e.htm#servic/.

———. 2000. *Status of China's Trade Commitments to the United States and Other Members* (GAO/NSIAD-00–142).

———. 2001a. "Report of the Working Party on the Accession of China." Available at www.wto.org/WT/MIN(01)/3/.

———. 2001b. "Report of the Working Party on the Accession of China, Part II—Schedule of Specific Commitments on Services." Available at www.wto.org/WT/MIN(01)/3/Add.2/.

Zhao, Xu. 2001. "Comparative Analysis of Efficiency Within the Chinese and Foreign Commercial Banks" (*Zhongwai shangye yinhang de xiaolu bijiao fenxi*). *World Economic Forum* 1: 39–44.

Part IV

Industrial and Agricultural Development

15

Openness and China's Industrial Locations

An Empirical Investigation

Ting Gao

Recent advances in economic geography stress the importance of access to markets and suppliers in choosing industry locations (Fujita, Krugman, and Venables 1999). In the presence of the demand for increasing returns to scale, and rising transportation and trade costs, firms have economic incentives to concentrate their production in locations that are close to their customers and suppliers. Therefore, when everything else is equal, locations with overall better access to markets and suppliers (domestic and foreign) tend to attract more production activity.

Changes in a country's openness to international trade and foreign direct investment (FDI) can thus cause adjustments in the location of industries within that country. Trade allows domestic firms to access foreign markets and suppliers. FDI brings in multinational firms that often have already established extensive networks in international markets. Liberalization of foreign trade and FDI may affect different regions' access to foreign markets, suppliers, and capital differently and induce changes in the spatial distribution of industries, especially in a geographically large country.

Other impacts of increased openness on the regional distribution of industries may come from the dynamic effects of international trade and FDI. International trade subjects domestic firms to foreign competition and provides additional incentives for them to improve efficiency and stay competitive. Trade is also a means for domestic firms to import advanced technologies, and FDI is believed to be an important vehicle of technology transfer. Regions that receive greater FDI are likely to benefit more from advanced foreign technologies and management. These benefits may also spill over to domestic firms through worker mobility and other informal channels. As a result, industries in regions with more trade and FDI can experience faster productivity growth. Uneven industrial growth across regions then will lead to changes in the pattern of industrial location.

This chapter examines the factors that may explain the pattern of industrial location in China and the recent changes, with specific attention to regional openness to trade and FDI. China opened up to trade and FDI in the late 1970s, and has transformed itself, though gradually, from a virtually closed economy into a major trading nation in the world. In 2000, China accounted for 3.4 percent of world trade and was a large FDI recipient in the developing world.

International trade and FDI are highly concentrated in China—southeast China conducts most of China's foreign trade and receives the majority of inward FDI. These patterns emerged from the beginning of China's "open-door" policy and still persist today, even though regional trade and FDI policies that initially favored the coastal regions have been largely removed. In the meantime, it is observed that significant changes in the regional distribution of industries have taken place in the last two decades or so, which will be discussed below in greater detail.

Is there a link between the location of industries and the pattern of regional openness in China? This chapter attempts to address this question. The findings will help us understand China's regional industrial development, and have policy implications for China's regional development strategy. It will also shed useful light on future changes for industrial locations in China as the nation continues to reform itself and become further integrated with the rest of the world.

Literature

Under increasing returns to scale, transportation and trade costs affect the location of production. Firms tend to economize on transportation and trade costs by locating close to customers and suppliers. Even in the absence of fundamental differences across regions, an uneven distribution of production activity can arise. This is a key insight of recent research in economic geography.

Paul R. Krugman (1991) illustrates agglomeration of an increasing returns to scale sector in a model with two identical regions and factor mobility. In an international context, Paul R. Krugman and Anthony J. Venables (1995) show that a core-periphery pattern of industry, which implies the inequality of nations, emerges among countries when there exist demand and cost linkages in the increasing returns sector. In a theoretical model that stresses the importance of openness, Raul Elizondo and Paul R. Krugman (1996) suggest that third world mega cities (such as Mexico City) with a large concentration of economic activity can be the consequences of firms serving small domestic markets under restricted foreign trade policy.

Empirically, Gordon Hanson (1998) studies the impact of economic integration with the United States on the location of industries in Mexico and finds strong effects on trade in Mexican states that are closer to the United States, where industries experience faster employment growth. Karen Helene Midelfart-Knarvik et al. (2000, 2001) focus on the location of industries in European countries. They find that a country's market potential, a proxy for access to markets and suppliers, is indeed important in explaining industrial location in Europe, especially for industries with strong demand and cost linkages and with increasing returns to scale. However, they do not separately identify the effects of the market potential that can be attributed to international trade and FDI.

In the case of China, Ting Gao (2002) uses data on aggregate industrial output at the provincial level to examine the relationship between regional industrial growth, trade, and FDI, and finds that provincial industrial growth was strongly and positively associated with trade and FDI over the period of 1985–1995. In Gao (2004), data on more detailed two-digit Chinese industrial classification industries are used to investigate the roles of three broadly defined location factors behind regional industrial growth: natural advantage, dynamic externalities, and foreign trade and FDI. Regional trade and FDI again are found to have had strong positive effects on regional industrial growth over the period of 1985–1993.

China's Regional Trade, FDI, and the Distribution of Industries

Changes in China's policies toward foreign trade and FDI have been widely discussed in the literature (see, for example, Lardy 1992, Naughton 1996, and Fu 2000). Perhaps the most important policy step taken in the early stage of the open-door policy was to designate four cities (Shenzhen, Zhuhai, Shantou, and Xiamen) on the southeast coast as special economic zones in 1980, where incentive packages, such as duty-free imports of raw materials, income tax concessions, and various subsidies from local jurisdictions, were offered to attract foreign investors. Similar incentives to foreign firms were offered in fourteen other coastal cities in 1984. Later on, economic and development zones and other similarly designated areas popped up across China.

Table 15.1

Regional Shares of Population and Industrial Output (selected years)

	1985	1987	1989	1991	1993	1995	1997
Population							
Coast	0.413	0.413	0.412	0.413	0.412	0.412	0.412
Southeast	0.233	0.233	0.233	0.233	0.233	0.234	0.235
Other coast	0.180	0.180	0.179	0.180	0.179	0.178	0.177
Inland	0.587	0.587	0.588	0.587	0.588	0.588	0.588
Industrial output							
Coast	0.579	0.611	0.622	0.637	0.707	0.660	0.653
Southeast	0.310	0.353	0.357	0.374	0.422	0.427	0.414
Other coast	0.269	0.258	0.265	0.263	0.285	0.233	0.240
Inland	0.421	0.389	0.378	0.363	0.293	0.340	0.346

Source: Calculations are based on data from the *Statistical Yearbook of China* (various years).
Note: The coastal region includes Beijing, Tianjin, Hebei, Liaoning, Shanghai, Jiangsu, Zhejiang, Fujian, Shandong, Guangdong (including Hainan), and Guangxi. The southeast coast includes Shanghai, Jiangsu, Zhejiang, Fujian, Guangdong (including Hainan), and Guangxi.

However, the gradualism adopted in China's opening up apparently has given the coast regions a head start and, to some extent, contributed to the concentration of trade and FDI on China's southeast coast.

Table 15.1 gives the population shares of coastal and inland regions. The coastal region includes eleven provinces (Hainan is treated as part of Guangdong and Chongqing as part of Sichuan province for data purposes).[1] The region accounted for a little more than 41 percent of China's population in 1985, and that percentage remained steady throughout the sample period of 1985–1997. Within the region, the southeast coast had about 23 percent of China's population, as the upper part of Table 15.1 shows.

The coastal region had a share of industry greater than its share of population even at the beginning of the sample period, producing about 58 percent of China's industrial output. And the output share increased significantly over 1985–1997, rising to 65 percent in 1997. Much of that increase occurred on the southeast coast, which experienced a dramatic surge in share from 31–41 percent. The rest of the coastal region and the inland region both witnessed declines in their shares. Thus, there was a significant shift in the distribution of industry, with the industrial center moving toward the southeast coast.

It must be made clear that output share changes only imply the industrial sector grew at different speeds in different regions. A decline in share does not necessarily mean a decrease in the level of output. In fact, over the sample

Table 15.2

Regional Shares of FDI, Exports, and Imports (selected years)

	1985	1987	1989	1991	1993	1995	1997
FDI							
Coast	0.896	0.893	0.922	0.904	0.875	0.879	0.859
Southeast	0.734	0.673	0.718	0.713	0.701	0.685	0.638
Other coast	0.161	0.213	0.204	0.191	0.173	0.194	0.221
Inland	0.104	0.107	0.078	0.096	0.125	0.121	0.141
Exports							
Coast	0.807	0.726	0.736	0.723	0.840	0.872	0.891
Southeast	0.384	0.423	0.463	0.491	0.672	0.677	0.707
Other coast	0.423	0.303	0.272	0.232	0.167	0.195	0.184
Inland	0.193	0.274	0.264	0.277	0.160	0.128	0.109
Imports							
Coast	0.874	0.853	0.841	0.851	0.870	0.876	0.916
Southeast	0.670	0.656	0.627	0.702	0.683	0.642	0.694
Other coast	0.203	0.197	0.214	0.149	0.188	0.234	0.222
Inland	0.126	0.147	0.159	0.149	0.130	0.123	0.084

Source: Calculations are based on data from the *Statistical Yearbook of China* and *The Almanac of China's Foreign Trade and Economic Relations* (various issues).
   Note: The regional divisions are the same as in Table 15.1.

period, the inland region and the non-southeast coast also enjoyed decent industrial growth rates, and their declining shares only reflect the much faster growth on the southeast coast.

Participation in foreign trade and FDI varied greatly from region to region. Table 15.2 shows the regional shares of FDI, imports and exports for the same regional breakdown as in Table 15.1. For the selected years shown in the table, the coastal region attracted the majority of FDI inflows into China, exceeding 85 percent each year. And over 60 percent of FDI in China found its way to the southeast coast, which had about 23 percent of China's population and 41 percent of industrial output in 1997.

The coastal region was also responsible for more than proportional shares of both imports and exports (92 and 89 percent respectively in 1997). Once again, the southeast coast conducted the majority of foreign trade in China. The export share of the southeast coast exploded from 38 to 71 percent, making the region the de facto export center of China.

The concentration of FDI and trade in southeast coastal China may not be entirely due to regional preferential trade and FDI policies. Coastal regions have the natural advantages of lower costs of shipping goods to and from foreign markets as well as a better transport and telecommunication infrastructure. These advantages are magnified by the overall poor transport system within China, which makes the trade costs of inland regions with markets outside China much higher, and therefore significantly hampers the inland regions' ability to conduct foreign trade and attract FDI.

Two additional factors may also explain the uneven distribution of trade and FDI. The coastal region historically has been more industrialized, as evident in its share of industrial output at the beginning of the reform period. Furthermore, the southeast coast, Guangdong and Fujian provinces in particular, have stronger cultural ties with and enjoy geographical proximity to Hong Kong and Taiwan, which, somewhat coincidentally, rose rapidly in the 1980s as important sources of FDI in Asia.

Let us turn next to the distribution of individual manufacturing industries across the three regions, as shown in Table 15.3. The southeast's share of industrial output increased in twenty-four out of twenty-six manufacturing industries. The inland region, on the other hand, lost ground in twenty-five out of twenty-six industries. The other coastal region also saw decreases in its output share in nineteen out of twenty-six industries. Consistent with the observation made previously that the southeast coast was fast becoming the export center of China, the region experienced large increases in output share in China's exporting industries, such as the Apparel and Other Textile Products industry, and the Leathers, Furs, Down, and Related Products industry. The evidence seems to suggest that a broad shift in the distribution of manufacturing in China (or, perhaps, an agglomeration of industry on the southeast coast) is taking shape.

What explains the patterns of manufacturing industries and their changes in recent years? How important is the role of regional openness? The remainder of this chapter provides empirical evidence on these issues.

Empirical Specifications and Variables

The following equation is used to examine the pattern of industrial location in China,

$$s_{ij} = \beta_0 + \beta_1 Pop_j + \beta_2 L_j + \beta_3 T_j + \beta_4 C_j + \beta_5 DM_j + \beta_6 O_j + \varepsilon_{ij,} \qquad (1)$$

where i is the industry index, j is the province index, s_{ij} is province j's share of industry i in the nation, Pop_j is population, which is to measure the size of province j, L_j is labor quality, T_j is a proxy for transportation infrastructure, C_j is a proxy for telecommunication infrastructure, DM_j is a constructed measure of province j's access to domestic markets, O_j is openness, and ε_{ij} is an error term.

In equation (1), the openness variable (O_j) is to capture a province's access to foreign markets and suppliers. DM_j, a domestic equivalent of O_j, is also included in the equation to account for province j's access to domestic

Table 15.3

Regional Shares of Output in Manufacturing Industries, 1985 and 1997

Industry	Southeast Coast			Other Coast			Inland		
	1985	1997	Change	1985	1997	Change	1985	1997	Change
Food Manufacturing	0.332	0.348	+	0.205	0.263	+	0.462	0.388	–
Beverage Manufacturing	0.286	0.329	+	0.208	0.240	+	0.506	0.431	–
Tobacco Processing	0.211	0.184	–	0.165	0.078	–	0.624	0.738	+
Textile	0.438	0.530	+	0.267	0.207	–	0.295	0.263	–
Apparel and Other Textile Products	0.397	0.676	+	0.283	0.178	–	0.320	0.146	–
Leather, Furs, Down, and Related Products	0.329	0.614	+	0.276	0.200	–	0.395	0.186	–
Timber Processing, Bamboo, Cane, Palm Fiber, and Straw Products	0.287	0.429	+	0.167	0.156	–	0.545	0.415	–
Furniture Manufacturing	0.358	0.431	+	0.234	0.229	–	0.407	0.339	–
Papermaking and Paper Products	0.399	0.391	–	0.176	0.268	+	0.425	0.341	–
Printing and Record Processing	0.333	0.429	+	0.267	0.208	–	0.400	0.362	–
Stationary, Education, and Sports Goods	0.595	0.766	+	0.242	0.144	–	0.162	0.090	–
Petroleum Processing	0.253	0.265	+	0.404	0.394	–	0.342	0.341	–
Chemical and Allied Products	0.317	0.384	+	0.297	0.238	–	0.386	0.378	–
Medical and Pharmaceutical Products	0.374	0.378	+	0.235	0.241	+	0.389	0.381	–
Chemical Fibers	0.557	0.672	+	0.226	0.141	–	0.215	0.186	–
Rubber Products	0.336	0.398	+	0.304	0.329	+	0.359	0.271	–
Plastic Products	0.514	0.587	+	0.226	0.181	–	0.260	0.232	–
Building Materials and Other Non-metal Mineral Products	0.325	0.335	+	0.253	0.245	–	0.422	0.421	–

(continued)

Table 15.3 (continued)

Industry	Southeast Coast			Other Coast			Inland		
	1985	1997	Change	1985	1997	Change	1985	1997	Change
Smelting and Pressing of Ferrous Metals	0.242	0.288	+	0.346	0.335	–	0.410	0.377	–
Smelting and Pressing of Nonferrous Metals	0.254	0.319	+	0.210	0.164	–	0.534	0.517	–
Metal Products	0.379	0.513	+	0.287	0.236	–	0.333	0.250	–
Ordinary Machinery	0.345	0.412	+	0.271	0.279	+	0.384	0.309	–
Transportation Equipment	0.230	0.402	+	0.268	0.219	–	0.502	0.378	–
Electrical Equipment and Machinery	0.470	0.587	+	0.229	0.215	–	0.302	0.197	–
Electronic and Telecommunication Equipment	0.549	0.634	+	0.210	0.224	+	0.240	0.141	–
Instruments, Meters, Cultural, and Office Machinery	0.449	0.665	+	0.219	0.173	–	0.333	0.162	–

markets. DM_j is defined as the distance-weighted sum of GDP's of other provinces (in logarithm), that is,

$$DM_j = ln(\sum_{k \neq j} \frac{1}{dist_{jk}} \frac{GDP_k}{\overline{GDP}}),$$

where $dist_{jk}$ is the distance between provinces j and k, and other provinces' GDPs are expressed as shares in total national GDP ($\overline{GDP}$). The labor quality, transportation, and communication variables in equation (1) are intended to capture other location advantages of a province that might matter for manufacturing production.

Let us now turn to changes in the distribution of industries. Spatial adjustments in industrial location are a result of uneven growth across provinces. Therefore, variables that are potentially important for industrial growth should be considered in explaining the changes. The empirical specification for this purpose is

$$\Delta s_{ij} = \gamma_0 + \gamma_1 s_{ij} + \gamma_2 L_j + \gamma_3 T_j + \gamma_4 C_j + \gamma_5 O_j + \gamma_6 S_j +$$

$$\gamma_7 ||I|| E_{ij}^1 + \gamma_8 E_{ij}^2 + \gamma_9 E_{ij}^3 + \mu_{ij}, \tag{2}$$

where Δs_{ij} is the change in s_{ij} between 1985 and 1997. All of the explanatory variables are measured at the beginning of the sample period from 1985 to 1997 (e.g., s_{ij} is the initial distribution of industry i in 1985) to minimize the potential problem of reverse causality. If numbers for 1985 are not available for a particular variable, the variable is then measured for the year that is the closest to 1985 with available data.

In addition to s_{ij}, L_j, T_j, C_j and O_j, four other variables are added to the right-hand side of equation (2). The first one is the share of state-owned enterprises in industrial output for 1985 (S_j). The rationale for including this variable is that state-owned enterprises in China are overall less efficient, and plagued by incentive problems as well as excessive social responsibilities. Maintaining a large state sector drains resources that could be otherwise directed to more productive uses, and therefore reduces industrial growth.

In addition, three variables, E_{ij}^1, E_{ij}^2, E_{ij}^3, and, measuring three possible types of dynamic externality arising from local specialization, local competition, and local industrial diversity, are added to the list of explanatory variables. E_{ij}^1 is a proxy for the Marshall-Arrow-Romer externality, which may explain the growth of an industry in a specific location. The concentration of a single industry due to local specialization facilitates knowledge spillovers through, among others, copying, spying, and worker mobility (Glaeser, Kallal, Scheinkman, and Shleifer 1992; Henderson, Kuncoro, and Turner 1995). E_{ij}^1 is defined as

$$E_{ij}^1 = \left(\frac{y_{ij}}{y_{\cdot j}}\right) \bigg/ \left(\frac{y_{i\cdot}}{y_{\cdot\cdot}}\right),$$

where y_{ij} is the output of industry i in province j, $y_{\cdot j}$ is the output of all industries in province j, $y_{i\cdot}$ is the output of industry i in the nation, and $y_{\cdot\cdot}$ is total industrial output of all industries in the nation. Thus, E_{ij}^1 measures the weight or importance of industry i in province j relative to the national average. If E_{ij}^1 is greater than 1, province j is more specialized in industry i than is the rest of China. A greater measured E_{ij}^1 also indicates that province j is more specialized in industry i.

E_{ij}^2 is a measure of the degree of local competition defined as

$$E_{ij}^2 = \left(\frac{n_{ij}}{y_{ij}}\right) \bigg/ \left(\frac{n_{i\cdot}}{y_{i\cdot}}\right),$$

where n_{ij} is the number of firms in industry i in province j, and $n_{i\cdot}$ is the number of firms in industry i nationwide. In fact, E_{ij}^2 is (the inverse of) the average output of a firm in industry i in province j relative to the national average. The greater E_{ij}^2 is, the smaller are industry i's firms in province j—industry i in province j is thus believed to be more competitive (Porter 1990). A higher degree of competition pushes firms to work harder to innovate and therefore accelerate productivity growth.

Finally, E_{ij}^3 captures the notion of Jane Jacobs (1969) that greater local industrial diversity leads to a higher degree of interindustry knowledge spillover or cross fertilization. Jacobs, in her work on city growth, argues that cross fertilization among a large variety of industries is the engine of growth in the city. E_{ij}^3 is a Herfindahl-Hirschman index of industries, defined as

$$E_{ij}^3 = \sum_{k \neq i} s_{kj}^2$$

where $s_{kj} = y_{kj}/y_{\cdot j}$ is the share of industry k in total industrial output in province j.

Whether these externalities are present in Chinese industries is an empirical question. Even if they are, whether they contribute significantly to regional industrial growth depends on a number of conditions. First, firms must

Table 15.4

Variables and Definitions

Variable	Definition
Province j's share of industry i (s_{ij})	(industry i's output in province j/industry i's national output)
Openness (FDI)	(FDI in province j/GDP in province j)
Openness (trade)	(sum of exports and imports in province j/GDP in province j)
Domestic access (DM_j)	$D_j = \sum_{k \neq j} \dfrac{1}{dist_{jk}} \dfrac{GDP_k}{\overline{GDP}}$
Labor quality (L_j)	percentage of workers with junior high school education or above
Transportation (T_j)	(total length of railway, highway, and waterway/area of province j)/(total length of railway, highway, and waterway/area in China)
Telecommunication (C_j)	(number of telephones/population in province j)/(number of telephones/population in China)
State sector (S_j)	share of state-owned enterprises in industrial output in province j
Local specialization (E_{ij}^1)	$E_{ij}^1 = \left(\dfrac{y_{ij}}{y_{\cdot j}} \right) / \left(\dfrac{y_{i\cdot}}{y_{\cdot\cdot}} \right)$
Local competition (E_{ij}^2)	$E_{ij}^2 = \left(\dfrac{n_{ij}}{y_{ij}} \right) / \left(\dfrac{n_{i\cdot}}{y_{i\cdot}} \right)$
Local diversity (E_{ij}^3)	$E_{ij}^3 = \sum_{k \neq i} s_{kj}^2$ where ($s_{kj} = y_{kj}/y_{\cdot j}$)

be driven by the right incentives to improve efficiency and increase productivity. This requires the existence of the market mechanism and a significant degree of competition. Second, these externalities must be to some extent localized to have a greater impact on local industrial growth.

The definitions of the variables used in equations (1) and (2) are gathered in Table 15.4 for easy reference.

Data and Results

Data Sources

The analysis discussed in this chapter uses data on the industrial output of two-digit (Chinese industrial classification) manufacturing industries by province. Data for 1985 are from the officially published 1985 *People's Republic of China Industrial Census Materials*, and data for 1997 are taken from the 1998 *China Industrial Economy Statistical Yearbook*. There are a total of twenty-six manufacturing industries in the data. Information at the provincial level on GDP, the education attainment of workers, transportation (length of railways, highways, and waterways), telecommunication (number of phones), and the output of state-owned enterprises is found in various issues of the *Statistical Yearbook of China*. Numbers for provincial exports, imports, and FDI are available from the *Almanac of China's Foreign Economic Relations and Trade* and the *Statistical Yearbook of China*. Since data on Hainan and Chongqing for 1985, the beginning of the sample period, are not available, Hainan is treated as part of Guangdong province, and Chongqing as part of Sichuan province.

Results and Discussion

Evidence on the relationship between the cross-province distribution of industries and the pattern of openness for 1997 is shown in Table 15.5, which collects regression results based on equation (1). In this set of regressions, data for 1997 are used for all the explanatory variables (except the number of phones which is for 1995 due to data availability). The dependent variable is province *j*'s share of industry *i* (measured in fractions). The population of a province (in logarithm), a proxy for the size of the province, is positive and highly significant in all regressions. An increase of 1 percent in population raises the province's share of an individual industry by more than 0.0002 (or 0.02 percentage point).

When openness (either trade or FDI) is included in the regression, it is positive and statistically significant at the 1 percent level, as shown in columns (1) and (2). Take the coefficient on FDI in column (1) for example. A one-percentage-point increase in the FDI/GDP ratio raises the province's share of an industry by 0.013. Given the large differences in the ratio across the provinces, this result implies a large effect of FDI on industrial location. The same can be said for trade based on the estimate in column (2). The sample correlation between trade and FDI is very high at 0.85 for 1997, so a multicollinearity problem arises when both of them are included in the explanatory variables. Therefore, in all of the reported regressions, trade and FDI are entered separately.

This, however, does not complicate our interpretation of the results on openness too much because trade and FDI are highly correlated for a straightforward reason—much of China's international trade is conducted by foreign-invested firms. For example, foreign-invested firms were responsible for 42.4 percent of export growth in southeast China over the period of 1984–

Table 15.5

Openness and the Regional Distribution of Industries, 1997

Dependent variable: Province j's share of industry i in China (S_{ij})

	(1) OLS	(2) OLS	(3) OLS	(4) OLS	(5) OLS	(6) OLS	(7) IV	(8) IV
Constant	-0.172***	-0.174***	-0.186***	-0.207***	-0.173***	-0.200***	-0.169***	-0.197***
	(0.014)	(0.013)	(0.019)	(0.018)	(0.025)	(0.024)	(0.025)	(0.025)
Population (1997)	0.023***	0.023***	0.023***	0.022***	0.029***	0.024***	0.028***	0.025***
	(0.002)	(0.002)	(0.002)	(0.002)	(0.002)	(0.002)	(0.002)	(0.003)
Openness (FDI)	1.307***		1.279***		0.460***		0.728***	
	(0.090)		(0.004)		(0.130)		(0.221)	
Openness (trade)		0.220***		0.215***		0.181***		0.161***
		(0.011)		(0.011)		(0.020)		(0.060)
Domestic access			0.004	0.012***	-0.002	0.011**	-0.002	0.009
			(0.004)	(0.004)	(0.004)	(0.004)	(0.004)	(0.006)
Labor quality					-0.100***	-0.070***	-0.094***	-0.074***
					(0.016)	(0.016)	(0.017)	(0.020)
Transportation					0.004**	0.001	0.004**	0.002
					(0.002)	(0.002)	(0.002)	(0.002)
Telecommunication					0.020***	0.008**	0.017***	0.010
					(0.004)	(0.004)	(0.004)	(0.006)
R^2	0.340	0.445	0.341	0.454	0.422	0.471	0.419	0.440
N	696	696	696	696	696	696	696	696

Note: Standard errors are in the parentheses.
*** = 1 percent significance; ** = 5 percent significance; * = 10 percent significance.

1993 based on numbers in Barry Naughton (1996). As recently as 2001, they accounted for 51 percent of China's total foreign trade. Therefore, much of the measured trade openness can be attributed to FDI in China.

In columns (3) and (4) of Table 15.5, variable DM_j is also added to the regression. Although the coefficient on DM_j is positive, its statistical significance depends on which openness measure is used.

Provincial labor quality, transportation, and telecommunication are included in columns (5) and (6). The coefficients on transportation and telecommunication are positive and mostly statistically significant, indicating that the location of industries is positively influenced by provincial transportation and telecommunication infrastructure. However, labor quality, measuring the percentage of workers with junior high school education or higher, is negative and significant at the 1 percent level in both regressions. Changing the measure of the variable to other education attainment levels of workers (such as senior high school and above, and college and above), it is still found that the coefficient remains negative and its statistical significance varies (in some cases, the coefficient become insignificant). Therefore, there is no evidence that the location of industries is positively associated with labor quality measured in education.

Both trade and FDI remain positive and highly significant with the inclusion of the other explanatory variables, although the magnitude of the coefficients on trade and FDI is somewhat reduced (the coefficients still imply that trade and FDI are important economically). Overall, the evidence suggests that the geographic distribution of manufacturing industries is positively associated with the cross-province pattern of openness to trade/FDI.

Since the estimated partial correlation between industrial location and openness is contemporary, it is natural to question whether the relationship is causal. In other words, does the pattern of openness have a causal effect on the location of manufacturing industries? The concern is that there may be some unobserved factors that lead to greater shares of industries in province j and also more trade and FDI in the same province, and thus the correlation does not imply causality in any direction. To address this concern, some geographic attributes of a province are used to instrument openness. Taking a hint from Shang-Jin Wei and Yi Wu (2001), the minimum of the distances from a province to Shanghai and Hong Kong and a cost dummy are used as instruments. The instrumental variables (IV) estimates are shown in column (7) and (8), which are similar to the OLS (ordinary least squares) ones. No results are significantly changed in the IV estimates.

Let us now turn to the changes in the location of industries between 1985 and 1997. The dependent variable in Table 15.6 is the change in province j's

Table 15.6

Openness and Changes in Regional Distribution of Industries, 1985–1997

Dependent variable: Change in province j's share of industry i in China (DS_{ij})

	(1)	(2)	(3)	(4)	(5)	(6)
Constant	0.001	0.003*	0.127***	0.136***	0.126***	0.147***
	(0.002)	(0.002)	(0.009)	(0.010)	(0.012)	(0.013)
S_{ij} (1985)	–0.233***	–0.211***	–0.309***	–0.364***	–0.385***	–0.491***
	(0.032)	(0.039)	(0.034)	(0.037)	(0.046)	(0.049)
Openness (FDI)	0.290***		0.302***		0.291***	
	(0.027)		(0.025)		(0.027)	
Openness (trade)		0.047***		0.077***		0.081***
		(0.016)		(0.016)		(0.017)
Labor quality			–0.028**	–0.058***	–0.020*	–0.044***
			(0.011)	(0.012)	(0.012)	(0.013)
Transportation			0.002	0.004***	0.003**	0.005***
			(0.001)	(0.001)	(0.001)	(0.001)
Telecommunication			–0.006***	–0.003**	–0.007***	–0.005***
			(0.001)	(0.001)	(0.002)	(0.002)
State sector			–0.139***	–0.148***	–0.151***	–0.163***
			(0.011)	(0.011)	(0.011)	(0.012)
Specialization					0.004**	0.007***
					(0.002)	(0.002)
Competition					–0.001	–0.000
					(0.001)	(0.001)
Diversity					0.002	–0.145
					(0.086)	(0.091)
R^2	0.170	0.042	0.431	0.336	0.440	0.367
N	696	696	696	696	646	646

Note: Standard errors are in the parentheses.
*** = 1 percent significance; ** = 5 percent significance; * = 10 percent significance.

share of industry i. The initial distribution of industry i (s_{ij} in 1985) is included to account for the persistence in industrial location. It may thus capture the lasting effects on industry location of state planning prior to the economic reforms. This variable is always negative and significant at the 1 percent level, indicating that provinces with larger shares of industry i initially tended to experience declines in share over the period of 1985–1997.

FDI and trade are highly significant and positive in explaining the changes in industrial location, as one can see in columns (1) and (2). Data for the beginning year (1985, or the year closest to 1985 if data for 1985 are not available) for all explanatory variables are used in this set of regressions to avoid possible reverse causality.

No positive effects of labor quality and telecommunication are found on output share changes in columns (3) and (4). In fact, these two variables are negative and statistically significant. Transportation is positive in the two regressions and significant in one of them. The size of the state sector is negative and highly significant, indicating that industries grow more slowly in provinces with bigger state sectors.

Finally, the three externality variables in the regressions are included in columns (5) and (6). Only the specialization variable (E_{ij}^1) is positive and significant at the 5 percent level, showing provincial specialization in manufacturing industries is positively associated with growth and supporting the Marshall-Arrow-Romer externalities. The other two externality variables are both insignificant, and therefore there is no evidence of externalities arising from local competition and industrial diversity.

Thus, the strong and positive effects of openness on the adjustments in industrial location are robust to the inclusion of the additional explanatory variables. In addition, it is also found that industries in provinces with a smaller state sector grew faster and thus gained in share, and that a better transportation system helped industrial growth, both of which are consistent with the findings in Gao (2004).

Implications and Extensions

The primary focus of this chapter is on the role of openness in China's industrial locations. The evidence indicates that provinces that are more open to trade and FDI also have greater shares of industries, after adjusting for province size. In addition, over the period of 1985–1997, provinces with more trade and FDI experienced faster industrial growth, and thus gained in their shares of industries.

It should be noted that, although government policies have played a role, the variations in openness across provinces are not entirely due to the regional preferential trade and FDI policies in China. In other words, even if all provinces had adopted the same set of policies toward trade and FDI, the regional concentration of trade and FDI would still have occurred, for the geographic proximity to FDI sources and cultural ties with them vary from province to province. Geography and culture have been found to be important in explaining trade and FDI in numerous empirical studies (see, for example, Rauch and Trindade 2002 and Gao 2005).

One lesson to be drawn from this study is that the uneven distribution of industries in China is likely to persist even after the trade and FDI policy bias toward the coastal provinces is removed. A possible scenario is that southeast China will emerge more prominently as China's industrial center. To a large extent, the degree of openness depends on geography and other exogenous factors that cannot be altered by policy. Given the large effects of openness on industrial location, provinces that enjoy natural advantages of better access to foreign markets, suppliers, and capital will continue to do well in attracting foreign firms and conducting foreign trade. And these advantages can be magnified by China's further integration with the rest of the world through its WTO membership.

This work can be potentially extended in at least two directions. First, although data on twenty-six two-digit manufacturing industries are used in our study, it does not take into account industry characteristics, which differ from industry to industry and may have implications for the location of individual industries. For example, skill-intensive industries tend to locate in regions with abundant supplies of skilled labor, whereas industries with strong input-output linkages tend to locate in regions with high market potential. Recent studies by Midelfart-Knarvik et al. (2000, 2001) on European industrial location have found empirical significance of the interactions between industry characteristics and regional characteristics in explaining the pattern of industrial location. Placed in their frameworks, openness would have greater effects on Chinese industries with increasing returns and input-output linkages, for it works through a region's market potential. Due to a lack of data on industry characteristics, this point is not pursued in the present study.

Another possible extension of this work is to use province-industry specific openness. In China, some industries receive more trade protection or face more trade restrictions than others do. FDI has also been restricted in some industries. However, our study only uses data on provincial aggregate FDI and trade, not data with an industry breakdown. Thus, the same measure of openness is applied to all industries in a province. If finer data on trade and FDI at the province-industry level are available, the effects of openness on industrial location can be estimated from both cross-province and cross-industry variations.

Note

1. For convenience, all thirty-one provinces, autonomous regions, and municipalities are referred to as provinces.

References

Almanac of China's Foreign Economic Relations and Trade. Various years. Beijing: China Foreign Economic Relations and Trade Publishing House.
China Industrial Economy Statistical Yearbook. Various years. Beijing: China Statistics Press.
Elizondo, R.L., and P.R. Krugman. 1996. "Trade Policy and Third-World Metropolis." *Journal of Development Economics* 49, no. 1: 137–50.

Fu, J. 2000. *Institutions and Investments: Foreign Direct Investment in China during an Era of Reforms*. Ann Arbor: University of Michigan Press.

Fujita, M., P.R. Krugman, and A.J. Venables. 1999. *The Spatial Economy: Cities, Regions, and International Trade*. Cambridge, MA: MIT Press.

Gao, T. 2002. "The Impact of Foreign Trade and Investment Reform on Industry Location: The Case of China." *Journal of International Trade and Economic Development* 11, no. 4: 367–86.

———. 2004. "Regional Industrial Growth: Evidence from Chinese Industries." *Regional Science and Urban Economics* 34, no. 1: 101–24.

———. 2005. "Foreign Direct Investment in China: How Big Are the Roles of Culture and Geography?" *Pacific Economic Review* 10, no. 2: 153–66.

Glaeser, E.L., H.D. Kallal, J.A. Scheinkman, and A. Shleifer. 1992. "Growth in Cities." *Journal of Political Economy* 100, no. 6: 1126–52.

Hanson, G.H. 1998. "Regional Adjustment to Trade Liberalization." *Economic Journal* 28, no. 4: 419–44.

Henderson, V., A. Kuncoro, and M. Turner. 1995. "Industrial Development in Cities." *Journal of Political Economy* 103, no. 5: 1067–90.

Jacobs, J. 1969. *The Economy of Cities*. New York: Random House.

Krugman, P.R. 1991. "Increasing Returns and Economic Geography." *Journal of Political Economy* 99, no. 3: 483–99.

Krugman, P.R., and A.J. Venables. 1995. "Globalization and the Inequality of Nations." *Quarterly Journal of Economics* 110, no. 4: 857–80.

Lardy, N.R. 1992. *Foreign Trade and Economic Reform in China*. New York: Cambridge University Press.

Midelfart-Knarvik, K., H. Overman, and A. Venables. 2001. "Comparative Advantage and Economic Geography: Estimating the Determinants of Industrial Location in the EU." Center for Economic Policy Research Discussion Paper no. 2618.

Midelfart-Knarvik, K., H. Overman, S. Redding, and A. Venables. 2000. "The Location of European Industry." Report prepared for the Directorate General for Economic and Financial Affairs, European Commission.

Naughton, B. 1996. "China's Emergence and Prospects as a Trading Nation." *Brookings Papers on Economic Activities* 2: 273–344.

People's Republic of China 1985 Industrial Census Materials. 1989. Beijing: China Statistics Press.

Porter, M.E. 1990. *The Competitive Advantage of Nations*. New York: Free Press.

Rauch. J., and V. Trindade. 2002. "Ethnic Chinese Networks in International Trade." *Review of Economics and Statistics* 84: 116–30.

Wei, S.J., and Y. Wu. 2001. "Globalization and Inequality: Evidence from Within China." National Bureau of Economic Research Working Paper 8611, Cambridge, MA.

16

Agricultural Policy Developments After China's Accession to the WTO

Francis Tuan, Agapi Somwaru, and Xinshen Diao

China submitted its application for membership in the World Trade Organization (WTO) in 1986. After sixteen years of holding party meetings and bilateral and multilateral negotiations, the country finally became an official member of the world trade community in December 2001 (see Table 16.1 for China's WTO chronology).

Upon accession to the WTO, China committed to reducing trade-distorting barriers and practices that fall into three main categories: nontariff trade barriers, domestic agricultural support, and export subsidies. At the conclusion of the final multilateral agreement, China committed to elimination of all nontariff trade barriers, leaving tariffs as the only measure affecting imports (Table 16.2). Nontariff measures, such as sanitary inspection, biotechnology-related testing, and domestic taxes, such as value-added tax, will comply with WTO rules. China reduced tariffs on more than 3,300 items and removed state trading controls on 367 commodities in 1993 and carried out another round of tariff reductions in 1996 (Wailes, Fang, and Tuan 1998). Tariffs on all agricultural products dropped from an average of 22 percent in 2001 to 17 percent in 2004, and tariffs on agricultural products with high export priorities for the United States (such as animal products, fruits, and dairy products) also fell to 14.5 percent.

Tariff-rate quotas (TRQs) are established for a number of bulk commodities, including wheat, corn, rice, cotton, and soybean oil (Table 16.2). For

Table 16.1

China's WTO Chronology

1986	China applies for GATT membership.
1989	Tiananmen Square incident derails trade negotiations.
1994	China begins a new push to join GATT.
1997	China cuts import duties on many goods, but maintains high tariffs on others.
1999	U.S.-China negotiators reach a bilateral agreement that will allow China to join the WTO.
1999	In June, the United States and China reach agreement on China's farm subsidies at a maximum of 8.5 percent of its total agricultural output value.
1999	In September, the United States Senate passes legislation establishing permanent normal trade relations with China.
2001	In September, multilateral negotiations on China's WTO accession concluded.
2001	In December, China officially joins the WTO.

goods subject to TRQs, a specified quantity of imports (i.e., a quota) may enter at a low tariff rate, and additional imports (i.e., over the quota) are assessed at a higher rate. The quantities allowed at the low tariff (within TRQs) were set to increase annually from 2002 through 2004, and the vegetable oil quotas were set to remain through 2005. There are no minimum purchase requirements and the negotiated TRQs do not represent minimum purchases. China can increase TRQ amounts as domestic demand surges. But China does not have to import the full TRQ amount, although China did agree to establish regular grain purchases from the United States in 1999. By cutting tariffs on specified quantities of imports, these quotas open the market for imports when domestic demand exceeds supply.

An important commitment associated with the TRQs is that China's government agreed to extend a portion of its trading rights to non-state trade entities. This would add transparency and competition to China's agricultural trade by phasing out the monopolistic power of state trade enterprises (STEs). STEs controlled all trade in some key agricultural commodities, particularly grains, prior to the WTO accession. Private sector participation and competition in trade would be encouraged by setting shares of imports to be allocated to non-state trading entities. For many agricultural commodities, including oilseeds and oilseed products, cotton, and medium and short grain rice, half or more of the import quotas are set to be allocated to non-state entities. Trade in major grains, including wheat and long grain rice, will continue to be channeled primarily through state trade enterprises. The non-STE share of corn imports was set to rise to 40 percent in 2004. Private sector trading rights were seen as one of the key terms negotiated in the U.S.-China bilateral agreement and were expected to have a profound impact on Chinese markets in future years.

Table 16.2

China's Tariff Rate Quota System for Major Agricultural Products after WTO Accession

Commodity	Unit	2002	2003	2004	2005
Wheat					
Total TRQ quota level	1,000 tons	8,468	9,052	9,636	
In quota tariff	Percent	1	1	1	
Over quota tariff	Percent	71	68	65	
Allocated to non-state trade	Percent	10	10	10	
Rice					
Total TRQ quota level	1,000 tons	3,990	4,655	5,320	
Short & medium grain quota	1,000 tons	1,995	2,328	2,660	
In quota tariff	Percent	1	1	1	
Over quota tariff	Percent	60	50	40	
Allocated to non-state trade	Percent	50	50	50	
Long grain quota	1,000 tons	1,995	2,328	2,660	
In quota tariff	Percent	1	1	1	
Over quota tariff	Percent	60	50	40	
Allocated to non-state trade	Percent	10	10	10	
Corn					
Total TRQ quota level	1,000 tons	5,850	6,525	7,200	
In quota tariff	Percent	1	1	1	
Over quota tariff	Percent	60	50	40	
Allocated to non-state trade	Percent	33	36	40	
Cotton					
Total TRQ quota level	1,000 tons	818.5	856.3	894	
In quota tariff	Percent	4	4	4	
Over quota tariff	Percent	54	47	40	
Allocated to non-state trade	Percent	67	67	67	
Soybean oil					
Total TRQ quota level	1,000 tons	2,518	2,818	3,118	3,587.1
In quota tariff	Percent	9	9	9	9
Over quota tariff	Percent	48	35	22	9
Allocated to non-state trade	Percent	66	74	82	90
Soybeans					
Bound tariff	Percent	3	3	3	
Soymeal					
Bound tariff	Percent	5	5	5	
Palm oil	1,000 tons	2,400	2,600	2,700	3,168
Bound tariff	Percent	9	9	9	9
Rapeseed oil	1,000 tons	878.9	1,018.6	1,126.6	1,243
Bound tariff	Percent	9	9	9	9

Source: Office of the United States Trade Representative (www.ustr.gov).

Note: All were fully implemented by 2004, except for vegetable oils, which runs through 2005, and after which it converts to a bound, tariff-only regime.

In addition, China has agreed to eliminate sanitary and phyto-sanitary (SPS) barriers that are not based on scientific evidence. For example, China lifted its ban on imports of U.S. wheat and other grains from the Pacific Northwest and now allows the import of U.S. wheat that meets specific tolerances for the TCK fungus.

China also agreed to eliminate export subsidies for farm products and to reduce and cap trade-distorting domestic farm subsidies. However, Chinese farmers are entitled to and may still sell unlimited amounts of surplus grain to the state at protection, or support, prices. China was unwilling to enter the WTO as a "developed economy," which would require reductions in trade distorting subsidies whenever their value exceeded 5 percent (re WTO-defined *de minimus* level) of the total farm value of that commodity. This limit is set at 10 percent for developing countries. China considers its support of farm products to be a crucial domestic policy instrument that protects farm household income and prevents social and political instabilities. A compromise was eventually reached in June 2001, setting China's subsidy limit at 8.5 percent of its total agricultural output value in the multilateral agreement and in the final protocol.

China's Trade in Major Agricultural Commodities

With all the above commitments agreed to by the Chinese government as the country joined the WTO, most trade analysts saw better opportunities for foreign agricultural products (including corn, wheat, cotton, and soybean oil) to have greater access to China's domestic market.

As a result, trade analysts, in both Western countries and in China, expected that China's domestic agricultural markets would face greater competition from imported agricultural commodities, particularly because the prevailing international commodity prices were significantly lower than China's domestic prices at the time. Most analyses predicted that, beginning in 2002, China would experience a gradual increase in imports of major bulk commodities, especially wheat and soybeans, although levels of imports were not projected to exceed the TRQ levels. Also, China's corn exports, at the least, were expected to decline because of the elimination of export subsidies (Lohmar et al. 2002; Ma and Lang 2002).

Immediately after accession to the WTO, China's trade of major agricultural products ran counter to expectations. China's imports of corn, wheat, and soybeans did not expand as estimated. Before China's accession to the WTO, most analytical studies forecast an increase in corn imports, particularly by southern China, a traditionally corn-deficit region. Soybean imports to China were also expected to steadily increase because of strong demand for soybean oils and rapid development of China's domestic soybean crush capacity during the two or three years before its accession to the WTO. This is on top of a low fixed tariff rate of 3 percent and no TRQ restrictions. Finally, wheat imports to China were also expected to gradually increase due to the country's two consecutive years of below par harvests as well as its long-term demand for high protein quality wheat, mainly for blending purposes.

According to trade statistics compiled by China's Customs Administration, in 2002 China imported limited corn, less than 8,000 tons, or only 0.1 percent of that year's TRQ for corn imports. With the elimination of direct export subsidies, the country was, nevertheless, able to not only continue but also expand corn exports in 2002 and 2003, reaching a record of 11.7 and 16.39 million tons, respectively, or 95 and 173 percent higher than the 2001 export level. In particular, after its WTO accession, China surpassed Argentina to become the world's second-largest corn exporter (Figure 16.1).

In the case of soybean imports, as soon as it became a member of the WTO, China officially promulgated its biotechnology regulations in January 2002. All foreign traders believed that the newly announced biotech regulations were mainly aimed at reducing or controlling the rapidly surging growth of soybean imports during the two or three years before its accession to the WTO. Trade statistics from China's Customs Administration revealed that, in 2002, China's total soybean imports were down to 11.3 million tons, 2.6 million tons less than the 2001 record of nearly 14 million tons (Figure 16.2). China's soybean imports, however, increased in 2003, reaching a historical high of 20.7 million tons, because of surging demand for soybean oils and rapid development of the livestock sector.

More astonishingly, in 2002 and 2003, not only did China not import much wheat, but the country surprised many wheat exporters by shipping about 690,000 and 2,237,000 tons, respectively, of feed wheat to its neighboring countries. This compares with a total import of 630,000 and 424,000 tons, or 7.5 and 4.7 percent of the respective year's wheat TRQ (Figure 16.3). Historically, China has never been a net wheat exporter, except when shifting relatively small quantities of feed wheat to neighboring Asian markets.

Policies Affecting Trade of Bulk Commodities in 2002 and 2003

Why was China's trade of major agricultural commodities so different from what most economic models previously estimated it would be after accession to the WTO? In general, we realize that most trade forecasting models are built with long-term average yields and sown areas to project crop output. Trade projections for major agricultural products depend heavily on pro-

Figure 16.1 **Corn Exports: China and Argentina, 1992–2003**

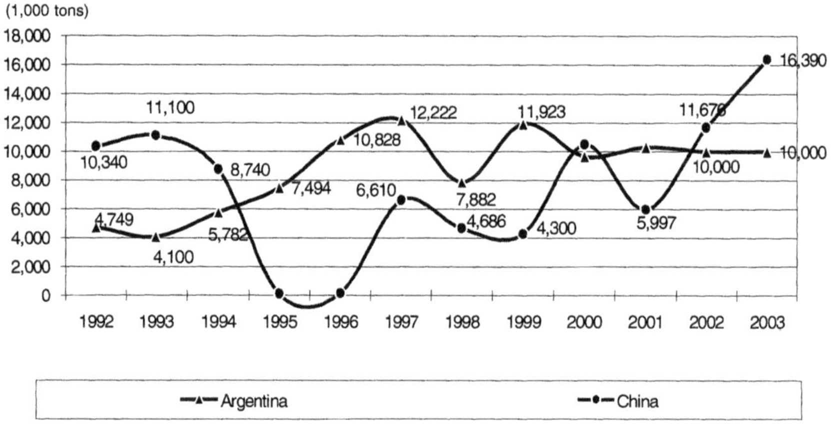

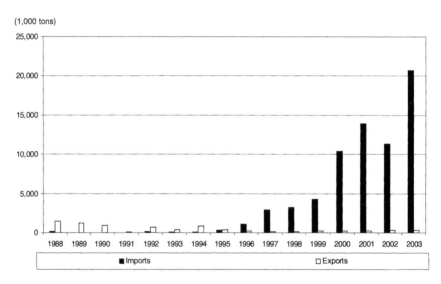

Source: PRC General Customs Administration, various years.

Figure 16.2 **The Decline of China's Soybean Imports, 1988–2003**

(1,000 tons)

Source: PRC General Customs Administration, various years.

jected domestic and world reference prices. Although China's new tariff rates, TRQs, and elimination of export subsidies were incorporated into the fore-casting framework, many new policy measures or regulation changes imple-mented by the government, particularly those after China joined the WTO,

Figure 16.3 **China: A Net Wheat Exporter in 2003**

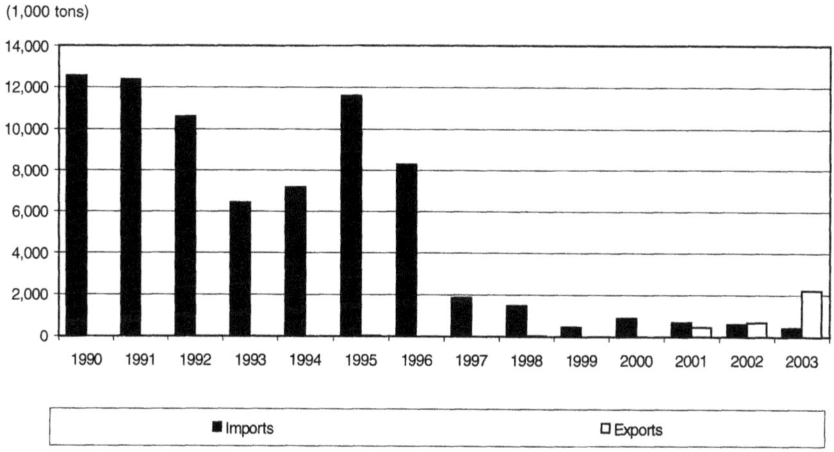

(1,000 tons)

■ Imports   □ Exports

Source: PRC General Customs Administration, various years.

were never incorporated into the models. These new policies or post–WTO accession reform adjustments adopted by the government, as well as changes in world market conditions, such as unanticipated significant short-term price fluctuations in international commodity markets, were all critical to China's agricultural trade after its accession and especially during 2002. More importantly, China, although it joined the WTO in 2001, still held on tight to the old mentality in dealing with agricultural trade. The mentality was, as in the past, to find more policy measures that would facilitate agricultural exports and to issue new regulations or procedures that would control or reduce imports. These types of policy measures, new trade requirements, and unexpected changes in world market conditions are briefly described and analyzed in two categories, one facilitating agricultural exports and the other reducing or controlling imports of major agricultural products:

Category 1. The following changes in policy measures and international market conditions facilitated China's exports of its agricultural products:

(a) In the late 1990s, China began piling up its grain stocks, including wheat, corn, and rice. The huge stocks chiefly resulted from several consecutive years of favorable weather and from the previous governors' grain bag policy imposed by the central government in 1995. This policy requires the governor of each province in China to be responsible for the supply of its food/grain needs without regard for efficient allocations of agricultural inputs or natural resources. The size of grain stocks remained a state secret even after China joined the WTO. Although traders and the United States Department of Agriculture have adjusted China's grain stock estimates upward twice over the past two years, the actual level of grain stocks in China has remained a mystery. China's wheat and corn stocks during the late 1990s and early 2000s apparently were considerably higher than many Western traders and commodity analysts estimated. In fact, even though China experienced significantly sub-par harvests over the period 2000 to 2003, or a drop of 230 million tons of grain output altogether compared with the 1999 total grain output, the country was still able to continue exporting corn and avoid wheat imports.

(b) In addition to very large grain stock levels, two tax-related policies implemented in 2002 enabled China to continuously draw down its stocks and export more corn and wheat to Asian markets. These two changes together kept China's export prices competitive, even with the elimination of direct export subsidies after joining the WTO. Chinese officials have long been using VAT to influence agricultural trade. While some Chinese agricultural tariffs are relatively low under WTO regulations, most imported agricultural products are assessed a VAT of 13 percent to make imported commodities less competitive. The same VAT, however, is also to encourage exports of Chinese agricultural products by offering rebates to traders. In 2002, China's government reimposed reimbursements of the VAT to trading corporations exporting corn and wheat. In addition, the government waived the railroad construction tax and fees for grains directed to ports for foreign destinations. According to a recently published annual report by China's State Grain Administration, the magnitude of reimbursement resulting from these two tax-related changes has been similar or larger than the direct export subsidies that China's government provided to exporters before accession to the WTO. China previously subsidized grain exports, reportedly from US$25 to US$40 per ton depending on types of products. In mid-2003, China's government also announced that VAT reimbursement would also be applied to soymeal exports retroactive to January 1, 2003.

(c) An unexpected change in the international agricultural commodity markets, after China's accession to the WTO, drastically changed China's trade opportunities and the competitiveness of its major agricultural products. Significant increases in the prices of most agricultural commodities in world markets in late summer 2002, because of severe droughts in the United States, Canada, and Australia, provided favorable opportunities for China's grain trade authorities to export their overstocked corn, wheat, and other commodities during the second half of 2002. The bulk of these farm products were previously procured by the central government with higher-than-market protection prices set in the late 1990s for encouraging farmers to produce more food grains and to maintain farmers' income levels. These grains had long been stocked in state-owned grain warehouses and would otherwise had been difficult to sell either to the domestic or international markets. For instance, according to reports published by China's Ministry of Agriculture, in October 2002, average cash market prices for wheat increased 45 percent in international markets over the previous year's levels. For corn the price rose 30 percent, for rice 13 percent, and for soybeans 25 percent.

Category 2. The following policy adjustments and trade-related regulations adopted by China's government reduced imports of agricultural products:

(a) Shortly after it joined the WTO, China's government announced its biotechnology regulations to be put in effect in March 2002. Some market analysts looked at this new set of regulations as a policy that aimed at controlling or reducing the country's surging soybean imports. China's soybean imports in 2000 and 2001 amounted to 10.2 and 13.7 million tons, respectively, compared to 4.3 million tons in 1999. The Chinese government rushed to put the biotechnology regulations and labeling requirements in place, according to China's Ministry of Agriculture, mainly for reasons of food safety. Foreign governments and trading companies, however, surmised that the timing, vagueness, and unreasonable time frame of the application procedures reflected China's intention to use the regulations to restrain or control the pace of soybean imports as well as imports of other agricultural products, such as corn, in the future. For instance, they stipulate that the total length of time needed to obtain an approval of an application for an import safety certificate for shipping biotech soybeans into China can take up to 270 days. Besides, each shipment of biotech soybeans would still need to obtain an individual and separate safety certificate. After consultations between the U.S. and Chinese governments, China agreed to accept a temporary import certificate for the transition period from March 2002 through April 2004. As a result, soybean imports were not seriously interrupted during the second half of 2002 and throughout 2003. China imported a record 20.7 million tons of soybeans in 2003.

(b) Another important production-related policy change that may have negatively affected the potential for importing food grains, such as wheat, is the ongoing structural adjustment of China's crop production. China began a major structural adjustment of grain production in 2000, before its accession to the WTO. Emphasis has been first put on grain crops, particularly wheat and rice. In general, production of low quality wheat and rice, such as those only usable for livestock feeding, has been gradually phased out or reduced. For instance, China's northeastern region has reduced its low-quality spring wheat area by about 40–50 percent over the past several years. Another major wheat area in the North China Plains also has increased planting of higher quality wheat, mainly for flour milling purposes. The new varieties of wheat produced in the two areas do not match the quality of Canadian or U.S. high protein wheat, but growing production has significantly reduced the imports of wheat from foreign sources. For the last several years, China, long recognized as a high-quality-wheat–deficient country, has bought minimal wheat from other countries. In fact, China imported less than 1 million tons of wheat between 1999 and 2003, compared with an average of over 10 million tons of wheat imported in the first half of the 1990s (Figure 16.3).

(c) Although China's low wheat imports in the early 2000s were related to the increasing supply of domestically produced high quality wheat, many wheat millers in south China were reportedly always searching for higher quality wheat from foreign sources. It was especially true when wheat prices were significantly lower in international markets in the early months of 2002. Nevertheless, the slow establishment of China's TRQ system and implementation of allocation of the TRQs prevented the wheat millers in south China from importing the better quality wheat they preferred. Even as the TRQs were eventually allocated to small wheat millers, it is reported that 10 percent of China's annual total wheat import TRQs, as allowed by China's WTO commitments, was distributed to a large number of small flour millers. The small flour millers then found out later that it was not economical to import the small quantity of wheat allotted by the government. In 2004, China finally resumed importing significant quantities of wheat, about 8 million tons, because of low stocks of high-quality imported wheat.

Long-Term Implications of Other Alternative Policies

The previous discussions on changes in policy measures and newly announced trade regulations or requirements are important, particularly to China's short-term trade performance in the first two or three years after accession to the WTO. Nonetheless, it is crucial to understand that some alternative policies including those being formulated or already implemented during the last few years could have long-term implications for China's trade of major products. These alternative policies or reform adjustments are briefly stated and analyzed as follows:

1. *Direct payments to farm producers (versus subsidies to marketing channels or price).* Facing a growing gap between urban and rural household incomes over the past ten or fifteen years, the central government has made increasing farmers' income one of the most important policy goals

in agricultural development. In the 1980s and early 1990s, China tried to raise farm income through increased procurement prices when the compulsory procurement system for major farm products was still in place. During the late 1990s, China carried out a program in which "protection prices" were guaranteed for part of farmers' total production. The protection prices were much higher than the prevailing market prices at the time. In 2002, after China's accession to the WTO, the central government began an experiment in which direct payments would be paid to farmers in some counties in Jilin and Anhui provinces. In early 2004, Guangdong and Zhejiang provinces also announced plans to use direct payments to farmers who grow grain crops in 2004. This kind of subsidy is unprecedented in China's farming history. Before China joined the WTO, government subsidies were provided to either consumers or food grain and oilseeds handlers or processors, while farmers were taxed by the government (Tuan and Cheng 1999; Tian et al. 2002). However, the details of the experimental program of direct payment to farmers, including the magnitude of the subsidy and the commodities eligible for the support, are not published. Our personal contacts with China's government researchers in early 2004 revealed that cash payments have not been provided directly to farm producers in any of the experiment areas. Instead, subsidies have been given to farm households in the form of providing free quality seeds (soybeans in Jilin province) or grain procured with higher-than-market government guaranteed protection prices (Henan province).

The Chinese government, in fact, had been considering the direct payment program for several years. But the government was not ready to try out the program earlier because of technical issues and administrative costs associated with the program. This includes the difficulties of paying subsidies to recipients in more than 200 million farm households widely spread out over China's vast rural and mountainous areas. Other reasons include the huge government budget needed to support so many farm households and the total cost of administering the program.

2. *Reform of the rural and agricultural taxation system.* A tax reform that consolidates various types of fees and taxes collected in rural areas into a new single agricultural tax has been introduced into provinces across China during the last several years. Furthermore, the central government decided that the rate of this new agricultural tax was to be reduced by one percentage in 2004.

The earliest experiment of this tax reform on China's agricultural taxes and fees began in Anhui province in 2001. The experimental tax reform afterwards expanded to twenty provinces in 2002. The purpose of the reform is primarily to standardize the rural taxation system and reduce the farmers' financial burden. To implement the reform, local governments began: (1) eliminating township or villages' collection of fees used for paying part of the salary of village cadres, (2) abolishing administrative fees and funds collected for carrying out rural compulsory education, (3) eliminating hog slaughtering taxes, all fees imputed or converted from public or voluntary service, and (4) eliminating farmers' contributions to specific activities approved by village committee meetings. The reform combines the previous agricultural tax with the new agricultural tax. The newly combined total tax should not exceed 7 percent of the annual agricultural output on an average year of production; adjusts the agricultural specialty product tax; reforms methods used to collect village reserves from village and township enterprises; and limits additional fees, which are not to exceed 20 percent of the new agricultural tax. To promote and implement the tax reform, both the central government and certain local governments provide financial support for the rural experiment areas. In general, total rural taxes and fees collected in areas under the experimental tax reform were reduced by an average of one-third from the previous tax and fee levels. In some areas, such as Shanghai and Zhejiang province, the agricultural specialty product tax was totally or partially eliminated. According to the central government, this reform program was implemented across the country starting in 2003.

3. *Increased government support for agricultural research and rural infrastructure.* China is shifting its financial support for the agricultural sector from marketing to WTO-defined green box (subsidies that do not affect production and distort trade) programs that support agricultural production. China's agricultural support in recent years can generally be characterized by low overall levels of support, with heavy support for the marketing segment:

(a) Low overall levels of support. China's aggregate measurement of support (AMS) calculations for 1996 through 2000 were at RMB108.3, 126.7, 182.6, 170.9, and 220.0 billion, respectively, according to China's Ministry of Agriculture. And its shares of the corresponding annual total agricultural output values were 4.9, 5.3, 7.4, 7.0, and 8.8 percent, respectively. Using the same calculations, the agricultural support of developed countries averaged between 30 and 50 percent. For developing countries, such as Pakistan, Thailand, India, and Brazil, the percentage shares are between 10 to 20 percent. Among the twelve various areas of policies defined under WTO green box support, China used only six of them (expenditure of general government services, food safety stocks, domestic food aids, natural disaster assistance or aids, protection of the natural environment, and regional development assistance). China's "amber box" support (subsidies that affect production and distort trade) calculated for the base years (1996–1998) averaged only

RMB29.7 billion per year, accounting for 1.23 percent of the total agricultural output value. Compared to the level of support permitted by the WTO, China could have used another RMB144.3 billion (see China's Ministry of Agriculture [MOA 2003a] at www.agri.gov.cn).

(b) Heavy support for the marketing segment. In the 2004 reform, major agricultural subsidies in China mainly concentrated on the marketing segment of farm products such as grains, cotton, oils, and sugar. Since 1998, annual government subsidies on marketing these farm products averaged RMB50 to RMB70 billion, accounting for 30 to 50 percent of the total annual agricultural support. In 2001, China's total agricultural support was RMB204.8 billion. Of the total, agricultural infrastructure, agricultural development, and poverty reduction expenditures totaled RMB67.8 billion; agricultural production supports, together with agriculture, forest, and water conservancy department expenditures, added up to RMB70.8 billion; and subsidies for the marketing of agricultural products amounted to RMB61.7 billion. Each of the above three categories accounted for 33.1, 34.1, and 30.1 percent, respectively, of the government's total expenditures in agriculture (MOA 2003b).

With low agricultural support levels and plans to increase so-called green box subsidies, the government intends to move major government supports from marketing (currently about RMB70 billion per year) to the production segment. If successful, according to China's MOA, these are the supports that can be used to directly subsidize farmers and farm production as discussed in the previous section. As a result, the marketing channel subsidies formerly classified under the amber box will then be converted to green box subsidies.

4. *Regional specialization in crop production.* In addition to the production structure adjustments of major agricultural products as discussed in the previous section, China's Ministry of Agriculture announced its first ever five-year (2003–7) regional plans for production of specialized farm products to accommodate China's accession to the WTO. The new specialized production plans are obviously aimed at capturing regional comparative advantages in order to produce farm products that would be more competitive, both in prices and quality. The new regional plans clearly indicate that China believes that specialized farm production is the direction needed for future production and development in order to stay competitive in a more globalized agricultural trade environment.

In brief, China's regional plans for specialized farm production include eleven varieties or types of farm products in which China's agricultural experts believe some regions hold particular advantages. Three of the specialized crops are:

(a) Specialty wheat. The plan is to expand production of special varieties of wheat bred by Chinese experts. The new varieties of wheat reportedly have gluten content close to those produced in the United States and Canada. Growing regions for the special varieties of wheat include the Yellow River Basin, the Huai River Valley, lower reaches of the Yangtze River, and the foot of the Daxinganling Mountain in the western part of China's northeastern region.

(b) Specialty corn. China is one of the world's major corn producing and consuming countries, with annual production ranked second only to the United States. Although China's government officials have foreseen its domestic demand for corn increase rapidly because of continued development of the livestock industry and industrial uses, the country also realizes that there are consistent annual imports of 35 million tons of corn by its neighboring countries, particularly in East Asia. These imports account for roughly 50 percent of total world corn trade. In the regional plans, China's Ministry of Agriculture and the central government specified its particular interest in supplying non–genetically modified (GM) corn to these neighboring markets. Major corn areas designated by the plan to grow the special corn are in the northeastern China–Inner Mongolia corn-belt region and in the North China Plains. In the same plans, although government officials emphasize the importance of shifting corn production from northern China to the south, they also predict that imports of corn in south China will be inevitable in the longer run. They presented the fact that total quantities of corn imported to the south are currently bound by the corn TRQs under the WTO commitments, but government administrative restrictions and biotechnology regulations could be applied to restrict corn imports if necessary.

(c) High oil soybeans. Soybean production originated in China. Once the largest soybean producing and exporting country in the world, China's demand for foreign imported soybeans and oils has risen rapidly over the last few years. China believes that its high oil content soybean varieties, particularly those grown in the northeastern region, are as competitive as U.S. soybeans. China, however, can only grow soybeans efficiently and economically in the northeastern region, and again China plans to develop the region into a GM-free high soybean oil–producing area. Nonetheless, China will need to maintain relatively high levels of soybean imports for the foreseeable future because of limited land availability and because of competition with other crops, particularly corn, in the long run.

There are eight other special farm products, including cotton, double-low rapeseed (low erucic acid and low glucosinolates), double-high sugarcane (high sugar content and high yield), citrus, apples, beef cattle and sheep, cow's milk, and aquatic products included in the regional plans, but discussion of these is beyond the scope of this chapter.

5. *Liberalization of the grain market in grain consumption areas.* In 2001, one year prior to China's entry into the WTO, the country began to further liberalize its grain markets. The liberalization process began in the grain consumption areas, including Guangdong, Hainan, Fujian, Zhejiang, and Jiangsu provinces, as well as in Shanghai, Beijing, and Tianjin municipalities. In these grain consumption areas, where the quantities of grain consumed are larger than that produced, producers will no longer need to deliver grains to the central and local governments; grain prices are chiefly determined by market demand and supply conditions; and all eligible enterprises are permitted to buy and sell grains. In other words, this policy adjustment again reflects that the market reforms would allow China's grain producing regions or provinces to grow more grains, exploiting their regional comparative advantages of high unit yields and low production costs. The governors' grain bag responsibility policy, which required all provincial governors to be responsible for producing enough food grains for their own uses, had been largely revoked at the time when grain market liberalization was instituted. This is another indication that signals China's market development is being pushed by market forces and by the country's determination to become a more market-oriented economy.

6. *Recent revision of China's agriculture law.* The National People's Congress revised China's agriculture law in early 2003 and the revised law has been in effect since March 1, 2003. The newly revised law for the first time stipulates that, in compliance with the WTO protocol, China's government will financially support farmers' agricultural production through measures of direct payment. However, details of the supporting measures are not stated in the context of the revised law, but will be formulated later by the State Council. In addition to policies and regulations related to production and marketing of agricultural products, other programs included in the new law encompass areas such as food security, input investment, agricultural technology and education, agricultural resources and environmental protection, farmers' rights, and rural economic development.

In summary, all the above policies and reform adjustments have been formulated and carried out to achieve a set of policy goals that include increasing farm household incomes, self-sufficiency in food grains, and compliance with WTO regulations. These policies will also be crucial to China's production, marketing, consumption, and trade of major agricultural products, particularly grains and major oilseeds and oilseed products in the years to come.

Perspectives on China's Long-Term Trade in Major Agricultural Products

In the long run, China will have to gradually increase imports of food grains and oilseeds, mainly because of increases in incomes and population growth, and because of limited resources (cultivated areas and water). China may sporadically export some surplus grains and import moderate quantities of oilseeds, but, on average, China is expected to import more land-intensive products and export labor-intensive output.

We agree with most previous studies that in the long run China, a labor abundant but land scarce nation, is very unlikely to remain a net grain exporter as trade liberalizes under its WTO obligations. During the late 1990s, several years of bumper harvests, together with reemphasis on grain-security/self-sufficiency policies using higher-than-market government-guaranteed protection prices and the governors' grain bag policy, built up China's enormous grain stocks. The accumulated stockpiles resulted in China's desperate need to export these grains in the last few years. It is, however, important to note that China did become a net wheat exporter in 2002 and 2003, shipping not only feed wheat but also a small quantity of higher quality flour-milling wheat to neighboring Asian markets. While China was not expected to retain its net wheat export status in 2004, wheat traders in the West still should pay close attention to China's policy adjustments, such as the regional planning program and its implications for high-quality wheat trade in the future. Given that more progress is expected to be achieved in the regional production of special products in the next few years, China's long-term demand for foreign quality wheat may not be as much as many traders previously estimated.

As to corn exports, the buildup of China's corn stocks during the late 1990s was obviously underestimated. China's corn-producing regions, particularly Jilin province, were able to ship more corn to the neighboring Asian countries. These exports, chiefly induced by regional surpluses, are expected to continue until the pace of structural changes in livestock production picks up, that is until more backyard feeding shifts toward specialized feeding and commercialized feedlots. We believe that it is also important to point out that China's feed corn use has likely been greatly overestimated over time by many commodity analysts in Western countries. This, together with underestimated levels of corn stocks, was likely the major reason why corn traders in the Western world did not expect China to be able to provide corn shipments to Asian markets for so many years.

As to how China could manage to reduce soybean imports in the first year after its accession to the WTO, it has been widely recognized that the major force behind the smaller shipments was China's promulgation of biotechnology regulations and food labeling requirements in early 2002. Although China's government officials claimed their main reason for implementing the regulations was to protect consumers, most commodity analysts and commodity traders believe that the new regulations were put in place to slow down the rapid growth of China's soybean imports in 2000 and 2001. Another obvious reason was the government's goal of providing at least temporary increases in domestic soybean prices before the sowing season, to encourage expansion of soybean areas in China's northeast region. Because of the new regulations, China's total soybean imports in 2002 were more than 2.5 million tons less than the previous year. In 2002, soybean areas did increase because of the announced biotech regulations, but output did not significantly rise because of widespread droughts. In contrast to the decline in soybean imports, soybean oil imports were up significantly in 2002 because of discrepancies between the total demand for edible oils and the lower soybean imports. In 2003, soybean imports topped 20 million tons, surpassing the country's annual production for the first time and reflecting the rapidly growing market demand for soybean oil. China's soybean oil imports, meanwhile, also surged and exceeded that of the 2002 level by about 1 million tons, reaching 1,884,400 tons.

In the long run, China will continue to depend upon soybean imports, mainly because of its limited capability of growing more soybeans. China has encouraged farmers to grow more soybeans in the northeastern region, which is competitive with the midwest area of the United States (Fang and Fabiosa 2002). But growing more soybeans will definitely be at the expense of corn production, because the two crops compete in land use. Another major reason for China's large quantities of imported soybeans is that crush capacity for beans has continued expanding. According to a recent estimate by the State Grain and Oils Information Center, crush capacity expanded to 57 million tons by the end of 2003, a significant increase from about 45 million tons in the previous year (*NGOIC Daily Report,* 2004).

Wheat and Soybean Imports Expected to Grow Despite Short-term Disruptions

China officially became a WTO member in December 2001 and committed to reducing policy distortions that fall into three main categories: nontariff trade barriers, domestic agricultural support, and export subsidies. For market access, a system of tariff-rate quotas was established for a number of bulk commodities, including wheat, corn, rice, and soybean oil. There are no minimum purchase requirements and the TRQs do not represent minimum purchases. In any year, China does not need to import the full TRQ amount. An important commitment associated with the TRQs is that China's government agreed to extend a portion of its trading rights to non-state trading entities. This adds transparency and competitiveness to China's agricultural trade by phasing out the monopolistic power of state trade enterprises, which controlled almost all trade in some key agricultural commodities, particularly grains, prior to the WTO accession.

After accession, China's trade of major agricultural products first ran counter to expectations. China's imports of corn did not increase as expected. Before accession, most analytical studies expected China to end its heavily subsidized corn exports to neighboring markets and imports of corn from foreign sources, particularly those to south China, were expected to gradually rise. On the contrary, China's corn exports totaled 11.7 and 16.4 million tons in 2002 and 2003, respectively, or 95 and 173 percent higher than the 2001 level. In addition, soybean imports to China were also expected to continue because of strong growing demand for soybean oils and rapid development of China's domestic soybean crush capacity during the two or three years before its accession to the WTO. This is on top of a low fixed tariff rate of 3 percent and no TRQ restrictions. But China's imports of soybeans for 2002 actually declined by about 2.6 million tons to 11.3 million tons, before soybean imports surged in 2003. Finally, wheat imports to China were also expected to gradually increase due to the country's two consecutive years of below par harvests and its long-term demand for high-quality wheat, mainly for wheat flour blending purposes. Not only did China not import more wheat, instead it became a wheat net exporter in both 2002 and 2003, even exporting a small share of flour-milling wheat to some Asian markets. Only in 2004 did China begin importing significantly more high-quality wheat.

The unexpected trade outcomes could generally be attributed to the post–WTO accession changes in domestic policy measures, new trade-related regulations or requirements, as well as sudden increases in commodity prices in the world agricultural markets. The short-term changes in international market conditions were greatly favorable to China's expansion of corn and wheat exports in 2002, after joining WTO, particularly given China's large grain stocks. Other than the market condition changes, China's government also imposed new policy measures, trade regulations, and requirements that made Chinese grain export prices more competitive. For instance, China rebated VAT to traders for exported grain and waived transportation construction fees for grains transported to foreign destinations. In contrast to measures adopted by the Chinese government to expand agricultural exports, new biotechnology regulations, TRQ allocation procedures, and production structural changes instituted by China's Ministry of Agriculture controlled or reduced imports of bulk commodities. China's announcement of biotech regulations and food safety requirements, as well as delayed TRQ allotments to small wheat millers, cut soybean imports and prevented small flour millers from importing wheat in 2002 and 2003. This took place in a situation in which a large share of China's TRQs for grains, such as 90 percent of wheat imports, was under the control China's state trade entities.

Other policy reforms being formulated or that have been imposed by the Chinese government since before accession to the WTO may also have significant long-term implications for China's agricultural trade. These policies, including programs for direct payments to grain and oilseed producers, reform of the rural and agricultural taxation system, increased government investment in agricultural research and infrastructure, regional specialization of crop production, liberalization of grain markets in consumption regions, and newly revised agriculture laws, may gradually increase China's long-term trade competitiveness and reduce distortions to both domestic as well as international trade. We need to understand that China's preference for food self-sufficiency may slow the transition to a market-oriented economy. However, the country's latest policy changes and reform adjustments are expected to have significant implications for the trade of its major agricultural products in the years to come.

In conclusion, China might be able to reverse its short-term trade performance within a few years after joining the WTO and its integration into the world economy. But in the long run, with more liberalized reforms and market-oriented policy adjustments in place, China should be able to allocate its resources and produce farm products more efficiently. China probably realizes that while it may steer clear of significant increases in imports of land-intensive products, it will be unlikely to be able to completely avoid the long-term trend of gradual increases in imports of those bulk commodities.

References

Chen, Xiwen. 2003. "Joining the WTO and Our Country's Agricultural Development." State Council, Beijing. Available at the Web site of the Development Research Center, www.drcnet.com.cn.

Fang, Cheng, and Jay Fabiosa. 2002. "Does the U.S. Midwest Have a Cost Advantage Over China in Producing Corn, Soybeans, and Hogs?" MATRIC Research Paper 02–MRP 4 (August). Iowa State University, Ames.

Lohmar, Bryan, James Hansen, Hsin-Hui Hsu, and Ralph Seeley. 2002. "WTO Accession Will Increase China's Agricultural Imports." *Agricultural Outlook* (April). Washington, DC: Economic Research Service, U.S. Department of Agriculture.

Ma, Xiaohe, and Haitao Lang. 2002. "A Study of Our Country's Agricultural Support After Joining the WTO." State Council, Beijing. Available at the Web site of the Development Research Center, www.drcnet.com.cn.

Ministry of Agriculture (MOA). 2003a. "Agricultural Law of the People's Republic of China." Available at www.agri.gov.cn.

———. 2003b. "Regional Planning of Farm Products with Growth Potential (2003–2007)." Available at www.agri.gov.cn.

NGOIC Daily Report. 2004. China's National Grain and Oils Information Center, Beijing (in Chinese).

Tian, Weiming, Liqin Zhang, and Zhangyue Zhou. 2002. "Experiences and Issues in Measuring the Level of Agricultural Support in China." *Agricultural Policies in China After the WTO Accession.* Paris: OECD.

Tuan, Francis, and Guoqiang Cheng. 1999. "A Review of China's Agricultural Trade Policy." Paper prepared for the IATRC Summer Meeting on China's Agricultural Trade and Policy: Issues, Analysis, and Global Consequences, San Francisco, June 25–26.

Tuan, Francis, and Hsin-Hui Hsu. 2001. "U.S.-China Bilateral WTO Agreement and Beyond." *China: Agriculture in Transition, Agriculture and Trade Report*, WRS-01-2 (November). Washington, DC: Economic Research Service, U.S. Department of Agriculture.

Wailes, Eric, Cheng Fang, and Francis Tuan. 1998. "U.S.-China Agricultural Trade: Constraints and Potential." *Journal of Applied and Agricultural Economics* 30, no. 1 (July): 113–26.

17

The Impact of China's Accession to the WTO on Chinese Agriculture and Farmers

Xiao-shan Zhang

Agricultural problems in China after accession to the World Trade Organization (WTO) in 2001 are manifold and complicated. They should be analyzed with respect to different regions, different products, and different farming groups. Staple food producers living in the northeastern and middle parts of China would not benefit from WTO accession, while cash crop producers, who are mostly living in the coastal areas, would. In the first quarter of 2002 the import and export situation already bore this out. In terms of sorting, grading, packing, quality control, quarantine, and so on, China has a lot of work to do to meet international standards and overcome nontariff barriers. It will be key for China's economic success to avoid the worst-case scenario, where land- and water-intensive products, such as cotton, wheat, or soybeans, are slowly moving into China, but labor-intensive Chinese products cannot find a similar international export market, leaving millions of Chinese producers unable to sell their products or forcing them to sell at prices below cost. Without alternative employment opportunities, they would have to return to subsistence farming.

To meet the challenges presented by China's accession to the WTO, a whole set of institutional arrangements must be established and a national policy framework needs to be formed. The rural economic situation has offered favorable opportunities in the past for Chinese farmers to organize themselves into farmers' trade associations, rural specialized cooperatives, or other similar organizations. It is important for Chinese farmers to enter the domestic and world markets as a group in order to protect their own interests when facing nontariff barriers or trade wars initiated by foreign countries. In China's socialist market-oriented economy, there continues to be an economic and social rationale for farmers to continue to build on these cooperatives or trade associations.

This chapter discusses the impacts of China's accession to the WTO on Chinese agriculture and farmers.

The Background of Globalization

In September and October 1999, the National Intelligence Council of the United States (NIC) initiated two unclassified workshops and developed four alternative future global scenarios—inclusive globalization, pernicious globalization, regional competition, and post-polar world. "In all but the first scenario, globalization does not create widespread global cooperation. Rather, in the second scenario, globalization's negative effects promote extensive dislocation and conflict, while in the third and fourth, they spur "regionalism" (NIC 2000).

A World Bank report pointed out that "earlier political interests in rural development (e.g., securing food for urban areas) have not been met in most regions. Today the political voice of the rural poor is even more neglected" (Csaki 2003). The policy reform agenda in many countries is still far from complete.

There is also little debate that globalization has contributed to an increase in inequality among countries. Average per capita income of the poorest countries is now 1.9 percent of that of the richest countries, down from 3.1 percent several decades ago (World Bank 2000).

A very important development around the turn of the twenty-first century is the emergence of multinational and transnational corporations. The transnational corporations have already controlled more than 70 percent of world trade and international investments, while the economic capacity of one super transnational corporation, for instance, like Microsoft, could surpass that of a medium-sized country.

In terms of the globalization issue, it is a crucial issue to enable those vulnerable groups or poor people to share the benefits which were gained from the globalization process. As Amartya Sen, a Nobel laureate in economics, said in 2002, "to say the poor gets poorer does not solve the problem. We have to see that the wealth is created and the distribution of wealth is fair. Therefore, we need to create a situation that encourages the masses

Table 17.1

The Structure and Change of the Chinese Rural Labor Force (unit: 10,000)

	Rural labor force	Agricultural labor force	Non-agricultural labor force	TVE* labor force	Change in the agricultural labor force
1986	37,989.8	30,467.9	7,521.9	7,696.34	116.4
1991	43,092.5	34,186.3	8,906.2	9,366.03	849.9
1992	43,801.6	34,037.0	9,764.6	10,326.3	149.3
1993	44,255.8	33,258.2	10,997.6	12,059.9	−778.8
1994	44,654.1	32,690.3	11,963.8	11,757.00	−567.9
1995	45,041.8	32,334.5	12,707.3	12,548.54	−355.8
1996	45,288.0	32,260.4	13,027.6	13,172.29	−74.1
1997	45,961.7	32,434.9	13,050.4	n.a.	174.5
1998	46,432.2	32,626.4	13,805.8	12,262.64	191.5
1999	46,896.5	32,911.8	13,984.7	12,270	285.4
2000	47,962.1	32,797.5	15,164.6	12,819	−114.3

Source: *Statistical Year Book of China*; *Rural Statistical Year Book of China*.
*Town and Village Enterprises.

to participate in the process of globalization" (*Financial Express*, January 6, 2002).

China's Macroeconomic Situation: The Unemployment Issue

China is now at a stage where both industrialization and information technology development are important and coexist side by side. It is important to upgrade China's economic structures that promote the substitution of capital for labor. The demand for unskilled and low-educated labor is gradually decreasing. In China, we have almost an unlimited supply of unskilled and cheap labor from the rural areas.

Two issues are important here: the presence of the rural surplus labor force and a stable macroeconomic situation. The Chinese rural population is not included in the national social security network; therefore they are not calculated into the unemployment statistics. Serious problems of hidden unemployment or disguised employment exist within the vast numbers of the rural labor force.

From Table 17.1, it is clear that during 1997, 1998, and 1999, the agricultural labor force was increasing, which meant that urban and rural nonfarming sectors were unable to absorb the newly emerging rural working population, let alone the existing agricultural surplus labor force.

Due to the dual structure of Chinese society, the problems of agriculture could not be solved within the agriculture sector alone. The impact of China's WTO membership on agriculture should be connected with the macroeconomic situation and overall governmental policies. The key issue is whether economic development can provide Chinese farmers with more non-farming employment opportunities and at the same time can raise the competitiveness of the farming sectors.

Potential Losers in China's Accession to the WTO

Chinese farmers (the rural population) are now no longer homogeneous. They are highly heterogeneous with diversified occupations, and, according to the agricultural general survey undertaken in 1997 (National Office of the Agricultural General Survey 2000), they can be roughly divided into several subgroups as follows.

1. Rural entrepreneurs. There were 1.39 million standard town and village enterprises (TVEs) whose selection was based on certain criteria.[1] If there were two or three decision makers selected in each enterprise, there should be at least three or four million reputable rural entrepreneurs. Those people, together with village leaders, formed the rural elites among the subgroups.
2. Village leaders (cadres). There were more than 730,000 administrative villages and 3.8 million village leaders.
3. Small holders. There were 24.65 million individual industrial and commercial households among the rural population.
4. Regular TVE workers. There were about 56 million rural labor forces working in the standard TVEs.
5. Farmers shifting to urban areas. It is difficult to accurately calculate the shifting population, but according to the agricultural survey, 72 million rural laborers worked outside of their home county.
6. Seasonal or temporary TVE workers. They were approximately 70 million.
7. Pure farming households. By the end of 1996, there were 213.83 million rural households. Among them, there were 126.72 million pure farming households that accounted for 59.26 percent of total rural households. The majority of them are small-scale farmers. Only a few of them are large-scale specialized farming households.
8. First type of part-time farming households.[2] By the end of 1996, there were 39.01 million first type of part-time farming households that accounted for 18.24 percent of total rural households.

Table 17.2

The Structure of Rural Households

	East	Middle	West
Total (10,000)	8,725.8	7,061.0	5,596.0
Pure farming households (%)	48.4	63.6	70.7
1st type of part-time farming (%)	17.9	18.9	17.9
2nd type of part-time farming (%)	17.8	11.3	6.9
Non-farming households (%)	15.9	6.2	4.5

Source: All-China Agricultural Survey, 1998.

In light of the different rural enterprise occupations discussed above, it becomes clear that the impacts of China's WTO membership on agriculture should be analyzed according to different regions, different products, and different farming groups in order to determine possible beneficiaries and losers.

If every agricultural laborer were engaged in cultivating the land, there would be a surplus labor force of more than 180 million, most of them hidden in the pure farming and first type of part-time farming households (Ministry of Agriculture 2001). Their livelihood is influenced by the prices of agricultural products and agricultural structural adjustment. After China's accession to the WTO, they would be the first rural groups to be affected. The staple food producers living in northeastern and central China will potentially be the possible losers, and thus, those engaged in pure farming and first type of part-time farming should be the target groups for policy support.

Heilongjiang province (in northeastern China) is the main soybean production area and its yield accounts for a third of total soybean production. The annual yield of soybeans in China is around 17–18 million tons. In 2000, China imported 12 million tons of soybeans and, according to the WTO agreement, the imported quota of soybean oil in the year of 2002 would be 2.51 million tons, equal to about 15 million tons of soybeans. If the quota were fully met, it would have a great impact on Chinese soybean producers. In fact, in 2003, China imported 20.74 million tons of soybeans, 1.88 million tons of soybean oil, and 954,000 tons of cotton (Chinese Academy of Social Sciences 2004, 105). And, in 2004, China imported 20.23 million tons of soybeans, 2.52 million tons of soybean oil, 7.23 million tons of wheat, and 1.98 million tons of cotton. China's unfavorable balance of agricultural trade reached US$4.64 billion in 2004, the first time China's trade balance was negative in this sector since 1984 (Chinese Academy of Social Sciences 2005). It seems quite difficult for China's small-scale stable food producers to compete with foreign producers in terms of product prices and quality. Some scholars believe that China's entry into the WTO will force many arable farmers (i.e., more than 4 million) to withdraw from the agriculture sector in 2005 according to some conservative estimates (Chinese Academy of Social Sciences 2000, p. 61).

Is This Approach Viable?

Because China has scarce supplies of arable land and water available to agriculture, but abundant surplus rural labor, it seems intuitively clear that it should import more land- and water-intensive products (such as corn and wheat, among others) and export labor-intensive products (such as horticultural products, fruit, poultry and meat products, and so on). In this way, this strategy of importing land and water products while exporting labor products (Chinese Academy of Social Sciences 2000, 13) allows the concept of comparative advantage in China to materialize.

The cash crop producers who are mostly living in the coastal areas are the potential beneficiaries in light of China's membership in the WTO. There are several obstacles that need to be overcome. First, imports and exports in the first quarter of 2002 confirmed that the projected losers have been the actual losers and that it would not be so easy for the possible beneficiaries to gain benefits in reality. As a newcomer to the world agricultural products market, China must compete with the Netherlands, Israel, the Taiwan region, and so on, in terms of flowers, fruit, and other cash crops to gain world market share. It is by no means an easy task. Second, in terms of sorting, grading, packing, quality control, and quarantine, among other aspects, China has a long way to meet international standards and overcome nontariff barriers (green barriers). The viability of the approach based on comparative advantage needs some conditions which are not so easy to be satisfied. China should avoid the situation whereby farmers are unable to find other employment, but have to return to subsistence farming.

Deepening the Reform—Institutional Arrangements and Organizational Innovation

The World Bank report correctly pointed out that "the question of how national policies contribute to greater inclusion or exclusion from the benefits of globalization is critical" (Csaki 2003, 3). The most important task for China is to deepen internal reforms and undertake policy adjustments through institutional changes and organizational innovations in order to meet the challenges of globalization. Emphasis should be on the "governance" issue. That is, reforms of policies and institutions are needed to provide incentives for the initiatives and investments for sustaining growth.

To meet the challenge of China's accession to the WTO, a number of institutional arrangements with a national policy framework should be set up. Among the most important considerations are:

1. Whether or not China's modernization can be realized depends on its ability to transfer millions of rural labor force to nonfarming sectors. Various approaches should be taken to generate employment opportunities for the surplus rural labor force.

2. The problems of China's rural areas, agriculture, and farmers are not the result of a market-oriented economy or China's accession to the WTO but, rather, the result of the drawbacks in the country's institutions. Approaches should be taken to deepen reforms and to adjust the redistribution of national income.

3. The reform of the national policy framework should include two approaches. First, the country needs to develop a demand-driven and rights-based approach. That is, it is important to initiate a social protection network for vulnerable groups (e.g., those who are disabled, aging, sick, etc., especially in rural areas) and to provide basic entitlements of welfare (essential social services) to the people as their "rights," not just according to their "needs" or "citizenship."[3] Second, we need to develop a human resources investment approach that encourages opportunity-based growth. It is important to provide equal access to opportunities among marginalized groups (such as migrants, shifting populations, minorities, women, etc.) to get access to resources (land, human capital, financial capital).

4. Deepening the reforms of the land tenure system. In China's case, it is critical to ensure that villagers can secure land use rights and their fair share of the added value resulting from changes in land use from farming to nonfarming purposes.

5. More effort is needed on human capital enhancement. As Amartya Sen has said, "We need to make our education system more effective as education provides economic, social, and political opportunities" (*Financial Express,* January 6, 2002). China needs to reform its education system to enable the children of the rural poor to obtain a basic education and to provide training programs for adults to improve their employment opportunities. In addition, reforms of the public health system would enable the rural people to have basic medical care, thereby reducing the number of rural adults sinking into poverty due to severe illness.

6. If rural labor cannot be combined with capital, it will be difficult for them to develop their own business and create more employment opportuni-

ties. Therefore, more rapid financial reform is needed to promote the diversified rural financial institutions to solve the contradiction between abundant labor force and scarce capital and to meet the institutional diversity. One important aspect is crowding-out informal finance by means of developing specific non-profit financial organizations (Carsten 2002).

7. Because regional disparities are widening and civil servants' salaries vary according to region and government sector, fiscal reform is needed to establish regular and transparent vertical and horizontal financial transfers. The objective of the reform is to balance responsibilities and fiscal capacities and ensure that different regions and localities receive minimum social provisions (primary education, public health, security, social relief, etc.) and that civil servants at the same rank in different sectors or at different levels receive relatively equal treatment.

8. Promotion of the formation of social and organizational capital. Farmers' autonomous economic organizations should be initiated and promoted. The present rural economic situation has offered a favorable opportunity for Chinese farmers to organize themselves into farmers' trade associations, rural specialized cooperatives, or other types of organizations, which enable farmers in the marketplace to become a countervailing power as a group. Farmers can protect their own interests through group efforts when facing nontariff barriers or trade wars initiated by foreign countries. Chinese farmers should have the right to choose alternatives to forming cooperatives. Even after forming or joining cooperatives, they should also have the right to withdraw and establish other organizational forms. In China's market-oriented economy, there exists an economic and social rationale for developing farmers' cooperatives. The ultimate goal is to establish an equal partnership relationship with the government, agribusiness, and other farmers' economic organizations.

Notes

1. Among more than 20 million TVEs, only those that meet one of the following three criteria were included in the first agricultural general survey: (1) licensed as a corporate legal person; (2) in the absence of such a license, the enterprise meets the following four criteria: (a) it has a fixed production and management organization, place, equipment, and staff; (b) in one year the production and management should last for, at least, three months; (c) it has an independent accounting system and accounts; (d) its business license was issued by the local industrial and commercial administrative office; (3) if it is licensed as a rural individual industrial or commercial household, it has eight or more employees.

2. According to the criteria set by the first agricultural general survey, the first type of part-time farming household refers to household in which the number of members who were engaged mainly in agriculture surpassed the number who were engaged mainly in nonagricultural activities.

3. All the people in a region, whether local inhabitants or migrants, have the "right" to enjoy equal basic social welfare.

References

Carsten, Herrmann-Pillath. 2002. "Disparities of Chinese Economic Development: A Comparison of Analytical Approaches on Different Levels of Aggregation." *Economic Systems* 26, no. 1: 31–54.

Chinese Academy of Social Sciences and Rural Social and Economic Survey Department, Rural Development Institute, National Bureau of Statistics. 2000, 2004, 2005. *Annual Report on Chinese Rural Economic Development: Rural Economic Green Book.* Beijing: Social Sciences Documentation Publishing House.

Csaki, Csaba. 2003. *Reaching the Rural Poor: A Renewed Strategy for Rural Development.* Washington, DC: World Bank.

Ministry of Agriculture, Project Team. 2001. "Report on the Application of Agricultural General Survey to Agricultural Policies and Development Program."

National Intelligence Council (NIC). 2000. "Global Trends 2015: A Dialogue About the Future with Nongovernment Experts." NIC 2000–2. Available at www.cia.gov/nic/NIC_globaltrend2015.html.

National Office of the Agricultural General Survey. 2000. *Comprehensive Abstract of China's First Agricultural General Survey Data.* Beijing: China Statistics Press.

World Bank. 2000. *World Development Report 1999/2000: Entering the Twenty-first Century.* New York: Oxford University Press.

18

Recent Development of the Petroleum Industry in China

Wai-Chung Lo

For decades, petroleum accounted for about 20 percent of the total production of energy in China. Not only was it an important source of energy, it was also a vehicle for generating foreign exchange. Since the 1990s, with China's spectacular economic growth, the demand for petroleum has been increasing rapidly, particularly the demand for transportation fuel. However, petroleum production has lagged behind. This imbalance in demand and production has caused China to become a net importer of oil since 1993. The ratio of net imports to total production increased steadily. In 2000, net imports were 46.5 percent of the total production. According to a forecast by the Energy Information Administration, a research branch of the U.S. Department of Energy, in 2005 China will produce 3.7 percent of the world total output of petroleum but consume 6.8 percent. By 2020, these figures will be 2.6 percent and 8.6 percent respectively. The gap between domestic oil supply and demand will continue to widen.

Under the pressure of the widening production-consumption gap, China's policymakers realized the necessity for an energy policy adjustment. In a speech delivered in 1997 on the strategic change in energy policy, Li Peng, then premier, called for establishing a stable crude oil import and export market channel to ensure long-term security for oil and gas supplies,[1] implying that China will rely more on foreign oil resources. Li Peng's speech signified a fundamental strategic change in oil policy, which became an overture to the oil industry's extensive restructuring in 1998. The goal is to build a national industry capable of competing in the international arena so as to warrant a stable supply of oil.

Compared to the industry's recent structural reform, the pace of reform in the pricing system has been relatively slow. Price reform in the oil sector since the 1980s can be described as zigzagging. To date, oil prices in China are still administered by the state agency, and the trading system is still insulated from the world market. With the accession to the World Trade Organization, China's oil prices will be more closely linked to those of the international markets, provoking a more urgent need for price reform. Naturally, the price system in effect at time of accession was not responsive enough to fast changes in market conditions, thus providing ample arbitrage opportunities. In April 2004, the State Council approved the trading of fuel oil in the Shanghai Futures Exchanges. The new derivative product is expected to provide an effective tool for price discovery as well as risk management.

The Institutional Reform

The petroleum industry was believed to be a strategic sector for the Chinese government. In the early years after establishment of the People's Republic of China, the industry was under control of the Bureau of Petroleum, a division of the Ministry of Fuel. This bureau rose to be the Ministry of the Petroleum Industry (MPI) in 1955, merged with the Ministry of Coal and Ministry of the Chemistry Industry in 1970, and was separated again in 1975. Prior to the open-door policy and subsequent economic reform of the early 1980s, the Ministry of Petroleum controlled the production of oil, and the refining was split among the ministry and a number of government bodies (Hornell 1997, 41). It should be emphasized that oil production was modeled after the Soviet style of central planning. Before the 1980s, all these changes were merely changes in administrative hierarchy.

The economic reform that started in the early 1980s imposed an authentic shakeup in the industry. As a measure to decentralize the industry, the government created the China National Offshore Oil Corporation (CNOOC) in 1982 for offshore petroleum exploration and production, and the Petrochemical Corporation of China (Sinopec) in 1983, to be responsible for petroleum refining, production of petrochemical products, and marketing of refined products. In 1985, China National Petroleum Corporation (CNPC) was founded to replace MPI's function in production. MPI was dissolved in 1991; its administrative duties taken over by the newly established Ministry of Energy, which was in turn dissolved in 1994, to be taken over by the State Development Planning Commission (SDPC). In essence, all these reforms meant a reshuffling of responsibility within the state sector, consistent with the policy that petroleum is a strategic sector that must remain under the firm control of the central government.

Before the economic reform in the late 1970s, self-reliance was the guiding policy for economic development. This, together with the weak domestic demand and stagnant economy, allowed China to have surplus for export. In fact, exporting crude oil was a means to generate much-needed hard currency. The rapid growth subsequent to the economic reform has changed China's domestic supply-demand balance of oil. Table 18.1 shows the domestic supply and demand for petroleum in China from 1985–2001. With oil consumption rising at an annual rate of 6.9 percent, and oil production at only 1.6 percent, China became a net importer of oil in 1993. The fact that the domestic supply-demand imbalance would keep widening in the foreseeable future forced China to review her long-term oil policy.

In 1997, Premier Li Peng delivered an official speech on strategy for future development in the energy sector. He announced fundamental policy changes in the nation's petroleum industry. The emphasis on self-reliance was replaced with an emphasis on international trade, ultimately to be integrated with the world market. Specifically, China would rely more on oil imports, especially for crude oil. This announcement was followed by a significant industry restructuring in 1998. A major feature included a series of asset swaps between CNPC and Sinopec. Before the asset swaps, CNPC had been a major producer of crude oil, with its domain in inland oil extraction, including both exploration and development, while Sinopec was assigned the refinery domain. In 1998, CNPC transferred eight southern oil fields to Sinopec, while Sinopec transferred four northern refineries to CNPC. The asset swaps created two giant petrochemical groups, effecting the integration of upstream and downstream, internal and external trade as well as production and marketing, for international competition. The strategy was that CNPC could focus on northern and western regions while Sinopec could focus on eastern and southern regions. These two vertically integrated gigantic oil enterprises were endowed with a size and scope of operations comparable to international competitors. It should be noted that since the two enterprises have distinct territories, they have become essentially the monopolists of the regions.

Simultaneous to this restructuring, substantial changes were also made in the state's central administrative structure in order to accommodate the new role of the state-owned petrochemical groups. The Ministry of Oil Industry and the Ministry of the Chemical Industry were dissolved. Part of their administrative functions was shifted to the newly established State Administration of Petroleum and Chemical Industries under the State Economic Planning Commission. These departments serve as regulatory bodies as well as coordinators for operations of the state petrochemical groups.

Table 18.1

Production, Imports, and Exports of Oil (10,000 metric tons), 1985 and 1990–2001

	Production	Imports	Exports	Stock changes in the year	Quantity available for consumption	Consumption	Net exports (exports minus imports)
1985	12,489.5	90.0	3,630.4	244.6	9,193.7	9,168.8	3,540.4
1990	13,830.6	755.5	3,110.4	−40.8	11,434.9	11,485.6	2,354.9
1991	14,009.2	1,249.5	2,930.3	−52.3	12,276.1	12,383.5	1,680.8
1992	14,209.7	2,124.7	2,859.6	78.3	13,553.1	13,353.7	734.9
1993	14,517.4	3,615.7	2,506.5	−699.2	14,927.4	14,721.3	−1,109.2
1994	14,608.2	2,903.3	2,380.2	−252.4	14,878.9	14,956.0	−523.1
1995	15,000.5	3,673.2	2,454.5	−151.0	16,068.2	16,064.9	−1,218.7
1996	15,733.4	4,536.9	2,696.0	81.8	17,656.1	17,436.2	−1,840.9
1997	16,074.1	6,787.0	2,815.2	−395.2	19,650.7	19,691.7	−3,971.8
1998	16,100.0	5,738.7	2,326.5	174.0	19,686.2	19,817.8	−3,412.2
1999	16,000.0	6,483.3	1,643.5	124.6	20,964.4	21,072.9	−4,839.8
2000	16,300.0	9,748.5	2,172.1	−1,244.6	22,631.8	22,439.3	−7,576.4
2001	16,395.9	9,118.2	2,046.7	−262.7	23,204.7	22,838.3	−7,071.5

Source: National Bureau of Statistics, *China Statistical Yearbook*, various years.

Table 18.2

Imports and Exports of Crude Oil, 1990–2002

	Imports		Exports		Net imports	
	(mn metric tons)	(bn US$)	(mn metric tons)	(bn US$)	(mn metric tons)	(bn US$)
1990	24.91	3.82	24.91	3.82	0.00	0.00
1991	25.16	3.27	25.16	3.27	0.00	0.00
1992	11.36	1.72	21.83	2.79	−10.47	−1.07
1993	15.67	2.32	19.60	2.39	−3.93	−0.07
1994	12.35	1.57	18.80	2.08	−6.46	−0.51
1995	17.09	2.36	17.25	2.06	−0.16	0.30
1996	22.62	3.41	0.00	0.00	22.62	3.41
1997	35.47	5.46	0.00	0.00	35.47	5.46
1998	27.32	3.27	0.00	0.00	27.32	3.27
1999	36.61	4.64	0.00	0.00	36.61	4.64
2000	70.27	14.86	0.00	0.00	70.27	14.86
2001	60.26	11.67	0.00	0.00	60.26	11.67
2002	69.41	12.76	0.00	0.00	69.41	12.76

Source: Yearbook of China's Foreign Economic Relations and Trade, various years; *Almanac of China's Foreign Economic Relations and Trade*, various years.

Some features of the 1998 restructuring are noteworthy. First, the reform is essentially a continuation of the central government's strategy to shift control of the oil industry from the ministries to state enterprises, without losing grip on the direction of development. Second, the reform would create a few giant corporations with size and scope comparable to international oil majors. For example, through CNPC, China outbid international competitors, acquired the right to develop two oilfields in Kazakhstan in exchange for her commitment to build a 3,000–kilometer pipeline from her oilfields to Xinjiang province, and a 250–kilometer pipeline to the border of Iran. In early 2002, CNPC bought a 30 percent stake from the European Bank for Reconstruction and Development in two oilfields in Azerbaijan. The state-owned oil enterprise plans to double its overseas oil production to 256 million barrels in 2005 ("CNPC Buys Overseas Oilfields" 2002). The restructured oil enterprises would implement a balanced development strategy by fully utilizing and improving the existing refining capacity as well as securing the long-run stability of crude oil. Tables 18.2 and 18.3 reflect the supply and demand of crude oil and finished oil products respectively. China has stopped exporting crude oil since 1996; imports have increased almost threefold from 27.3 million metric tons in 1998 to 69.4 metric tons in 2002. In contrast, exports of finished oil products have increased from 4.7 million tons in

Table 18.3

Imports and Exports of Finished Oil Products, 1990–2002

	Imports		Exports		Net imports	
	(mn metric tons)	(bn US$)	(mn metric tons)	(bn US$)	(mn metric tons)	(bn US$)
1990	5.39	1.11	2.49	3.82	5.39	−2.71
1991	5.21	0.99	2.52	3.23	5.21	−2.24
1992	7.68	1.39	4.60	0.78	3.08	0.61
1993	17.29	2.99	4.79	0.85	12.50	2.14
1994	12.89	1.96	5.13	0.88	7.76	1.08
1995	14.39	2.07	5.33	0.92	9.06	1.14
1996	15.83	2.38	4.17	0.87	11.65	1.52
1997	23.79	3.68	5.59	1.20	18.21	2.48
1998	21.74	2.41	4.36	0.74	17.38	1.67
1999	20.88	4.64	6.45	1.10	14.42	3.55
2000	18.05	3.66	8.27	2.13	9.77	1.53
2001	21.45	3.77	9.22	2.13	12.23	1.64
2002	20.34	3.80	10.68	2.38	9.65	1.41

Source: *Yearbook of China's Foreign Economic Relations and Trade*, various years; *Almanac of China's Foreign Economic Relations and Trade*, various years.

1998 to 10.4 million tons in 2002, with imports stabilized at around 3.5 million metric tons. The trade balance of crude oil and finished oil products is shown in Figure 18.1. While there is a steady increase in the net imports of crude oil, the net imports of finished oil products remains relatively stable, indicating that the oil enterprises have improved their refining capacity. Finally, industrial reform has created two regional monopolists, namely, CNPC and Sinopec. The sheer fact that a few regional monopolists dominate the industry poses profound implications for domestic market competition.

Price Reform

The central government believes petroleum is a strategic commodity. Prior to the 1980s, the central government monopolized trading of oil from upstream to downstream, keeping all prices administered. Under the administered price system, upstream industry sold crude oil to downstream at state-controlled low prices, guaranteeing all losses would be subsidized by the central government. As a first step for price liberalization, a three-tier pricing system on oil products was introduced in 1983. Oil products were sold at "in quota" low prices, "in quota" high prices, and market prices. Under this pricing system, a portion of high-end products was allowed to trade in the free market.

Figure 18.1   **Net Imports of Crude Oil and Finished Oil Products, 1990–2002**

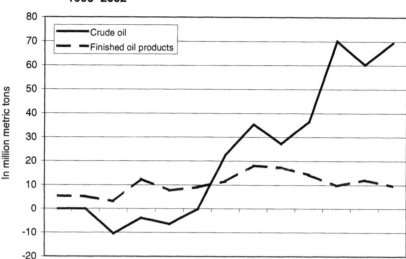

Source: Caltex Oil Hong Kong Ltd.

Price Reform in the Early 1990s

Under the three-tiered price system, the proportion of market-priced finished products increased from 10 percent in 1983 to 65 percent in 1993 (Wang 1999, 56). For further market liberalization, oil exchanges were established in several cities to trade oil futures. Meanwhile, demand for oil products continued to surge. To overcome the shortage in domestic supply, the regions with a surplus in hard currency were allowed to meet their demand from overseas markets, and foreign retailers were permitted to import non-tariff oil products directly from abroad. As a result, oil imports increased almost threefold, from 0.8 billion metric tons in 1990 to 3.6 billion metric tons in 1993. The sudden increase in oil imports at substantially lower prices put tremendous pressure on domestic oil enterprises, which were still operating inefficiently. The price differential between foreign and domestic oil products also created opportunities for arbitrage.[2] The impact of cheaper imports on domestic refineries was so detrimental that the central government decided to halt the price liberalization. In 1994, the State Council announced a series of measures that essentially led the industry back to Soviet-style central planning. Specifically, CNPC would propose the plan of supply and demand, including imports of crude oil and finished products. The State Planning Commission, collaborating with the State Economic and Trade Commission (SETC), would compile the material balance of the crude oil and finished oil products to establish the plan for imports and exports. To bring imports under control, approval of import quotas would be centralized by the SDPC, while import rights would be granted to only two state-owned firms supervised by the SDPC. Foreign firms were denied licenses to import oil. Furthermore, the state would strictly regulate prices of finished oil products, which in the major cities were to be administered by the SDPC. For the rest of the markets, prices would be administered by the local government according to prices set by the SDPC. The switch in policy aroused much speculation and brought chaos to the futures market. Finally, in 1995, the government ordered closure of the oil exchanges.

Pricing Mechanisms Since 1998

Before 2000, the SDPC set the prices of major oil products, both wholesale and retail, based on its assessment of domestic supply and demand conditions. In May 2000, it announced a new pricing mechanism. The SDPC would adjust the benchmark prices monthly, based on the spot price in Singapore. The new pricing system intended to link domestic oil prices to those of the international market, in spite of criticism that this pricing mechanism would encourage arbitrage, as the monthly benchmark price announcements could easily be forecast by market conditions in Singapore. In October 2001 the SDPC announced a new pricing system. In addition to the Singapore market, the f.o.b. prices in the Rotterdam market and New York market were incorporated. The pricing formula would take ratios of 60 percent, 30 percent, and 10 percent from Rotterdam, New York, and Singapore respectively. Instead of making monthly adjustments, the SDPC would only intervene when the prices of the three markets exceeded certain acceptable ranges, which were not disclosed to the public. The new pricing mechanism would take domestic supply and demand conditions into consideration. Domestic oil could collate and stipulate its retail prices within the range of plus or minus 8 percent of the guideline prices.

Although the pricing mechanism aimed at linking oil prices to international markets, domestic prices were still substantially higher than the world market prices. For example, in April 2002 the wholesale price of diesel was US$33.3/barrel (bbl), while its world market price was around US$22 bbl. Figure 18.2 shows the graphs of the prices of diesel in Shenzhen, Rotterdam, New York, and Singapore from October 2001 to April 2002. Shenzhen prices

Figure 18.2   **Diesel Prices in Shenzhen, New York, Rotterdam, and Singapore (SP), October 2001–April 2002**

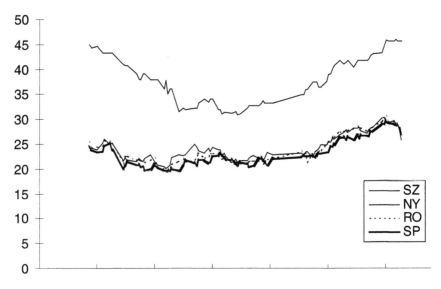

Source: Caltex Oil Hong Kong Ltd.
Note: SZ = Shenzhen; NY = New York; RO = Rotterdam; SP = Singapore.

Table 18.4

Descriptive Statistics on the Prices of Diesel Oil in Shenzhen, New York, Rotterdam, and Singapore, 2001–2002

	Shenzhen	New York	Rotterdam	Singapore
Mean	37.75	24.25	23.93	23.13
Maximum	45.98	30.45	30.47	29.55
Minimum	30.84	20.21	19.82	19.51
Variance	22.7	7.15	8.57	7.94

Source: Caltex Oil Hong Kong Ltd.

clearly diverged from those in other markets. Table 18.4 shows the descriptive statistics of the prices in the four markets. Not only were the Shenzhen prices substantially higher, but they were also more volatile. To show how Shenzhen prices diverge, we subtract the prices in Rotterdam from the prices in the other three markets. Figure 18.3 shows the graphs of the price differ-

Figure 18.3 **Price Differentials in Shenzhen, New York, and Singapore Using Rotterdam Prices as a Benchmark**

(U.S.$/bbl)

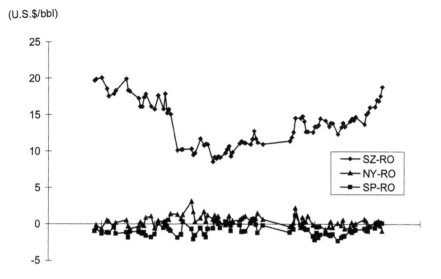

Source: Caltex Oil Hong Kong Ltd.

entials. While the price differentials in the Singapore and New York markets were small and relatively stable, the price differentials in the Shenzhen market showed much higher volatility. For example, the Shenzhen price differential in November 2001 was about US$20/bbl, down to US$8.5/bbl in January 2002 and up again to US$20/bbl in April 2002. This indicates that domestic conditions, in addition to the prices in international markets, were important considerations when the SDPC set the benchmark price.

Market Opening Under WTO Membership

The WTO accession signified China's interest in further market opening. Under the WTO agreement, China made a series of concessions (Table 18.5). Tariffs on oils had to be either removed or significantly lowered. Before accession to the WTO, tariffs on most petrochemical products stood at the level of 13 percent to 18 percent. These are to diminish significantly by 2008. There were also concessions on import quotas. Specifically, quotas and licenses on the imports of crude oil and refined products would increase at an annual rate of 15 percent and would be eliminated by 2004. As for the domestic retail market, retail distributions were to be open to foreign suppliers of refined products three years after China's WTO accession. Barriers to

Table 18.5

Tariff Reductions in the Sino-U.S. WTO Agreement

	Before 2001	Under Sino-U.S. agreement	Effective year
Crude oil	(RMB16/tonne) 2%	0%	2000
Gasoline	9%	5%	2001
Diesel	6%	6%	2000
Kerosene	9%	6%	2000
Naphtha	5%	6%	2000
Heavy fuel oil	12%	6%	2000
Ethylene	5%	2%	2003
Stylene	9%	2%	2005
MEG	14%	7%	2003
LDPE/HDPE	16%	6.50%	2008
PP	16%	6.50%	2008
PVC	16%	6.50%	2008
ABS	16%	6.50%	2008
ABC resin	16%	6.50%	2008
Fertilizers	5%	4%	2000

Source: *China's Giant Oil Duo*, HSBC, Hong Kong.

wholesale distribution of crude oil and refined products were to be removed in five years. These include geographic, quantity, or ownership restrictions. In short, the WTO accession required a full-fledged opening of China's oil market to foreign competitors by 2008.

Removal of tariffs on crude and refined oil products should have little impact on the upstream industry because China had already implemented a low tariff policy on crude and refined oil products. For example, the pre-WTO tariff on crude oil was 0.8 percent. Lifting the import ban would only have limited effect on crude oil because China was planning to increase the import of crude oil anyway, in response to the widening gap between domestic consumption and production. The price impact on the downstream industry might be deemed more significant, due to substantial decreases in tariffs. Gradual reduction of tariffs softened the impact.

Under WTO rules, China must remove restrictions on distribution, including wholesale, retail, and transportation. With respect to the domestic retail market, the strategy of the Chinese government was to strengthen the position of CNPC and Sinopec in order to preempt domestic retail outlets before the market could be opened to foreign competition. For example, in August 2001 the SETC stipulated that only CNPC and Sinopec would be permitted to build new gas stations ("Sinopec, CNPC Braced for Looming Rivalry" 2001). The objective was to enhance the two petrochemical groups' competitiveness ahead of the country's accession to the WTO.[3] Accordingly, the two petrochemical groups aggressively acquired retail outlets. Sinopec planned to expand its market share of the domestic retail business to 60 percent, whereas CNPC targeted a market share of 30 percent by 2005. Curiously, though the central government intended to coordinate the two petrochemical groups' development, as evidenced by appointing them distinct territories, competition still existed between the two firms, particularly in the downstream sector.[4] As the two domestic petrochemical groups aggressively expand their retail networks, foreign firms must cooperate with them to gain entrance to the domestic retail business.[5]

As for the wholesale market, the central Chinese government will maintain control through the issue of import/export licenses and will also retain the "specified trading rights" for crude oil and refined products, so that all imports of these products can only be conducted through assigned state-owned petroleum firms. Under this trading system, four companies were designated as state importers of crude oil and oil products: Sinochem, Unipec, China Oil, and Zhuhai Zhenrong. The three companies designated as state exporters are Sinochem, Unipec, and China Oil.[6] The WTO agreement allows for some non-state-controlled imports. At the time of accession, the maximum non-state import allowance for crude oil and oil products amounted to 52.7 million bbl and 29 million bbl respectively, with an annual growth rate of 15 percent. The rate for increasing imports of crude oil would be renegotiated in ten years, but for oil products the import quotas were lifted on January 1, 2004. Under the WTO agreement, China's oil industry will be subjected to severe foreign competition in both wholesale and retail sales. Apparently the strategy of the central government is to strengthen the position of state enterprises to dominate domestic markets before fully opening them to foreign competition.

Relaunching Oil Futures

As discussed in the previous section, when the government began to relax control of the price of domestic finished oil products in 1998 to reduce the divergence between domestic and world market prices, prices in the Singapore market were used as benchmarks for setting domestic prices. After criticism for relying solely on the Singapore market, in which a few traders could easily influence prices, prices in New York and Rotterdam were also incorporated into the pricing mechanism starting in October 2001. The prices in New York, Rotterdam, and Singapore were assembled to compute a benchmark for domestic prices for a more transparent pricing mechanism. However, the new pricing mechanism was criticized for its arbitrage potential as domestic prices would lag behind international prices in a predictable manner.

A causality test was conducted to examine whether the criticism was justified. The test examines whether the price change of a market would lead to a price change in another market. Daily prices of diesel in New York, Rotterdam, Singapore, and Shenzhen from October 2001 to April 2002 were compiled.[7] Bilateral causality relationships between New York and Shenzhen, Rotterdam and Shenzhen, and Singapore and Shenzhen were tested. The results from the causality test showed that for a lag of three business days or less, the price effect of New York, Rotterdam, and Singapore on Shenzhen is statistically significant. When the lag increases to four business days, prices in New York and Rotterdam lead the price in Shenzhen. When the lag increases to six business days, the price in Rotterdam leads the price in Shenzhen. In all cases, price change in Shenzhen does not have any effect on the international markets. These results indicated that on average Shenzhen prices lagged international prices for seven business days. The causality test confirms the perception of market participants that under that particular pricing mechanism the domestic price indeed lagged international prices. When international prices rose, speculators would hoard domestic products at a lower price to be sold later when the domestic price increased. If the international prices fell, speculators would sell domestic products and purchase later when the domestic price subsequently declined. As such, the price mechanism created a profiteering condition for speculators at the expense of users, and there was a strong demand for a pricing system that could rectify this deficiency. In April 2004, the State Council approved the Shanghai Futures Exchange's application to trade heavy fuel oil futures.

In fact, there have been incessant voices in recent years urging the relaunching of the trading of oil futures. The major argument is that it would help to establish a pricing mechanism that would be more reflective of domestic demand.

It is well established in the literature that futures trading serves the function of price discovery and risk management (Deaves and Krinsky 1991; Moosa and Al-Loughani 1994). Efficient futures markets are able to reveal prices of the underlying commodities and hence provide valuable information for pricing in the spot market. The question is: Given market conditions in China, would the futures serve the intended purpose?

From the perspective of market participants, the primary purpose of trading futures is risk management. In the United States, demand for fuel oil futures is strong. The history of the oil futures in NYMEX shows that strong demand for hedging is a necessary condition to support successful futures trading. The NYMEX heating oil futures serve various users: fuel oil distributors want to lock in the delivery price; wholesalers want to protect physical inventories and to hedge the forward purchases of supply; and large commercial users of heating oil and transportation fuel want to hedge against increases in the cost of diesel fuel and jet fuel. Demand from utility companies for hedging is particularly strong. In fact, informal markets in New York had been very liquid before the introduction of oil futures, indicating that there was strong demand for hedging. In contrast, most oil futures launched in Singapore were unsuccessful. As the hub in Asia for oil trading, in the last two decades Singapore has aimed to launch oil futures in its exchanges. The first fuel oil contract was launched in 1987, which lasted until 1999. A gasoline futures contract was launched in 1991, failed, relaunched in 1992 but failed again. A Brent Crude Oil contract was launched in 1995 and again did not perform well. Dubai crude futures were launched in November 2002. The performance was again disappointing, with open interest declining to half in the first six months after launching. The futures were delisted in October 2004. In depicting the Singaporean oil market, Paul Hornell (1997) pointed out that before the formal market was launched in 1989, trading in the informal paper market in Singapore was scanty. This was an indication that there was little demand for hedging (Hornell 1997, 232). He observed that, "there is no example in oil futures of any contract both surviving and growing without the existence of an already high liquidity informal market, and numerous examples where they have failed even when the informal markets existed" (233). Strong demand for hedging is predicted in China due to surging domestic consumption. Chinese oil companies need an effective instrument for risk management. However, owing to the immature nature of the banking system, domestic informal markets are not in place, although there are signs Chinese oil companies are beginning to participate in the informal market in Singapore for hedging. This could be an indication that the demand for hedging is growing.

The demand for risk management is also related to the industrial structure. In this regard, the experience in agricultural futures is revealing. The Chengzhou Commodity Exchange (CZCE) provides valuable experiences for successful futures markets. Two fundamental factors accounted for the success of the agricultural futures, the mungbean futures in particular. First, agricultural markets are basically liberalized. The proportion of procurement at market price since 1992 has been around 80 percent (Guo 1995), a clear indication that agricultural markets have been highly liberalized. Second, agriculture markets are highly competitive. For example, mungbean planters are typically small producers. The industrial structure of the oil industry, on the other hand, is highly concentrated. To date, the industry is dominated by three giant enterprises, CNPC, Sinopec, and CNOOC. In particular, CNPC and Sinopec control the domestic supply of finished oil products. Moreover, out of approximately 500,000 petroleum stations nationwide, about 60 percent are either owned by the two giants directly or controlled by their subsidiaries. In short, the markets for finished oil products are hardly competitive. This would be a big concern for the effectiveness of a futures market for risk management and price discovery. In this regard, the launching of heavy fuel oil futures is a pilot test. Heavy fuel oil is normally consumed in the textile industry, by power plants, and by ships. The product is 100 percent imported. The government does not regulate fuel oil prices, which are determined by the market and closely follow international prices. The performance of the futures has been quite steady, with open interests remaining around 250,000 tonnes since its launching in September 2004.

Price Liberalization: An Unfinished Reform

The 1998 restructuring made the oil industry one of the best-prepared sectors for the WTO accession, which required China to open its market to foreign competitors. The restructuring improved the industry's efficiency as well as created a few sizable petrochemical enterprises for international competition, deemed vital for the nation's long-term energy security. The WTO accession has stepped up the integration of domestic oil markets with international markets. The most challenging task will be price reform. The pricing system established in 1989 and revised in 2001 was the initial step to liberalize the domestic market. As the upheaval of the oil futures in the mid-1990s plainly exhibited, without a genuine commitment to price liberalization, government would respond by price intervention in an attempt to maintain industrial stability when oil prices became too volatile. The brief history of oil futures from 1993 to 1995 showed that a futures exchange would not be able to function properly without a fully liberalized and competitive domestic market. Price liberalization in the oil market ended abruptly in 1995, which, in retrospect, was due to the gradual approach in reform. Although China had begun to introduce market forces to the oil industry as early as 1982, the true state-owned enterprise reform did not take place until the mid-1990s. The government intended to use market liberalization as an impetus to improve the efficiency of the oil industry. Yet the gradualism in reform required the government to maintain the status quo and to protect the interests of existing oil companies from undesirable effects of market liberalization. To date, the retail prices of distillate products such as gasoline and diesel are still heavily regulated. In short, retail prices in China are still subject to controls and the distortion in resources continues.

Apendix 18.1

Granger Causality Test on the Lead-Lag Relationship Between the Pricing of Diesel Oil in New York (NY), Rotterdam (RO), Singapore (SP), and Shenzhen (SZ).

The Granger causality test is conducted by running the following regression:
$Y_t = a_i X_{t-i} + b_i Y_{t-i} + u_i.$

X Granger-causes Y, i.e., X leads Y, if all a_i's are jointly insignificant. The choice of the order of the lag in the regression is arbitrary. We run the regression from the lag equal to 1 to 15. When the lag order is 8 or higher, all the a_i's are insignificant. In this table, the following table reports the results of the lag order up to 8.

Null hypothesis	F-statistic	P-value
Lag order = 1		
NY leads SZ	11.034	0.001
RO leads SZ	18.991	0.000
SP leads SZ	10.272	0.002
SZ leads NY	0.000	0.989
SZ leads RO	0.008	0.927
SZ leads SP	0.303	0.584
Lag order = 2		
NY leads SZ	6.138	0.003
RO leads SZ	10.663	0.000
SP leads SZ	6.140	0.003
SZ leads NY	1.172	0.315
SZ leads RO	1.924	0.153
SZ leads SP	0.512	0.601
Lag order = 3		
NY leads SZ	4.448	0.006
RO leads SZ	7.043	0.000
SP leads SZ	4.361	0.007
SZ leads NY	1.080	0.363
SZ leads RO	1.120	0.346
SZ leads SP	0.505	0.680
Lag order = 4		
NY leads SZ	2.649	0.040
RO leads SZ	4.348	0.003
SP leads SZ	2.426	0.055
SZ leads NY	0.922	0.456
SZ leads RO	1.027	0.399
SZ leads SP	1.954	0.110

(continued)

Apendix 18.1 *(continued)*

Null hypothesis	F-statistic	P-value
Lag order = 5		
NY leads SZ	2.069	0.079
RO leads SZ	3.346	0.009
SP leads SZ	1.963	0.095
SZ leads NY	0.719	0.612
SZ leads RO	0.759	0.583
SZ leads SP	2.334	0.051
Lag order = 6		
NY leads SZ	1.706	0.133
RO leads SZ	2.889	0.014
SP leads SZ	1.479	0.198
SZ leads NY	0.741	0.619
SZ leads RO	0.598	0.731
SZ leads SP	2.021	0.075
Lag order = 7		
NY leads SZ	1.636	0.141
RO leads SZ	2.851	0.012
SP leads SZ	1.369	0.233
SZ leads NY	0.651	0.712
SZ leads RO	0.782	0.605
SZ leads SP	1.599	0.151
Lag order = 8		
NY leads SZ	1.245	0.289
RO leads SZ	1.890	0.078
SP leads SZ	1.716	0.112
SZ leads NY	0.539	0.822
SZ leads RO	0.646	0.736
SZ leads SP	1.450	0.194

Notes

1. "Development in the petroleum sector should rely on two markets and two resources, i.e., both domestic and international. China will widen the diversified collaborations with foreigners, be involved in petroleum exploitation and development overseas, and get construction projects and services abroad. A stable crude oil import/ export market channel should be established to provide security for national oil and gas supply in the long run" ("Zhongguo de nengyuan zhengce" [China's energy policy], *People's Daily* [overseas edition], May 30, 1997).

2. With the relaxation on imports, imported oil products flooded the Shenzhen market. According to a report by a Hong Kong–based newspaper, while the twenty-four retail outlets owned by foreigners in Shenzhen imported approximately only 150,000 tons of oil products in 1993 for local consumption, total imported oil products available in the Shenzhen market amounted to over 2 million tons (*Economic Journal* 1994, Hong Kong).

3. For example, an official with the State Economic and Trade Commission said that allowing only Sinopec and CNPC to open new gasoline stations was expected to reinforce the two companies' positions in the Chinese oil retail markets before opening it up to foreign competition.

4. In the 2002 annual report, which is available at Sinopec's Web site (http://english.sinopec.com/index.jsp), Li Yizhong, the chairman of Sinopec, reveals that the company is planning to increase the number of retail outlets beyond its principal market, implying that there will be some competition with PetroChina.

5. Li Yizhong, chairman of Sinopec, openly expressed the view that "foreign competitors will have to cooperate with us in an attempt to further explore the domestic market as long as we control more gasoline stations" ("Sinopec, CNPC Braced for Looming Rivalry," *China Daily*, July 31, 2001).

6. China Oil and Sinochem, subsidiaries of CNPC, and Unipec, a subsidiary of Sinopec, are among the small number of state-specified firms being granted the right to import and export crude oil and refined products.

7. The author is indebted to Edmond Hui of Caltex Oil Hong Kong Ltd. for providing this data.

References

Balabanoff, Stefan. 1995. "Oil Futures Price and Stock Management: A Cointegration Analysis." *Energy Economics* 17, no. 3 (July): 205–10.

Barros-Luis, Jorge. 2001. "The Estimation of Risk-Premium Implicit in Oil Prices." *OPEC Review* 25, no. 3: 221–59.

"CNPC Buys Overseas Oilfields." 2002. *China Daily*, January 25.

Deaves, Richard, and Itzhak Krinsky. 1991. "Costs and Benefits of Using NYMEX Crude Oil Futures." *Energy Studies Review* 3, no. 2: 142–50.

Fleming, Jeff, and Barbara Ostiek. 1999. "The Impact of Energy Derivatives on the Crude Oil Market." *Energy Economics* 21, no. 2 (April): 135–67.

Guo Jianying. 1995. "The Weights and Changes of the Three Forms of Pricing." *Zhongguo wujia* (China Price) 79: 8–12.

Gulen, S. Gurcan. 1998. "Efficiency in the Crude Oil Futures Market." *Journal of Energy Finance and Development* 3, no. 1: 13–21.

Hornell, Paul. 1997. *Oil in Asia: Markets, Trading, Refining and Regulation.* Oxford: Oxford University Press.

Moosa, Imad. 2000. "Arbitrage, Hedging, Speculation, and the Pricing of Crude Oil Futures Contracts." *Keio Economics Studies* 37, no. 1: 53–61.

Moosa, Imad, and N.E. Al-Loughani. 1994. "Unbiasedness and Time Varying Risk Premium in the Crude Oil Futures Market." *Energy Economics* 16, no. 2 (April): 99–105.

"Sinopec, CNPC Braced for Looming Rivalry." 2001. *China Daily*, July 31.

Tse, Yimun, and G. Geoffrey Booth. 1997. "Information Shares in International Oil Futures Markets." *International Review of Economics and Finance* 6, no. 1: 49–56.

U.S. Department of Energy, Energy Information Administration. 2002. *International Energy Outlook.* Washington, DC.

Wang, H. H. 1999. *China's Oil Industry & Market.* New York: Elsevier.

World Bank. 2001. *Modernizing China's Oil and Gas Sector Structure and Regulation.* Joint report of the World Bank and China's State Council for Restructuring the Economic System. Washington DC.

.

About the Editors and Contributors

The Editors

Hung-Gay Fung is Dr. Y. S. Tsiang chair professor of Chinese studies at the College of Business Administration, University of Missouri-St. Louis. His research covers a wide range of international finance and Chinese financial markets. He is the editor of two journals—*China and World Economy* and *The Chinese Economy*.

Changhong Pei is professor of the Graduate School of the Chinese Academy of Social Sciences and chair professor of the University of International Business Economy. His research focuses on international trade, investment, and Chinese financial markets. He has published over one hundred articles in leading academic journals and five books.

Kevin H. Zhang is associate professor of economics at Illinois State University. He received his PhD in economics from the University of Colorado in 1996, and has been a post-doctoral fellow at Harvard University and a consultant at the Harvard Institute of International Development for a year. His research focuses on international trade and foreign direct investment, especially in China and developing countries.

The Contributors

Xinshen Diao is a research fellow at the Development Strategy and Governance Division, International Food Policy Research Institute in Washington, D.C. He specializes in international trade and development. He received his doctoral degree in 1995 from the University of Minnesota.

Ting Gao is an assistant professor in the Department of Economics and Finance at the City University of Hong Kong. His research interest focuses on the industrial structure and economic development of the Chinese economy.

He taught at the University of Missouri-Columbia before joining the City University of Hong Kong.

Wai Kin Leung is professor at the Chinese University of Hong Kong. He received his doctoral degree from the University of Texas-Austin. His research interest has been on international finance, real estate issues, and financial issues in China.

Kun Li received a master's degree in finance at Southern Illinois University. Currently, he is a lecturer at the Business School of Sichuan University, and is also a PhD Candidate in finance at Sichuan University.

Mei Liao is the vice president of the Economics and Management School, Beijing Polytechnic University. Her research focuses on economic issues and management of Chinese enterprises. She has published extensively in many academic journals and has also published numerous books.

Qingfeng "Wilson" Liu is an assistant professor at James Madison University. He taught at University of Redlands, where he received an Outstanding Teaching Award for 2002–2003. His research focus is on investments, international finance, and risk management.

Ying-Qiu Liu is vice president of the Graduate School of the Chinese Academy of Social Sciences. His major studies are on China's macro-economy and especially on development in the western area of China. He has published more than one hundred papers and books.

Wai-Chung Lo is a professor at the Open University of Hong Kong. He graduated from the University of Georgia. Currently, his research focuses on international finance and economic issues.

Penelope B. Prime is professor of economics in the Department of Economics and Finance and director of the China Research Center at Kennesaw State University in the University of Georgia system. She has also taught at Emory University, Georgia State University, and Carleton College. She earned her PhD in economics at the University of Michigan. Dr. Prime's research focuses on China's economy and business, including China's business environment, foreign trade and investment, industrial and technological progress, and provincial development.

Jinjian Shen is an associate research fellow, deputy director of the Research Office for International Cooperation, Chinese Academy of Social Sciences.

His major studies focus on Chinese foreign trade and investment as well as the financial market. He is in charge of the publication of Social Sciences and Humanities Forum.

Agapi Somwaru is a senior agricultural economist in the Economic Research Service (ERS) at the U.S. Department of Agriculture where she works in the area of applied agricultural trade and policy analysis research. Her work focuses on international policy and trade, intersectoral linkages, regional trade integration, and WTO issues as well as risk and agricultural production–related issues.

Francis Tuan is a senior economist and leader of the China Project, Market and Trade Economics Division, Economic Research Service, U.S. Department of Agriculture. He joined ERS in 1979 and his current research focus is in the area of China's agricultural and agricultural trade policies. He has co-edited several books in both English and Chinese and published many professional journal articles. He received his PhD in agricultural economics from the University of Illinois.

Yan-Zhong Wang is deputy director, Bureau of Research Coordination and professor of the Graduate School, Chinese Academy of Social Science. His major studies focus on social security and the industrial economy. He has published five books and many scholarly papers.

Xiaodong Wu joined the Department of Economics at the University of North Carolina at Chapel Hill in fall of 1999. He received a doctoral degree from Princeton University in May 2000. His areas of interest are international economics, development, political economy, and applied microeconomics. Currently, his research focuses on the behavior and regulation of multinational firms as well as the related political and institutional issues.

Nini Yang is an associate professor at San Francisco State University. Her research focuses on international business issues and she has published many high-quality papers in scholarly journals.

Jian Zhang received her doctoral degree from the University of Hawaii at Manoa in 2003 and worked as a postdoctoral research fellow at the University of Florida for one year. Since June 2004, Zhang has worked as a researcher at the Abdus Salam International Center for Theoretical Physics (ICTP), which is a joint program of UNESCO, IAEA, Fondazione Eni Enrico Mattei (FEEM), and the Royal Swedish Academy of Sciences.

Ju-Wei Zhang is deputy director of the Institute of Population and Labor Economics at the Chinese Academy of Social Sciences. His major studies focus on demographic and labor economics in China.

Xiao-shan Zhang is director of the Institute of Rural Development, Chinese Academy of Social Sciences. His major research interest is the agricultural economy, the theory and practice of the cooperative economy, rural organizations, and institutions in the Chinese economy.

Changwen Zhao is chair professor of finance, Business School of Sichuan University. He serves as the assistant to the president at Sichuan University. He was a visiting scholar at the University of Michigan.

Bing-Wen Zheng is director of the Institute of Latin-American Studies and a professor of the Graduate School of the Chinese Academy of Social Sciences (CASS). Earlier, he served as deputy director at the Institute of European Studies, CASS. His major studies are on social security and macroeconomics.

Stanley J. Zhu is an analyst at OCI-Prudential Asset Management Ltd. He graduated from the University of Hong Kong in 2004. His research interest is financial issues in China.

Index

Agricultural Bank of China (ABC),
  146–50, 158, 209, 210f
Agricultural labor force
  economic growth impact, 136–39
  global economy, 274–75
  household structure, 276–77, 280n2
  institutional arrangements, 273–74,
    278–80
  labor demand, 134–35
  labor supply, 134–35, 275–76, 277–78
  national policy framework, 273–74,
    278–80
  organizational innovation, 273–74,
    278–80
  per capita income, 105
  town and village enterprise (TVE), 276,
    280n1
  unemployment, 275–76
  WTO membership impact, 25t, 38–39,
    97–98, 104–5, 139–40, 273–74,
    276–78
Agricultural trade policy
  agriculture law, 267
  biotechnology, 261, 268–69, 270–71
  direct payment program, 262–63
  forecasting models, 256–59, 269–71
  liberalization, 267, 268, 271
  livestock feed, 261–62, 268
  long-term performance, 262–67
    perspectives on, 268–69
  major trade commodities, 256–62
    exports, 256, 257, 258f, 259–61,
      268, 270, 278

Agricultural trade policy
  major trade commodities *(continued)*
    imports, 253–54, 255t, 256–57,
      258f, 261–62, 266, 268–70,
      271, 277, 278
    specialty crops, 265–67
  sanitary inspections, 256
  short-term performance, 257–62
  state trade enterprise (STE), 254, 270
  subsidies, 262–63, 264–65
    exports, 256, 257
  tariff-rate quota (TRQ), 253–54, 255t,
    256–57, 258–59, 262, 266,
    269–71
  taxation, 260, 263–64
  World Trade Organization (WTO)
    commitments, 130, 253–54, 255t,
      256, 259–62, 265, 266, 267,
      269–71
    membership impact, 253, 256–59,
      268–71
  See also specific commodity
All-China Federation of Trade Unions,
  118
Apples, 266–67
Arab Banking, 154
Argentina, 258f
Asian Financial Crisis (1997), 145, 149,
  196, 197t
Asset management companies (AMCs),
  148, 149, 196, 218, 230n7
Australia, 41, 109–10
Austria, 110

Automobile industry
  foreign direct investment (FDI), 25*t*,
    26, 54, 98
  WTO commitments, 25*t*, 26, 44–45, 46

Banking system assessment
  central bank
    functions, 211–13, 230n5
    structural organization, 208–9, 210*f*
  commercial banks
    capital property structure, 213–14
    corporate control system, 214
    operational efficiency, 215–19
    organizational structure, 215
    system structure, 208–9, 210*f*
  credit cooperatives, 209, 230n3
  currency, 12, 46–47, 146, 153, 157–59,
    208, 219–20, 223–24
  foreign banks
    inferior treatment, 219–20
    market access, 219–21, 222–25,
      226–29
    structural organization, 208–9,
      210–11
    supranational treatment, 219,
      220–21
  foreign direct investment (FDI), 25*t*,
    26, 31
  perspectives on, 207–8
  stockholding banks, 208–9, 210*f*
  structural organization, 208–11
    overview, 210*f*
  urban cooperative banks, 208–10
  See also Capital structure; Small-
    business debt financing; *specific
    institution*
Banking system reform
  asset management companies (AMCs),
    148, 149, 196, 218, 230n7
  auditors, 150
  bank branches, 147, 153, 215
  capital inadequacy, 145–46
  capital injection, 147–48
  conclusion, 161–62
  corruption, 149–50
  debt-for-equity swaps, 147–48

Banking system reform *(continued)*
  economic growth, 145, 146, 147, 154,
    155*t*, 162n7, 187
  economic partnerships, 147, 153–54
  initial public offering (IPO), 149–50,
    151–52
  interbank market, 152–53
  interest rates, 146–47
  liberalization policy, 223–24, 225–26
  moral hazard, 145–46, 149–50
  nonperforming loan (NPL), 145–46,
    147–50, 196, 218
  privatization, 151–52, 162n4
  small-business debt financing, 195–96,
    197*t*, 198, 201–2, 203
  state-owned banks, 146–50, 152–54
  WTO commitments, 25*t*, 39, 46–47,
    130, 145–46, 147, 161–62,
    220–21, 223–30
  See also General Agreement on Trade
    in Services (GATS)
Bank of China (BOC), 91, 146–50, 158,
  209, 210*f*
Bank of Communications, 158
Bank of Shanghai, 151–52
Beef cattle, 266–67
Belgium, 110, 216
Biotechnology, 261, 268–69, 270–71
Bonds, 168, 170, 172, 173*t*, 176–78, 180

Canada
  capital structure, 167*t*, 197
  corporatism, 109–10
  foreign direct investment (FDI), 122
  foreign trade, 122, 124, 262
Capital markets
  A-share market, 174–75
  bond market, 176–78
  B-share market, 176
  equity market, 173–76, 179, 180, 181
  financing costs, 178–80
  H-share market, 176*f*
Capital structure
  bank loans, 165, 168, 169–70, 172,
    180, 181
  bonds, 168, 170, 172, 173*t*, 176–78, 180

Capital structure *(continued)*
  conclusion, 180–81
  debt financing, 165, 166*t*, 168
  debt-to-asset ratios, 168, 169*f*
  developed countries, 164–68
  developing countries, 164–66
  equity financing, 165–66, 168–69,
    170, 173–76, 179, 180, 181
  external financing, 164–68, 170, 172
  financing patterns, 165–68
  fixed asset investment, 170, 171*t*
  government role, 164–65
  internal financing, 164–68, 170, 172
  pecking order theory, 164, 165,
    166–68
  securities market, 164, 167–68
  short-term financing, 168, 169–70
  static tradeoff theory, 164
  stock market, 165, 170, 172, 179–80
    A-shares, 168, 173–75, 177–78,
      179*t*
    B-shares, 168, 173–76, 177–78,
      179*t*
    H-shares, 168, 173–74, 176*f*
    initial public offering (IPO),
      168–69, 173–76, 177–78, 181
    seasoned equity offering (SEO),
      168–69, 173–76, 181
  See also Small-business debt financing
Central Banking Regulatory
  Commission, 46
Central Bank Law, 211–13
Chase Manhattan, 216, 218
Chengzhou Commodity Exchange
  (CZCE), 295
China Banking Regulatory Commission
  (CBRC), 148, 151–52, 162, 229
China Construction Bank (CCB),
  146–50, 158, 209, 210*f*
China Investment Bank, 209
China Merchants Bank, 151, 158
China Minsheng Bank, 151–52, 162n3,
  201, 209
China National Petroleum Corporation
  (CNPC), 283, 284, 286–87, 288–89,
  292–93, 295–96, 299n4

China Securities Depository and
  Clearing Corporation (CSDCC),
  158–59
China Securities Regulatory Commission
  (CSRC), 168
China Society for WTO Studies, 41, 42
China Technology and Equity Exchange
  (CTEE), 150, 160–61
Chinese Agricultural Development Bank,
  197–98
Chinese-Foreign Joint Venture Law
  (1979), 31
Chinese Import and Export Bank,
  197–98
Cinda, 148, 161
Citibank, 151–52, 158, 216, 218
Citrus products, 266–67
Closer Economic Partnership
  Arrangement (CEPA), 147, 153–54
Collective-owned enterprise, 67–68
Commercial Banking Law, 209, 213, 215
Corn
  exports, 257, 258*f*, 259–61, 268, 270
  imports, 253–54, 255*t*, 256, 257, 266,
    269–70
  specialty crop, 266
Corporatism
  economic system relationship, 110–19
  labor unions
    collective bargaining, 112, 115–19
    neo-liberalism, 113
    trade union law, 108, 114–19
  prevalence of, 111–12
  social democracy, 110, 112, 114
  social security system, 110–16
    modernization of, 117–19
  social values, 113–14
  social welfare system, 110–16
    modernization of, 117–19
  tripartite partnerships, 111–12, 115–16,
    118–19
  Western corporatism, 108–10, 111–12
  Western social welfare, 108–10,
    111–12
    decommodification, 109–10
    pensions, 109, 110

Corruption
  banking system, 149–50
  securities market, 155, 157
Cotton
  imports, 253–54, 255t, 277
  specialty crop, 266–67
  subsidies, 265
Credit cooperatives, 209, 230n3
Credit rating system, 191, 202
Credit Suisse First Boston, 150
Currency, 12, 46–47, 146, 153, 157–59,
    208, 223–24

Denmark, 110
Deutsche Bank, 151
Distribution services, 25t, 39
Doha Ministerial Conference (2001),
    124, 132

Economic growth
  banking system, 145, 146, 147, 154,
    155t, 162n7, 187
  employment impact, 135, 136–39
  foreign direct investment (FDI), 23–24,
    27–28, 31–32, 33–34
  global economy, 3, 12, 18, 19–20, 97
  industrial labor force, 83–84, 87–89
  securities market, 146, 154, 155t, 156t,
    160
  Trade Related Investment Measures
    (TRIMs), 121, 124, 127–32
  WTO membership perspectives, 96,
    97–100, 104–6
  See also Foreign trade; Gross domestic
    product (GDP)
Education
  agricultural labor force, 279
  foreign direct investment (FDI), 57, 59
  industrial labor force, 88, 91–92
Electronics
  exports, 9, 12, 18, 20–21, 86
  foreign direct investment (FDI), 58–59,
    98
Employment
  challenges to, 134–35
  economic growth impact, 135, 136–39

Employment (continued)
  elasticity, 135, 136–41
  employment transfer, 88, 91
  growth rate
    foreign direct investment (FDI),
      66–68
    industrial labor force, 87–88
    labor demand/supply, 134–41
  layoffs, 135
  manufacturing industry, 136–39, 140
  service sector, 136–39, 140–41
  WTO membership impact, 139–41
  See also Agricultural labor force;
    Industrial labor force
Ernst & Young, 150
European Union (EU)
  corporatism, 109
  foreign direct investment (FDI), 26
  foreign trade, 8, 17–18, 21, 31, 99t,
    237
    Trade Related Investment Measures
      (TRIMs), 123–24, 129–30, 132
  WTO compliance-monitoring, 41
Exports. See Foreign trade

Financial leasing, 202
Financial system. See Banking system
    assessment; Banking system reform;
    Capital structure; Securities market
    reform; Small-business debt
    financing
Finland, 110, 167t
Foreign direct investment (FDI)
  advantages, 24–28, 30–32
  barrier-hopping, 26
  disadvantages, 23–24, 27–30, 32–34
  economic growth impact, 23–24,
    27–28, 31–32, 33–34
  foreign trade impact, 3, 14–15, 19,
    23–24, 26, 27, 28, 31, 32, 33
  industrial labor force, 86–87
  inflow features, 24–27
  introduction, 63–65
  investor conflict, 27–30
  liberalization policy, 23, 24, 27, 30
  manufacturing industry, 24, 26, 27

Foreign direct investment (FDI)
    (continued)
  mergers-acquisitions, 27, 33
  overview, 34–35
  research-development (R&D), 27, 32, 33
  technology transfer, 26, 27–28, 31–32, 33
  wage effects
    collective-owned enterprise, 67–68
    employment growth, 66–68
    foreign trade, 68–69, 71, 78–79
    income inequality, 33–34, 64–65, 66, 68–69, 70f, 71–79
    Intellectual Property Rights (IPR), 70–71, 72
    per capita income, 63, 65, 78
    policy implications, 63–64, 77–79
    product differentiation, 69–71, 72–74, 79n2
    profit margin, 71–72, 80n4
    real wage growth, 69, 70f, 75, 78
    sector differentiation, 73–76, 78
    skilled-unskilled labor, 64–65, 68–79
    state-owned enterprise (SOE), 66, 67–68
    technological-labor intensive production, 68–79
    technology transfer, 64, 65, 71–74
    theoretical predictions, 71–74
    theoretical support, 74–77
    uniform effects, 68–69, 70f
    WTO membership impact, 64, 66, 68, 77, 79
  World Trade Organization (WTO)
    commitments, 25t
    membership impact, 24–27, 32–34, 64, 66, 68, 77, 79
    membership perspectives, 98, 106
  See also Industrial locations; Trade Related Investment Measures (TRIMs); Western China investment
Foreign funded enterprise (FFE)
  labor unions, 116–17
  wage effects, 65–66, 78–79

Foreign investment enterprise (FIE)
  foreign direct investment (FDI), 23–24, 26, 29t
  foreign trade, 6, 14–15, 23–24
  industrial labor force, 87, 92–94
Foreign Investment Review Act (FIRA) (Canada), 122
Foreign trade
  characteristics
    export contributions, 4–10
    foreign-owned enterprise (FOE), 17
    major trade partners, 6, 8, 16t, 17–18, 20, 21, 97t, 99t
    non state-owned enterprise (SOE), 6, 15, 17
    processing and assembling products (PAP), 5–6, 7t, 15
    regional contributions, 9, 10f
    2002, 4–10
    2003, 15–21
  economic growth impact, 4, 19–20
  export duties, 11
  export growth
    1980–2001, 84–85, 86, 87, 92–94
    1998–2002, 5f
    2002, 4–15, 97
    2003, 15–21.97
  export licenses, 38, 293
  export markets (2002), 8, 9f, 21, 31
  export refund policy, 3, 10–11
  export regulation, 37, 38
  export value
    future potential, 105
    1980–2001, 84, 85t, 86t, 87, 93, 98
    2002, 3, 6, 9–11, 15
    2003, 15, 17–18, 20, 21t
  growth factors
    domestic economy, 3, 10, 19–20
    export refund policy, 3, 10–11
    foreign direct investment (FDI), 3, 14–15, 19, 23–24, 26, 27, 28, 31, 32, 33
    global economy, 3, 12, 18, 19–20, 97
    overview, 3–4, 21–22
    trade services, 3, 13–15

Foreign trade
  growth factors *(continued)*
    trade structure, 3, 11–12, 18, 20–21
    2002, 3–4, 10–15, 19, 23–24, 26,
      27, 28, 31, 32, 33
    U.S. dollar depreciation, 3, 12,
      18–19
  import growth
    1998–2002, 5f
    2002, 4–9, 12–13
    2003, 15–21
  import licenses, 289, 291, 293
  import quotas, 4–5, 44–45, 122–24,
    131
    agriculture, 253–54, 255t, 256–57,
      258–59, 262, 266, 269–71, 277
    petroleum industry, 289, 291, 293
  import regulation, 38
  import tariffs, 4–5, 19, 43, 130
    agriculture, 253–54, 255t, 256–57,
      258–59, 262, 266, 269–71
    petroleum industry, 291, 292
  import value
    1980–2001, 85t, 98
    2002/2003, 3, 4, 6, 15, 17–18, 20,
      21t
  industrial labor force, 84–85, 86, 87,
    92–94
  Intellectual Property Rights (IPR), 39,
    124, 132
  trade balance, 19, 103t
  trade barriers, 38, 97–98, 291–92
  trade surplus, 4, 5f, 8, 9f, 19
  trading rights, 38
  wage impact, 68–69, 71, 78–79
  World Trade Organization (WTO)
    commitments, 37–38, 39–40, 42–47
    membership impact, 3, 10, 12–13,
      21–22
    membership perspectives, 96,
      97–98, 99t, 101–4, 105
  See also Agricultural trade policy;
    General Agreement on Trade in
    Services (GATS); Industrial
    locations; Petroleum industry;
    specific commodity; Trade Related
    Investment Measures (TRIMs)

France, 110, 167t, 192, 216, 217
Fund management industry, 159, 160t

Garment industry, 9, 94, 98, 131, 240
General Agreement on Tariffs and Trade
  (GATT), 100–101, 121–24, 126
General Agreement on Trade in Services
  (GATS)
  Article I, 221–22
  Article II, 222
  Article III, 222
  Article VI, 228
  Article XII, 224
  Article XVI, 222–23, 224–25, 226–29
  Article XVII, 224–25, 226–29
  Article XX, 226
  banking system reform
    capital account convertibility,
      225–26
    currency, 223–24, 225, 227
    government role, 227–28, 229
    market access, 220–21, 222–25,
      226–29
    national treatment, 221, 222–23,
      224, 225, 226–29, 231n8
    protection evasion measures,
      226–29
    service-supply modes, 221–22, 224,
      231n10
    taxation, 226–27
    transparency, 222
    WTO commitments, 208, 220–21,
      223–30
  provisions, 221–23
  regulation interpretation, 224–30
Germany
  banking system, 216, 217
  capital structure, 167t, 197
  corporatism, 110
  foreign trade, 8, 9f, 97t
Global economy
  agricultural labor force, 274–75
  foreign trade, 3, 12, 18, 19–20, 97
  gross domestic product (GDP), 97
  industrial labor force, 92–94
Goldman Sachs, 151, 158
Great Wall, 148, 161

Greenfield investment, 27
Gross domestic product (GDP)
  banking system, 147, 154, 155*t*, 162n7,
    187
  employment, 135, 138*f*
  foreign trade, 4
  global economy, 97
  industrial labor force, 83–84, 88–89
  securities market, 154, 155*t*, 156*t*, 160
  United States, 12

Half-floor investment, 202
Holland, 110
Hong Kong
  banking system reform, 147, 151–52,
    153–54, 162n6
  capital markets, 174, 176
  foreign direct investment (FDI), 26, 30,
    240
  foreign trade, 8*f*, 9*f*, 21, 97*t*
Hong Kong & Shanghai Banking
    Corporation (HSBC), 151–52, 158,
    216, 218
Hong Kong Stock Market, 150
Hua'an Innovation Fund, 159
Huarong, 148, 161
Huaxia Bank, 151

Imports. *See* Foreign trade
Income. *See* Foreign direct investment
    (FDI); Wages
Indonesia, 99*t*
Industrial and Commercial Bank of
    China (ICBC), 146–50, 158
Industrial labor force
  economic growth impact, 83–84, 87–89
  future prospects, 94
  global cooperation, 92–94
  labor export, 92–94
  labor supply
    educational level, 88, 91–92
    employment growth, 87–88
    employment transfer, 88, 91
    wages, 89–92
  liberalization policy, 94
  production expansion
    competitive advantages, 85–87

Industrial labor force
  production expansion *(continued)*
    foreign direct investment (FDI),
      86–87
    foreign trade, 84–85, 86, 87, 92–94
    industrial evolution, 83–84
    technology transfer, 87
    world-factory designation, 85–87,
      94
  production modernization, 89, 90
  WTO membership impact, 83, 92–94
Industrial locations
  liberalization policy, 235, 236, 237–38,
    246–48, 249*t*, 250–51
  regional differences
    foreign direct investment (FDI),
      237–40, 246–51
    foreign trade, 237–40, 246–51
    industrial output, 238–39, 241–42*t*
    manufacturing industries, 241–42*t*
    population, 238
  research data, 245–46
  research implications, 251
  research methodology, 240, 243–45
  research results, 246–50
  research review, 236–37
  research variables, 240, 243–45
    definitions, 245*t*
  technology transfer, 235–36
Initial public offering (IPO)
  banking system reform, 149–50,
    151–52
  capital structure, 168–69, 173–76,
    177–78, 181
Innovation Fund for Small Technology-
    based Firms (IFSTF), 198, 199*t*,
    200*t*
Insurance industry, 25*t*, 26, 27, 31, 39
Intellectual Property Rights (IPR)
  foreign trade, 39, 124, 132
  wage impact, 70–71, 72
  WTO commitments, 37, 39, 41, 42, 45
Interest rates, 146–47, 186, 191–92,
    193–94, 196, 201–2
International Bank of Asia, 154
International Finance Corporation (IFC),
    151–52, 164–65, 187

Iraq war, 19
Ireland, 109–10
Italy
  banking system, 216, 217
  capital structure, 167t
  corporatism, 110
  export market, 8, 9f

Japan
  capital structure, 167t, 197
  corporatism, 109–10
  foreign direct investment (FDI), 26, 68
  foreign trade, 8, 9f, 17–18, 21, 97t, 99t,
    100, 123–24, 132
  WTO compliance-monitoring, 41
Jiang Zemin, 43
Joint-venture firms, 161
JP Morgan, 159

Labor force. See Agricultural labor force;
    Employment; Industrial labor force
Labor unions
  corporatism
    collective bargaining, 112, 115–19
    neo-liberalism, 113
    trade union law, 108, 114–19
  foreign trade, 101, 103
Law on Banking Regulation and
    Supervision (2003), 148–49
Lianhua Synthetic Fiber, 161
Liberalization policy
  agricultural trade, 267, 268, 271
  banking system reform, 223–24, 225–26
  foreign direct investment (FDI), 23, 24,
    27, 30
  industrial labor force, 94
  industrial locations, 235, 236, 237–38,
    246–48, 249t, 250–51
  petroleum industry, 287, 288–89, 295,
    296
  Trade Related Investment Measures
    (TRIMs), 127, 132
  World Trade Organization (WTO)
    commitment compliance, 36, 37, 38,
      39
    membership perspectives, 96

Logistics industry, 130–31
Lu Fuyuan, 42

Macao, 147, 153–54, 162n6
Malaysia, 8f, 9f, 97t, 99t
Manufacturing industry. See Industrial
    labor force; Industrial locations;
    specific industry
Mechanical products, 9, 12, 18, 20–21, 86
Mergers-acquisitions, 27, 33
Mexico, 98, 99t, 237
Milk, 266–67
Morgan Stanley, 158
Multinational corporation (MNC). See
    Foreign direct investment (FDI)
Multinational enterprise (MNE), 5–6,
    14–15

Nanhua Bank, 152
Nanjing City Commercial Bank, 151–52
National Development Bank, 197–98
Natural resources, 53, 54, 59
Neoclassical economic theory, 127–28,
    131–32
Neo-liberalism, 113
Netherlands
  banking system, 216, 218
  corporatism, 9f, 110
  foreign trade, 8, 9f, 97t
  petroleum industry, 289–91, 293–95,
    297–98
New York Stock Exchange (NYSE), 174
New Zealand, 109–10
Nomura, 158
Nonperforming loan (NPL), 145–46,
    147–50, 161, 196, 218
Norway, 110

Oil industry. See Petroleum industry
Organization for Economic Cooperation
    and Development (OECD), 124
Oriental, 148, 161

Pecking order theory, 164, 165, 166–68
People's Bank of China (PBOC), 157,
    214, 215

People's Bank of China (PBOC)
  (continued)
  banking system reform, 146–50,
    152–53, 195, 201, 219–20
  functions, 211–13, 230n5
  structural organization, 208–9, 210*f*
Petroleum industry
  consumption, 282, 284, 285*t*, 286,
    288–89, 292, 294–95
  exploration/development, 284, 286–87
  institutional reform, 283–87, 288*f*
    administration, 283, 284
  oil exports
    crude oil, 282, 284, 285*t*, 293,
      298n1, 299n6
    finished oil products, 286–87, 293
    licenses, 293
  oil futures, 288, 289, 293–96, 299n8
  oil imports
    crude oil, 19, 282, 285*t*, 286*t*, 287,
      288–89, 291–92, 293, 298n1,
      299n6
    finished oil products, 287, 288–89,
      291–92, 293, 298n2
    licenses, 289, 291, 293
    quotas, 289, 291, 293
    tariffs, 291, 292
  price reform
    crude oil, 19, 283, 287–89
    diesel oil, 289–91, 293–95, 297–98
    finished oil products, 288–89
    international benchmark system,
      289–91, 293–94, 296, 297–98
    liberalization policy, 287, 288–89,
      295, 296
    three-tier system, 287–89
  production, 282, 284, 285*t*, 286,
    288–89, 292, 294–96
  WTO commitments, 25*t*, 291–93
Philippines, 99*t*
Plastic products, 9–10
Policy banks, 197–98, 208–9, 210*f*,
  230n2
PricewaterhouseCoopers, 150
Processing and assembling products
  (PAPs), 5–6, 7*t*, 15

Profit margin
  wage effects, 71–72, 80n4
  Western China investment, 54, 55,
    58–59
Pudong Development Bank, 151–52

Qualified Foreign Institutional Investor
  (QFII), 146, 157–59

Rapeseed, 255*t*, 266–67
Research-development (R&D), 27, 32, 33
Retail services, 25*t*, 26–27
Rice
  direct payment program, 263
  exports, 259–61, 268, 270
  imports, 253–54, 255*t*, 261, 268,
    269–70
  liberalization policy, 267
Russia, 8*f*, 21, 97*t*

Sanyuan Foods Co. Ltd., 161
SARS. *See* Severe acute respiratory
  syndrome (SARS)
Seasoned equity offering (SEO), 168–69,
  173–76, 181
Securities Investment Fund Law (2004),
  160
Securities Investment Fund Provisional
  Regulations (1997), 159
Securities market reform
  A-share market, 146, 154–55, 156*t*,
    157, 158–59, 161, 163n11
  B-share market, 146, 154–55, 156*t*,
    157, 158–59, 163n9
  conclusion, 161–62
  corruption, 155, 157
  currency, 146, 157–59
  economic growth, 146, 154, 155*t*, 156*t*,
    160
  introduction, 145, 146
  securities funds, 159–60
  stock market, 146, 154–55, 156*t*,
    157–61, 163n8
  WTO commitments, 25*t*
Securities Regulatory Commission, 157,
  158

Service sector, 39, 136–39, 140–41
  See also General Agreement on Trade
    in Services (GATS); *specific
    sector*
Severe acute respiratory syndrome
    (SARS), 19, 42, 158
Shanghai Futures Exchange, 283, 294
Shanghai Pudong Development Bank,
    151
Shanghai Stock Exchange, 151, 154,
    156*t*, 161, 173–74, 179–80
Sheep, 266–67
Shenzhen Development Bank, 151
Shenzhen Nanshan Risk Investment
    Fund, 159
Shenzhen Stock Exchange, 151, 154,
    156*t*, 161, 173–74, 179–80
Shoes, 9
Singapore
  capital structure, 197
  foreign trade, 97*t*
  petroleum industry, 289–91, 293–95,
    297–98
Sinopec, 284, 287, 292–93, 295–96,
    299n3
Small-business debt financing
  banking system reform, 195–96, 197*t*,
    198, 201–2, 203
  bank loans
    adverse selection, 186, 189, 191,
      196
    credit rating system, 191, 202
    equity financing, 184, 185
    financing costs, 185–86, 191–92
    half-floor investment, 202
    information asymmetry, 183–84,
      186, 189, 191
    institutional effect, 194–95
    interest rates, 186, 191–92, 193–94,
      196, 201–2
    loan approvals, 189, 190*t*
    loan collateral, 187, 192–93, 202
    loan guarantees, 192–93, 198, 201,
      202
    loan rejections, 189*t*
    moral hazard, 186, 189, 191

Small-business debt financing
    (continued)
  conclusion, 203
  financial depression, 193–95
  financial innovation, 184–85, 199*t*,
    200*t*, 202, 203
  financial leasing, 202
  financing gap, 185–96
    causation of, 185–86, 191–92
    reduction strategies, 186, 196–203
  government role, 197–202
  internal financing, 183, 187, 188*t*, 189
  non-state banks, 186, 201
  policy banks, 197–98
  research review, 184–86
  venture capital, 197–98, 199*t*, 200*t*
  WTO membership impact, 202–3
Social democracy, 110, 112, 114
Social security system
  corporatism, 110–19
  United States, 112, 119n1
Social values, 113–14
Social welfare system
  agricultural labor force, 279, 281n3
  corporatism, 110–19
  Western, 108–10, 111–12
South Korea
  capital structure, 197
  foreign trade, 8, 9*f*, 21, 97*t*, 99*t*, 100
Soybean oil
  direct payment program, 263
  imports, 253–54, 255*t*, 256–57, 261,
    268, 269–70, 277
  specialty crop, 266
  subsidies, 263, 265
Soybeans
  exports, 261
  imports, 255*t*, 256–57, 258*f*, 261,
    268–69, 270, 271, 277
  specialty crop, 266
Spain, 216, 217
Special Economic Zone (SEZ), 209,
    210–11, 220, 230n4, 237–38
Standard Chartered, 158
State Administration of Foreign
    Exchange, 157

State Council
  collective bargaining, 116
  financial system, 47, 149–50,
    211–12
  foreign trade, 11
  petroleum industry, 283, 288–89, 294
State-owned enterprise (SOE), 66,
  67–68, 135, 138
State trade enterprise (STE), 254, 270
Static tradeoff theory, 164
Stockholding banks, 208–9, 210*f*
Stock market
  A-shares
    capital structure, 168, 173–75,
      177–78, 179*t*
    securities market reform, 146,
      154–55, 156*t*, 157, 158–59,
      161, 163n11
  banking system reform, 149–52
  B-shares
    capital structure, 168, 173–76,
      177–78, 179*t*
    securities market reform, 146,
      154–55, 156*t*, 157, 158–59,
      163n9
  capital structure, 165, 168, 170, 172,
    173–76, 177–78, 179–80, 181
  H-shares, 168, 173–74, 176*f*
  initial public offering (IPO)
    banking system reform, 149–50,
      151–52
    capital structure, 168–69, 173–76,
      177–78, 181
    petroleum industry, 288, 289, 293–96,
      299n8
  seasoned equity offering (SEO),
    168–69, 173–76, 181
  securities market reform, 146, 154–55,
    156*t*, 157–61, 163n8
  See also specific exchange
Strategic trade theory, 127, 128–29,
  132
Subsidies, 256, 257, 262–63, 264–65
Sugar, 265, 266–67
Sweden, 110
Switzerland, 110, 158–59

Taiwan
  foreign direct investment (FDI), 26, 30,
    240
  foreign trade, 8, 9*f*, 97*t*, 99*t*, 100
  WTO accession, 100
Taiwan Fubon Financial Holding, 154
Taxation
  agricultural trade policy, 260, 263–64
  banking system reform, 226–27
Technology
  electronics, 58–59, 98
    exports, 9, 12, 18, 20–21, 86
  foreign direct investment (FDI)
    electronics, 58–59, 98
    wage effects, 68–79
    Western China, 55, 59, 60
  small business funding, 198, 199*t*, 200*t*
Technology transfer
  foreign direct investment (FDI), 26,
    27–28, 31–32, 33
  wage effects, 64, 65, 71–74
  industrial labor force, 87
  industrial locations, 235–36
Telecommunications industry, 25*t*, 26,
  31, 84, 131
Textile industry, 9, 98, 131, 240, 296
Thailand, 99*t*, 149, 162n2
Tourism industry, 130
Town and village enterprise (TVE), 276,
  280n1
Trade. *See* Foreign trade
Trade-Related Aspects of Intellectual
    Property Rights (TRIPS), 39, 124,
    132
Trade Related Investment Measures
    (TRIMs)
  conclusion, 131–32
  defined, 124–27
  development of, 121–24
  Doha Ministerial Conference (2001),
    124, 132
  economic impact
    neoclassical economic theory,
      127–28, 131–32
    strategic trade theory, 127, 128–29,
      132

Trade Related Investment Measures
    (TRIMs)
  economic impact *(continued)*
    WTO membership, 121, 124,
        129–31, 132
  export performance requirements, 123,
      124–25, 126, 128
  international trade policy, 121–24, 126
  liberalization policy, 127, 132
  local content requirements (LCRs),
      123, 124–25, 126, 128
  trade distortion, 123, 125–26
  Uruguay Round (1992), 121–24, 125,
      132
Trade Union Law Amendment (2003),
    108, 114–19
Transportation industry, 27, 31, 39, 130

United Kingdom
  banking system, 216, 217
  capital structure, 167–68, 192, 198,
      202
  corporatism, 109–10
  export market, 8, 9f
United States
  banking system, 216
  capital structure, 164, 165, 166–68,
      192, 198
  corporatism, 109–10, 112, 119n2
  dollar depreciation, 3, 12, 18–19
  foreign direct investment (FDI), 26,
      66–67, 68, 237
  foreign trade, 8, 9f, 17–18, 21, 31,
      43–45, 47, 237
    agricultural policy, 253–54, 256,
        260, 262, 269
    market access agreement (1999),
        207
    petroleum industry, 289–91, 292t,
        293–95, 297–98
    top exporters, 102t
    top exports, 104t
    top importers, 102t
    top imports, 104t
    trade balance, 19, 103t
    trade deficit, 101, 103

United States
  foreign trade *(continued)*
    trade partners, 97t, 98, 99t, 101–4,
        105
    Trade Related Investment Measures
        (TRIMs), 122, 123–24, 129,
        130, 132
  General Accounting Office (GAO),
      37, 39, 41
  gross domestic product (GDP), 12
  Iraq war, 19
  social security system, 112, 119n1
  social welfare system, 109–10, 112
  World Trade Organization (WTO)
    compliance-assessment, 43–45
    compliance-monitoring, 37, 39,
        41–42
Urban cooperative banks, 208–10
Uruguay Round (1992), 121–24, 125, 132

Wages
  industrial labor force, 89–92
  labor unions, 116
  per capita income, 52–53, 63, 65, 78,
      104–5
  See also Foreign direct investment
      (FDI)
Wen Jiabao, 42, 46
Western China investment
  advantages, 51–53
    labor costs, 53
    land values, 52
    natural resources, 53, 54, 59
    per capita income, 52–53
    population diversity, 53
  current investment (2001–2003),
      53–55, 56t
  geographic area, 51–52, 53, 57, 60n1
  obstacles
    educational levels, 57, 59
    geography, 57
    ideological, 58
    industrial infrastructure, 57
    institutional, 58
  patterns
    investment size, 55

Western China investment
patterns *(continued)*
  profit margin, 54, 55, 58–59
  technology investment, 55, 59, 60
strategies
  first-mover advantages, 54, 58–59
  industrial-educational investment,
    59
  market expansion, 60
  production, 60
  resource development, 59
  value-added products, 60
Wheat
  exports, 257, 259*f*, 260–61, 268, 270
  imports, 253–54, 255*t*, 256, 257,
    261–62, 269–70, 271, 277
  specialty crop, 266
Wholly foreign-owned enterprise
  (WFOE), 26
World-factory designation, 85–87, 94
World Trade Organization (WTO)
  accession chronology, 100–101, 253,
    254*t*
  commitment challenges
    agricultural trade policy, 130,
      253–54, 255*t*, 256, 259–62,
      265, 266, 267, 269–71
    automobile industry, 25*t*, 26, 44–45,
      46
    banking system reform, 25*t*, 39,
      46–47, 130, 145–46, 147,
      161–62, 208, 220–21, 223–30
    distribution services, 25*t*, 39
    foreign direct investment (FDI), 25*t*
    foreign trade, 37–38, 39–40, 42–47
    insurance industry, 25*t*, 39
    Intellectual Property Rights (IPR),
      37, 39, 41, 42, 45
    petroleum industry, 25*t*, 291–93
    retail services, 25*t*
    securities market, 25*t*
    service sector, 39
    telecommunications industry, 25*t*
    transportation industry, 39, 130
  commitment compliance
    China assessment, 42, 43–45

World Trade Organization (WTO)
  commitment compliance *(continued)*
    China concessions, 46–47
    future challenges, 47–48
    global assessment, 42–45
    global monitoring, 40, 41–42
    implementation costs, 40, 48n3
    information deficiency, 45, 48n13
    infrastructure facilitation, 40–42
    introduction, 36–37
    liberalization policy, 36, 37, 38, 39
    time schedule, 37, 42–45
    WTO Affairs Consulting Center, 40
    WTO Inquiry Center, 40
    WTO Transition Review
      Mechanism, 40, 42
  membership impact
    agricultural labor force, 25*t*, 38–39,
      97–98, 104–5, 139–40,
      273–74, 276–78
    agricultural trade policy, 253,
      256–59, 268–71
    employment, 139–41
    foreign direct investment (FDI),
      24–27, 32–34, 64, 66, 68,
      77, 79
    foreign trade, 3, 10, 12–13, 21–22
    industrial labor force, 83, 92–94
    small-business debt financing,
      202–3
  membership perspectives
    agricultural trade policy, 268–69
    China, 42, 43–45, 96, 104–6
    compliance assessment, 42–45
    economic growth, 96, 97–100,
      104–6
    foreign direct investment (FDI), 98,
      106
    foreign trade, 96, 97–98, 99*t*,
      101–4, 105
    global, 42–45, 96, 97–100, 106
    liberalization policy, 96
    United States, 96, 101–4
Wuhan Securities Investment Fund, 159

Xiamen International Bank, 151–52

For Product Safety Concerns and Information please contact our EU
representative GPSR@taylorandfrancis.com
Taylor & Francis Verlag GmbH, Kaufingerstraße 24, 80331 München, Germany